LITERATURE, SATIRE AND THE EARLY STUART STATE

Andrew McRae examines the relation between literature and politics at a pivotal moment in English history. He argues that the most influential and incisive political satire in this period may be found in manuscript libels, scurrilous pamphlets, and a range of other material written and circulated under the threat of censorship. These are the unauthorized texts of early Stuart England. From his analysis of these texts, McRae argues that satire, as the pre-eminent literary mode of discrimination and stigmatization, helped people make sense of the confusing political conditions of the early Stuart era. It did so partly through personal attacks, and partly also through sophisticated interventions into ongoing political and ideological debates. In such forms satire provided resources through which contemporary writers could define new models of political identity and construct new discourses of dissent. This book will be of interest to political and literary historians alike.

ANDREW MCRAE is Senior Lecturer in the School of English at the University of Exeter. He is the author of *God Speed the Plough: The Representation of Agrarian England, 1500–1660* (Cambridge, 1996) and *Renaissance Drama* (2003), and co-editor of *The Writing of Rural England, 1500–1800* (2003).

LITERATURE, SATIRE AND THE EARLY STUART STATE

ANDREW McRAE

University of Exeter

PUBLISHED BY THE PRESS SYNDICATE OF THE UNIVERSITY OF CAMBRIDGE
The Pitt Building, Trumpington Street, Cambridge, United Kingdom

CAMBRIDGE UNIVERSITY PRESS
The Edinburgh Building, Cambridge, CB2 2RU, UK
40 West 20th Street, New York, NY 10011-4211, USA
477 Williamstown Road, Port Melbourne, VIC 3207, Australia
Ruiz de Alarcón 13, 28014 Madrid, Spain
Dock House, The Waterfront, Cape Town 8001, South Africa

http://www.cambridge.org

First published 2004

Printed in the United Kingdom at the University Press, Cambridge

Typeface Adobe Garamond 11/12.5 pt   *System* LATEX 2$_\varepsilon$ [TB]

A catalogue record for this book is available from the British Library

Library of Congress Cataloguing in Publication data
McRae, Andrew.
Literature, satire, and the early Stuart state / Andrew McRae.
p.   cm.
Includes bibliographical references and index.
ISBN 0 521 81495 2
1. Satire, English – History and criticism.   2. English prose literature – Early modern, 1500–1700 –
History and criticism.   3. Great Britain – History – Early Stuarts, 1603–1649 – Historiography.
4. Politics and literature – Great Britain – History – 17th century.   5. Literature and state – Great
Britain – History – 17th century.   I. Title.
PR934.M38   2003
827′.409358–dc21   2003053189

ISBN 0 521 81495 2 hardback

Contents

Acknowledgements

This book began as a more general study of Renaissance satire, but developed into the first of two projected books when I discovered the sheer wealth of relatively untouched material relating to early Stuart politics. As a consequence, I am particularly grateful to the institutions that afforded me the time and resources in which to make those decisions and pursue those interests. In the early phases of research, which demanded a lot of time in archives around the world, I was generously supported by the Australian Research Council and the University of Sydney. More recently, I have received assistance from the University of Exeter and the Arts and Humanities Research Board.

The work has also benefited from the comments and criticisms of colleagues, and happily bears the marks of my movement from Sydney, to Leeds, to Exeter. In Sydney, I learned much from Mary Chan, Conal Condren, Andrew Fitzmaurice, Anthony Miller, Michael Wilding and other members of the Early Modern Studies Group. Since my move to England, the project has benefited from my contact with Katharine Craik, Karen Edwards, Regenia Gagnier, Paul Hammond, Nick McDowell, Philip Schwyzer and Alex Walsham. In addition, Harold Love made helpful early suggestions, Bradin Cormack and Michelle O'Callaghan offered perceptive comments on drafts, Gerald MacLean and the other anonymous Cambridge University Press reader made some acute points of criticism, and Kevin Sharpe was supportive throughout. I am also grateful to those who invited me to speak at their universities, or who discussed my work at seminars and conferences: in particular, to audiences at the universities of Exeter, Leeds, Monash, Oxford Brookes, Reading, Warwick and York. And several people generously offered advice on sources and access to unpublished work: most notably, Alastair Bellany, Stephen Clucas and Nigel Smith.

Finally, this book may never have been possible without Kristin Hammett, who made sacrifices beyond any call of duty, and endured more than she ever deserved. Nor would its final stages have been so rewarding, expeditious, and simply enjoyable without Jane Whittle. Throughout, my mother has also been a constant source of support.

Earlier versions of Chapters 1 and 5, respectively, have been published in *Modern Philology*, 97 (2000), 364–92; and *Review of English Studies*, 54 (2003), 336–64. Parts of Chapter 5 are incorporated into 'The Poetics of Sycophancy: Ben Jonson and the Caroline Court', in David Brooks and Brian Kiernan, eds., *Running Wild: Essays, Fictions and Memoirs Presented to Michael Wilding* (Sydney, 2003), pp. 29–42.

Conventions

Much of the research on which this book is based involves libels: licentious poems on individuals and political events, which were typically circulated anonymously in manuscript form. Since most of these poems are difficult to access, and many have never before been published, I have co-edited (with Alastair Bellany) an edition of them, which will be published electronically as 'Early Stuart Libels: An Edition of Political Poems from Manuscript Sources', in *Early Modern Literary Studies* <http://purl.oclc.org/emls/emlshome.html>. Consequently, for ease of cross-referencing between the book and the database, all citations of poems here include (either in the text or footnotes) a first line, and all poems in the database are searchable by first line. As in the database, I make no claims to be providing a definitive text of any poem. Since these poems circulated widely, and were often altered in the process, the goal of identifying original texts is not only extremely difficult but also of uncertain value (given that this study is less concerned with questions of authorial intention than with texts as they circulated). So, while the database provides the necessary information for researchers who wish to compare different versions of a particular poem, the book typically focuses on just one version, as it was read and copied by contemporaries.

The editorial method employed with primary material from both manuscript and print sources is identical to that used in the database, and is intended to provide texts which are at once reliable and readable. As a result, standard scribal abbreviations and contractions are expanded without comment, and conflations of u/v and i/j are routinely modernized. In all other respects original spelling and punctuation are retained.

When citing printed texts published in the sixteenth or seventeenth century, the place of publication is London unless otherwise stated. Biblical quotations are from the Authorized (King James) Version.

Abbreviations

Beinecke	Beinecke Library, Yale University
Bodleian	Bodleian Library, University of Oxford
BL	British Library
CSPD	*Calendar of State Papers, Domestic Series*
CUL	Cambridge University Library
DNB	*The Dictionary of National Biography*, ed. Sir Leslie Stephen and Sir Sidney Lee (22 vols., London, 1917)
Folger	Folger Shakespeare Library
Huntington	Henry E. Huntington Library, San Marino
NLS	National Library of Scotland
OED	*Oxford English Dictionary*, 2nd edn, prepared by J. A. Simpson and E. S. C. Weiner (20 vols., Oxford, 1989)
Poems and Songs	*Poems and Songs Relating to George Villiers, Duke of Buckingham; and his Assassination by John Felton*, ed. Frederick W. Fairholt (Percy Society, London, 1850)
'Poems from a Seventeenth-Century Manuscript'	'Poems from a Seventeenth-Century Manuscript with the Hand of Robert Herrick', ed. Norman Farmer, *Texas Quarterly*, 16.4 (1973), supplement
PRO	Public Record Office, London
Rosenbach	Rosenbach Museum and Library, Philadelphia
STC	*A Short Title Catalogue of Books Printed in England, Scotland, and Ireland . . . 1475–1640*, compiled by A. W. Pollard and G. R. Redgrave, 2nd edn (3 vols., London, 1976–91)

Introduction

This is a study of literature and politics in the early decades of the seventeenth century. It considers how the resources of satire, the pre-eminent literary mode of discrimination and stigmatization, helped people make sense of the confusing political conditions of the early Stuart era. Throughout, therefore, it brings into conjunction sets of questions from two distinct academic disciplines. From a tradition of literary history, it asks what happened to satire in the decades after the Bishops' Ban of 1599, which evidently brought an abrupt end to a vigorous, late-Elizabethan outpouring of verse satire by writers such as John Donne, Joseph Hall and John Marston. In search of the following generation of satirists, it looks to the 'strange *Monstrous Satyrs*' that contemporaries encountered all around them.[1] I argue that unconventional and uncanny forms of satire, though less visible than Elizabethan verse within the terms of a literary history concerned with print culture and canonical authors, were in fact vital and influential products of early Stuart culture. And from a tradition of political history, the book investigates changes in the language of politics, which enabled the articulation of radical new notions of ideological difference and political confrontation. Like many recent historical studies of the early seventeenth century, *Literature, Satire and the Early Stuart State* is thus concerned with the ways in which an orthodox Tudor commitment to consensus and harmony gave way by the 1640s to some of the most devastating political ruptures of English history.[2]

More specifically, this book examines the *unauthorized texts* of early Stuart England. My use of this term is intended to identify a range of writing, in various textual forms, that rejects the dominant assumption in

---

[1] Arthur Wilson, *The History of Great Britain, Being the Life and Reign of King James I* (1653), p. 290.

[2] The word 'literature' in the title of this book, which might in some respects seem redundant, is not in any way intended to suggest a narrowly canonical approach to writing of the period. On the contrary, the book challenges such suppositions about literature and literary culture, and focuses on the functions of satire throughout English political culture.

early Stuart political culture that all authority to speak was derived from the monarch.[3] Models of speech at court and from the pulpit were founded on this powerful political fiction, while the period's various structures of censorship aimed to enforce it much more widely. Most writers within this context struggled to define for themselves positions of orthodoxy and legitimacy; increasingly, however, many rejected the system's constraints, and constructed new modes of illicit expression. Numerous writers and readers entered into political action through libels: licentious poems on individuals and political events, typically circulated anonymously within manuscript culture. Others explored politics in published poems, prose pamphlets, sermons and drama. Some such texts provocatively tested the uncertain constraints on public speech, while other authors and publishers evaded censorship by employing fugitive models of publication and speech. It is largely for this reason that the book does not look in any detail beyond the effective collapse of censorship early in the 1640s, after which modes of writing and political expression changed markedly.[4] Meanwhile, the only significant exception to the book's focus on the unauthorized is the work of Richard Corbett. Though determinedly orthodox and loyal, I suggest that Corbett's outspoken poetics of satire and sycophancy, which so forthrightly confront the nation's multiplying voices of dissent, serve to clarify the very lines of division he so fears.

It is no coincidence that Corbett is one of the few writers to be considered here who has survived, albeit on the fringes, in traditional narratives of literary history. When canons are constructed, it is advantageous for an author to be authorized and identifiable, working within established literary and cultural conventions. Yet I want to suggest that satire, more than most literature, is often most pertinent when it stretches conventions and challenges authority. Moreover, the book sets aside the concern with textual form that dominates many studies of literary genre, following some of the best recent work on satire by considering it not in accordance with neo-classical standards and conventions, but rather as a 'mode' that informs 'an astonishingly wide range of vastly varied works'.[5] This approach opens to scrutiny a plethora of texts previously considered only within the narrower

---

[3] See Kevin Sharpe, *Reading Revolutions: The Politics of Reading in Early Modern England* (New Haven, CT and London, 2000), p. 27.

[4] On this period, see especially James Loxley, *Royalism and Poetry in the English Civil Wars: The Drawn Sword* (London, 1997); David Norbrook, *Writing the English Republic: Poetry, Rhetoric and Politics, 1627–1660* (Cambridge, 1999); Nigel Smith, *Literature and Revolution in England, 1640–1660* (New Haven, CT and London, 1994).

[5] Brian A. Connery and Kirk Combe, 'Theorizing Satire: A Retrospective Introduction', in *Theorizing Satire: Essays in Literary Criticism*, ed. Connery and Combe (Basingstoke and London, 1995), p. 9.

terms of political history. As Kevin Sharpe has observed, 'much recent work on pamphlets, news and ballads' has made the mistake of reading 'complex texts as straightforward documents', and has consequently overlooked much of their significance.[6] Crucially, I argue that while satirists do not necessarily see themselves involved in a rational and open debate, and rarely make any direct claim to a place in the history of political thought, satire nonetheless helps to shape the very contours of political debate. As one recent theorist argues, it is a mode committed to the production of difference, creating clarity and hierarchy out of complexity and uncertainty.[7] And it is precisely its textual and rhetorical resources – of provocation, outspokenness, indirection, wit – that can make it so effective.

I want to consider at once how satire adapts to the political and cultural circumstances of these decades, and how in turn it informs contemporary discourse. I argue that satire became, in many respects, pervasive: as much an attitude or an inflection as a literary genre.[8] Hence, in the narrative of one contemporary pamphlet, a decision to become 'a perfect *Satyrist*' involved an act of self-fashioning. 'Cource *Cynical* diet *sowr'd* my disposition,' the pamphlet's speaker reflects, and 'bitter'd all my thoughts, by eating passage for my *Gaul*, to overflow my *Heat*: and *Custom* setled my mind in affection of that, which before seem'd *unnaturall* to it'.[9] As we shall see in Chapter 3, some writers, such as George Wither, struggled to maintain satire as a public and authorized mode, distinct from the licentious and libellous. But most accepted that such distinctions were effectively valueless in the early Stuart context, and that satire might instead be forced into 'strange' and 'monstrous' shapes. In such shapes, I argue, it provided a vehicle through which existing political discourses could be fractured and reset. This is not to say that satire was necessarily 'oppositional'; indeed, binary models structured around poles such as monarch and opposition, court and country, absolutism and republicanism, can for this period be as crude when dealing with language as when discussing political alliances. Rather, and more fundamentally, satire provided the resources for the establishment of differences and the imagination of alternatives. As a result,

---

[6] *Reading Revolutions*, p. 5.
[7] Fredric Bogel, *The Difference Satire Makes: Rhetoric and Reading from Jonson to Byron* (Ithaca and London, 2001), stated esp. at p. 42. Cf. Lawrence Manley, who observes that Renaissance satire 'defined itself as *the* medium for discrimination, for the moral and social judgement that could establish differences no longer given or apparent in contemporary social life' (*Literature and Culture in Early Modern London* [Cambridge, 1995], p. 373).
[8] Cf. George A. Test's more general approach to satire (*Satire: Spirit and Art* [Tampa, 1991], esp. p. 4).
[9] T. M., *The Life of a Satyrical Puppy, Called Nim* (1657), p. 58. On the dating and authorship of this pamphlet, see below, pp. 29–30 and n.

it assumed unquestionable significance within a culture becoming increasingly anxious, and undeniably curious, about the phenomena of dissent and division.

In recent decades, the critical movements in literary studies of new historicism and cultural materialism have transformed the ways in which we read early modern texts. But while critics have focused superbly on genres such as epic, pastoral and love poetry, satire has somehow faded into the background. Perhaps it has seemed already too obviously historical; perhaps it has suffered from the new historicism's desire to find politics where we might least expect it. Whatever the case, apart from some suggestive reassessments of literary culture in the 1590s, readers of satire remain perforce heavily reliant on formalist and New Critical studies.[10] Moreover, consideration of satire in the following decades has been informed by a widespread perception that the Bishops' Ban drove satirists 'underground': becoming, as a result, more a concern for historians and archivists than literary critics.[11] Given my commitment to combining the archival and the critical, and my alignment with a form of cultural history concerned with 'the processes by which meaning is constructed', I want to outline at this stage some of the relevant literary issues for an historicized study of this mode.[12] In line with my approach throughout the book, it will be worth attending to contemporary perceptions of satire, the functions it served within its culture, and the conventional stances and strategies adopted by satirists. It will even be possible to glance towards the most vexed question of all: the very definition of this protean mode.

The satirists of the 1590s saw themselves as pioneers, bringing a classical genre to their native country. While Joseph Hall's 1597 claim to be the first English satirist is questionable on many grounds, it certainly highlights an

[10] On the 1590s, see especially Richard Helgerson, *The Elizabethan Prodigals* (Berkeley, 1976); Lorna Hutson, *Thomas Nashe in Context* (Oxford, 1989); and Neil Rhodes, *Elizabethan Grotesque* (London, 1980). The works of literary history that continue to influence this field include: Gilbert Highet, *The Anatomy of Satire* (Princeton, 1962); Alvin Kernan, *The Cankered Muse: Satire of the English Renaissance* (New Haven, 1959); John Peter, *Complaint and Satire in Early English Literature* (Oxford, 1956); and Raman Selden, *English Verse Satire, 1590–1765* (London, 1978).

[11] This narrative, which I will contest, continues to be rehearsed in studies of satire (see, for example, Connery and Combe, 'Theorizing Satire', p. 2). For the most important historical engagement with it, see Thomas Cogswell, 'Underground Political Verse and the Transformation of English Political Culture', in Susan D. Amussen and Mark A. Kishlansky, ed., *Political Culture and Cultural Politics in Early Modern England: Essays Presented to David Underdown* (Manchester, 1995), pp. 277–300.

[12] Roger Chartier, *Cultural History: Between Practices and Representations*, trans. Lydia G. Cochrane (Cambridge, 1988), p. 14. In this respect the present book develops upon the interdisciplinary approaches of my *God Speed the Plough: The Representation of Agrarian England, 1500–1660* (Cambridge, 1996).

emergent mood of generic purification. For Hall and his contemporaries, satire was literature at its most unashamedly moralistic and unabashedly instructive: writing with 'Truth on my side', he sets out to 'unmask' the 'ugly face of vice'.[13] Renaissance satire is thus founded on comfortable assumptions about the relation between texts and contexts. Satirists aim to 'speake the truth', using their powers of forensic inquiry to expose vice, and their conventions of outspokenness and didacticism to 'heale with lashing'.[14] Although, as Alvin Kernan has convincingly demonstrated, much satire of this decade is informed equally by Calvinistic anxieties about the speaker's own sinfulness, poets almost universally assume that there is sin out there to be identified, and that their audience will agree on its definition.[15] Satire is concerned with acts of revelation rather than strategies of fabrication, and with attacks on agreed sins rather than particular sinners. Consequently, even what might initially appear libellous and scurrilous, and what might seem merely gratuitous descriptions of sinfulness, are supposedly underpinned by the most soundly orthodox of moral principles.

In general, the satire of this decade is not recognizably political: though this is in part because contemporary discourses of politics themselves require such efforts of reconstruction and historicization.[16] Donne's fourth satire, for instance, focuses attention on the court, but does so with a moralist's disgust in the face of rampant self-interest and dissimulation. After a tour of the court, the poem's speaker calls on preachers to 'Drown the sins of this place'; like so much other satire of this decade, Donne's suggests that the political realm requires no more, and no less, than a moral reformation.[17] The Bishops' Ban, however, alerts us to other possible ways in which satires may have been functioning politically. While the opinions of literary historians remain divided on the intent of the Ban, some of the more stimulating interpretations have highlighted the political ramifications of Elizabethan satire.[18] Cyndia Susan Clegg, for instance, argues that a discrete set of political events, relating especially to the Earl of Essex's unsuccessful Irish campaign, changed the ways in which certain satires were

[13] *Virgidemiarum*, Book 1 Prologue; in *Collected Poems*, ed. Arnold Davenport (Liverpool, 1949), p. 11.
[14] Everard Guilpin, 'Satyre Preludium', lines 76, 71; in *Skialetheia or A Shadowe of Truth, in Certaine Epigrams and Satyres*, ed. D. Allen Carroll (Chapel Hill, 1974), p. 61.
[15] This is Kernan's central argument in *The Cankered Muse*.
[16] See esp. John Guy, ed., *The Reign of Elizabeth I: Court and Culture in the Last Decade* (Cambridge, 1995); and Paul E. J. Hammer, *The Polarisation of Elizabethan Politics: The Political Career of Robert Devereux, 2nd Earl of Essex, 1587–1597* (Cambridge, 1999).
[17] 'Satire 4', line 239; in *The Complete English Poems*, ed. A. J. Smith (London, 1986), p. 170.
[18] The text of the Ban is published in Richard A. McCabe, 'Elizabethan Satire and the Bishops' Ban of 1599', *Yearbook of English Studies*, 11 (1981), 188–93.

read in 1599. The generalized moralism of the satirists thereby became, albeit briefly, politically sensitive, so the mechanisms of censorship were mobilized in an effort to ease tensions.[19] While she almost certainly underestimates the political motivations of some poets, her analysis highlights the notorious grey area between attacks on corruption and attacks on the corrupt: a field which early Stuart poets would inhabit far more knowingly. Douglas Bruster, who considers the full list of works banned in 1599, which also included prose pamphlets and Ovidian erotica, argues that the authorities were responding to 'an intensively familiar approach to others' bodies and identities'.[20] Though somewhat speculative and intuitive, his argument too directs attention to the political potential of satire, especially at a time when personal and factional identities were so thoroughly intertwined with any more abstract notions of politics or ideology. Whatever the intentions of the banned poets of the 1590s, their successors were consistently more explicit in their attention to particular individuals, yet also more rigorous in their commitment to look for causes and principles beyond the individual.

Although the effects of the Ban were localized, and conventional moral satires continued to pass through the London presses, this book argues that satiric practices under the Stuarts changed in subtle yet decisive ways. Consequently, approaches and questions that were appropriate for Elizabethan satire now need to be rethought and revised. What happens to satire, we might ask, when dominant cultural assumptions about the relation between morality and power are opened to question? What happens when satirists abandon their commitment to revealing truths, in favour of a willingness to shape perceptions and delineate confrontations? What happens when moralizing attacks on corruption at court give way to a consideration of radical political alternatives? And what happens when royalism is translated from a universal assumption into a discourse of division? Unquestionably, many writers in these years maintained Elizabethan principles; however, many others accepted the necessity of change. As one commented, 'This is a wondrous witty age that sees / Beyond the truth of things, forty degrees'.[21] Seeing 'beyond the truth', as this poet anxiously begins to perceive, involves accepting that literature shapes realities as much as it merely reflects them, and that satire might now be revealing itself as interested

---

[19] *Press Censorship in Elizabethan England* (Cambridge, 1997), pp. 198–217.
[20] 'The Structural Transformation of Print in Late Elizabethan England', in Arthur F. Marotti and Michael D. Bristol, ed., *Print, Manuscript, and Performance: The Changing Relations of the Media in Early Modern England* (Columbus, OH, 2000), p. 49.
[21] Thomas Scot, *Philomythie or Philomythologie* (1622), sig. B1r.

and polemical rather than disinterested and aloof. I would suggest that a recognition of these possibilities may underpin a newly historicized analysis of political satire in this period.

Satire that sees 'beyond the truth', or that helps to construct its culture's truths, is especially valuable under conditions of censorship, which work to suppress more open and rational discussion of political issues.[22] The extent and mechanics of censorship in the reigns of James and Charles remain matters of dispute. Most recently, Clegg has argued against perceptions of a 'single abusive authoritarian system' of censorship in the early Stuart period, and has sought instead to demonstrate the importance of local circumstances, individual personalities and sheer chance.[23] Clegg's research is often compelling, and helps to explain the vicissitudes experienced by a poet such as Wither, who was variously punished, rewarded, or simply ignored by the state in the course of his prolific publishing career.[24] Yet she tends to underestimate the undeniable fear of repression which informs writing throughout the period. Writers were imprisoned, interrogated, fined and pilloried in this period; and even those who escaped such treatment were constantly aware of the risks they ran. Indeed for the present study, concerned as it is with textual practices rather than publication histories, the consciousness of censorship in the minds of writers is in most respects more significant than its actual achievements.[25] To take one example, the pamphleteer Thomas Scott, looking back on the 1623 Spanish Match negotiations, recalled that 'the dore began to wax narrow, at which the Protestants sent out . . . their labours for the presse'.[26] Like so many other writers in these years, Scott quite simply felt the constraints of censorship, and shaped his writing and publishing career accordingly.

The writing produced in these circumstances exists in a dialectical relationship with its context: informed by the prevailing conditions, and in turn helping to give definition to them. Of course, there were strong native traditions of political satire, stretching back through Donne, Sir Thomas Wyatt, John Skelton, and into the Middle Ages. It is also true that satire informed some of the most prominent political literature of the Elizabethan

---

[22] Cf. Dustin Griffin, *Satire: A Critical Reintroduction* (Lexington, KY, 1994), p. 138.

[23] *Press Censorship in Jacobean England* (Cambridge, 2001), quote at p. 118.

[24] *Press Censorship in Jacobean England*, pp. 45–50, 113–16; on Wither, see below, Chapter 3.

[25] Cf. David Norbrook, *Poetry and Politics in the English Renaissance*, revised edn (Oxford, 2002), p. 310; and Anthony Milton, 'Licensing, Censorship, and Religious Orthodoxy in Early Stuart England', *Historical Journal*, 41 (1998), 637.

[26] *Vox Dei* (1623), p. 69; reprinted in Scott, *Works* (1624); facsimile edn (Amsterdam, 1973). Cf. John Reynolds, *Vox Coeli* (1624), sig. A4v.

years, produced by writers such as Edmund Spenser and Sir Philip Sidney.[27] But the early Stuart decades produced distinctly new kinds of satiric writing. Most notably, the libel, a form with established popular and courtly roots, flourished in the reign of James, providing perhaps the single most important textual site for interaction between political and literary cultures. And not only was the libel ideally suited to a reign marked by court scandals and notorious favourites, it was also malleable enough to invite further reflection on ideological conflicts and political contestation. Similarly, the pamphlet had emerged by the end of the sixteenth century as a distinct, though almost infinitely versatile, textual form.[28] The achievements of the anti-episcopal Martin Marprelate tracts, published anonymously in the late 1580s, established a vital precedent for satiric voice and political insurgency.[29] In the following decades, authors and printers alike explored ways of developing upon this precedent, especially by intervening in matters of political debate. While the term 'pamphlet' is in many respects a loose, catchall word denoting a wide range of writing – including poetry, prose, news reports, dialogues and sermons – an intention to stretch the parameters of popular political interaction is consistent across a whole range of cheap printed texts. Although I selectively glance beyond these principal sources – towards letters, speeches, history writing, religious tracts, and the most scandalous political play of the period, Thomas Middleton's *A Game at Chess* – the book is founded on a perception that libels and pamphlets were the most vital and influential vehicles for early Stuart political satire.

Given its focus on satire within a discrete historical context, this is not a book that makes bold claims to define the mode. Definitions have a tendency to become reified and ahistorical, whereas my contention is that satire is malleable, adaptable and sometimes most incisive when it fails even to announce itself. Nonetheless, like other recent studies this book is committed to challenging the residual influence of John Dryden's Restoration definition of the mode, which works so hard to establish clear boundaries between the native and the neoclassical, the scurrilous and the moral, the libellous and the properly satiric.[30] In search of a definition less overloaded with formal and aesthetic concerns, more than one scholar has adopted Edward

---

[27] See esp. Norbrook, *Poetry and Politics*, pp. 53–139; and Blair Worden, *The Sound of Virtue: Philip Sidney's* Arcadia *and Elizabethan Politics* (New Haven, CT and London, 1996).
[28] See esp. Sandra Clark, *The Elizabethan Pamphleteers* (London, 1982); and Alexandra Halasz, *The Marketplace of Print: Pamphlets and the Public Sphere in Early Modern England* (Cambridge, 1997).
[29] *The Marprelate Tracts*, ed. William Pierce (London, 1911).
[30] See Dryden's 'Discourse concerning the Original and Progress of Satire', in *The Works of John Dryden, Volume IV: Poems 1693–1696*, ed. A. B. Chambers and William Frost (Berkeley, 1974), pp. 3–90; and Griffin's summary and critique of Dryden, in *Satire*, pp. 14–21.

Rosenheim, Jr.'s definition of satire as an 'attack by means of a manifest fiction upon discernible historical particulars'.[31] This helpfully suppresses the moral imperative claimed by both Dryden and the Elizabethans, and creates a space for serious analysis of libels. But Rosenheim's apparent assumption that a text will present itself unproblematically as a satire remains biased towards modern notions of literature and authorship, and might cause one to neglect occasional and tactical deployments of satire in the early Stuart decades. Moreover, his perception of 'discernible historical particulars' is overly simplistic, neglecting the extent to which texts help to shape their contexts, and thereby give definition to history itself. Even the seemingly historical facts of individual identity may be manipulated (as we shall see in Chapter 2), while political alignments and confrontations depend on a language of discrimination. In this book, therefore, satire is perceived at once as more fluid and available throughout its contemporary culture, and also as more active and influential in its political interventions. This is a study, that is, of a literary mode in action.

As a result, I would also suggest that debates over whether satire is conservative or radical are, at least within this specific historical context, reductive.[32] The very terms 'conservatism' and 'radicalism' assume an uncomplicated binary model of power, while the sense that 'satire' might somehow be consistent in its politics posits an unrealistically restrictive model of textual production. Nonetheless, it is fair to say that early Stuart satire had distinctly radical effects on political discourse: not because it dared on occasion to challenge the status quo, but because it helped to delineate entirely new discourses of politics. It was radical, that is, because it turned its techniques of discrimination upon a politics resting shakily on assumptions of consensus. What particular 'side' a satire might take is in this respect relatively unimportant: in part because the whole notion of sides is so loose and shadowy when applied to early Stuart politics, and in part because the satiric act of discrimination is itself more fundamental, no matter what the particular politics of any text. Satire is radical, in other words, to the extent that it lends contemporaries the resources to move beyond existing political structures.

These arguments in turn help to situate the book in relation to questions that have dominated studies in seventeenth-century political history for

<hr/>

[31] *Jonathan Swift and the Satirist's Art* (Chicago, 1963), p. 31. Cf. Kirk Combe, 'The New Voice of Political Dissent: The Transition from Complaint to Satire', in *Theorizing Satire*, ed. Combe and Connery, p. 75; and Bogel, *The Difference Satire Makes*, p. 8.
[32] On this debate, see Griffin, *Satire*, pp. 149–60.

the past twenty-five years. Crucially, the revisionist movement challenged previously accepted ideas that there were clear lines of political division in early Stuart England, evident especially by the late 1620s and 1630s, and often defined in terms of 'court' and 'country'. Though there is hardly the space here to do justice to their arguments, revisionists spoke of a nation that valorized consensus, and enjoined their colleagues against importing anachronistic terms to describe a pre-modern political world.[33] Conflict, to the extent that it existed, was primarily seen as a struggle to define the boundaries of orthodoxy, rather than to confront or challenge orthodoxy. But these arguments, though effective in demonstrating the false assumptions of earlier historiography, left many questions unanswered and many sources unexamined. In particular, in their intensive scrutiny of the mechanics of government, revisionists tended to neglect evidence of popular opinion and political language.[34] The best post-revisionist work has returned to such issues, and has championed some of the sources that form the basis of the present study. Above all else, such work has prompted researchers to rethink their very definitions of the political.

Perhaps most importantly, post-revisionist reassessments of the politics of court corruption and scandal create a context for my own engagement with a wealth of texts concerned with the early Stuart court. As Linda Levy Peck has argued, in this period 'the language of corruption', though overtly traditional and moralistic, in fact 'provided an essential vocabulary with which to criticize the early Stuart government'.[35] Similarly, the revisionist neglect of court scandals has been challenged for its 'curiously limited definition of the political'.[36] Indeed certain events and individuals became undeniably controversial in these years, producing distinct waves of satirical commentary; and at this stage it is worth outlining, however sketchily, some of the most significant of these. In the 1610s, the most notorious scandal centred on James's favourite, Robert Carr, and his wife, Frances Howard. After being married to the Earl of Essex as a child, Howard obtained a divorce on grounds of her husband's impotence, after a salacious legal process

---

[33] See esp. Kevin Sharpe, ed., *Faction and Parliament: Essays in Early Stuart History* (Oxford, 1978); John Morrill, *Revolt in the Provinces: The People of England and the Tragedies of War*, 2nd edn (London and New York, 1999), pp. 1–74; and Conrad Russell, *Parliaments and English Politics 1621–1629* (Oxford, 1979), pp. 1–84.

[34] See esp. Kevin Sharpe's review of early Stuart historiography, in *Remapping Early Modern England: The Culture of Seventeenth-Century Politics* (Cambridge, 2000), pp. 3–37.

[35] *Court Patronage and Corruption in Early Stuart England* (London, 1993), p. 11.

[36] Alastair Bellany, *The Politics of Court Scandal in Early Modern England: News Culture and the Overbury Affair, 1603–1660* (Cambridge, 2002), p. 14.

in which the king's intervention helped to sway the result. She then married Carr, but they were soon embroiled in further controversy, which led to their political ruin, when the courtier Sir Thomas Overbury was murdered in the Tower, allegedly on the couple's instructions. Though dismissed in revisionist narratives as a matter of personality rather than politics, more recent studies have convincingly reinserted discourse on these events into the political sphere, arguing for its significance within a culture increasingly concerned about the foundations and legitimacy of authority.[37] In the 1620s, the Spanish Match negotiations provided a focus for recurrent anxieties about the influence of papists in government policy, and prompted many commentators to challenge James's classification of issues of foreign policy as *arcana imperii*.[38] Further, political observers at this time focused on individuals who seemed in various ways to epitomize the excesses of the court: from Sir Francis Bacon, impeached in the 1621 Parliament, to George Villiers, Duke of Buckingham, whose intimacy with James and apparent stranglehold on power made him the most talked-about individual of the entire early Stuart period. Like the libellous commentary on Carr and Howard, that on Buckingham, especially after his assassination in 1628, furthered an ongoing interrogation of authority in England, and provided occasion for more radical, even republican, comment.[39] By the 1630s, attention turned particularly to Archbishop William Laud, who seemed to many to be undermining the foundations of the English Church. Far from being merely a religious matter, or from demonstrating the inability of contemporaries to distinguish between the religious and the political, I argue in Chapter 6 that attacks on Laud include some of the most acute political comment of the period.

Parliaments claim slightly less prominence in the current context: not because I would want to endorse the revisionist position that they were mere events, which aimed above all to reach consensus and to avoid confrontation with the court, but rather because most parliamentary speech was withheld within authorized bounds. Satire was available to members of parliament, and on occasion helped them to sharpen barbs of criticism; however, its use in this forum remained an exceptional and noteworthy occurrence. Nonetheless, early modern parliaments were in many respects more important than the records of debates might sometimes suggest, and

[37] See esp. Bellany, *Politics of Court Scandal.*

[38] Thomas Cogswell, *The Blessed Revolution: English Politics and the Coming of War, 1621–1624* (Cambridge, 1989).

[39] See esp. James Holstun, "'God Bless Thee, Little David!': John Felton and his Allies', *ELH*, 59 (1992), 513–52; and Norbrook, *Writing the English Republic*, pp. 50–8.

this book participates in an ongoing reconsideration of their wider cultural significance.[40] Throughout the early Stuart decades, parliamentary years provided the stimuli for a wealth of discussion, documented in manuscript and printed sources, about the limits of authorized political comment and the status of the political subject. Free speech, as we shall see in Chapter 3, is an issue on which the interests of parliamentarians and poets coalesce, and therefore a series of satires published by Wither may be seen to amplify arguments which dominated the parliaments of 1614 and 1621.[41] Moreover, it is becoming increasingly clear that parliamentary debates were echoed across the nation, and translated by satirists into newly pointed and libellous idioms. Hence, for example, parliament's repeated projects of impeachment, which is itself a strategy of stigmatization, are decisively reiterated, and grotesquely distorted, in the waves of libels to be examined here.[42]

Other historians have revised ideas about political identities in the period by focusing afresh on the languages of politics. Most importantly, J. G. A. Pocock and Quentin Skinner have turned attention within the field of intellectual history from political ideas to the language in which such ideas were expressed.[43] Republicanism, for example, is reconceived in this model as a political language rather than a programme.[44] This approach enables more dynamic models of political conflict, usefully complicating the otherwise valuable structure of competing theories propounded by historians such as J. P. Sommerville.[45] Hence the scholarly project of identifying particular individuals as 'republicans' or 'royalists', among the many other classifications afforded by the period's political discourse, may be problematized by a perception of 'republicanism' and 'royalism' as discourses which were available to different people, in different forms, at different times. One person

[40] See esp. Stephen Clucas and Rosalind Davies, ed., *1614: Year of Crisis: Studies in Jacobean History and Literature* (Aldershot, 2002). I am grateful to Dr Clucas for providing me with copies of essays from this volume before its publication.

[41] On the debates in 1621, see Christopher Thompson, *The Debate on Freedom of Speech in the House of Commons in February 1621* (Orsett, Essex, 1985); and Robert Zaller, *The Parliament of 1621: A Study in Constitutional Conflict* (Berkeley, 1971).

[42] Robert Zaller makes the point about impeachment as an act of stigmatization in 'The Concept of Opposition in Early Stuart England', *Albion*, 12 (1980), 233. See further below, pp. 135–7.

[43] See esp. Pocock, *Politics, Language and Time* (London, 1972), and *Virtue, Commerce and History* (Cambridge, 1985); Skinner, 'Meaning and Understanding in the History of Ideas', *History and Theory*, 8 (1969), 3–53; and J. H. Tully, ed., *Meaning and Context: Quentin Skinner and his Critics* (Cambridge, 1988).

[44] Pocock, 'Introduction' to *The Political Works of James Harrington* (Cambridge, 1977), p. 15: quoted in J. C. D. Clark, *Revolution and Rebellion: State and Society in England in the Seventeenth and Eighteenth Centuries* (Cambridge, 1986), p. 106.

[45] *Royalists and Patriots: Politics and Ideology in England 1603–1640*, 2nd edn (London and New York, 1999); cf. the comments of Glenn Burgess, in *The Politics of the Ancient Constitution: An Introduction to English Political Thought, 1603–1642* (Basingstoke and London, 1992), p. 113.

might hold competing discourses in his or her head at any one moment; one text might bring such discourses into collision, for either rhetorical or polemical purposes. But Pocock and Skinner have rightly been criticized for their exclusive attention to the great, canonical texts of political theory, and as a result they have arguably underestimated both the extent and sophistication of radical political thought in early Stuart England.[46] They also, I argue, underestimate the extent to which religious radicalism, even in evidently populist forms, may be translated into political radicalism.

Within this context, studies of news, rumour and libel have usefully extended our appreciations of political discourse. Although printed reports of domestic news were officially banned throughout our period, 'corantoes' containing news from the continent, especially during the Thirty Years' War, provided a vital framework for popular political engagement.[47] Moreover, fresh scrutiny of manuscript news networks has revealed the extent to which English men and women, across the country, were involved in political discussions.[48] As we have learned, the business of newsgathering was centred on the nave and aisles of St Paul's Cathedral – 'the great Exchange of all discourse' and 'the Synod of all pates politicke' – and was subsequently filtered through various newsmongers, intelligencers and scribes.[49] Fact and rumour, prose and verse circulated alike in the city and court, and then reached the provinces, where it was assessed, discussed, and occasionally disseminated further in letters, or committed thoughtfully to the pages of private diaries. Significantly, the readers of news were absorbed by instances of political conflict, and preoccupied by the careers of controversial figures such as Buckingham. In the light of such evidence, certain historians have challenged revisionist arguments, and have prompted a reassessment of the

[46] Kevin Sharpe, *Politics and Ideas in Early Stuart England: Essays and Studies* (London and New York, 1989), p. 5; Markuu Peltonen, *Classical Humanism and Republicanism in English Political Thought 1570–1640* (Cambridge, 1995), pp. 6–7.

[47] See J. Frank, *The Beginnings of the English Newspaper, 1620–1660* (Cambridge, MA, 1961); Michael Colin Frearson, 'The English Corantoes of the 1620s' (unpublished Ph.D dissertation, University of Cambridge, 1993); Joad Raymond, ed., *News, Newspapers, and Society in Early Modern Britain* (London and Portland, 1999); Joad Raymond, *The Invention of the Newspaper: English Newsbooks, 1641–1649* (Oxford, 1996); and C. John Sommerville, *The News Revolution in England: Cultural Dynamics of Daily Information* (New York and Oxford, 1996).

[48] See esp. Ian Atherton, 'The Itch Grown a Disease: Manuscript Transmission of News in the Seventeenth Century', in Raymond, ed., *News, Newspapers, and Society in Early Modern Britain*, pp. 39–65; Richard Cust, 'News and Politics in Early Seventeenth-Century England', *Past and Present*, 112 (1986), 60–90; Dagmar Freist, *Governed by Opinion: Politics, Religion, and the Dynamics of Communication in Stuart London, 1637–1645* (London, 1997); Harold Love, *The Culture and Commerce of Texts: Scribal Publication in Seventeenth-Century England* (Amherst, 1998), pp. 9–22; Adam Fox, *Oral and Literate Culture in England 1500–1700* (Oxford, 2000), pp. 335–405.

[49] John Earle, *Micro-cosmographie* (1628), sig. iiiv; cf. Francis Osborne, *Traditionall Memoryes on the Raigne of King James* (1658), pp. 64–6.

origins of political opposition in the years before the Civil War. Although I do not intend to enter these arguments directly, my own analysis of the discourses of politics demonstrates further a contemporary fascination with discord and contestation. In this respect, we will find that some of the most interesting evidence concerns not those who were developing passionate views of different kinds, but those who traced lines of debate and assessed competing arguments in the privacy of their own studies.

Such people were rethinking the meaning of politics, and evidence of their thought has in turn prompted a number of scholars to revise pre-existing models of early modern political engagement. In particular, Jürgen Habermas's notion of the 'public sphere', which he identifies first in the coffee houses of late seventeenth-century London, has recently been applied to earlier periods. For Habermas, the public sphere is a socially inclusive realm which facilitates the free exchange of ideas and opinions in a manner governed by principles of reason.[50] In many respects, efforts to relocate his theory underscore our growing appreciation of the sophistication of political culture in the early Stuart period; however, in other respects the existence of a public sphere depends heavily on the ways in which any particular person chooses to manipulate Habermas's suggestive theory. There is indeed a danger, as Alastair Bellany has also appreciated, of identifying the first emergence of a public sphere becoming something of an academic game.[51] As I hope to show, it is perhaps more interesting to examine the ways in which contemporaries tried to think their way towards something that we might choose to call a public sphere, but which for them was unclear and untested. Moreover, in this process Habermasian 'reason' is perhaps less useful, and less illuminating, than forms of unreason. As Joad Raymond has argued, at this time 'reason was not generally recognized as an arbiter of debate'; and, as the period's satiric writing reveals time and again, new discourses of dissent and division are often formulated first in experimental and provocative idioms.[52] Similarly, while I do not claim that a new model of citizenship simply replaced existing notions of subjecthood in this period, I want to remain alert to critical shifts and tensions, as contemporaries chipped away at

---

[50] Habermas, *The Structural Transformation of the Public Sphere: An Inquiry into a Category of Bourgeois Society*, trans. Thomas Burger (Cambridge, MA, 1991). See also Love, *Culture and Commerce of Texts*, pp. 203–7; Michelle O'Callaghan, *The 'shepheards nation': Jacobean Spenserians and Early Stuart Political Culture* (Oxford, 2000), pp. 5–8; Peter Lake and Steven Pincus, eds., *The Public Sphere in Early Modern England* (Manchester, forthcoming); and David Zaret, *Origins of Democratic Culture: Printing, Petitions, and the Public Sphere in Early Modern England* (Princeton, 2000).

[51] Bellany, *Politics of Court Scandal*, p. 18.

[52] 'The Newspaper, Public Opinion, and the Public Sphere in the Seventeenth Century', in Raymond, ed., *News, Newspapers, and Society in Early Modern Britain*, p. 122.

the foundations of a constrictive order.[53] As Patrick Collinson has written, 'citizens' were at this time 'concealed within subjects'.[54]

These directions of historical inquiry have in turn informed approaches to the politics of early Stuart literature. In the wake of the revisionist debate, several rigorously historical studies of poetry and politics set out to prove the existence, or otherwise, of conflict. For Kevin Sharpe, for example, Caroline literature articulated values of consensus; for David Norbrook, on the contrary, traditions of opposition could be traced right back into the sixteenth century.[55] Norbrook's recent publication of a revised edition of his *Poetry and Politics in the English Renaissance* signals at once a continued interest in the issues it raises, and the ways in which the field has developed.[56] Among other notable advances, Michelle O'Callaghan has explored the politics of early seventeenth-century Spenserian poetry, particularly that written against a backdrop of mounting anxiety in England over court politics and apparent struggles between king and parliament.[57] Meanwhile, Norbrook has expanded on his argument for an existence of a republican tradition before the Civil War, and James Loxley has led a reassessment of a royalist poetic tradition, in a study that intelligently stretches back into the 1630s.[58] Others, such as Arthur Marotti and Timothy Raylor, have added clarity to our appreciation of the politics of manuscript culture.[59] Given the new sources being opened to consideration, and the new range of questions that literary scholars are asking of the period, there will undoubtedly be much more to come.[60]

[53] On theories of citizenship, see esp. Peltonen, *Classical Humanism and Republicanism*.
[54] 'De Republica Anglorum: Or, History with the Politics Put Back', in *Elizabethan Essays* (London and Rio Grande, 1994), p. 19.
[55] Sharpe, *Criticism and Compliment: The Politics of Literature in the England of Charles I* (Cambridge, 1987); Norbrook, *Poetry and Politics* (first published London, 1984). For other important critiques of revisionism from the direction of literary studies, see esp. Martin Butler, *Theatre and Crisis 1632–1642* (Cambridge, 1984); Margot Heinemann, *Puritanism and Theatre: Thomas Middleton and Opposition Drama under the Early Stuarts* (Cambridge, 1980); and Annabel Patterson, *Censorship and Interpretation: The Conditions of Writing and Reading in Early Modern England* (Madison, 1984). Norbrook usefully surveys this context in his revised edition of *Poetry and Politics*, pp. 270–89.
[56] See Norbrook's survey of relevant publications since the first edition of his book (pp. 298–315); and note also his decision to revise the chapters which are of most concern in the present context: on Jonson, the Spenserians, and the years 1617–28.
[57] O'Callaghan, *The 'shepheards nation'*.
[58] Norbrook, *Writing the English Republic*; Loxley, *Royalism and Poetry*.
[59] Marotti, *Manuscript, Print, and the English Renaissance Lyric* (Ithaca and London, 1995); Raylor, *Cavaliers, Clubs, and Literary Culture: Sir John Mennes, James Smith, and the Order of the Fancy* (Newark, 1994).
[60] It is hoped that the study of libels, in particular, will be advanced by the publication of 'Early Stuart Libels: An Edition of Political Poems from Manuscript Sources', ed. Alastair Bellany and Andrew McRae, *Early Modern Literary Studies* (forthcoming).

Some of this work, like many of the recent historical investigations, will doubtless attend to England's place in a wider international context. James I and Charles I were, after all, kings of Scotland and (more problematically) Ireland as well as England and Wales, while each man was also drawn into the struggles and intrigues of an entire continent which was at war from 1618 until nearly the end of Charles's life. One of the most impressive studies of James explicitly situates him within this context, while some of the more enlightening post-revisionist work has attended to the English people's perception of their nation.[61] Discussion of the Thirty Years' War, in particular, provided occasion for a wealth of discourse insisting on the English nation's international ties and responsibilities. Yet in the present book, while international concerns consistently impinge upon political comment, and while many interventions in the debates surrounding the Thirty Years' War employ satire, the overwhelming focus of the texts under consideration repeatedly draws one back to England. Satire in this period, that is, tends to be introspective, brooding on the government and political structures of the nation rather than looking beyond that nation's borders. Spain is typically depicted simply as a locus of all that is not English, while Scotland and Ireland are barely even mentioned. James's homeland had its own national literary culture, with its own traditions of satire and scurrility; however, connections between Scottish and English writers, and the interest of each in the political contexts of the other, appear to have been slight.[62]

The book's chapters ask distinct yet overlapping questions, and are concerned with distinct yet overlapping bodies of material. All are concerned with the functions of satire within political culture, and all argue that this literary mode helped contemporaries to reconstruct their discourses of politics, yet each takes a particular approach to a particular set of texts. It is not, therefore, a narrative. Although there is a certain chronological momentum, and although certain dates assume special significance – the Parliament of 1614, the Spanish Match negotiations in 1623, the assassination of Buckingham in 1628, the trial of John Bastwick, Henry Burton and William Prynne in 1637 – this is not a subject best tackled in narrative form. Changes in the discourses of politics are too erratic and piecemeal; rather than a history of even and unfolding development, we find different people at different

[61] See W. B. Patterson, *King James VI and I and the Reunion of Christendom* (Cambridge, 1997); Cogswell, *The Blessed Revolution*; Peter Lake, 'Constitutional Consensus and Puritan Opposition in the 1620s: Thomas Scott and the Spanish Match', *Historical Journal*, 25 (1982), 805–25.
[62] One exception is provided by William Drummond of Hawthornden, whose work and interests will be mentioned occasionally throughout.

times trying to make sense of their circumstances. Hence the reasons behind the book's structure are partly chronological, partly generic and partly thematic. I attempt to consider the full range of texts that has presented itself in my research, and to examine particular texts within their appropriate contexts. And I attempt to bring to bear upon these texts questions of concern to both literary and political historians.

The first part, 'Personal politics', is concerned specifically with libels. The remarkable proliferation of libels in the early Stuart period has long been recognized; however, only recently have these poems begun to receive the sort of attention they deserve. The chapters in Part I are intended as a major step forward, not only in bringing the poems into the public domain, but also setting them within their literary and political contexts. The first, 'The culture of early Stuart libelling', argues that these texts warrant consideration as the most successful and influential forms of satire produced in the early seventeenth century. Despite claims to the contrary made by some historians, there is evidence that libels were not merely written by hack writers in order to score cheap political points, but were rather products of a sophisticated literary culture. Consequently, rather than labelling these poems as unproblematic expressions of popular opinion, or claiming them simply as evidence of a tradition of opposition, we should first try to understand more about how they work as poems, and how they relate to satiric traditions. The following chapter, 'Contesting identities: libels and the early Stuart politician', examines some of the ways in which libels intervened in a political culture centred on prominent individuals. This chapter draws together some central concerns of recent literary studies of this period, and applies them to very real personal and political struggles. Libels, I argue, participated in processes of contestation over identity formation, which had critical consequences not only for the individuals involved, but also for the wider political system. Most notably, libellous discourse surrounding the Duke of Buckingham not only helped to create a context in which his assassination would widely be welcomed, but also stimulated more fundamental critiques of the system within which he had risen.

In the second part, 'Public politics', the range of sources is expanded, to include printed poetry and prose as well as some more libels. Chapter 3, 'Freeing the tongue and the heart: satire and the political subject', considers the relation between this literary mode and contemporary debates over free speech. The rhetorical stance adopted by the satirist is critical in this regard. While Wither, in his early works, struggles to accommodate the satirist within a traditional structure of loyal courtly counsel, the overwhelming momentum in political satire is towards a radically new subject position. In such works, for all their provocations and evasions, we may discern writers imagining a public sphere in England, within which citizens may openly debate political concerns. The fourth, and longest, chapter, 'Discourses of discrimination: political satire in the 1620s', focuses on texts from one turbulent and pivotal decade. It examines the ways in which contemporaries represented political identities and processes, and argues that the resources of satire informed some critical revaluations of contestation. In particular, I argue that discourses of religious division were powerfully clarified in this decade, and an increasing number of writers wilfully intertwined the political and the religious, in ways that established a framework for the more damaging conflicts of the following decades. Moreover, as an analysis of Middleton's *Game at Chess* demonstrates, this new appreciation of confrontation underpinned some significant revisions of the political process.

The chapters in the third part, 'The politics of division', are more discrete in focus, and look in turn at pivotal figures in the construction, respectively, of royalism and opposition. Chapter 5, 'Satire and sycophancy: Richard Corbett and Early Stuart royalism', focuses on one of the most influential poets operating in early Stuart manuscript culture. Corbett, who rose to the position of Bishop of Oxford under the patronage of the Duke of Buckingham, fundamentally rejects the orthodox position that poets, whether writing praise or blame, should endorse values of unity and harmony. While Ben Jonson struggled to maintain these fictions in the early years of James's reign, Corbett decisively rejected them, and fashioned instead a poetics of division, stridently setting the interests of himself and his patron against those of their perceived enemies. Chapter 6, 'Stigmatizing Prynne: puritanism and politics in the 1630s', examines the three men whose Star Chamber trial in 1637 helped to galvanize a movement of opposition to Laud and the court. While previous studies have considered the trial of Bastwick, Burton and Prynne, Chapter 6 begins by analysing their published works from the years leading up to the trial, considering the ways in which satire helped them to hone their perceptions of corruption and persecution in their nation. Subsequently, I turn to discourse surrounding the trial and punishment, and consider the ways in which their contested status, as martyrs or traitors, further polarized Caroline politics.

The book's temporal parameters are 1603 to, roughly, 1640. The latter date is commonly accepted as marking a watershed, in both political and literary culture, for reasons that remain sensible enough. Although the Civil War did not begin until 1642, the foundations of royal authority were undermined with the opening of the Long Parliament in November 1640, and the subsequent impeachment of Laud and Thomas Wentworth, Earl of Strafford. Crucially, the institutions of state censorship also collapsed, and as a result the presses produced a flood of new texts, in novel and unsettling forms. Literary historians, broadly speaking, rightly see these years as the start of a new era; however, as I hope the present book demonstrates, they have often overlooked the ways in which the writers of this era are indebted to those who came before them. Consequently, while satire of the 1640s and 1650s might well provide the subject for another book, my discussion in the Epilogue selectively glances towards the writing of these decades, and identifies some lines of continuity linking writing from before and after 1640.[63] If the book has a single conclusion it is, quite simply, that in the early Stuart period a literature of division was inextricably intertwined with a politics of division. The outbreak of warfare – a brutal historical fact which satire had helped make thinkable – effectively brings the book to a close, while instigating in turn a new era of political and textual engagement.

[63] Existing studies of satire in these decades include: Harold F. Brooks, 'Verse Satire, 1640–1660', *The Seventeenth Century*, 3 (1989), 17–46; Margaret Anne Doody, *The Daring Muse: Augustan Poetry Reconsidered* (Cambridge, 1985), pp. 30–57; Benne Klaas Faber, 'The Poetics of Subversion and Conservatism: Popular Satire, c.1640–c.1649' (unpublished DPhil. dissertation, University of Oxford, 1992); Loxley, *Royalism and Poetry*; Nigel Smith, *Literature and Revolution*, pp. 295–319; Zwicker, *Lines of Authority: Politics and English Literary Culture, 1649–1689* (Ithaca and London, 1993).

PART I

Personal politics

CHAPTER I

The culture of early Stuart libelling

The death in 1612 of the Lord Treasurer, Robert Cecil, Earl of Salisbury, prompted a cultural phenomenon that few observers of state affairs could have failed to notice. As the days passed, libellous verses on Cecil began to proliferate and circulate in unprecedented numbers.[1] The anxiety surrounding this wave of textual production is evident in the letters of John Chamberlain, who wrote that 'the memorie of the late Lord Treasurer growes dayly worse and worse and more libells come as yt were continually'.[2] Writing just three weeks later, however, John Donne provided a different view. He suggested, perhaps with a touch of irony, that many of the libels were so bad that they might have been written by Cecil's friends:

It is not the first time that our age hath seen that art practised, That when there are witty and sharp libels made which not onely for liberty of speaking, but for the elegancie, and composition, would take deep root, and make durable impressions in the memory, no other way hath been thought so fit to suppress them, as to divulge some course, and railing one: for when the noise is risen, that libels are abroad, mens curiositie must be served with something: and it is better for the honour of the person traduced, that some blunt downright railings be vented, of which every body is soon weary, then other pieces, which entertain us long with a delight, and love to the things themselves.[3]

Alongside Chamberlain's concern for biographical truth and political order, Donne shifts attention to the aesthetic qualities of libels. Adopting a Sidneian conception of the function of poetry – to teach and delight – he suggests that a libel will influence only to the extent that it 'entertain[s]' a reader.

---

[1] This phenomenon is documented in Pauline Croft, 'The Reputation of Robert Cecil: Libels, Political Opinion and Popular Awareness in the Early Seventeenth Century', *Transactions of the Royal Historical Society*, 6th series, 1 (1991), 43–69.

[2] *The Letters of John Chamberlain*, ed. Norman Egbert McClure (2 vols., Philadelphia, 1939), 1.364.

[3] *Letters to Severall Persons of Honour* (London, 1651), pp. 89–90.

Donne's letter raises important questions about the functions of libels. A scurrilous poem circulated in news networks immediately after the death of a statesman has a clear strategic purpose; the Cecil libels certainly prompted Chamberlain to reassess his opinion of the man, as he wondered 'whether yt be that practises and juglings' were in truth coming 'more and more to light'.[4] Its status might therefore appear to be close to that of graffiti, a form of invective as ephemeral as it is topical. Evidence supporting Donne's divergent appreciation of the libel, however, may be derived from manuscript sources in which the poetry is preserved. In numerous verse miscellanies libels were transcribed, often many years after their composition, alongside the work of the greatest poets of the age.[5] The compiler of BL MS Egerton 2230, for example, transcribed a series of Cecil libels in a section of epigrams. Rosenbach MS 1083/16 is even more concerned to read libels in literary terms; titled by its compiler 'MISCELLANIES: OR A collection of Divers Witty and pleasant Epigrams, Adages, poemes Epitaphes &c: for the recreation of the overtravelled Sences: 1630', it includes a selection of libels from across the previous thirty years, along with poems by Donne, Ben Jonson, Thomas Carew and Robert Herrick, and others. It is even possible to discern an application of literary judgement, along the lines suggested by Donne, among the men and women who kept miscellanies. The most sophisticated of the Cecil libels, a poem often attributed to Sir Walter Raleigh, survives in more sources than any other.[6]

These details of textual transmission and reception alert us to the importance of examining both literary and political contexts when considering early Stuart libels. To date, most scholarship on libels has been conducted by historians, concerned with issues of public opinion and political culture. Thomas Cogswell, for example, argues that the poems document 'the emergence of popular political awareness'; similarly, Pauline Croft interprets them as 'valuable evidence for a lively public opinion, emanating

---

[4] *Letters of John Chamberlain*, 1.364.

[5] On the manuscript verse miscellany, and its relation to the commonplace book, see Peter Beal, 'Notions in Garrison: The Seventeenth-Century Commonplace Book', in W. Speed Hill, ed., *New Ways of Looking at Old Texts: Papers of the Renaissance English Text Society, 1985–1991* (Binghamton, 1993), pp. 131–47 (esp. 142–4).

[6] I will consider this poem, 'Here lyes old Hobinol, our shephard while heare', further below. Copies exist in: Bodleian MS Rawlinson poet. 26, fol. 78r; Bodleian MS Eng. poet. e.14, fol. 79v; Bodleian MS Eng. poet. f.10, fols. 97v–98r; Bodleian MS Tanner 299, fol. 12v; BL MS Egerton 2230, fol. 34r; BL MS Harley 1221, fol. 74r; BL MS Harley 6038, fol. 18r; BL MS Harley 6947, fol. 211r; Folger MS v.a.345, p. 110; and 'Poems from a Seventeenth-Century Manuscript', 41–3. It is attributed to Raleigh in Bodleian Rawlinson poet. 26 and Folger v.a.345; Croft discusses the matter of authorship in 'Reputation', 62.

from London but not confined to the capital'.[7] Work by literary scholars on
political poetry of the early seventeenth century has tended to avoid general
questions about the mode, focusing rather on individual poems or groups
of poems.[8] At the outset of *Satire and the Early Stuart State*, therefore,
I want to consider as broadly as possible the practices of libelling, and the
qualities and functions of verse libels. For, as Donne's letter suggests, it
would be wrong to approach libels as no more than strategic statements,
directly reflecting popular opinion. Libels were also acknowledged as literary products, and it is important to appreciate the significance of literary
codes and expectations in the culture of early Stuart libelling. In accordance with the governing intent of this book, such an approach promises
also to illuminate the interaction between literary and political discourse in
the pre-revolutionary decades: as the political situation stimulated a wealth
of literature, and as literature helped to provide a language for emergent
divisions in the state.

This chapter initially seeks to contextualize early Stuart libelling, considering the literary origins of the form, its growth in the seventeenth century,
and its construction as a licensed mode. Subsequently, I analyse the major
sources for the study of libels, and argue that the culture of the verse miscellany contributed at once to the proliferation and developing characteristics
of the poems. The final section then considers the principal generic qualities
of the libel, and thus works towards an appreciation of its literary and political functions. As becomes apparent, while the practice of libelling overlaps

[7] Cogswell, 'Underground Political Verse and the Transformation of English Political Culture', in Susan
D. Amussen and Mark A. Kishlansky, eds., *Political Culture and Cultural Politics in Early Modern
England: Essays Presented to David Underdown* (Manchester, 1995), p. 278; Croft, 'Libels, Popular
Literacy and Public Opinion in Early Modern England', *Historical Research*, 68 (1995), 280. Other
work by historians on this material includes Alastair Bellany, *The Politics of Court Scandal in Early
Modern England: News Culture and the Overbury Affair, 1603–1660* (Cambridge, 2002), pp. 97–111;
Bellany, '"Raylinge Rymes and Vaunting Verse": Libellous Politics in Early Stuart England, 1603–
1628', in *Culture and Politics in Early Stuart England*, ed. Kevin Sharpe and Peter Lake (Basingstoke,
1994), pp. 285–310; Bellany, 'A Poem on the Archbishop's Hearse: Puritanism, Libel, and Sedition after
the Hampton Court Conference', *Journal of British Studies*, 34 (1995), 137–64. Adam Fox considers a
parallel tradition of libelling in localized disputes, in 'Ballads, Libels and Popular Ridicule in Jacobean
England', *Past and Present*, 145 (1994), 47–83 (revised in *Oral and Literate Culture in England 1500–1700*
[Oxford, 2000], pp. 299–34.).
[8] Arthur F. Marotti provides a valuable survey of the extant material in *Manuscript, Print, and the English
Renaissance Lyric* (Ithaca and London, 1995), pp. 75–133. See further Gerald Hammond, *Fleeting
Things: English Poets and Poems 1616–1660* (Cambridge, MA, 1990), pp. 41–66; James Holstun, '"God
Bless Thee, Little David!": John Felton and his Allies', *ELH*, 59 (1992), 513–52; and Holstun, *Ehud's
Dagger: Class Struggle in the English Revolution* (London, 2000), pp. 158–64, 178–86. Kirk Combe
considers a relatively small canon of poems as evidence of generic development from complaint to
satire ('The New Voice of Political Dissent: The Transition from Complaint to Satire', in Kirk Combe
and Brian A. Connery, eds., *Theorizing Satire: Essays in Literary Criticism* [Basingstoke and London,
1995], pp. 73–94).

with news culture, the libel demands specific strategies of interpretation. Whereas news claimed attention for its purported truth value, the libel was by nature excessive, proffering illicit truths but simultaneously stretching into satire's realm of manifest fiction.[9] This ambiguity invited on the one hand the detached aesthetic appreciation signalled by Donne, and on the other hand facilitated achievements of satiric discrimination and stigmatization which resonated throughout political discourse in the period.

LIBELS IN LITERARY CULTURE

The verse libel is unique as a literary mode in owing its definition to the law. William Hudson's Jacobean 'Treatise of the Court of Star Chamber' identified a wide range of libellous practices:

Libels are of several kinds; either by scoffing at the person of another in rhyme or prose, or by personating him, thereby to make him ridiculous; or by setting up horns at his gate, or picturing or describing him; or by writing of some base or defamatory letter, and publishing the same to others, or some scurvy love-letter to himself, whereby it is not likely but he should be provoked to break the peace.[10]

Francis Bacon was more attuned to the poetic dimension of libelling, noting in 1592 that libels are 'sometimes contrived into pleasant pasquils and satires, to move sport'.[11] By the seventeenth century, the libel was more specifically understood to be an unauthorized and controversial text, generally in poetic form, on a person or topical issue. Hence a poem attacking George Villiers, Duke of Buckingham would clearly be classified as a libel, but so too would a piece eulogizing his assassin or defending the act of assassination.[12]

At the outset of the seventeenth century, practices of libelling were informed by both popular traditions and literary antecedents. Legal minds were principally concerned with cases in which libellous poems were employed in local disputes, often linked to traditional shaming rituals and riots. Details of such cases survive in the records of church courts and

---

[9] I am adopting here Edward Rosenheim, Jr.'s definition of satire as an 'attack by means of a manifest fiction upon discernible historical particulars' (*Jonathan Swift and the Satirist's Art* [Chicago, 1963], p. 31).

[10] In *Collectanea Juridica. Consisting of Tracts Relative to the Law and Constitution of England* (2 vols., London, 1791), II.100.

[11] 'Certain Observations made upon a Libel Published this Present Year, 1592', in *The Works of Francis Bacon*, ed. J. Spedding *et al.* (14 vols., London, 1857–74), VIII.148.

[12] Cf. Bellany's suggestion that the category of libels should include 'all types of underground political verse, not solely those containing direct personal remarks' (*Politics of Court Scandal*, p. 97). For legal purposes, libellous epitaphs might not be actionable at common law, but fell within the Star Chamber's jurisdiction of controlling disorder (Hudson, 'Treatise', *Collectanea Juridica*, II.103).

the Star Chamber, to which cases were increasingly brought from the six-teenth century.[13] In literary and courtly circles, libellous verse was informed by popular traditions, but further shaped and justified according to loose generic categories. Early in the sixteenth century, John Skelton supported his personal attacks by reference to the classical authority of 'famous poet-tes saturicall'.[14] Vague notions that satire originated in Greek satyr plays, and the appreciation that at least Lucilius among the Roman satirists at-tacked his targets by name, underpinned such statements.[15] Satiric theory, especially before the concerted neoclassicism of the 1590s, commonly jus-tified 'taunting Darcklye certeyn men of state'.[16] Related literary modes also contributed to the development of libelling. Celtic satire was inter-twined with practices of incantation and cursing, and was believed to have tangible effects, even causing death.[17] The flyting, in which Skelton ex-celled, was appreciated as a vitriolic poetic exchange, highly performative and competitive.[18] And further support for libelling was derived from the sixteenth-century Roman practice of attaching anonymous topical verses to the statue of Pasquino.[19] The 'pasquil', as Bacon recognized in 1592, became a fashionable term for witty and libellous verses, particularly when distributed surreptitiously around the city and court.

The outpouring of formal verse satire in the 1590s served to clarify the status of the verse libel, largely through means of negative definition. As I have suggested elsewhere, libel was encoded as satire's other: a mode satirists regularly invoked against which to define their work, but which

---

[13] The libel cases surviving in Jacobean Star Chamber records are analysed in Fox, 'Ballads'. For a consideration of the relation between the poetry of the Star Chamber libels and Renaissance satire, see my 'The Verse Libel: Popular Satire in Early Modern England', in Dermot Cavanagh and Tim Kirk, eds., *Subversion and Scurrility: Popular Discourse in Europe from 1500 to the Present* (Aldershot, 2000), pp. 58–73.

[14] Quoted in Douglas Gray, 'Rough Music: Some Early Invectives and Flytings', in Claude Rawson, ed., *English Satire and the Satiric Tradition* (London, 1984), p. 43.

[15] Renaissance debates over the propriety of using real names in satire are covered at length in A. L. Soens, Jr., 'Criticism of Formal Satire in the Renaissance' (unpublished Ph.D dissertation, Princeton University, 1957), pp. 235–41, 308–12, 405–6.

[16] Richard Stanyhurst, discussing the work of classical satirists, in the dedication to his translation, *Thee First Foure Bookes of Virgil his Aeneis* (Leiden, 1582), sig. A2r.

[17] Robert C. Elliott argues for the significance of Celtic satire on the English development of the genre in *The Power of Satire: Magic, Ritual, Art* (Princeton, 1960), pp. 3–48.

[18] See Gray, 'Rough Music', p. 21.

[19] While it is clear that English writers were aware of the Roman practice, it is more difficult to find evidence of actual Italian texts circulating in English manuscript culture. The only example of this that I have found comes from north of the border, in the miscellaneous literary collections of William Drummond of Hawthornden (NLS, MS 2060, f. 9r). For a dramatic representation of libelling in Rome, see Barnabe Barnes, *The Devil's Charter*, ed. Jim C. Pogue (New York and London, 1980), I ii–iii.

could never satisfactorily be separated from their neoclassical genre.[20] The libel was figured as a debased mode, nurtured by popular traditions rather than classical authority, employing indigenous forms rather than satire's iambic pentameter couplet, attacking individuals rather than generalized types of vice, steeped in ephemeral topical issues rather than enduring moral struggles, and concerned with undermining authority rather than purging evil in the interests of authority. These arguments were pursued right through to John Dryden's classic essay on satire, which carefully distinguishes between poets who adhere to classical models and standards of generic decorum, and the 'multitude of Scriblers, who daily pester the World with . . . Lampoons and Libels'.[21] Although this process of discrimination was often tenuous, literary historians generally agree that it contributed to the construction of a native conception of satire. By extension, it also helped to establish the libel as an independent mode, requiring different strategies for writing, reading and circulation.

It is clear that writers appreciated these points of distinction, though equally clear that, even when the vogue for formal verse satire was at its height, many distinguished poets still chose to write libels. For example, the satirist Thomas Bastard was expelled from Oxford for his libels on university scandals, while Sir John Harington was both a collector and writer of scandalous verse.[22] A note in Harington's *Diary* records his intention to 'write a damnable storie and put it in goodlie verse about Lord A. He hath done me some ill turnes'. (Remarkably, the following sentence recoils to the Renaissance poet's accustomed position of moral orthodoxy: 'God keepe us from lyinge and slander worke.')[23] The rise of the satiric epigram around the turn of the century provided another vehicle for libellous writing. Harington's most successful poetic works were his epigrams and, like other epigrammatists of the period, many of his poems are unquestionably libellous in intent, though the use of nonce names avoided problems with the law.[24] At least one later poet was less careful; in 1615 William Goddard published two epigrams on the controversial marriage of Frances Howard and Robert Carr, Earl of Somerset, in which the latter is identified pointedly as 'the dunghill Carr'.[25] Such examples demonstrate that purported

[20] See 'The Verse Libel', p. 69.
[21] 'Discourse concerning the Original and Progress of Satire', in *The Works of John Dryden, Volume IV: Poems 1693–1696*, ed. A. B. Chambers and William Frost (Berkeley, 1974), p. 8.
[22] See Croft, 'Libels', 273.
[23] Quoted in C. J. Sisson, *Lost Plays of Shakespeare's Age* (Cambridge, 1936), pp. 187–8.
[24] See Harington, *Epigrams* (1618); facsimile edn (Menston, 1970).
[25] *A Neaste of Waspes* (Dort, 1615), sig. F4r.

disdain for libelling cannot necessarily be equated with a lack of interest in the mode; indeed even Dryden, in his *Discourse on Satire*, defends a poet's right to libel his enemies in self-defence.[26]

The Bishops' Ban of 1599, which called for the public burning of the works of certain satirists, undoubtedly affected the development of English satire.[27] Yet it would be simplistic to claim that satire was at this point forced 'underground', where it took shape afresh in the form of libels.[28] In fact there is little evidence that the ban was enforced much beyond the initial clampdown, and numerous satiric works (including countless volumes of epigrams) were published in the early years of the seventeenth century.[29] It is evident, however, that formal verse satire at this time became at once less fashionable and less relevant. It gradually lost its earlier attachment to the universities and Inns of Court, and turned away from the aggressive neo-classicism of the 1590s, towards a more accessible style and more traditional themes. At the same time, however, changes in political culture were creating a vital new context for the libel. James's rapid expansion of royal bounty, a number of notorious court scandals, a series of troubled parliaments, and ongoing problems of corruption in the government, fuelled increasing anxieties about the nation. Moreover, the prominence of royal favourites, and the incessant struggles between rival factions, increased the significance of individuals in political discourse. Contemporaries were coming to terms with distinctly Jacobean forms of political interaction, and were exploring new ways of articulating dissent. The pre-existent mode of the libel, enriched by the achievements of Renaissance satire and intertwined with the contemporary rise of the epigram, was an obvious vehicle for their efforts.

A pamphlet which was almost certainly written in the 1620s reflects valuably on this milieu. *The Life of a Satyrical Puppy, Called Nim*, published under the initials T. M., narrates a period spent in London's satiric culture

---

[26] 'Discourse concerning the Original and Progress of Satire', p. 59.
[27] See Richard A. McCabe, 'Elizabethan Satire and the Bishops' Ban of 1599', *Yearbook of English Studies*, 11 (1981), 188–93.
[28] This claim is made in Cogswell, 'Underground Verse', pp. 279–80.
[29] See, for example, C. G., *The Minte of Deformitie* (1600); Samuel Rowlands, *The Letting of Humours Blood in the Head-Vaine* (1600), in *Complete Works* (3 vols., Hunterian Club, Glasgow, 1880), vol. 1; John Weever's translations of satires by Horace, Persius and Juvenal, published in *Faunus and Melliflora* (1600), ed. Arnold Davenport (Liverpool, 1948); and the debates over satire conducted in a series of pamphlets around the turn of the century, collectively known as *The Whipper Pamphlets* (ed. Arnold Davenport [Liverpool, 1951]). My argument here is supported by Cyndia Susan Clegg's research, which suggests that the Bishops' Ban was a reaction to certain topical references rather than a considered assault on a literary genre (*Press Censorship in Elizabethan England* [Cambridge, 1997], pp. 198–217).

by a young man of small but independent means.[30] The speaker decides 'to turn *Satyrist*' in part through a fascination with emergent processes of political preferment, as 'the State at that time felt alteration; and divers great ones (plac'd before as *high* as Fortune her self could *reach*) sate then on her foot-stool, *humbled* below vulgar respect' (p. 49). When he surveys the work of his fellow satirists, he notes in particular their 'Fame-murdering Libells' (p. 65), including several poems that can be identified in surviving verse miscellanies. This was a time in which writers might be observed to

murmure in obscure Corners: who are fearfull even of speaking softly; therefore proclaim to others a *dumb silence* in their own *prattle*: who whisper with their pens, and darkly bring their thoughts to light in *Hieroglyphicall* words, personating Men in the natures of Beasts, whose names (*literally* or *allegorically*) doth sympathize with theirs, whom they aime at. (p. 64)

For T. M., the context of corruption and government surveillance is the principal determinant of poetry produced in the period. Within such a context, he suggests, libel becomes the only pertinent type of satire.

The evidence of T. M. might appear to support claims that libels were written by a 'literary species of . . . "pot poet"', a type situated 'somewhere between a court literati and a humble balladeer', ever prepared to pen a verse for cash or beer.[31] Certainly this representation of libellers is endorsed by those who attempted to rebut attacks on controversial figures; in their writings, the authors of libels were routinely figured as emanations from the 'heady Monster, Brayneles Multitude', led by blind 'fury . . . to Intrude / on princes rights'.[32] But it is always dangerous to accept a term of stigmatization at face value, and even more so when dealing with the febrile literary environment of early seventeenth-century London. In fact, an analysis of elite literary culture demonstrates that, for all its expressions of disgust, it consistently embraced many of the practices associated with libels. At a time when poets valorized qualities of wit, and seized on the epigram as a concise and memorable vehicle for praise or blame, the libel presented obvious attractions. As one moralist complained of court culture in 1629, 'malitious detraction' was then widely 'esteemed the quintessence of wit'.[33]

[30] The text, which was published in 1657, is usually catalogued as the probable work of Thomas May; however, Leonie J. Gibson, who valuably dates it to the 1620s, suggests Thomas Middleton ('Formal Satire in the First Half of the Seventeenth Century, 1600–1650' [unpublished DPhil. dissertation, University of Oxford, 1952], p. 305).

[31] Cogswell, 'Underground Verse', p. 281.

[32] Transcribed from Bodleian MS Rawlinson poet. 166, in Ted-Larry Pebworth, 'Sir Henry Wotton's "Dazel'd Thus, with Height of Place" and the Appropriation of Political Poetry in the Earlier Seventeenth Century', *Publications of the Bibliographical Society of America*, 71 (1977), 167.

[33] Nathanael Carpenter, *Achitophel, Or, The Picture of a Wicked Politician* (1629), p. 10.

Moreover, as Timothy Raylor has shown, within certain literary circles writers wilfully confused stylistic markers that might appear to separate high and low forms of poetry. Poetry 'that is designed to appear extempore and humorously shoddy', he writes, was 'a vital part of the courtly and would-be courtly culture of the age'.[34]

Investigation into available evidence regarding the authorship of libels further undermines the 'pot poet' thesis.[35] Robert Devereux, Second Earl of Essex, appears to have libelled Raleigh in the late 1590s, while Raleigh himself (as noted above) probably wrote at least one libel after the death of Cecil.[36] John Marston, despite maintaining in the 1590s that satire avoids personal attacks, instead using 'fained private names, to note generall vices', most likely wrote at least one distinctly pointed piece on Buckingham in the late 1620s.[37] William Drummond of Hawthornden had 'a taste and facility for coarse satire', and may have written one of the most incisive libels on the relationship between James and Buckingham.[38] James Smith, a poet at the centre of one of London's most active literary clubs, did likewise.[39] And at the universities – especially Oxford – libelling was part of a lively culture of manuscript verse circulation. Elizabethan miscellanies from the universities often include libels on local figures, and in the following century these are more commonly combined with poems on national politics.[40] Among other identifiable libellers at the universities, the Oxford scholar Zouch Townley wrote a panegyric on John Felton, Buckingham's assassin, while Alexander Gill, who was arrested for libelling in Oxford in 1628, was known in the 1630s for his Latin and Greek lyrics.[41] Finally, a case earlier in James's reign suggests that in some instances a considerable level of learning might even have been expected of a libeller. Edward Coke, Attorney-General in 1605, judged that a libellous epitaph pinned to the hearse of Archbishop Whitgift

---

[34] *Cavaliers, Clubs, and Literary Culture: Sir John Mennes, James Smith, and the Order of the Fancy* (Newark, 1994), p. 22.

[35] Cf. Bellany, *Politics of Court Scandal*, pp. 101–2.

[36] 'The Poems of Edward DeVere, Seventeenth Earl of Oxford and of Robert Devereux, Second Earl of Essex', ed. Steven W. May, *Studies in Philology*, 77 (1980), 'Texts and Studies' Supplement, 60.

[37] 'To him that hath perused me', in *Poems*, ed. Arnold Davenport (Liverpool, 1961), p. 176; R. E. Brettle, 'John Marston and the Duke of Buckingham', *Notes and Queries*, 212 (1967), 326–30.

[38] Robert H. MacDonald, 'Amendments to L. E. Kastner's Edition of Drummond's Poems', *Studies in Scottish Literature*, 7 (1970), 107. On 'The Five Senses', see below, pp. 75–82.

[39] Raylor, *Cavaliers*, pp. 55–6.

[40] For a representative Elizabethan volume (of courtly origin) including university libels, see *The Arundel Harington Manuscript of Tudor Poetry*, ed. Ruth Hussey (2 vols., Columbus, OH, 1960).

[41] Townley's poem, 'Enjoy thy bondage; make thy prison know', is printed in *Poems and Songs*, pp. 74–6. Gill is identified as an author of libels, and possibly of 'The Five Senses', in documents printed in *Original Papers Illustrative of the Life and Writings of John Milton*, ed. W. Douglas Hamilton (London, 1859), pp. 65–71.

could not have been written by the university graduate charged with the offence, 'for he is no scholar'.[42]

It becomes clear from such cases that libelling was more prevalent and also more important a phenomenon than an attribution to 'pot poets' might suggest. Some, such as Gill, were apparently motivated by a conviction that corruption at court was endangering the nation. Gill was in fact as close to a revolutionary as the 1620s affords, having been known to drink a toast to Felton, and declare that 'We have a fine wise King. He has wit enough to be a shopkeeper, to ask "What do you lack?" and that is all.'[43] In contrast with this political fervour, other writers may rather have followed 'the sway of the multitude', which Chamberlain suspected was behind the plethora of Cecil libels.[44] Certain waves of libelling had an undeniably self-generating character, and some writers perhaps seized merely an opportunity to perform. For instance, at least one person appears to have taken the death of Buckingham as a topic for a rhetorical exercise, writing epitaphs against and in commendation of the Duke, both of which survive on the same page of a miscellany.[45] And while it would be impossible to deny that some wrote poetry in exchange for money, even in such cases a piece-work economy (as posited by the 'pot poet' argument) shades into patronage exchanges, which were a fact of life for most of the leading poets of the age. Thus George Wither assumed that 'A *Libeller* is impudently bold, / When he hath *Times*, or *Patrons* to uphold / His biting *Straines*'.[46]

But while the libel had an identifiable status within patronage networks, it remained perforce an anonymous mode, and authors were rarely identified beyond a small coterie. The need for anonymity is evidenced by the experience of Townley, who was forced to flee the country when his authorship of the poem on Felton became known.[47] As well as being a practical restraint on a poet seeking recognition, however, anonymity should also be considered as a condition which contributed to the character of libellous verse. Most notably, it underset the rhetorically inflated, taunting voice

---

[42] *HMC: Calendar of Manuscripts of the Most Honorable the Marquis of Salisbury Preserved at Hatfield House* (24 vols., Dublin and London, 1883–1976), XVII.114: quoted in Bellany, 'Poem on the Archbishop's Hearse', 145.

[43] *Calendar of State Papers, Domestic Series, of the Reign of Charles I*, ed. J. Bruce (23 vols., London, 1858–97), item 116.56.

[44] *Letters*, 1.364.

[45] See the poems attributed to John Heape in Bodleian MS Ashmole 38, p. 14. Cf. a poem on Frances Howard, which is constructed as a rhetorical exercise and divided into equal sections headed 'Petitio' and 'Respontio' (BL MS Add. 25707, fol. 46r).

[46] *Britain's Remembrancer* (1628); facsimile edn (Spenser Society, New York, 1967), fol. 285v.

[47] See *The Court and Times of Charles I*, ed. Thomas Birch (2 vols., London, 1848), 1.427–8.

adopted by many of the writers. In one poem attacking Buckingham for
his leadership of the failed Isle of Rhé military expedition in 1627, the
author mocks the Duke, as he admits that he was himself injured in the
expedition and hence may almost be identifiable, but nonetheless exploits
his namelessness:

> Now I have said enough to thee, great George,
> If I were knowne, 'twould make thy radge disgorge
> Its venome on me; yet for all this hate
> Lett's on this distance expostulate.[48]

The 'distance' of anonymity is empowering. The 'expostulation' is thus by
nature evasive: inevitably more a protest or remonstration than a debate.[49]

Anonymity was reinforced by the libel's status as a manuscript mode.
A few libellous poems were printed, but the vast majority derived both
an audience and a reputation through means of manuscript publication.[50]
This characteristic further distinguishes the libel from formal verse satire,
which was emphatically a product of print culture. Apart from Donne, no
writer of satires chose to circulate work in manuscript; nor did collectors
transcribe such work, even after the Bishops' Ban removed many texts from
the marketplace.[51] Hence the claim that in commonplace books and verse
miscellanies the 'abstract satire of the literary world met and merged with
the popular verse libel' unjustly diminishes the significance of the libel.[52] As
I have already argued, the distinction between 'literary' satire and 'popular'
libel breaks down under analysis. Moreover, of the two modes only the
libel was prized by the men and women of high degree who were the
most common compilers of manuscript miscellanies. This would not only
have encouraged poets moving in literary circles at court, the universities
or the Inns of Court to compose libels; it would at the same time have

[48] 'And art return'd againe with all thy faults' (*Poems and Songs*, p. 22).
[49] Cf. *OED*, *sub* 'expostulate', meanings 2 and 3.
[50] For examples of libellous poems in print, see Goddard's poems cited above (*A Neaste of Waspes*, sig.
F4r); and for evidence of the punishment of men who printed a ballad celebrating the violent death
of Buckingham's physician, John Lambe, see *The Court and Times of Charles I*, 1.367–8. On the
notion of publication through means of manuscript distribution, see Harold Love, *The Culture and
Commerce of Texts: Scribal Publication in Seventeenth-Century England* (Amherst, 1998).
[51] This contradicts the entirely undocumented claims of John Wilcox ('Informal Publication of Late
Sixteenth-Century Verse Satire', *Huntington Library Quarterly*, 13 [1949–50], 191–200). My argument is confirmed by a survey of prominent 1590s satirists in Peter Beal's *Index of English Literary
Manuscripts. Vol. 1. 1450–1625* (2 parts, London, 1980). There are no listings of surviving manuscript
versions of the satires of major writers such as John Marston and Thomas Lodge, while the only
listing for Joseph Hall's satires is a reference to a volume of material on heraldry, in which the compiler has transcribed twenty-seven lines on the topic from the beginning of *Virgidemiarum* (1599),
IV.3 (BL MS Add. 26705, fol. 130r).
[52] Croft, 'Libels', 273.

discouraged 'popular' writers whose projects of self-promotion were bound to the medium of print.

The libel should therefore be situated in a peculiarly licensed discursive space. As we shall see in Chapter 3, some early Stuart poets struggled to reconcile satire with prevailing constraints on speech. Manuscript poetry, however, always offered greater scope. As David Colclough argues in his analysis of John Hoskyns, Jacobean parliamentarian and manuscript poet, authors and texts within this context

provide a way of exploring the area in which the shift occurs between liberality and excess of language; a liminal space whose instability is evinced in the dual implications of the words 'liberty' and 'licence/license' in the period. Frankness, or candid speech, is considered as a rhetorical figure in many classical and Renaissance handbooks and its name, *licentia*, carries a similar potential for slippage into licentiousness.[53]

Hence the undeniable political charge carried by the mode. Although neither the writers nor their poems were necessarily 'oppositional' in any organized sense, and although much manuscript poetry in fact favours courtiers and government policy, the practice itself wilfully exceeds the acknowledged bounds of authorized political discourse. It replaces orthodox values of consensus with a contrary perception of discord, and exchanges a voice of loyal counsel for that of fugitive dissent. James I had some appreciation of this, and wrote a poem attacking those 'That Kings designes darr thus deryde / By railing rymes and vaunting verse'. He warned such people rather to 'Hold . . . the publique beaten way / Wounder at Kings, and them obey'.[54] Ironically, James's poem was distributed through the same medium as libels, and is copied in several contemporary miscellanies along with libellous pieces.[55]

James also perceived that the inherent excess of libellous verse involved a slippage from illicit truths to malicious fictions. While 'God and Kings doe pace together', he argued, the 'Vulgar wander light as feather'.[56] Indeed the medium created an expectation of scurrility; as Harold Love suggests, it 'would have been hard' for a writer of manuscript verse on political topics

[53] '"Of the alleadging of authors": The Construction and Reception of Textual Authority in English Prose, *c.*1600–1630. With special reference to the writings of Francis Bacon, John Hoskyns, and John Donne' (unpublished DPhil. dissertation, University of Oxford, 1996), p. 107. See further Colclough's *Freedom of Speech in Early Stuart England* (forthcoming).
[54] *The Poems of King James VI of Scotland*, ed. James Craigie (2 vols., Scottish Text Society, Edinburgh and London, 1955–8), II.182.
[55] See, for example, BL MS Egerton 923 (James's poem at fols. 37r–38r); and Bodleian MS Malone 23 (James's poem at pp. 49–56).
[56] *Poems*, II.182.

'not to be obscene and not to traduce the great'.[57] Later in the century, the Earl of Rochester would claim that 'the lies in . . . Libels came often as Ornaments that could not be spared without spoiling the beauty of the *Poem*'.[58] Yet to equate early Stuart libelling with mere lies, or 'politically motivated falsehood', as Debora Shuger has done, diminishes their artful confusion of the categories of fact and fiction.[59] As becomes apparent in the best known of the Cecil libels, the poems operate most commonly in the shadowy discursive territory of rumour:

> Heere lyes old Hobinol, our shephard while heare
> That very duly, our fleeces did sheere.
> To please us he tyde up his Cur in a clog
> And was to us both shephard and dog.
> for his oblations to pan his manners were thus
> Him selfe give a trifle, and offered up us,
> And thus by his wisdom the providant swaine
> Kept himselfe on the mountaine and us on the plaine
> where many a Hornepipe he tun'd to his Phyllis
> And sweetly sung Walsingham to Amaryllis
> The whilst neither Tyger nor wolfe feard wee
> for he never let worse thing come near us then hee
> Till Atropos payd him (a pox on the Drab)
> for in spite of his tarbox hee dy'de of the scab.[60]

The poem is rather suggestive than forthright, shaped in part by numerous more outspoken libels. It moves through claims of financial exploitation, conventionally figured as an abuse of the minister's pastoral role, to the unsubstantiated sexual intrigue which linked Cecil with Catherine Countess of Suffolk and Lady Walsingham. The shepherd's concern with the treatment of 'scab' alludes to the allegation that Cecil died of venereal disease, despite the ministrations of one of the foremost physicians of the time.[61] Ultimately, the poem's success might be judged as much in literary as in political terms: as a text read and appreciated over succeeding decades as much as a text which swayed contemporary opinion of Cecil. It succeeds as a sophisticated piece of poetry; and, as I will argue in the following section,

[57] *Culture and Commerce of Texts*, p. 189.
[58] David Farley-Hills, ed., *Earl of Rochester: The Critical Heritage* (London, 1972), p. 54.
[59] 'Civility and Censorship in Early Modern England', in *Censorship and Silencing: Practices of Cultural Regulation*, ed. Robert C. Post (Los Angeles, 1998), pp. 91–4.
[60] *The Poems of Sir Walter Raleigh: A Historical Edition*, ed. Michael Rudick (Tempe, Arizona, 1999), pp. 120–1.
[61] Croft, 'Reputation', 58–9, 60–2; see further below, pp. 61–2.

it circulated among men and women who exhibited a comparable level of sophistication in their reading practices.

DISSEMINATORS AND COLLECTORS

The circulation of libels in early modern England has been well documented.[62] Some were strategically scattered or posted when first written, in order to gain a suitable impact; however, it is likely that all surviving works were subsequently transmitted in manuscript form, to varying degrees, around the court, city and country. Some may have been scribally reproduced for sale, but the majority circulated through less formal channels.[63] Much evidence of libelling in fact survives from the period's emergent manuscript networks for the spread of news.[64] But much more evidence survives in verse miscellanies, which drew upon a thriving news culture, yet laid claim to a less ephemeral and more literary status than that accorded to mere newsletters. An analysis of these sources offers a greater appreciation of the situation of libelling within literary culture. Such an approach also illuminates the textual practices of libellers, who commonly exploited the interaction between their work and the circulation of news. A libel was always less than and more than news: unreliable in its facts but intriguing in its fictions.

The news culture of early Stuart England had established oral and written dimensions. Its heart was St Paul's Cathedral, the acknowledged metropolitan centre for seekers and gatherers of news, and an obvious site at which libels might be passed into circulation.[65] The rapid transmission of libels into the provinces is documented by sources such as the regular newsletters written by the Cambridge academic Joseph Mead to a more isolated associate, and the news-diary maintained by the Suffolk clergyman John Rous: texts which have been central in studies of news and political awareness, and which are now familiar to historians.[66] Such sources also underline the danger libels posed to the reader according to contemporary law. In the opinion of the Star Chamber, 'it seemethe to be a perylouse thing to keepe

---

[62] The best account is in Bellany, *Politics of Court Scandal*, pp. 102–11.

[63] Bellany raises this possibility in *Politics of Court Scandal*, pp. 108–9.

[64] On the importance of news, see Richard Cust, 'News and Politics in Early Seventeenth-Century England', *Past and Present*, 112 (1986), 60–90.

[65] Cogswell, 'Underground Verse', p. 281.

[66] Mead, 'A Critical Edition of the Letters of the Reverend Joseph Mead, 1626–1627, Contained in British Library Harleian MS 390', ed. David Anthony John Cockburn (unpublished Ph.D dissertation, University of Cambridge, 1994); *Diary of John Rous, Incumbent of Santon Downham, Suffolk, From 1625 to 1642*, ed. Mary Anne Everett Green (reprint edn, New York, 1968).

a lybelle, epeciallye if it touche the state'. It was held instead to be imperative that libels be brought immediately to the attention of a magistrate, and ultimately be put before the Privy Council.[67] Mead was well aware of the dangers: when sending his correspondent one libel on Buckingham he commented, 'I know you will not think it fitt to be showen, though I send it you. If you do, at your owne perill. Ile deny it.'[68]

Consumers of news were also well aware that libels required different reading practices from those applied to prose reports.[69] News was assessed in terms of its truth value. As David Cockburn has shown, Mead was rigorous in his analysis, categorizing reports in terms ranging from 'information' or 'intelligence' for news considered to be reliable, down to the more suspect categories of 'report', 'relation', 'tale' or mere 'talk'.[70] By comparison, while the libel was tantalizing in its offering of truths beyond the public record, it remained an unquestionably suspect textual mode, valued for reasons other than newsworthiness. Rous, for example, transcribed a long poem about the Isle of Rhé expedition, but commented that, 'whether any more be sette downe then vulgar rumor, which is often lying, I knowe not'.[71] Though generally scornful of 'light scoffing wittes' who 'rime upon any the most vulgar surmises', however, Rous nonetheless recorded a significant number of libels. The 'scorne of witte' clearly held a certain appeal, despite the patrician rhetoric.[72] Sir Simonds D'Ewes, with the benefit of hindsight and greater capacities of literary analysis, was more appreciative when he discussed libels in his *Autobiography*.[73] The murder of Sir Thomas Overbury in 1613, he wrote, 'gave many satirical wits occasion to vent themselves in stingy libels'. Similar qualities were assumed in the readers: two libellous anagrams on the names of Frances Howard and Thomas Overbury at this time 'came . . . to my hands, not unworthy to be owned by the rarest wits of this age'.[74]

---

[67] *Les Reportes del Cases in Camera Stellata 1593 to 1609, From the Original MS. of John Hawarde* (London, 1894), p. 373.
[68] 'Critical Edition of the Letters of the Reverend Joseph Mead', p. 615.
[69] Andrew Mousley considers news as 'a problematic form of knowledge', in 'Self, State, and Seventeenth-Century News', *The Seventeenth-Century*, 6 (1991), 149–68.
[70] 'Critical Edition of the Letters of the Reverend Joseph Mead', pp. 94–104. As Mousley argues, the concern with the sources of news evident in the news-diaries of John Rous and Walter Yonge demonstrates similarly discriminating reading practices ('Self, State, and Seventeenth-Century News', 162–5).
[71] *Diary of John Rous*, p. 22.
[72] *Diary of John Rous*, p. 30.
[73] On Rous's capacity as a literary critic, see below, p. 181.
[74] The anagrams, which were circulated widely, were: 'Francis Howarde. Car finds a whore' and 'Thomas Overburie. O! O! a busie murther' (*The Autobiography of Sir Simonds D'Ewes*, ed. James Orchard Halliwell [2 vols., London, 1845], 1.87).

Some libels explored and exploited the implications of this ambiguous relation to news. One poem which enjoyed a distinct currency in news networks was intended, in the words of D'Ewes, 'to show the meanness of [Buckingham's client] Sir Nicholas Hyde, and to deliver the four preceding Chief Justices to be remembered by posterity'. Until the final line it functions almost as a memory-aid:

> Learned Coke, Court Montague,
> The aged Lea, and honest Crew;
> Two preferred, two set aside,
> And then starts up Sir Nicholas Hyde![75]

Rous in fact transcribed this piece in such a way as to reduce it to news: instead of including the barbed 'starts up' (or 'upstart' in other sources), his final line reads 'There's *now in place* sir Nicholas Hide'.[76] D'Ewes, however, considered the 'significant tetrastich' to be another product of 'wit', and recalled hearing it recited 'at the Bury Lent assizes in Suffolk, in 1627, upon the bench, the same Hyde then sitting in his robes there'; the reading 'so loud as I feared he would have overheard'.[77] And since Randolph Crew was 'set aside' for refusing to affirm the legality of forced loans, there are here undertones, at the very least, of more pointed political satire.[78]

Another poem of the early 1620s, titled variously 'A Proclamation' or 'The Cryer', adapts the conventions of official news distribution, in the public voice of a town-crier, to attack Sir Giles Mompesson, Sir Francis Michell and Sir Francis Bacon:[79]

> Oyes,[80]
>   Can any tell true tideinges
>   of a Monopolist

[75] *Autobiography*, II.48. The diarist William Whiteway noted the libel's occasion, though not the poem itself, in a note of November 1626: 'In this moneth, the Subsidy Roiall went about, which all the Judges refused to subscribe unto, and som of them were thereupon put from their places, as Sir Randall Crew, from being Lord cheife Justice to the kings Bench . . . In steed of Sir Randall Crew, Sir Nicholas Hide was made Lord chiefe Justice kings bench' (*His Diary 1618 to 1635* [Dorset Record Society, 1991], p. 85).

[76] *Diary of John Rous*, p. 8 (Rous's italics). The single word 'upstart' is used in *The Letters of John Holles 1587–1637*, ed. P. R. Seddon (3 vols., Nottingham, 1975–86), II.346; and *Diary of Walter Yonge, Esq.*, ed. George Roberts (Camden Society, London, 1848), p. 100. On the transmission of this poem, see further Bellany, *Politics of Court Scandal*, p. 103.

[77] *Autobiography*, II.48.

[78] *DNB*, *sub.* Crew.

[79] A fourth stanza, omitted here, concerns Sir Robert Floud. The four men are identified in marginal notes to a version of the poem in BL Add. MS 33998, fols. 65v–66r.

[80] '"Hear, hear ye"; a call by the public crier or by a court officer . . . to command silence and attention when a proclamation, etc., is about to be made' (*OED*).

Knight of the Post for rideing
'cause he wist,
It argued no small cunning
To make his leggs the instruments
To save his necke by running.[81]

Come forth
Thou bawdy house Protector
Pattentee of froth
Of signe posts the Erector[82]
Our true worth,
Thy Quorum shall not checke,
For thou shalt unto Newgate ryde,
With Canns about thy necke.

. . .

Sitt sure,
Thou quaking quivering Keeper,
A tent[83] thou must endure,
Least thy wounds grow deeper,
and past the cure,
For if thy faults prove comon
Thou soone shalt feele a Nimble Coke
Slice collops from thy Gammon.[84]

Whereas a crier is employed to disseminate a strictly authorized discourse, this poem translates news of political scandals into the idiom of popular balladry, setting the 'true worth' of the people against the misdeeds of courtiers. The endemic corruption in the Jacobean government's use of monopolies and patents as a means of regulating economic practice was one of the major issues of the 1621 Parliament, which brought about the impeachment of Mompesson and Bacon.[85] Within this context, the libel does not aim to simplify, but in fact assumes an informed reader, erecting around a series of witty allusions a carnivalesque mode of satire, aligned with popular shaming rituals. Hence the attack on Bacon plays predictably on his name, from his political wounds 'past the cure', to the attentions of the most zealous of his enemies in the Commons, Sir Edward Coke

---

[81] Mompesson fled the country when charges against him were laid.

[82] Michell was one of the patentees for alehouses, which explains the references to 'froth', 'signe posts', and possibly also to 'bawdy house(s)', since alehouses were often depicted as sites of sexual depravity.

[83] (Surgical) probe.

[84] BL MS Harley 4955, fol. 86r.

[85] Conrad Russell details the proceedings against monopolists and patentees, including the three attacked in this libel, in *Parliaments and English Politics 1621–1629* (Oxford, 1979), pp. 98–113.

(pronounced 'Cook'). Further, in its attention to Michell the poem ignores the elaborate shaming rituals to which he was subjected at court, in
favour of his subsequent procession through the London streets. According to a contemporary report, Michell 'was sent unto finsbury Jaile . . . and
made to ride on a leane jade backeward through london, holding the tail
in his hand having a Paper upon his forehead, wherein was written his
offence'.[86]

Despite this poem's obvious interaction with news culture, the sources
in which it survives suggest overlapping spheres of readership, shading into
an identifiably literary milieu.[87] In BL MS Harley 4955 it is transcribed
in a collection of poetry largely composed of the work of Jonson and
Donne; in BL MS Add. 33998, a carefully prepared verse miscellany dating
from the reign of Charles I, including all the major poets of the period
and a contemporary first-line index, it is one of only a handful of poems
which could be considered politically sensitive. This appropriation of a
topical poem into literary anthologies may be explained by examining the
practices and interests of contemporary readers.[88] As demonstrated above,
manuscript verse was highly prized in these years, with sites of greatest
activity including the universities, the court and the Inns of Court. Oxford and Cambridge remained the principal training grounds for writers
and readers throughout the period, while in London numerous informal
social and cultural associations proliferated in the city and at the fringes
of the court. One group, centred on John Hoskyns, which met at the
Mitre in Fleet Street early in James's reign, was responsible for pieces including 'The Parliament Fart', a widely read series of witty observations
on members of the House of Commons.[89] From the latter 1620s, further
groups of poets, playwrights and patrons formed into clubs in which political discourse could be volatile, if not directly oppositional.[90] One man

---

[86] Whiteway, *Diary*, p. 36. On such rituals, see Martin Ingram, 'Ridings, Rough Music and Mocking
Rhymes in Early Modern England', in Barry Reay, ed., *Popular Culture in Seventeenth-Century
England* (London and Sydney, 1985), pp. 166–97. For a ballad on his treatment at court, see 'The
Deserved Downfall of a Corrupted Conscience', in *A Pepysian Garland: Black-letter Broadside Ballads
of the Years 1595 to 1639*, ed. Hyder E. Rollins (Cambridge, 1922), pp. 147–8.

[87] My research has revealed only two contemporary sources; however, the final stanza on Bacon forms
the first eight lines of another eighteen-line poem, which survives in BL MS Add. 22118, fol. 38b;
and Beinecke MS Osborn b.197, pp. 182–3.

[88] On the manuscript miscellany, see esp. H. R. Woudhuysen, *Sir Philip Sidney and the Circulation of
Manuscripts* (Oxford, 1996), pp. 153–73.

[89] See Baird W. Whitlock, *John Hoskyns, Serjeant-at-Law* (Washington, DC, 1982), pp. 392–3, 283–8, and
his annotated text of 'The Parliament Fart', pp. 288–92. On the manuscript circulation of Hoskyns's
poems, see David Colclough, '"The Muses Recreation": John Hoskyns and the Manuscript Culture
of the Seventeenth Century', *Huntington Library Quarterly*, 61 (2000), 369–400.

[90] See Raylor, *Cavaliers*, pp. 84–110.

active in these circles was Robert Herrick, who is best known to literary historians as a committed royalist, but who was the probable compiler of a miscellany which is now one of our best sources of early Stuart political poetry.[91]

An interest in topical and libellous poetry thus informed literary tastes in the great period of English verse miscellany compilation, which lasted from around 1620 to the 1640s.[92] Miscellanies – private collections of poetry, often mixed with prose documents or notes – became the principal vehicles for the preservation and circulation of poetry among the elite. The vogue for the miscellany was a phenomenon centred on, though not restricted to, the universities. It helped to shape a canon of significant writers, and in turn informed the poetry of those seeking recognition and reward. Not surprisingly, apart from Donne no writer is more consistently represented in miscellanies than Richard Corbett, whose poetry is fundamental in the many surviving volumes associated with Christ Church, and also circulated widely beyond Oxford.[93] Other important poets in this context include William Strode, Henry King, Carew, Herrick and Jonson. Apart from the latter, these were poets who eschewed printed publication, and relied on the miscellany as a medium for establishing personal reputation and textual survival. It should not be forgotten, therefore, that libellous verse, though sometimes described as an 'underground' form, thrived in a literary context in which manuscript circulation was valorized by most major writers.

The cultural work of contemporary collectors of poetry helped to establish literary standards and generic conventions. Miscellanies, in which compilers variously selected, organized and annotated their material, are therefore best approached as active interventions in literary culture rather than documentary reflections of poetic activity. The majority of extant manuscripts which include political poetry simply mix such pieces with conventional collections of elegies, love poetry and occasional verse. Even this act is significant, however, as it situates libellous verse unproblematically within an established literary culture, inviting a reader to move from a Donne love lyric to an unattributed political libel. Other compilers attempted more actively to make sense of poems. BL Sloane MS 826 is perhaps the most notable collection on a single topic, gathering together prose

---

[91] Raylor, *Cavaliers*, pp. 87–90; 'Poems from a Seventeenth-Century Manuscript'.
[92] Marotti, *Manuscript*, p. 32; Woudhuysen, *Sir Philip Sidney*, p. 158.
[93] Mary Hobbs, *Early Seventeenth-Century Verse Miscellany Manuscripts* (Aldershot, 1992), p. 3. On Corbett, see below, Chapter 5.

documents and poetry relating to the life and death of Buckingham.[94] A number of other manuscripts contain sections devoted to particular topics, such as that in Bodleian MS Rawlinson D 1048, fol. 64r–v, headed 'Carres Ignomynye', and containing six libels on the scandal surrounding the marriage of Robert Carr and Frances Howard. Few such instances clearly indicate that the compiler wished to promote a particular political position. Rather, they suggest a certain detachment, often reinforced by a temporal distance from the controversy which produced a particular piece.

Many compilers also felt that libels required situating in generic terms. The compiler of Folger MS v.a.345 placed a collection of libels in a section devoted to epigrams, while Richard Boyle, Earl of Burlington, set a number of libellous epitaphs in a section otherwise devoted to laudatory elegies and epitaphs.[95] (Folger MS v.a.103 is more discriminating, as it separates a section of 'Laudatory Epitaphs' from a subsequent section of 'Epitaphs Merry & Satyricall'.) Bodleian Rawlinson Poet. 26, which has sectional headings for 'Verses. Poems. Sonnets. Moral and Divine', and 'Songs. Ballads. Libels', ranges across a period from the later sixteenth century to the early 1640s, but the ordering of material is by genre and topic rather than date. A similar sense of a compiler approaching libels with a view to establishing a canon of the best pieces from the early Stuart period is evident in the volume maintained by John Holles, Second Earl of Clare (BL MS Harley 6383). Much of this book consists of prose, including an account of the 1624 Parliament.[96] The poetry section is carefully compiled, with numbered pages and an index. Its collection of political poetry, much of which Holles identifies in headnotes as 'libels', might fairly be called discerning on literary grounds. The volume also has three poems concerned with the squabble between Ben Jonson and Inigo Jones (fols. 73r–76r), a fact which further suggests an identifiably literary interest in poetry of invective.

The process of canon formation is most clearly apparent in Bodleian MS Malone 23, which is composed almost entirely of early Stuart political poetry.[97] The consistent hand and the predominance of poems on Buckingham suggest that the volume was composed at one time, probably around

---

[94] This manuscript was by far the most important source for *Poems and Songs*.

[95] Folger MS v.a.125, fols. 1–19; the volume was compiled around 1630.

[96] This has been published as *The Holles Account of Proceedings in the House of Commons in 1624*, ed. Christopher Thompson (Orsett, Essex, 1985).

[97] Apart from the poetry, it includes a letter and prose notes, in Latin and English, concerning the rationale and morality of Felton's murder of Buckingham.

1630.[98] It contains about eighty poems, ranging in length from pithy epigrams to an extended beast satire, John Hepwith's *The Calidonian Forest* (pp. 67–102).[99] The material from early in the century reads as a selective survey of political controversy, though it is of course impossible to judge whether particular pieces were selected on factional or aesthetic grounds, or merely because they were all the compiler had to hand. For the 1620s it is more comprehensive; but although weighted, due to the nature of the mode, towards the scurrilous and subversive, it also includes James I's poem in response to Buckingham libels (pp. 49–56), and a strong selection of eulogistic epitaphs on Buckingham. The compiler appears to have been concerned to represent a range of the political poetry of the period, rather than to promote a coherent ideological position.

According to Arthur Marotti, who aligns this manuscript with an 'oppositionist critical perspective', its collection of poems both eulogizing and vilifying Buckingham is 'unusual'.[100] In fact my research indicates, on the contrary, that it is rather more unusual to find a miscellany with a consistent political position. This is not to say that some compilers did not hold identifiable political views; debate on Buckingham in the late 1620s was the single dominant issue in the nation, and there are certainly examples of miscellanies in which the compiler's opinion on such matters shaped a collection.[101] But it is instead characteristic of the miscellany at this period for compilers to gather together poems presenting arguments diametrically opposed. The miscellany thus characterizes a culture within which people were becoming increasingly fascinated by the emergent phenomena of political contestation and ideological division. Libels, which were often as much literary exercises as impassioned statements, encouraged writers and readers alike to experiment with discourses of dissent and division. Therefore, while it would risk overstatement to claim that libels delineate a 'starkly binary political vision', they were unquestionably creating the parameters for such a vision.[102] How they did so will

---

[98] Marotti claims that 'it looks like a presentation volume to a social superior', but offers no supporting evidence (*Manuscript*, p. 85).

[99] *The Calidonian Forest* was published in 1641; other manuscript copies are in Folger MS v.a.275, pp. 63–86, and BL MS Harley 6920, pp. 1–22.

[100] *Manuscript*, pp. 87, 108.

[101] See, for example, Bodleian MS Eng. poet. c.50, which contains only libels on Buckingham; and J. A. Taylor's discussion of Leicestershire County Record Office MS DG 9/2796, which contains rare poems in support of the Duke ('Two Unpublished Poems on the Duke of Buckingham', ed. Taylor, *Review of English Studies*, 40 [1989], 232–40). Cf. Colclough's analysis of the politics of Bodleian MS Rawlinson B.151 ('"The Muses Recreation"', 386–90).

[102] Cogswell, 'Underground Verse', p. 295.

become apparent through a closer examination of their textual strategies and conventions.

THE POETICS OF INFAMY

Although the libel received only the barest attention from contemporary poetic theorists, and encompasses a broad range of forms and styles, it is nonetheless possible to identify certain conventions which characterize it as a literary mode. It is hardly surprising that the poetic voice of the libeller is generally notable for vitriolic outspokenness. This point was commonly made by those attacking libels. The Elizabethan satirist Thomas Bastard depicted the libel as 'all rawe with indigested spite' and the libeller's pen as clumsily 'leak[ing] blots of spitefull infamie'; similarly, Ben Jonson slated Alexander Gill for his 'blatant Muse'.[103] But just as satirists were advised to adopt a 'low familiar way of speaking', so many libellers self-consciously embraced a quality of harshness.[104] One libel on Cecil begins with the invocation, 'Advance, advance, my ill-disposed muse, / With uncouth stile and ill-disposed verse'.[105] Another writer redraws indices of social transgression as marks of authority:

> Bridewell I come be valiant muse and strip
> ride naked in despite of Bridewells whip.
> Goe to the Court let those above us knowe
> they have theire faults as well as we belowe.[106]

The construction of poetic voice in terms of social degree is here figured as at once legitimating and empowering, as the speaker freely acknowledges the 'faults' of the common people but sets out to undermine the pretensions of their rulers. For another writer, libelling involves adopting a 'rurall pen' suited to his task, while another still claims that although 'I was not wont to scould and scawle', the subject's behaviour has forced him to 'dippe my penne in gall'.[107]

This principle similarly underpins choices of form. The construction of libels in song and ballad forms may in many instances have facilitated

[103] *Poems English and Latin*, ed. Alexander Grosart (Manchester, 1880), p. 39; *Ben Jonson*, ed. C. H. Herford, Percy Simpson and Evelyn Simpson (11 vols., Oxford, 1925–52), VIII.411.
[104] Daniel Heinsius, *De Satyra Horatiana* (1629); quoted in Dustin Griffin, *Satire: A Critical Reintroduction* (Lexington, KY, 1994), p. 14.
[105] 'Poems from a Seventeenth-Century Manuscript', 45.
[106] Bodleian MS Eng. poet. c.50, fol. 30r.
[107] 'O thou prodigious monster moste accurst' (BL MS Add. 22601, fol. 37v); 'I know not how it comes to passe' (BL MS Add. 23229, fol. 30r).

oral circulation; however, this need not mean that authors were directing their work principally at those of low degree. A song on the court of James, for example, usefully combines popular form and coterie allusion, as it scrutinizes the king's love of masculine entertainments:

> King James hath meat. King James hath men
> King James loves to be merry
> King James too is Angrie nowe and then
> But it makes him quickely wearie
> Hee dwells at Court wheare hee hath good sport
> Att Christmes hee hath daunceing
> In the Summer tyde abrode will hee ryde
> With a guard about him pranceinge.
> > With a hey downe downe &c.
>
> Att Royston and newmarkett hele hunt till he be leane
> But hee hath merry boys that with maskes and toyes
> Can make him fatt againe
> Nedd Zouch, Harrie Riche, Tom Badger
> George Goringe, and Jacke Finett
> These will dance A heate till they stinke of sweate
> As if the Devill weere in it.
> > With a hey downe &c.
>
> But o Jacke Maynard Jacke Milliscent
> Two Joviall boyes of the Rout
> For a maske or play beare the bell away
> If Jacke Milliscent be not out
> Alas poore Jacke money didst thou lacke
> When thou wert out at Saxum
> Thou wer't wont to have boldnes
> A pox on thy Coldnes
> Was cause that thou did'st lacke some
> > With a hey downe downe &c[108]

Despite the conventional ballad refrain, the poem belongs primarily in a context of manuscript distribution, at court and among observers of the court. Sir Anthony Weldon helps to contextualize the personal references, recalling the rise of 'pastimes and fooleries' at court during Buckingham's period of greatest influence in the 1620s:

in which Sir *Ed. Zouch*, Sir *George Goring*, and Sir *John Finit* were the chiefe and Master Fools... Zouch his part it was to sing bawdy songs, and tell bawdy tales; *Finit*, to compose these Songs... and *Goring* was Master of the game for

---

[108] Bodleian MS Malone 23, pp. 20–1.

Fooleries . . . But Sir *John Milliscent* . . . was commended for notable fooling, and so was he indeed the best extemporary foole of them all.[109]

Hence this libel, like many others, employs the same form as the 'bawdy songs' favoured among an allegedly debased courtly coterie. Within this frame, the poem establishes a suggestive nexus between courtly entertainments and sodomy, conveyed through provocative imagery and a consistently arch tone: as evidenced, for example, in the reference to the king's waxing 'fatt[ness]', and the suggestion of Jack Milliscent's financial loss due to his 'coldnes' with the king. The poem positions the reader as a person detached from this milieu, yet equipped nonetheless with a suitably worldly wit. 'But to dance with a man like a puritan', it continues, 'Tis a drie and ugly sport' (p. 21).

This poem, in a manner characteristic of the mode, operates by subverting discourses of hierarchy and praise. Whereas orthodox representations of courtly pleasures stress the dignity of the aristocracy and elevate the monarch above worldly concerns, the libel knowingly explores a world of 'sweat' and shame. This strategy is typified by the mock epitaph, the most common form employed by libellers. In Chapter 2 I will consider more closely the ways in which the mock epitaph contributes to cultural contestations over the significance of individual political figures. Here it is worth noting the form's dominant satiric strategies, as it relentlessly undermines established conventions through which the life of an individual may be situated within social and political structures. Its resources range from the cultivated poetry already observed in 'Here lies Hobinoll our Pastor while ere', down to the idiom of the popular jest book. One piece of bawdy misogyny on Penelope Rich (Sir Philip Sidney's 'Stella'), for example, has an air of hackneyed folk humour: 'One stone contents her, loe what death can doe, / That in her life was not content with two'.[110] Many other pieces confront conventions of lapidary brevity and decorum with a railing excess, as is evident in one Buckingham libel:

> Fortune's darling, king's content,
> Vexation of the parliament,
> The flatterer's deitie of state,
> Advancer of each money-mate,
> The divell's factor for the purse,

---

[109] *The Court and Character of King James* (1651), pp. 84–5.
[110] 'Here lyes the Lady Penelope Rich' (Folger MS v.a.345, p. 28). Other manuscripts preserve only the couplet quoted above, without the preceding two lines on Penelope Rich (e.g. Rosenbach MS 239/22, fol. 4r and Folger MS v.a.103, fol. 21v, which title the piece, respectively, 'On a lascivious woman' and 'On a lascivious Gentlewoman').

> The papist's hope, the common's curse,
> The saylor's crosse, the soldier's greife,
> Commission's blanke, and England's theife,
> The coward at the Ile of Ree,
> The bane of noble chivalrie,
> The night-worke of a painted dame,
> Confederate with doctor Lambe.
>> All this lies underneath this stone,
>> And yet, alas! heere lies but one.[III]

Like a number of other libels on Buckingham, the poem parodies a commonplace of contemporary epideictic epitaphs, 'the motif that one person contains all the different virtues'.[112] The poem's force is derived from the rhetorical accumulation of insult, met at the close by the ironic evocation of Buckingham's tombstone. As one supporter of Buckingham complained, the wave of libels had effectively appropriated the monumental decorum of the epitaph: 'But what good deeds we doe ar writt in sande, / What bad (though done by chance) in Marble stande.'[113]

Another poem on Buckingham's death, written by William Davenant, addresses more directly the way in which courtly discourse had sustained his power:

> But where are now his plumed Troopes? those high
> Cedars, which tooke swift growth but in his Eye?
> Those gilded Flatterers too that did torment
> Their Active Lungs, t'indeavour a consent
> An Eccho to his speech? are they all fledd?
>> . . .
> Whom supple knees adore for secrett ends,
> Greatness many followers hath but few friends.[114]

The ironic glances at 'supple knees' and 'secrett ends' posit panegyric as the pre-eminent mode of deceit. Consequently, as the excess of the libeller is counterposed against the courtly dissimulation of the 'gilded Flatterer', notions of truth in the construction of reputation are problematized, undermined by the confrontation of discursive models. As I will argue at greater length in Chapter 5, such statements typify a culture which was

---

[III] *Poems and Songs*, p. 65.
[112] Joshua Scodel, *The English Poetic Epitaph: Commemoration and Conflict from Jonson to Wordsworth* (Ithaca and London, 1991), p. 74.
[113] 'When Poets use to write men use to say' (BL MS Sloane 542, fol. 15v).
[114] 'Noe Poets triviall rage that must aspire' (BL MS Egerton 2725, fol. 80r–v); see also Davenant, *The Shorter Poems*, ed. A. M. Gibbs (Oxford, 1972), p.274.

becoming increasingly sceptical about the political ends of praise. According to several contemporary commentators, flattery and slander are equally duplicitous, diverging alike from an ideal of language that is 'single' and 'the very Image of our mind'. 'Lady flattery' is 'kinswoman, cosen germain to Dame sclaunder'.[115]

The play of irony in such poems thereby becomes a powerfully anarchic force, which carries the potential to erode the structures on which even the authority of the monarch was erected. One poem from 1614 demonstrates this effect in a commentary on the divorce of Frances Howard from the Earl of Essex, her subsequent marriage to Robert Carr, and the mysterious death of the courtier Sir Thomas Overbury.[116] The libel sets the scepticism of the politically powerless against the machinations of the powerful:

> Tis painefull rowing gainst the bigg swolne tide
> Nor dare wee say why Overburye dide
> I dare not marry least when I have layde
> Close by my wife seven yeare shee prove a mayde
> And that her greatness or the law consent
> To prove my weapon insufficient
> Some are made greate by birth some have advance
> Some clime by witt some are made greate by chance
> I know one made a lord for his good face
> That had no more witt then would bare the place.[117]

The poem panders to the bawdy humour and misogyny that surrounded the case; however, the ironic suggestion that 'greatness or the law' can conspire to 'prove' a man's 'weapon insufficient' touches significantly on the foundations of justice in the state. The commission which ultimately decreed Howard's virginity was constituted of the Archbishop of Canterbury, three other bishops, and six civilian lawyers and judges. When it was deadlocked, James added another two bishops to secure the decision he wanted.[118] The implication of the king in the corruption is reiterated in the final lines, which note the promotion of Carr to a 'place' for which he was manifestly unfit, merely on the grounds of 'his good face'. Later in his reign, James instructed his subjects to 'Content yourselves with such as I / Shall take near me, and place on high'.[119] Here, by contrast, his judgement

[115] *A Plaine description of the Auncient Petigree of Dame Slaunder* (1573), sigs. F3v, C4v.
[116] The dating is Bellany's (*Politics of Court Scandal*, p. 177).
[117] BL MS Egerton 2230, fol. 69r.
[118] David Lindley, *The Trials of Frances Howard: Fact and Fiction at the Court of King James* (London and New York, 1993), pp. 81–2; and Bellany, *Politics of Court Scandal*, pp. 52–3.
[119] *Poems*, II.184.

is figured as more fallible than inscrutable: swayed merely by the physical appearance of his favourite.

Other writers employ irony to shape artfully ambiguous poems, which challenge the claims of truth raised by opposing sides in political controversies. One epitaph on Sir Walter Raleigh slides treacherously in intent according to the weight laid on either half of the final line: 'Of Raleighs life and death the sum of all to tell / none ever livde so ill, that seem'd to dye so well'.[120] Another piece on Buckingham similarly holds criticism and panegyric in uneasy tension:

> Here lyes great George the Glory of our state
> Noe way, Our Kingdome did him hate,
> Wrong did he, non he writed, even
> Disloyall was he counted, never
> Faithfull he was, in any thing
> Unto his countrie, and to his Noble King
> He did deceave, both Rome, & spayne
> Then wish him Now alive againe.[121]

The poem translates the epitaph into a mode of comic instability. It endorses and exploits a culture of political controversy, collapsing the identity of the Duke between the play of competing discourses. Although unusual, the poem typifies the libellous attention to the fashioning of reputations, and mirrors the practices of the compilers of miscellanies, who transcribed together poems presenting diametrically opposed views.

This celebration of semantic and political instability provides further evidence of the sophistication of early Stuart libelling. Just as the practices of miscellany compilers evidence an appreciation of libels as literary texts which cannot merely be equated with news or popular opinion, so poets may be observed exploring the resources of the mode, which held the capacity for the bitterest of invective, or a more subtle irony. As expressions of dissent, therefore, libels are more complex than we might assume. Their political significance, I have been arguing, lies not necessarily in a straightforward commitment to 'a mode of oppositional rationality', but rather in a more fundamental commitment to stretching the bounds of commentary and reflection.[122] The culture of libelling was impelled by a prevailing spirit of destabilization and interrogation, as contemporaries sought to reconceive

---

[120] Folger MS v.a.418, fol. 5v.
[121] Huntington MS HM 116, pp. 47–8.
[122] Holstun, '"God Bless Thee, Little David!"', 517.

orthodox practices and discourses of political engagement. While this was not a concerted movement of opposition, and while many libellers would doubtless have been horrified by the radical arguments and forces which became apparent in subsequent decades, it contributed to a fundamental reassessment of English politics. Moreover, as I argue further in the following chapter, this culture attended to individual identities in ways that could not only reflect on wider ideological issues, but could also have the most brutal of consequences.

CHAPTER 2

Contesting identities: libels and the early Stuart politician

On 23 August 1628, when John Felton fatally stabbed George Villiers, Duke of Buckingham, he was attacking the most controversial political figure of the age. Buckingham had risen to the position of court favourite during the reign of James I in part through a careful manipulation and presentation of his own identity. He was skilled in the arts of self-fashioning required of the Renaissance courtier, and adept at nurturing his relationships with James and Charles, at a time when proximity to the monarch was critical in the struggle for power. In turn, his self was shaped by the authorizing hand of royal power, which bestowed upon him a succession of titles and offices. Over the course of a decade in positions of authority, however, Buckingham's identity increasingly became a matter of public contestation. While he was lauded in masques and patronage poems, and briefly represented as a hero in the aftermath of the failed Spanish Match negotiations, in his final years he was relentlessly refashioned as a self-interested usurper and Machiavellian schemer. Libels were central to this process. As Alastair Bellany has argued, Buckingham's 'libellous reputation . . . ensured that his death was popularly welcomed and that his assassin could plausibly be represented as a hero'.[1] At the time of his death, Buckingham was a man who had lost control over the fashioning of his own identity.

Buckingham's career demonstrates that the construction of identities at the early Stuart court was an unstable and precarious process. As much as a courtier or statesman might seek to control the semiotics of the self, and as much as the monarch might wish to inscribe clear meanings upon subjects, identity remained inherently contestable. Consequently, after arguing in Chapter 1 that libels contributed to a reshaping of the parameters of political discourse, in the present chapter I attend more closely to the ways in which these poems intervened in processes of identity formation. In their

[1] '"Raylinge Rymes and Vaunting Verse": Libellous Politics in Early Stuart England, 1603–1628', in Kevin Sharpe and Peter Lake, eds., *Culture and Politics in Early Stuart England* (Basingstoke, 1994), p. 305.

attacks on individual statesmen and courtiers, libels are at once carnivalesque and deadly serious: wittily exploding the glorious self-images of the great, yet shading menacingly into valorizations of violence and rebellion. Moreover, at a time when the spheres of the personal and the political were intricately intermeshed, libels were not only employed as weapons in struggles between individuals and factions, but also provided vehicles through which contemporaries could reassess the mechanics of power and the structures of ideology. An attack on Buckingham might thus prompt a critical consideration of the structures which supported his rise, or lead further to suggestions for sweeping changes in the nation. As a result, I want to argue, the libel emerged as a pivotal textual site for the development of radical politics.

The chapter's four sections examine different aspects of the politics of identity. The opening section situates practices of libelling in relation to a gathering mood of scepticism in English culture about the foundations of meaning and authority. While in theory the great men and women of the state enjoyed their status on account of inherent virtue, recognized and authorized by the monarch, poets in the early Stuart era were increasingly drawn into contests over the moral and political significance of particular lives. The subsequent section focuses on the body, which emerges in libels as the pre-eminent site of semiotic contestation. Indeed the body's deceptive and inconclusive nature consistently invites libellous inscriptions of meaning, which often speculate further on the invisible entities of the conscience or soul, marked indelibly yet imperceptibly by an authority even greater than the king. The third section extends this line of inquiry by considering libellous epitaphs, which continue the fashioning of identities beyond an individual's death. The liminal moment of death, in fact, urgently raises the stakes of interpretation, as the individual passes at once into the Christian afterlife and the nation's collective memory. And the final section analyses one poem, 'The Five Senses', which filters an attack on Buckingham through a powerful vision of the pollution of the monarch's body. This poem, more than any other of the period, demonstrates the subversive potential of the libel's attention to the corporeal, as it refashions not only the courtly image of Buckingham, but also authorized discourses of monarchical government.

THE ARTS OF DEGRADATION

Dominant theories of Renaissance poetry rested on assumptions of a society united by a commitment to certain common values. The art of the poet was thus perceived to be grounded in practices of epideictic rhetoric, which involved attacking vice and praising virtue; good poets, as one writer declared, 'give / Vertue and vice their titles'.[2] Within circles of power, however, such assumptions were placed under acute strain in early Stuart England. As much as the state attempted to fix authorized meanings on its subjects, typically equating a person's status with evidence of his or her virtue, observers were becoming increasingly sceptical. In particular, the period's spectacular rises and falls, and openly bitter rivalries, suggested to many observers that greatness may have other foundations, and very little to do with virtue. The poetry of praise and blame, in such circumstances, may be exposed as little more than a political tool. Indeed, while it would be absurd to claim that poetry was not politicized before the seventeenth century, early Stuart commentators rightly perceived an intensification of a trend. William Loe, for example, lamented a language of moral discrimination corroded by ambition and competition, and producing on the one hand 'Flatterie, that ayerie Chamaelion', and on the other hand 'Infamous Libels . . . that sow seditious, treacherous, and treasonable thoughts'.[3] In the light of this observation, it is worth considering the ways in which libels refashioned traditional poetic practices. Although libellers are commonly motivated by a profound moralism, I suggest, they participate in a poetics of rhetorical excess and violent contestation, committed to acts of degradation rather than discrimination.

One of the prime qualities of libels within this context, as suggested already in Chapter 1, is their radical scepticism about discourses of authority. Libels frequently operate through an ironic subversion of courtly panegyric, in the process seeking to expose skeletons of artifice sustaining identities formulated out of self-interest and opportunism. As one poet suggested, in the wake of one of Buckingham's failed military ventures, 'all that hope by flatterie / To be preferred, doe singe'. This degrades panegyric from the level of epideictic discrimination, underpinned by the legitimating authority of the monarch, to a discourse of popular fable:[4]

> They rancke the duke with Bevis,
>   This skirmish they doe place
> Before the cowe of Dunmowe heath,
>   And next to Chevy Chase:

---

[2] Richard Brathwaite, *A Strappado for the Divell* (1615); ed. J. W. Ebsworth (Boston, Lincs., 1878), p. 24.
[3] *Vox Clamantis* (1621), p. 10.
[4] I consider contemporary concerns about epideictic rhetoric – the rhetoric of praise and blame – further below, pp. 157–71.

And sweare that through our chronicles,
We farr and neere doe wander,
Before that such an one wee finde
Imployed as a commaunder.[5]

As in so many libels, this poem's pervasive irony propels a subtly incisive political comment. As Buckingham's court poets are initially figured as no more than balladeers, the identity of the Duke himself is lifted from an arena of military engagement, and enmeshed instead with the dubious narratives of England's national mythologies. The subsequent reference to chronicle histories develops the attack, placing England's current situation in a firmer historical context. The fruitless search for a fitting precedent to Buckingham thus hints at a more fundamental crisis of 'command' in the nation, which may have political as well as military consequences.

Such textual strategies are clarified in poems concerned with falls from power: moments at which authorized meanings themselves are mysteriously erased and rewritten. For example, one libel on Robert Carr, Earl of Somerset, written after he was implicated in the murder of Sir Thomas Overbury, considers the relation between impermanent marks of status and the ongoing life of the fallen subject:

Poore pylat thou art like to loose thy pincke
And by the Lack downe to the bottome sincke[6]
Thy lands are gone, alas they weere not thyne
Thy house likewise another saies is myne
Now wher's thy witt, alas its two yeares dead
And wher's thy wife another did her wedd
Art thou a man or but a simple part
Nothing thyne owne but thy aspiring hart
Rawley thy house, and Westmorland thy lands
Overbury thy witt, Essex thy wife demaunds
Like Esops Jay each Bird will have a feather
And leave the naked expos'd to the weather.[7]

The reference to Aesop (presumably to the fable 'Of the Crow and the Peacocks') underlines the libeller's point, as all the markers of office and

---

[5] 'Rejoyce, brave English gallants' (*Poems and Songs*, p. 17).

[6] These lines allude to another libel about Carr and his wife, Frances Howard ('From Katherin's dock there lanch't a Pinke'), which puns throughout on 'pink' (which may be either a boat or a whore). This widely copied poem is published in 'Poems from a Seventeenth-Century Manuscript', 75–9.

[7] Bodleian MS Malone 23, pp. 6–7. Since Carr was Scottish by birth, Bellany finds echoes in this poem of earlier libellous attacks on the Scots who accompanied James to England in 1603 (*The Politics of Court Scandal in Early Modern England: News Culture and the Overbury Affair, 1603–1660* (Cambridge, 2002), p. 170).

identity Carr had accrued in his rise are ruthlessly stripped away. Yet the poem is as much concerned with the mystery of what is left of Carr as it is with the details of his fall. The suggestion that Carr may be 'but a simple part' – either one useless portion of a body, or perhaps an allusion to the courtier's assumed theatrical role – is countered by the rhyme, which isolates his 'aspiring hart'. Carr is left 'naked' and 'expos'd', but with a curious residual vitality, figured at once in physical and psychological terms.

This reflection on Carr's fall betrays an informing anxiety about the foundations of identity, yet a willingness in the face of this epistemological void to pursue a politicized act of vilification. This informing tension, between interpretation and stigmatization, is evident in libellers' recurrent attention to names, which are a person's most basic cultural marker of identification. Names signify social status. Moreover, among the higher levels of society names carried a weight of tradition and authority, quite often fixed in place by acts of the state: just as 'Duke of Buckingham' was in fact a title attached to an adult subject by his devoted king. Within this context, many libels were little more than commentaries or satiric plays on names. In the months before Buckingham's death, for example, one libeller rewrote the favourite as an assassination target: 'Yet shalt I love to heare a cry / Of hounds when Buck-in-game shall dye'.[8] Other libellous attacks were made through the use of anagrams. Frances Howard was translated into 'Car finds a whore', while the despised Spanish ambassador Count Gondomar became 'Romane Dog'.[9] In accord with wider practices of libelling, such anagrams had an ambiguous function, appreciated widely as entertaining products of wit, but also offering themselves as 'keys to deeper . . . meaning', or unauthorized truths.[10]

This duality of function also informs the labelling of individuals in libels. One epigram attacked Sir Walter Raleigh in a two-line commentary on his name, headed 'Raw-lygh': 'The offence of the stomach, & the word of disgrace, / Is the name of the man with the brazen face.'[11] Here the task of interpretation gives way to an inscription of meaning on the public face of the target, while a quality of wit is inherent from the

---

[8] 'To hunte the Doctor I have refus'd' (Bodleian MS Ashmole 36, 37, fol. 174v).

[9] *The Autobiography of Sir Simonds D'Ewes*, ed. James Orchard Halliwell (2 vols., London, 1845), 1.87; BL MS Egerton 2725, fol. 47r.

[10] Bellany, *Politics of Court Scandal*, p. 107.

[11] Bodleian MS Malone 19, p. 52. John Manningham claims that this was written by one Noel, in reply to Raleigh's 'The word of deniall, and the letter of fifty / Makes the gent. name that will never be thrifty' (*The Diary of John Manningham of the Middle Temple 1602–1603*, ed. Robert Parker Sorlien (Hanover, N H, 1976), pp. 161–2).

outset in the very dismemberment of the name. Many other poems define
a person by a simple ascription of virtues or vices, in a manner that appropriates and exploits established epideictic strategies of discrimination.
For one epitaph written in support of Buckingham, the man was the ag-
gregate of his qualities: 'Honor, worth, greatnes, ar what partes so eare /
Conduc'd to make Nobilitie lies hear.'[12] Translating this moral anatomiza-
tion into licentious terms, another epitaph reinterprets Buckingham's
'partes':

> Pride lies heere, revenge and lust,
> Sorcerie and averice, all accurst:
> A great one base, a rich one poor,
> Hee that consum'd the kingdomes store;
> Alive and dead of all good abhorr'd,
> Because that all ill doe hee dar'd;
> The law to death had him condemn'd,
> Hee death and law both then contemn'd;
> His life not lov'd, nor mourn'd his death,
> 'Cause long hee drew condemned breath;
> Hee sinfull liv'd and dy'd with shame,
> His flesh now rotts, soe Buckingham.[13]

The opening lines satirically invoke the contemporary panegyric motif,
derived from Aristotelian thought, that one person might contain all human virtues.[14] Subsequently, the poem reduces Buckingham's identity to a
grotesque allegory of courtly ambition, epitomized in the paradoxes of 'A
great one base' and 'a rich one poor', and symbolized at last by the rotting
flesh in his grave. The poem's sheer excess of vituperation inevitably undermines its own claim to truth-value; its more significant achievement,
however, is its interrogation of the very determinants of true worth and nobility. It looks askance at authorized meanings, recalling instead the more
egalitarian wisdom of Solomon, that 'The memory of the just is blessed:
but the name of the wicked shall rot' (Proverbs 10.7).[15]

   An attack on Raleigh, written (possibly by Robert Devereux, Second
Earl of Essex) as a response to his anti-court satire 'The Lie', extends this

---

[12] Bodleian MS Ashmole 38, p. 14.
[13] *Poems and Songs*, p. 64.
[14] See Joshua Scodel, *The English Poetic Epitaph: Commemoration and Conflict from Jonson to Wordsworth*
   (Ithaca and London, 1991), p. 74.
[15] This text was invoked elsewhere in discussions of reputation and identity. See, for example, Charles
   Gibbon's *The Praise of a good Name. The reproch of an ill Name* (1594), which uses it as a title-page
   epigraph.

method of assault by adopting the rhetorical strategy of *accumulatio*, which is often employed in libels:[16]

> Courts scorne, states disgracing
> Potentates scoffe, goverments defacing
> Prelates nippe, churches unhallowinge
> Artes injurye, vertues debasinge
> Ages monster honours wastinge
> Beauties blemish, favours blastinge
> Witts excremente, wisdoms vomitte
> Physicks scorne, lawes concette
> Fortunes childe, natures defiler
> Justice revenger, frindshippes beguiler
>   Such is the songe, such is the author
>   Woorthy to bee rewarded with a halter.[17]

Authors of encomiastic epitaphs commonly aimed for brevity; according to George Puttenham, an epitaph should be 'pithie, quicke, and sententious'.[18] By contrast, as this poem methodically defines Raleigh in opposition to the ideals he claimed for himself as a courtier, the very accumulation of insult introduces an excessive quality, which undermines the gravity of its statements. This carnivalesque momentum is furthered in the poem's imagery of abjection; Raleigh, for example, is 'Witts excremente, wisdoms vomitte'. The significance of the poem thus lies not just in the labels, but perhaps even more in the contestatory spirit, which claims Raleigh's identity as a matter for rhetorical play. At least one manuscript miscellany preserves this libel alongside a poem written in reply, which presents Raleigh as 'Courts commender, states mantayner / Potentates defender, goverments gayner'.[19] Yet this merely works to reinforce the culture of contestation, which (as demonstrated in Chapter 1) is evident in numerous contemporary miscellanies.[20]

Like Buckingham, Raleigh's power was virtually inseparable from his carefully fashioned identity; also like Buckingham, however, his identity

---

[16] *Accumulatio*, or *synathroesmus*, is 'heaping up praise or accusation to emphasize or summarize points or inferences already made' (Richard A. Lanham, *A Handlist of Rhetorical Terms*, 2nd edn [Berkeley, 1991], p. 1).

[17] Bodleian MS Rawlinson poet. 212, fol. 91r. On the poem's authorship, see 'The Poems of Edward DeVere, Seventeenth Earl of Oxford and of Robert Devereux, Second Earl of Essex', ed. Steven W. May, *Studies in Philology*, 77 (1980), 'Texts and Studies' supplement, 60, 106–8.

[18] *The Arte of English Poesie*, ed. Gladys Doidge Willcock and Alice Walker (Cambridge, 1936), p. 56; quoted in Scodel, *English Poetic Epitaph*, p. 51.

[19] Bodleian MS Rawlinson poet. 212, fol. 91v.

[20] On the practice of collecting poems with opposing political views, see above, pp. 40–44.

was shaped by the libeller's arts of stigmatization, as well as his own strategies of self-presentation. Libels thus assumed a central position within a
context of heightened contestation over the meaning and significance of
individual lives. This was not necessarily a culture in which politics was
clearly polarized; it was, however, a culture in which poets were increasingly willing to challenge authorized meanings, bringing to the fashioning
of identities a freshly violent and contestatory spirit. And, for all of the
wit and rhetorical excess of such strategies (as I argue in the sections and
chapters to come), they provided critical tools for people struggling to give
definition to political conflicts.

THE POLITICS OF THE BODY

To stigmatize, in the words of a seventeenth-century dictionary, is 'to mark
with an hot iron, as we use to do Rogues, and notorious offenders'.[21] Indeed the early modern state's disciplinary regime consistently focused on
the body. As Michel Foucault demonstrates, the criminal's 'body, displayed,
exhibited in procession, tortured, served as the public support of a proce-
dure that had hitherto remained in the shade; in him, on him, the sentence
had to be legible for all'.[22] Further, in an age troubled by the mysteries
of salvation, such marking of the body might be interpreted as realizing
God's otherwise illegible discriminations between the godly and ungodly.
For Phillip Stubbes, adulterers and fornicators should thus be 'cauterized
and seared with a hot yron on the cheeke, forehead, or some other part of
their bodye that might be seene, to the end honest and chast Christians
might be discerned from the adulterous Children of Sathan'.[23] The consistent attention to the body in libels, meanwhile, evidences an illicit parallel
project of verbal violence. Its roots lay partly in the 1590s, when formal verse
satire contributed to a new mode of 'embodied writing', which 'aggressively
drew real and imaginary figures into print for potentially indecorous han-
dling'.[24] In the subsequent decades, libels consistently asserted a subversive
and demotic form of stigmatization, as they relentlessly inscribed alternative
meanings upon the magnificent bodies of courtiers and statesmen.

---

[21] Thomas Blount, *Glossographia* (1656), *sub.* 'stigmatize'.
[22] *Discipline and Punish: The Birth of the Prison*, trans. Alan Sheridan (London, 1991), p. 43.
[23] *Anatomie of Abuses* (1583); quoted in Peter Stallybrass, 'Reading the Body: *The Revenger's Tragedy* and
the Jacobean Theater of Consumption', *Renaissance Drama*, 18 (1987), 122.
[24] Douglas Bruster, 'The Structural Transformation of Print in Late Elizabethan England', in Arthur
F. Marotti and Michael D. Bristol, eds., *Print, Manuscript, and Performance: The Changing Relations
of the Media in Early Modern England* (Columbus, OH, 2000), p. 50.

Physiognomy was itself controversial at this time. Protestant moralists exhorted people not to 'jest' at another's 'infirmities': 'For he that is deformed in his body, may conceale a generous spirit within, like unto a tottered ship, which containes within it more goods then tenne such ships are worth.'[25] But others were more equivocal, and acutely conscious that the body was scripted by forces beyond human comprehension. Bacon's essay 'On Deformity', for example, concedes a measure of 'consent between the body and the mind', despite arguing thereafter that 'the stars of natural inclination are sometimes obscured by the sun of discipline and virtue'.[26] His latent assumption of a 'natural inclination' of deformity, linking the body and the mind, aligns further with traditional attitudes and practices. In examinations for witchcraft a woman might be 'stripped and her whole body shaved in an attempt to find a "witch's mark"', while even on less controversial bodies mere scars left by injuries or disease 'must greatly have prejudiced the individual's chances of appearing clear and unspotted before the world'.[27] In circles of power, by the reign of James the English were entirely familiar with the example of Richard III, who became a pre-eminent 'vehicle for the doctrine that villainy in the soul was predicated by a correspondent deformity in the body'.[28] As represented by Shakespeare's Queen Margaret, who serves as a spokesperson for what would become the orthodox Tudor interpretation, Richard was a man upon whom 'Sin, death, and hell have set their marks'.[29]

For Robert Cecil, the dominant statesman during James's first decade of power in England, the historical precedent provided by Richard's allegedly hunched back was particularly unfortunate. One libeller simply claimed Cecil's own similar characteristic as a symbol of oppression: 'Richard, or Robert, which is the worse? / A Crookt back great in state is Englands curse'.[30] Another wrote, after Cecil's death:

> The divell now hath fetcht the Ape
> Of crooked manners, crooked shape.

---

[25] William Vaughan, *The Spirit of Detraction Conjured and Convicted in Seven Circles* (1611), p. 343.

[26] *The Essays*, ed. John Pitcher (London, 1985), p. 191.

[27] Katharine Eisaman Maus, *Inwardness and Theater in the English Renaissance* (Chicago and London, 1995), p. 115; Margaret Pelling, 'Appearance and Reality: Barber-Surgeons, the Body and Disease', in A. L. Beier and Roger Finlay, eds., *London 1500–1700: The Making of the Metropolis* (London and New York, 1986), p. 89.

[28] John S. Wilks, *The Idea of Conscience in Renaissance Tragedy* (London and New York, 1990), p. 19.

[29] *Richard III*, I iii 291; in *The Norton Shakespeare*, ed. Stephen Greenblatt *et al.* (New York and London, 1997). See also Christopher Brooke's poem on Richard, published shortly after Cecil's death, which revives this tradition of vilification for a Jacobean context (*The Ghost of Richard III* [1614]).

[30] 'Heere lieth Robbin Crookt back, unjustly reckond' (Bodleian MS Tanner 299, fol. 13r).

> Great were his infirmities,
> But greater his enormities.
> Oppression, lechery, blood & pride
> He liv'd in; & like Herod he di'd.[31]

The poem deftly parallels the corporeal and the moral, 'shape' and 'manners'. It thus moves, in accordance with accepted cultural logic, from a consideration of the physical feature which reduced Cecil to the status of an 'ape', to an inventory of sinfulness and political corruption: 'Oppression, lechery, blood & pride'. The final line invokes the death of Herod Agrippa, who was struck down 'because he gave not God the glory: and he was eaten of worms, and gave up the ghost' (Acts 12.23). Consequently, while Cecil's family erected for him an ornate funeral monument, in an effort finally to determine his meaning, the libel instead asserts the contrary proverbial wisdom, that 'the name of the wicked will rot'.[32]

This poem's allusion to the death of 'Herod' also highlights the extent to which attacks on Cecil were informed by the damage that his final illness wrought upon his body. Disease was often seen as a correcting instrument of God, which should prompt the sufferer to 'labour to find the cause why and to what purpose God doth follow you in such a kind'.[33] In the terms of this model, Cecil's condition, apparently like that of Herod Agrippa, and definitely like that suffered by his grandfather Herod the Great, was particularly inauspicious. Herod the Great's numerous symptoms included 'an intolerable itching of the whole skin', as well as an 'inflammation of the abdomen and gangrene of the privy parts', which was believed to have in fact 'produced worms', which commenced a grotesque process of bodily decay before the moment of his death.[34] Like both Herods, Cecil was at the height of his political powers when he collapsed into his fatal illness, probably suffering in his final months 'from an advanced state of scurvy, together with tumours, almost certainly cancerous, in the stomach, liver and neck'. The symptoms of his disease were 'repellant, especially the ulcerous and weeping sores which produce a bloody fungus . . . and . . . unbearably

---

[31] Bodleian MS Tanner 299, fol. 11r.

[32] On Cecil's tomb, see Claire Gittings, *Death, Burial and the Individual in Early Modern England* (London and Sydney, 1984), pp. 129, 195.

[33] Nehemiah Wallington, in BL MS Sloane 922, fol. 66r: quoted in Andrew Wear, 'Puritan Perceptions of Illness in Seventeenth-Century England', in Roy Porter, ed., *Patients and Practitioners: Lay Perceptions of Medicine in Pre-Industrial Society* (Cambridge, 1985), p. 71.

[34] Josephus, *The Jewish War, Books I–III*, trans. H. St J. Thackeray (Loeb Classical Library, Cambridge, MA, 1967), pp. 311–13; Joesphus, *Jewish Antiquities, Books XV–XVII*, trans. Ralph Marcus, ed. Allen Wikgren (Loeb Classical Library, Cambridge, MA, 1963), p. 449. I am grateful to Garry Trompf for assistance with this point.

foetid breath'.[35] Sir Anthony Weldon, looking back on this death, noted that Cecil left 'a marke of ignominy on himselfe by that *Herodian* disease'.[36] At the time, one particularly virulent libel graphically imaged the 'filthie froath' of scurvy, another (probably written by Raleigh) diagnosed death 'of the scab', while others still noted the stench which presaged his death.[37] This attention to bodily decay is pursued further in representations of the corpse:

> Heere lieth interred for wormes meate;
> Little Robbin that was soe great.
> Not Robbin goodfellow, nor Robbin hood,
> But Robbin the devill, that never did good.
> A monster sent by cruell Fate,
> To plague the country, & the state.[38]

The corrupt body here signifies a category of monstrosity that carries intertwined moral, spiritual and political implications. For the libeller, prepared in the interests of the oppressed 'country' to confront one marked by authority as 'great', Cecil's death exposes the hidden truths of a devilish life.

Given the state of contemporary medical knowledge, it was also inevitable that Cecil would be stigmatized as suffering from venereal disease. The pox was widely appreciated as a sign of social transgression; it was a self-inscribed mark of immorality, roughly comparable in its impact to legal punishments of stigmatization.[39] In this respect it was critical to the work of Renaissance satirists, as they scoured society for indices of corruption, and mocked attempts made by men and women to hide telltale traces of the disease. Similarly triumphant notes are evident in libellous representations of Cecil, which almost uniformly stamp the reputation of venereal disease, with all of its moral connotations, upon their subject. The poem that figures Cecil as monstrous concludes:

> As for his soule, I cannot tell,
> Whither it went to heaven, or hell.
> But sure I am, they have earthed the foxe,
> That stanke alive, & di'd of the poxe.[40]

[35] Pauline Croft, 'The Reputation of Robert Cecil: Libels, Political Opinion and Popular Awareness in the Early Seventeenth Century', *Transactions of the Royal Historical Society*, 6th series, 1 (1991), 60–1.
[36] *The Court and Character of King James* (1651), p. 12.
[37] 'O Ladies, ladies, howle & cry' (Bodleian MS Tanner 299, fol. 12r); *The Poems of Sir Walter Ralegh: A Historical Edition*, ed. Michael Rudick (Tempe, Arizona, 1999), p. 121; 'This Taper, fedd, & nurst with court-oyle' (Bodleian MS Tanner 299, fol. 11r).
[38] Bodleian MS Tanner 299, fol. 12r.
[39] Pelling, 'Barber-Surgeons', p. 99.
[40] 'Heere lieth interred for wormes meate' (Bodleian MS Tanner 299, fol. 12v).

The poet's rigorously corporeal focus overtly renders issues of spiritual life irrelevant, while nonetheless suggesting an element of divine judgement in his bodily stench and marks of the pox. In this context it is also significant that the pox was perceived as 'flowing matter' within the unstable humoral body of Galenic physiology, which thus evaded the best efforts of physicians and undermined the arts of even the most skilful of courtly self-fashioners.[41] It was a mark that could neither be arrested nor dissembled; as one Cecil libel commented of the statesman's physician Dr Poe: 'For though the man be very cunning, / He canne not stay the poxe from running'.[42]

Like so many corporeal conditions, the pox thus directed attention to the mysterious interior spaces of the body. The menace of the disease was indeed accentuated by the fact that it was believed not merely to touch the body's surface, but instead to lodge ineradicably deep within 'the very bones and marrow' of the sufferer.[43] The perception of such marks hidden beneath the surface stimulated profound contemporary anxiety about the legibility of selves. Not surprisingly, however, libels respond by developing licentious discourses of forensic inquiry, which grotesquely parallel the violent investigation of the early modern anatomist, who 'cuts, dissects, flays, tears, and rips the body apart in order to know it'.[44] As one commentator wrote, in an image that fuses the moral with the corporeal, the ambitious man is deceptively 'faire and comely without, but within, nothing but rotten bones, and corrupt practises'.[45] Moreover, while such statements may appear primarily figurative, it is equally clear that they carry more than merely metaphorical weight, and as a result may alert us to a nexus of ideas concerning the relation between bodily, moral, spiritual and political corruption. One scurrilous pamphlet on the Elizabethan court, for example, observes pointedly of Francis Walsingham that 'in his end, his uryne came foorth at his mouth, and nose, with so odious a stench, that none could endure to come near him'.[46] In the reign of James, the Spanish ambassador's anal fistula prompted numerous comparable exercises in scandalous revelation. A fistula, 'a long, narrow, suppurating canal of morbid origin' (*OED*), is a sign of corruption not only hidden from the observer's view, but also reaching malevolently into the interior of the body; as the Elizabethan

---

[41] Pelling, 'Barber-Surgeons', p. 99.
[42] 'O Ladies, ladies, howle & cry' (Bodleian MS Tanner 299, fol. 12r).
[43] William Cornwallis, *Essayes of Certaine Paradoxes* (1617), sig. E2v.
[44] Devon L. Hodges, *Renaissance Fictions of Anatomy* (Amherst, 1985), p. 5; cf. Jonathan Sawday, *The Body Emblazoned: Dissection and the Human Body in Renaissance Culture* (London, 1995).
[45] I. T., *The Just Down[fall] of Ambition, Adultery and Murder* (1616), sig. A1v.
[46] *A Declaration of the True Causes of the Great Troubles, Presupposed to be Intended against the Realme of England* (Antwerp, 1592), p. 54.

polemicist Stephen Gosson argued, 'there is more peril in close fistulas, than outward sores'.[47] At a time when Count Gondomar was one of the most prominent men in English political affairs, his condition became a matter of public discussion, and prompted Thomas Middleton to describe him as 'the fistula of Europe'.[48] A contemporary libel more specifically challenged the Jacobean state's amicable relations with Gondomar by declaring that while Gondomar's 'foreparts cleare', his true 'sting is in his taile'. Looking further inward, the poem discovers a metaphor for England's political naivety, warning that 'Spaine is his heart, treating of peace, [but] for warre / Closely providing'.[49]

In libellous representations of female bodies, conventional strains of misogyny fuse with discourses of unauthorized revelation. The female sexual organs held their feared threat of contagion within; Elizabeth I herself had employed, as parallel images of veiled corruption, a man with a fistula in his thigh and his 'wife' who 'cancer hathe in secret hidden place'.[50] In the early Stuart period, the most notable case of alleged female sexual impropriety was that of Frances Howard, who was declared by a commission of inquiry to be still a virgin despite seven years of marriage to the Earl of Essex. The commission itself, which embarked on a physically and emotionally invasive investigation, represented the state's determination to elicit incontrovertible facts about Howard's identity. Its declaration in her favour, however, was shadowed by numerous libellous acts of stigmatization.[51] In one particularly venomous manuscript ballad, Howard is a 'lusty filly':

> Though I have praisd Her, shee is faulty.
>   [Come listen to me, and you shall heare]
> She has some Tricks, are counted naughty,
>   Yet serve her Turne [for other geare]
> In her foal-age shee began to wince
>   [Come listen to me, and you shall heare]
> And hath been a striker ever since.
>   Which serves her Turne [for other geare]
> Resty shee is. Her taile was burn'd.
>   [Come listen to me, and you shall heare]
> With a hott iron cramm'd, as Butter's churnd

---

[47] *The Schoole of Abuse* (1582), sig. C4v; quoted in Maus, *Inwardness*, p. 45.

[48] *A Game at Chess*, ed. T. H. Howard-Hill (The Revels Plays, Manchester, 1993), II ii 46.

[49] 'Why? what means this? England, & Spaine alike' (Bodleian MS Tanner 465, fols. 81v–82r).

[50] *The Poems of Queen Elizabeth I*, ed. Leicester Bradner (Providence, Rhode Island, 1964), p. 59.

[51] On the case, and the representation of Howard, see Bellany, *Politics of Court Scandal*; and David Lindley, *The Trials of Frances Howard: Fact and Fiction at the Court of King James* (London and New York, 1993).

> To serve her Turne [for other geare]
> Her dock and heeles have Mangie and scratches,
> [Come listen to me, and you shall heare]
> Her tinderbox is full of French matches
> To serve to burne some other's geare.[52]

The libel's speech-act of unauthorized disrobing is lent a demotic note by the ballad refrain, 'Come listen to me, and you shall heare', with its suggestion of illicit news escaping in spite of the state's legalistic obfuscation. Suitably, then, the poem directs the reader's gaze to bodily parts otherwise hidden from view, such as the 'heeles' (which were associated with wantonness), the 'dock' (accepted slang either for the vagina or anus), and the 'taile'.[53] The threat of contagion is prefigured in the description of 'Mangie and scratches', and subsequently centred in the 'tinderbox' of Howard's vagina, crammed with the 'matches' of the disease commonly known as the French pox.

In the face of profound anxiety about the determination of corporeal truths, libels on Howard thereby offer a self-consciously transgressive substitute. Another poem seizes upon the female use of cosmetics as an index of dissimulation, as it refers to 'She that consisted all of borrowed grace', who 'Could paint her heart as smoothly as her face'. Subsequently, her manipulation of her identity, from the surface of her face to the internal substance of her heart, is yoked to the vexed issue of her virginity, which is figured as 'a false-stamped, adulterate maidenhead'.[54] To 'stamp' was to impress a device onto an object: most notably, at this time, to fix a mark of royal authority onto a coin. The image thus indicates a political price to be paid for courtly corruption, as it links Howard's paradoxically 'adulterate maidenhead' with the threat of counterfeit coinage, stamped with false (and therefore devalued) images of the king. In the physical presence of this obdurate courtier, therefore, the libeller identifies a fundamental challenge to the king's capacity to determine, and stabilize, meaning in his realm. The misogynist ballad quoted above deploys similar imagery in a concluding claim that Howard and Carr 'cannot be currant till Tyburn shall stampe / The print of justice under their Eare'.[55] Here the only truly reliable mark, like the royal stamp that authenticates 'current coin', is that left by the

---

[52] 'In England there lives a jolly Sire' (BL MS Add. 15476, fol. 91r); the ballad refrain is contracted in the manuscript, but expanded here.

[53] Gordon Williams, *A Dictionary of Sexual Language and Imagery in Shakespearean and Stuart Literature* (3 vols., London and Atlantic Highlands, 1994), II.657, and I.399.

[54] 'She with whome troops of bustuary slaves' (BL MS Sloane 1792, fols. 2v–4r); transcription in Beatrice White, *Cast of Ravens: The Strange Case of Sir Thomas Overbury* (London, 1965), p. 224.

[55] 'In England there lives a jolly Sire' (BL MS Add. 15476, fol. 91r).

hangman's halter.[56] The libel hankers after such a mark of 'justice', which will authoritatively 'brand the victim with infamy'; yet it intimates, nonetheless, a realm in which an anonymous libeller's stigmatizing scars may assert altogether less corruptible codes of judgement than those administered by the government.[57]

Given the extent to which contemporaries suspected the arts through which the body could be manipulated, the search for evidence of sinfulness ultimately directed the attention of libellers beyond the flesh, towards the foundational sites of identity posited by protestant theology. As one godly manual noted, 'men first look to the outward behavior, and hence descend to judge of the heart'.[58] Historians in the sixteenth century had been more restrained; as Debora Shuger notes, Raphael Holinshed argued that 'the heart is not available for human inspection', and therefore 'the historian's gaze reaches only to matters "publicklie doone"'.[59] By comparison, the more incisive commentators of the following century were impelled by a perception that while all else may be dissembled, the heart bears indelible marks of the individual character. For corruption, according to one writer, may be 'concealed in a man's heart, as like unto a tree, which in outward appearance seemeth to be most beautiful, and is full of fair blossoms, but inwardly is rotten, worm-eaten, and withered'.[60] Significantly, the heart remained in the early seventeenth century a site rich with both physical and metaphysical significance, informed in part by Aristotle's location within it of sensory knowledge, memory and imagination.[61] As Robert Erickson argues,

the word 'heart' had come to mean a variety of things: the centre of all vital functions, the source of one's inmost thoughts and secret feelings or one's inmost being, the seat of courage and the emotions generally, the essential, innermost, or central part of anything, the source of desire, volition, truth, understanding, intellect, ethics, spirit.[62]

The biblical language of the heart, as interpreted by protestant theologians, further asserted this organ as an irreducible text of subjectivity, knowledge of which promised to unlock the uncertainties of predestination.

[56] *OED, sub.* 'current', 5.
[57] Foucault, *Discipline and Punish*, p. 34.
[58] John Dod and Robert Cleaver, *A Plaine and Familiar Exposition of the Ten Commandments* (1604), pp. 29–30; quoted in Maus, *Inwardness*, p. 10.
[59] 'Civility and Censorship in Early Modern England', in Robert C. Post, ed., *Censorship and Silencing: Practices of Cultural Regulation* (Los Angeles, 1998), p. 102.
[60] William Vaughan, *The Golden-Grove, Moralized in Three Books* (1600), sig. L4r; quoted in Maus, *Inwardness*, p. 5.
[61] See Robert A. Erickson, *The Language of the Heart, 1600–1750* (Philadelphia, 1997), p. 4.
[62] Erickson, *Language of the Heart*, p. 11.

The heart was a tablet on which God 'actively inscribes his divine image and essence'.[63] According to Richard Hooker, even people who have no access to the 'written law of God' nonetheless 'carry written in their hearts the universal law of mankind, the law of reason'.[64] More specifically, the word 'heart' could signify the conscience. As the Jacobean puritan Jeremiah Dyke explains, invoking Jeremiah 17.1, 'Conscience prints and writes so surely, so indelebly, yea it writes mens sinnes as *Judah* his sinne was, *with a pen of iron, with the point of a diamond, and they are graven upon the table of their hearts.*'[65] His image, like so many contemporary libels, thus identifies a level of identity unaffected by the guiles of courtly self-fashioning, and standing witness to God as a record of the Christian life.[66] As I argue in Chapter 3, this discourse held the capacity to set a profoundly individualized site of authority against existing structures of power, and as a result men and women appealed to the conscience in order to legitimize a whole raft of illicit political commentary. In the present context, meanwhile, concerns about the consciences of others, and especially those in positions of authority, fuelled wave after wave of libels.

Libels therefore participated in processes of scrutiny and inscription. While God is the only perfect anatomist, and the true '*anatomizing* of the heart' thus 'remaynes for the worke of that last and great day', contemporaries were nonetheless tempted to speculate about the consciences of others, especially within the fraught environment of the court.[67] One Tacitean commentator simply noted the folly of the courtier 'that weareth his heart in his fore-head, and is of an overt and transparent nature', whereas others scrutinized identities that were more closely guarded.[68] As a supporter of Buckingham claimed, libellers examined his 'Actions' and 'thoughts', and 'where no signe of faulte suspicion founde', turned their attention to his

---

[63] Erickson, *Language of the Heart*, p. 38.

[64] *Of the Laws of Ecclesiastical Polity*, ed. Arthur Stephen McGrade (Cambridge, 1989), p. 124.

[65] *Good Conscience: Or a Treatise Shewing the Nature, Meanes, Marks, Benefit, and Necessity thereof* (1624), pp. 12, 14. (Jeremiah 17.1: 'The sin of Judah is written with a pen of iron, and with the point of a diamond: it is graven upon the table of their heart, and upon the horns of your altars.')

[66] Erickson, *Language of the Heart*, p. 38. Erickson, however, does not pursue the relation between the heart and the conscience.

[67] Thomas Adams, *Workes* (1629), p. 488. He is working from Romans 2.15–16. ('Which shew the work of the law written in their hearts, their conscience also bearing witness, and their thoughts the mean while accusing or else excusing one another;) In the day when God shall judge the secrets of men by Jesus Christ according to my gospel'.)

[68] Robert Dallington, *Aphorismes Civil and Military, amplified with authorities and exemplified out of the first quarterne of Guicciardini* (1613), p. 314; quoted in J. H. M. Salmon, 'Stoicism and the Roman Example: Seneca and Tacitus in Jacobean England', *Journal of the History of Ideas*, 50 (1989), 217.

'Inward conscience & . . . fayth'.[69] One libel, presented as Buckingham's confession from the grave, exemplifies this strategy. Admitting that his plots aimed to effect 'the ruine of heaven's favourite, / Reform'd religion', he exclaims: 'Oh! my Sinon's art, / To seeme to bee, and not to bee in heart'.[70] Sinon, who persuaded the Trojans to accept the gift of a wooden horse, is a suitable example of courtly dissimulation (and figures elsewhere in early modern texts as a quintessential court flatterer), while the evocation of the horse itself furthers the poem's imagery of concealed menace.[71] In the same poem, Buckingham reveals his project 'To gett possession of my sove-raignes heart', and subsequently to search 'the royall cabbinett / Of secrets' (pp. 38–9). The threat posed by his own corrupt conscience is thus com-pounded by his efforts to undermine that of the king, which is perceived as a site of national as well as individual significance.

The libellous attention to the conscience is even more consistently ap-parent in poems on Raleigh, who bore a popular reputation for atheism.[72] Raleigh himself looked inward in 'The Passionate Mans Pilgrimage', which expresses a wish for 'No Conscience molten into gold'.[73] In response, li-bellers turn his own imagery against him. In one poem, 'The dispairinge Complainte of wretched Rawleigh for his Trecheries wrought against the worthy Essex', the dramatic figure of Raleigh wonders: 'Wherefore I will my clogged conscience cleere / by true confession of my treachery'.[74] An-other admits less hope of redemption; Raleigh's 'conscience now is seared / That knowes not Jove, nor Plato ever feared'.[75] The metaphor, derived from 1 Timothy 4.2, is explained by William Perkins: a 'seared conscience', he writes, is 'that which doth not accuse for any sinne; no not for great sinns'. It is a conscience found 'in such persons as are become obstinate heretickes and notorious malefactours'.[76] Interestingly, the image also has corporeal connotations; as Dyke explains, 'When a lim is cut off, Chirurgions use to seare that part of the body from whence the other is taken with hot

[69] Transcribed from Bodleian MS Rawlinson poet. 166, in Ted-Larry Pebworth, 'Sir Henry Wotton's "Dazel'd Thus, with Height of Place" and the Appropriation of Political Poetry in the Earlier Seventeenth Century', *Publications of the Bibliographical Society of America*, 71 (1977), 168.

[70] 'The argument is cold and sencelesse clay' (*Poems and Songs*, p. 42).

[71] On Sinon as flatterer, see [William Cavendish], *A Discourse Against Flatterie* (1611), p. 70.

[72] See Franklin B. Williams, Jr., 'Thomas Rogers on Raleigh's Atheism', *Notes and Queries*, 213 (1968), 368–70.

[73] *Poems of Sir Walter Ralegh*, p. 127.

[74] 'To whome shall cursed I my case complaine' (Bodleian MS Ashmole 36, 37, fol. 11v).

[75] 'Where Medwaye greetes old Thamesis silver streames' (Bodleian MS Don.c.54, fol. 19v).

[76] *Of Conscience*, in *Works* (Cambridge, 1603), p. 660. (1 Timothy 4.2: 'Speaking lies in hypocrisy; having their conscience seared with a hot iron.')

yrons'.[77] Like a later poem on Buckingham, in which the Duke confesses 'that sinne through custome cauteriz'd my soule', it suggests an insidious form of self-mutilation, hidden from the observer's view but visible always to the eye of God. The corrupt courtiers have alike made their hearts 'thunder profe gainst all contrition', and thereby fashioned themselves on earth for eternal damnation.[78]

The early modern body, though it might initially seem unconnected to matters of state, is thus consistently inscribed into political discourse. Faced with the decaying body of Cecil, libellers respond with vitriolic claims of interconnected moral and political corruption; faced with the outwardly splendid bodies of Howard or Buckingham, they speculate about hidden flaws. Ultimately, in their attention to the conscience, libellers use a vocabulary of corporeality to identify a foundational site of identity. In this regard, they bring religious discourse into conjunction with politics, repeatedly asserting the priority of a form of identity which is beyond both the shaping hand of the courtier and the authorizing stamp of the monarch. It remains critical when considering these poems, however, to appreciate the way that libels consistently combine earnest projects of discrimination with a commitment to inherently violent acts of stigmatization. Hence Philip Massinger parallels the violent aim of invective with the uncanny bodily stains left by the pox, as he boasts:

> nor shall the brand
> of infamie stamp't on thee by my hand
> bee washt of[f] by thy Barbers subtillest arte
> but still growe fresher.[79]

Like a virulent case of venereal disease, Massinger suggests, the libel's infamy becomes a living mark, 'growe[ing] fresher' with the passage of time, and impinging constantly on the identity of its subject. In the political sphere, having once rejected authorized meanings as deceptive fictions, libellers accept that political truths are rather matters to be shaped through discursive struggle, and engage as a result in wilfully excessive and carnivalesque processes of contestation. The bodies of statesmen and courtiers, as we have seen, become principal battlegrounds for these conflicts.

---

77 *Good Conscience*, p. 39; Beza, Dyke claims, 'translates and expounds' 1 Timothy 4.2 as 'A Conscience cut off as it were with a Chirurgions Instrument'.
78 'Ye gastly Spiritts that haunt the gloomy night' (Bodleian MS Ashmole 36, 37, fol. 7v).
79 Peter Beal, 'Massinger at Bay: Unpublished Verses in a War of the Theatres', *Yearbook of English Studies*, 10 (1980), 197.

MEMORY AND MEMORIALIZATION

For the protestant, identity does not end with death, but is rather fixed at that moment for eternity. Indeed, as the Reformation abolished the concept of purgatory and stripped away all sense of interaction between the realms of the living and the dead, the English devoted increasing energies to practices of memorializing, such as funeral services and monuments.[80] They were 'forced to devise new ways of accommodating [themselves] to the experience of mortality', and within this context poetry became a critical vehicle for acts of remembrance.[81] Not surprisingly, verse miscellanies from the period are especially rich in elegies and epitaphs, many written on the deaths of statesmen and courtiers; as Francis Osborne wrote, it had been 'the fashion of the Poets all my daies, to summe up great mens virtues or vices upon their Graves'.[82] Eulogistic epitaphs, which were often placed on hearses or coffins, aim to define identities clearly and unproblematically. By comparison, libellous epitaphs subvert authorized acts of memorialization. Commonly informed by a profound sense of the futility of earthly judgements, such poems look sceptically upon the assessments of Church and State, and proffer instead transgressive and licentious acts of discrimination. Moreover, although only few pieces posit clearly identifiable political agendas, the very act of placing a life in context may prompt subtle comments on wider political forces: as becomes evident especially in the wake of Buckingham's assassination in 1628.

Libellous poems written after a person's death range greatly in form and tone, from pithy epitaphs, through comic dialogues situated in hell, to lengthy speeches of confession. Some of the most effective pieces, however, are characterized not by an earnestly forensic search for truth, but rather by a wilful confusion of material and spiritual realms. One, on the death of Cecil, appropriates a conventional image of the soul:

> This Taper, fedd, & nurst with court-oyle,
> Made great, & mighty by rapine, & spoile
> Of ruined subjects; which did shine of late,
> And flashed with glorie thorough the state,

---

[80] Michael Neill, *Issues of Death: Mortality and Identity in English Renaissance Tragedy* (Oxford, 1997), pp. 39–40.

[81] Neill, *Issues of Death*, p. 38; Scodel, *English Poetic Epitaph*, p. 21. See also Matthew Greenfield, 'The Cultural Functions of Renaissance Elegy', *English Literary Renaissance*, 28 (1998), 75–94.

[82] According to Mary Hobbs, the funeral elegy is 'the form which outnumbers all except song lyrics in early seventeenth-century verse miscellanies (*Early Seventeenth-Century Verse Miscellany Manuscripts* [Aldershot, 1992], p. 35); *Traditionall Memoryes on the Raigne of King James* (1658), p. 132.

> Unable now to spredd more light about,
> Like a lampe dying, stanke, & went out.[83]

The flame of Cecil's life is relentlessly materialized, 'nurst' not by God but by 'court-oyle': an image that satirically conflates a sense of 'oil' as either a fuel or an item used in religious and state ceremony, with established figurative senses suggestive of flattery or bribery. The stink of his corrupted body is consequently aligned with an extinguished lamp, which amounts to nothing beyond its brief moment of earthly brilliance. A slightly more crude piece similarly concentrates on the odour of disease and death:

> You say that Malefacit was dead:
> Some wicked spirit brake the thread
> I sweare thou wert a witty divell,
> To flie from such a stinking will.[84]

This libeller presents the stench of bodily corruption as, quite simply, definitive of Cecil's identity. His 'stinking will' informed his actions in life and is taken with him into death, like a damaged conscience or a stained soul.

For Cecil's supporters, the authors of such libels were simply incapable of distinguishing between body and soul:

> Well might thy body be a soule to those
> Whose more gross earthen soules did late compose
> Blacke libels gainst thy fame, and rak'd so low
> Into thy purged excrements to know
> What foule disease durst kill thee.[85]

While seventeenth-century epitaphs 'often divide the deceased into his or her body, soul, and fame', libellers are here figured as men incapable of grasping such distinctions, falsely fixated instead on the material.[86] Whereas a true interpreter of Cecil's life would look to his soul, the libellers are ultimately drawn, like anatomists pursuing a debased coronial inquiry, from the corpse to Cecil's 'excrements'. Yet the satire of the libels is more subtle than this critic allows. Significantly, libellers exploit existing ambiguities in Christian doctrine on death, which are evident most clearly in 1 Corinthians 15:

42.   So also is the resurrection of the dead. It is sown in corruption; it is raised in incorruption.

---

[83] Bodleian MS Tanner 299, fol. 11r.
[84] Bodleian MS Tanner 299, fol. 12r.
[85] Thomas Scot, *Philomythie and Philomythologie* (1622), sig. L5r.
[86] Scodel, *English Poetic Epitaph*, p. 79.

43.   It is sown in dishonour; it is raised in glory: it is sown in weakness; it is raised
in power:
. . .
50.   Now this I say, brethren, that flesh and blood cannot inherit the kingdom of
God; neither doth corruption inherit incorruption.[87]

The latent pun on 'corruption' offered fertile ground for libellers. In the
Cecil libels, in particular, the statesman's political corruption is linked to
his physical corruption, and the corrupt corpse is claimed as emblematic of
his soul. If 'corruption' cannot 'inherit incorruption', then Cecil's identity
must remain eternally bound to his stinking corpse. This context lends
further resonance to apparently trite statements in libellous epitaphs, that
'now the wormes this Robbin eat'.[88] Just as Herod's body engendered its
own worms in its living state of corruption, and just as the conscience may
be 'compared to a worme that never dieth, but alwaies lies gnawing and
grabbing, and pulling at the heart of man', so, after death, the worms of
the grave can assert a gruesome continuity of suffering within the ongoing
being of the corrupt man.[89]

Although libels on the occasion of Buckingham's assassination could
not charge their subject with bodily corruption at the point of death, they
commonly suggest instead his own inability to distinguish the spiritual
from the secular. One strikingly concise epitaph, for example, satirizes his
personal investment in an accumulation of offices, wryly suggesting that
the essence of the man was inseparable from his worldly position: 'This
little grave embraces, / One duke and twentie places'.[90] In one of several
poems written as dialogues between Buckingham and Charon, the Duke
himself fails to grasp the significance of death:

> *Duke.* Nay, prithee stay, sweet Charon, thou shalt see
> That if George liveth all shall come to thee.
>   *Charon.* Pish! come, I say: my boate shall stay for none,
> Thy sweet perfumed sinnes will fill't all alone:
> If not, thy titles.[91]

The satire of Charon's response is derived from a confusion at once of material and immaterial qualities, and also of moral and cultural attainments;
his 'sinnes', appropriately adorned with the courtier's 'perfume', are figured
being tossed into a heap along with his 'titles'. Though the political charge

---

[87] Caroline Walker Bynum draws attention to the significance of this passage in *The Resurrection of the
Body in Western Christianity, 200–1336* (New York, 1995), pp. 3–7.
[88] 'Heere Robbin consteth in his last neast' (Bodleian MS Tanner 299, fol. 13r).
[89] Perkins (extrapolating on Mark 9.44–8), *Works*, p. 641.
[90] *Poems and Songs*, p. 63.
[91] 'At Portsmouth, duke, I will no longer stay' (*Poems and Songs*, p. 56).

of the poem remains understated, the dismissive treatment of the honours
bestowed upon him by successive monarchs gestures distinctly towards an
anti-court radicalism. Another poem achieves a similar effect by representing the courtly vices that Buckingham epitomized being obliterated by the
assassin along with his body. It declares: 'Live ever Felton: thou hast turn'd
to dust, / Treason, ambition, murther, pride and lust'.[92]

The best-known libel on Buckingham, which was widely transcribed in
miscellanies and has received recent critical attention, takes the form of a
meditation on the corpse of his assassin, and subtly juxtaposes consideration
of the respective bodies and souls of the two men.[93] After his execution,
Felton's body was taken back to Portsmouth, the scene of the crime, and
hung up in chains just outside the town.[94] Foucault remarks that early
modern justice 'pursues the body beyond all possible pain'; in fact, though,
the state was in this case pursuing more than merely the body.[95] As well as
serving as a symbolic reassertion of political order and a warning to Felton's
many sympathizers, the judgement denied Felton a posthumous place in
the Christian nation. A study of early modern Germany suggests that the
objective of such practices 'was the radical extermination and annihilation
of a malefactor of whom no trace – either memory or grave – must remain'.
The exposure of the corpse to the birds at once signified and ensured that
the felon's 'soul would not be granted peace'.[96] By effacing the physical
site of a grave, the practice also aimed to deny the criminal the right to
epitaphs; the author of 'Felton's Epitaph', however, seizes on this point as
a stimulus:[97]

> Heere uninterr'd suspends (though not to save
> Surviving frends th' expences of a grave,)

[92] 'Awake, sad Brittaine, and advance at last' (*Poems and Songs*, p. 67).
[93] See Gerald Hammond, *Fleeting Things: English Poets and Poems 1616–1660* (Cambridge, MA., 1990),
pp. 65–6; James Holstun, '"God Bless Thee, Little David!": John Felton and his Allies', *ELH*, 59
(1992), 541–2; Holstun, *Ehud's Dagger: Class Struggle in the English Revolution* (London, 2000),
pp. 184–6; and David Norbrook, *Writing the English Republic: Poetry, Rhetoric and Politics, 1627–1660*
(Cambridge, 1999), pp. 55–6. The poem is anthologized in *The Penguin Book of Renaissance Verse*,
selected by David Norbrook, ed. H. R. Woudhuysen (London, 1992), pp. 148–9.
[94] Roger Lockyer, *Buckingham: The Life and Political Career of George Villiers, First Duke of Buckingham
1592–1628* (London and New York, 1981), p. 459.
[95] *Discipline and Punish*, p. 34.
[96] Richard van Dülmen, *Theatre of Horror: Crime and Punishment in Early Modern Germany*, trans.
Elisabeth Neu (Cambridge, 1990), pp. 88, 97.
[97] The poem has been attributed to Henry Cholmley (e.g. in Margaret Crum, ed., *First-Line Index
of English Poetry 1500–1800 in Manuscripts of the Bodleian Library Oxford* (2 vols., Oxford, 1969),
1.357); however, the only contemporary evidence for this attribution is at best ambiguous. In BL
MS Add. 15226, fol. 28r–v, there is a copy of the poem, and also a copy of an answer to it (which I
discuss below), and the attribution to Cholmley follows the latter. The unpublished first-line index
to manuscript poetry in the British Library does not recognize the answer poem as a separate piece.

Felton's dead earth; which to the world must bee
It's owne sadd monument, his elegie;
As large as fame, but whether badd or good
I say not: by himselfe 'twas writt in blood;
For which his body is entomb'd in ayre,
Archt o're with heaven, sett with a thousand faire
And glorious diamond starrs. A sepulchre
That time can never ruinate, and where
Th' impartiall worme (which is not brib'd to spare
Princes corrupt in marble) cannot share
His flesh; which if the charitable skies
Embalme with teares; doeing those obsequies
Belong to men: shall last, till pittying fowle
Contend to beare his bodie to his soule.[98]

The body itself, which is 'It's owne sadd monument, his elegie', lends substance to the poem, which explores the relation between corporeality and identity, in both political and metaphysical contexts. Since the formalities of Christian burial have been denied the body, the poet appropriates natural and pagan motifs of mourning and renewal. The body is 'entomb'd in ayre' and 'embalme[d] with teares', as the skies observe the 'obsequies' which properly 'Belong to men'. The apotheosis of the corpse is presaged in the image of 'heaven, sett with a thousand faire / And glorious diamond starrs', which claims for a Christian context classical traditions in which great men and women were metamorphosed after death into stars. The final conceit returns to this suggestion, as it transforms the carrion 'fowle' into servants of God, reuniting body and soul beyond the earth.

The poem's sardonic glance at greatness, meanwhile, is loaded with significance. The 'impartiall worme' invokes a long tradition of satire directed against the pretensions of wealth and power, enlisted in many of the libellous epitaphs of the early Stuart period. Yet the lines at this point also allude more specifically to complaints about Buckingham's abuses of authority, and thereby posit Felton as an equally impartial judge, who has purged the nation of its greatest canker. The subsequent parenthetical comment further subverts the funerary order imposed by the government in the respective cases of Buckingham and his assassin. In a manner that evokes 1 Corinthians 15, the phrase 'princes corrupt in marble' conflates bodily and political 'corruption', intimating by extension 'the vainglorious physicality of princes' tombs'.[99] The poet's grammatically irregular use of 'corrupt', which may be functioning either as a verb or an adjective, reinforces the

---

[98] *Poems and Songs*, p. 78.
[99] Norbrook, *Writing the English Republic*, p. 56.

Pauline pun within a contemporary context of political complaint. The choice of 'princes' is in part justified by Buckingham's burial in King Henry VII's chapel in Westminster Abbey, where 'he lay surrounded by monarchs and princes of the blood royal, the first commoner to be honoured in this way'.[100] Yet the word is also more pointed, as it introduces into the poem resonances that are profoundly subversive of existing political structures. While Felton's body is exposed to heaven, 'princes' continue to 'corrupt': within marble palaces, perhaps, as much as in tombs.[101] The poem could hardly be categorized on this basis as an explicitly republican statement; however, as David Norbrook argues, it bears 'signs of more critical analysis of the basic structures of monarchical power'.[102] As may be observed in other contemporary libels, its provocative challenge to authorized meanings prompts a more searching analysis of the institutions and ideologies which set those meanings in place.

A hitherto undocumented poem written in response to 'Felton's Epitaph' attempts to reassert order:

> Here uninterd suspends, (doubtles to save
> hopefull, and freindles, th'expences of a grave
> Feltons curst corps, which to the world must bee
> It's owne fowle Monument his Elegie
> wider then fame, which whether badd or good
> Judge by himself, bee-smear'd in faultles blood
> For which his bodie is intombd i'th Aire
> Shrowded in Clowds, blacke as his Sepulchere
> Yet time is pleas'd; and thine partiall worme
> Unbribd to Spare, this wretches wretched Urne
> His fleshe which ever memorable Skyes
> Enbalme, to teache us and Posterities
> T'abhorre his fact: shall last till Harpies fowle
> Through Stix shall dragge, his Carkas to his sowle.[103]

This poem undoes the rich paradoxes of the original, reinscribing on the assassin's body the Caroline government's authorized meaning. Accordingly, while the natural world is stripped of spirituality and conceived instead as cold and threatening, the corpse is interpreted as a lesson, 'to teache

---

[100] Lockyer, *Buckingham*, p. 458. Lockyer documents the government's struggle to maintain suitable decorum in the burial. He was eventually buried at night, and one report suggests that 'the coffin which was carried in the procession was empty, the corpse having been interred privately on the previous day' (pp. 457–8).

[101] Cf. Holstun, *Ehud's Dagger*, p. 185.

[102] *Writing the English Republic*, p. 55.

[103] BL MS Add. 15226, fol. 28r–v.

us and Posterities / T'abhorre his fact'. Given the poem's attempt to de-
mythologize Felton, the weight on 'fact' is apt, as it centres the reader's
attention squarely on the sinful act of murder. Yet in the fevered environment of the late 1620s the impact of this reply was negligible, and it never
achieved anything like the wide circulation enjoyed by that in favour of the
assassin.[104]

'THE FIVE SENSES': WRITING THE KING'S BODY

The monarch was generally insulated against libellous attacks. Criticism
of kings tended to be conducted in oblique and allusive satire, rather
than through the libel's strategies of stigmatization and vilification.[105] Yet
James was not entirely misguided when he expressed a personal anxiety
about the effects of 'railing rymes and vaunting verse'.[106] Indeed, one of
the most accomplished political poems in manuscript circulation in the
1620s, although founded on declarations of loyalty, amply demonstrates
the libel's subversive potential. 'The Five Senses' is presented as a prayer
for the king's welfare, and much of the text focuses conventionally on
the dangers posed by corrupt counsellors and foreign papists. In accordance with an established tradition of political satire, however, this poem
uses its explicit purpose to veil a devastating critique of corruption at the
very centre of the political system. Crucially, the 'five senses' are those
of the king's own body, and the poem depicts each as a site of potential pollution. 'The Five Senses' therefore employs a number of strategies
familiar from other contemporary libels in order to explore forms of corruption threatening not only the individual monarch, but also his entire
nation.

This poem warrants a position at the centre of early Stuart literary culture. While some conjecture remains about its authorship and date, it was
most likely written by William Drummond in 1623. Those scholars who
have contested this attribution have uniformly failed to acknowledge that
it is directly ascribed to him in one contemporary miscellany, while only

---

[104] My research has revealed only one extant copy of the poem, compared to at least twenty-four of
'Heere uninterr'd suspends (though not to save'. (See further the discussion of sources for the latter
in Holstun, *Ehud's Dagger*, p. 184n.)

[105] One notable exception, Corneille de Breda's *Is. Casauboni Corona Regia* (1615), which salaciously
purports to reveal James's sexual exploits, was published in Latin and circulated on the continent.
For evidence of James's sensitivity to this tract, see Cyndia Susan Clegg, *Press Censorship in Jacobean
England* (Cambridge, 2001), p. 88.

[106] *The Poems of James VI of Scotland*, ed. James Craigie (2 vols., Scottish Text Society, Edinburgh and
London, 1955–8), II.182.

Robert H. MacDonald has acknowledged the poet's unquestionable interest in the poetics of invective.[107] Although Drummond's writings on politics were generally more moderate and scholarly, he was thus well aware of the capacities of political satire, and quite capable of questioning the decisions of his kings. In the wake of the failed Isle of Rhé expedition, for instance, he penned the couplet, 'Charles, would yee quaile your foes, have better lucke; / Send forth some Drakes, and keep at home the Ducke'.[108] 'The Five Senses' itself is modelled on a song in Ben Jonson's masque *The Gypsies Metamorphosed*, which was presented by Buckingham and his wife in honour of James in 1621. The politics of this masque have been the subject of critical debate; however, while it is arguable that Jonson's representation of Buckingham as a gypsy was open to satiric interpretation, it is difficult to accept that the entire text functioned as satire.[109] In the masque, Jonson's song is situated towards the end, and serves as a lightly comic assertion of political order, as the masquers pray that James should be protected from various nominal dangers, such as spoiled food, tobacco, or 'a lady that doth breathe / Worse above than underneath'.[110] The only threats

[107] The poem was tentatively attributed to Drummond in L. E. Kastner's edition of his poems (*Poetical Works*, 2 vols., Edinburgh, 1913), on the basis of its existence in the poet's notes, and in line with previous editions of his work. For the subsequent debate over the poem's authorship, see Allan H. Gilbert, 'Jonson and Drummond or Gil on the King's Senses', *Modern Language Notes*, 62 (1947), 35–7; C. F. Main, 'Ben Jonson and an Unknown Poet on the King's Senses', *Modern Language Notes*, 74 (1959), 389–93; and MacDonald, 'Amendments to L. E. Kastner's Edition of Drummond's Poems', *Studies in Scottish Literature*, 7 (1970), 107, 118. On Drummond's politics, and his relationship with Charles, see Joseph A. Taylor, 'The Literary Presentation of James I and Charles I, With Special Reference to the Period *c.*1614–1630' (unpublished DPhil. dissertation, University of Oxford, 1985), ch. 9; and on his interest in Roman pasquils, see above, p. 27n. Another candidate for the poem's authorship may more easily be dismissed. On the basis of research in the State Papers Domestic, W. Douglas Hamilton attributes the poem to Alexander Gill and dates it 1628 (*Original Papers Illustrative of the Life and Writings of John Milton* [Camden Society, London, 1859], p. 67). A review of his evidence, however, is inconclusive, since a report in the State Papers may indicate merely that this poem was in Gill's possession when he was arrested and examined in 1628 (PRO, State Papers Domestic 16/111/51). While no contemporary verse miscellany attributes it to Gill, one of the best sources for early Stuart libels attributes it to Drummond (Bodleian MS Eng. poet. c.50, fol. 25v), while another lists it as the work of James Johnson (Folger MS v.a.345, p. 59). Three miscellanies date the poem, and in each case the date is 1623 (Bodleian MS Rawlinson Poetry 26, fol. 72r; BL MS Stowe 962, fol. 144v; and Folger MS v.a.345, p. 59). The poem is discussed in Bellany, *Politics of Court Scandal*, pp. 258–60; and Paul Hammond, *Figuring Sex Between Men from Shakespeare to Rochester* (Oxford, 2002), pp. 141–3.

[108] Taylor, 'Literary Presentation of James I and Charles I', p. 280.

[109] A satiric interpretation of *The Gypsies Metamorphosed* is posited by B. J. Randall, *Jonson's Gypsies Unmasked* (Durham, NC, 1975). For a compelling critique of Randall, however, see Richard Helgerson, *Self-Crowned Laureates: Spenser, Jonson, Milton, and the Literary System* (Berkeley and Los Angeles, 1983), p. 178.

[110] *Ben Jonson: The Complete Masques*, ed. Stephen Orgel (New Haven, CT and London, 1969), pp. 367–9.

to Jacobean authority, it suggests, are trivial assaults on the king's refined sensibility.[III]

By comparison, 'The Five Senses' presents a far more troubling vision of corporeal frailty:

'The Five Senses'

1. Seeinge
From such a face whose Excellence
May captivate my Soveraignes sence
And make him Phœbus like his throne
Resigne to him younge Phaëton
Whose skillesse and unsteaddie hand   5
May prove the ruine of a land
Unlesse great Jove downe from the skye
Beholding Earthes Calamitie
Strike with his hand that cannot err
The proud Usurping Charioter   10
And cure though Phœbus greive our woe
From such a face that cann worke soe
Wheresoere thou hast a beeing
Blesse my Soveraigne, and his seeing.

2. Heareinge
From Jeasts prophane, from flattering tongues   15
From bawdy tales from beastly soungs
From after supper suits that feare
A Parliament or Councells eare
From Spanish treaties that may wound
Our Countries peace the gospell sound   20
From Jobs false frends that would entice
My Soveraigne from Heavens paradise
From Prophetts such as Ahabs weere
Whose flatteringes sooth my soveraignes eare
His frownes more then his makers fearing   25
Blesse my soveraigne and his heareing.

3. Tastinge
From all fruite that is forbidden
Such for which old Eve was chidden
From bread of Laborers sweat, and toyle

[III] Another poem written on the model of Jonson's song accords with the sanguine politics of the original. Clearly associated with Christmas revels, it implores 'good Phœbus' to protect the singers 'on this our 12th day', from ills which range from 'silent and strangled farts', to 'Gundemore's breech, and the Spanish Itch' ('Since grizly old Janus hath suddenly ta'ne us' [BL MS Add. 22603, fols. 55v–56r]).

From the widdowes meale, and oyle   30
From the [candied]¹¹² poyson'd baites
Of Jesuites and their deceipts
Italian Salletts, Romish druggs
The milke of Babells proud whore duggs
From wyne that can destroye the braine   35
And from the daingerous figg of Spaine
Att all banquetts, and all feasting
Blesse my Soveraigne, and his tasting.

　4. Feelinge
From prick of Conscience such a sting
As staines the Soule, heavens blesse my King   40
From such a bribe¹¹³ as may with drawe
His thoughts from equitie, and lawe
From such a smooth, and beardlesse chinn
As may provoke, or tempt to sinn
From such a hand whose moyst palme may   45
My soveraigne lead out of the way
From things polluted, and uncleane
From all thats beastly, and obsceane
From what may sett his Soule a reeling
Blesse my Soveraigne, and his feeling.   50

　5. Smellinge
Where Mirrhe, and Frankinsence is throwne
The altars built to Gods unknowne
Oh lett my Soveraigne never smell
Such damn'd perfumes are fitt for hell
Let noe such scent his nostrills staine   55
From smells that poyson may the braine
Heavens still preserve him, Next I crave
Thou wilt be pleas'd great God to save
My Soveraigne from a Ganimede
Whose whoreish breath hath power to lead   60
His excellence which way it list
O lett such lipps be never kist
From a breath soe farr excelling
Blesse my Soveraigne and his smelling.

　on all the Sences
And just God I humblie pray   65
That thou wilt take the Filme away
That keepes my Soveraignes eyes from vieweing

---

¹¹² The MS has 'canded'.
¹¹³ The MS has 'tribe'; however, other sources give 'bribe', which is clearly a preferable reading.

The things that wilbe our undoeing
Then lett him *Heare* good God the sounds
Aswell of Men, as of his hounds   70
Give him a *Taste* and tymely too
Of what his Subjects undergoe
Give him a *Feelinge* of there woes
And noe doubt his royall nose
Will quickely *Smell* those rascalls forth   75
Whose blacke deeds have ecclips't his worth.
These found, and scourg'd for their offences
Heavens blesse my Soveraigne and his sences.[114]

Although it uses no names, the poem's repetition of the word 'such' is
the slightest of veils covering criticism of Buckingham. The 'face' which,
the opening lines declare, 'May captivate my Soveraignes sence', is certainly that of Buckingham (lines 1–2); and this identification is reinforced
by the subsequent image of a 'skillesse and unsteaddie hand' directing the
nation (line 5), which evokes conventional representations of the ship of
state in a manner also used in another libel on Buckingham.[115] In the fourth
stanza the image of a particular hand is recalled, with more pointed intent,
as that hand's 'moyst palme may / My soveraigne lead out of the way'
(lines 45–6). Relations between James and his favourite were at the very
least erotically charged, and widespread rumours of homosexual activity
probably had some substance, especially in the early years of their association.[116] Moreover, the 'moyst palme' may easily function synecdochi-
cally, figuring for an informed readership the spectre of sodomy, with
all of its intertwined moral and political connotations. The accusation
is underlined in the poem's fifth stanza, which presents the threat of a
'Ganimede' with 'whoreish breath' (lines 59–60). In the Renaissance, the
name of Ganymede, cupbearer to Zeus, became a popular euphemism for a
'catamite': the passive partner in a homosexual coupling.[117] Moreover, the title was especially applicable to Buckingham given that one of his first official

[114] Bodleian MS Malone 23, pp. 28–31.
[115] 'When onely one doth rule and guide the shipp' (*Poems and Songs*, pp. 33–4); see further below, pp. 142–3.
[116] See Lockyer, *Buckingham*, p. 22. On the representation of royal sodomy, see Hammond, *Figuring Sex Between Men*, pp. 128–50; James Knowles, 'To "scourge the arse / Jove's marrow so had wasted": Scurrility and the Subversion of Sodomy', in Dermot Cavanagh and Tim Kirk, eds., *Subversion and Scurrility: Popular Discourse in Europe from 1500 to the Present* (Aldershot, 2000), pp. 74–92; Curtis Perry, 'The Politics of Access and Representations of the Sodomite King in Early Modern England', *Renaissance Quarterly*, 53 (2000), 1054–83; and Michael B. Young, *King James and the History of Homosexuality* (New York, 2000).
[117] The word 'catamite' was in fact derived from 'Ganymede'. See further James M. Saslow, *Ganymede in the Renaissance: Homosexuality in Art and Society* (New Haven, CT, 1986).

positions at court was as cupbearer to James: a fact that prompted snide comments, right up to his death, about his 'Ganimedian lookes' and 'courting lady-hand'.[118]

Yet 'The Five Senses' is also a poem about James himself. Medieval kingship theory inherited by the Stuarts acknowledged the human physicality and fallibility of a monarch through the notion of the king's two bodies.[119] The divinely ordained body politic 'is a Body that cannot be seen or handled, consisting of Policy and Government', whereas the body natural belonged to the quotidian world and was 'subject to all Infirmities that come by Nature or Accident'.[120] Theorists generally agreed, however, that there dwelt within the body politic 'mysterious forces which reduce, or even remove, the imperfections of the fragile human nature'. The entities existed in a perfect union, controlled by the immutable and angelic character of the body politic.[121] A product of a more sceptical age, 'The Five Senses' works to subvert this theory of kingship, representing the king's senses as agents of a corruption which threatens to spill beyond the corporeal site of the body natural. Notably, James's body is figured as inherently porous and corruptible, open alike to 'bawdy tales' and 'Spanish treaties', 'wyne that can destroye the braine' and the 'poyson'd baites / Of Jesuites' (lines 16, 19, 35, 31–2). More topically, the reference to the 'daingerous figg of Spaine' perhaps alludes to the Spanish match (the fig being considered an aphrodisiac, and a word sometimes used euphemistically for the vagina), which threatened to erode the protestant rectitude of both Prince Charles and the English people (line 36).[122] Throughout, the definitive danger is that James will be led by the promptings of his senses into paths that will damage at once his soul and his subjects' liberties. Around the spectre of royal sodomy, therefore, the poet fashions a narrative of national calamity, as the 'moyst palme' draws him 'out of the way' of both sexual propriety, godly government and religious integrity.[123]

---

[118] Lockyer, *Buckingham*, p. 17; 'Pale death with firm hand hath struck a blowe' (*Poems and Songs*, p. 49).

[119] See Ernst H. Kantorowicz, *The King's Two Bodies: A Study in Mediaeval Political Theology* (Princeton, 1957); and Glenn Burgess's assessment of the theory in the context of the early seventeenth century, in *The Politics of the Ancient Constitution: An Introduction to English Political Thought, 1603–1642* (Basingstoke, 1992), pp. 163–4.

[120] Edmund Plowden, *Commentaries or Reports* (1816), p. 212a: quoted in Kantorowicz, *King's Two Bodies*, p. 7.

[121] Kantorowicz, *King's Two Bodies*, pp. 8–9.

[122] Williams, *Dictionary of Sexual Language and Imagery*, I.480–1.

[123] Cf. Bellany, whose reading of the poem prioritizes rather the threat of popery (*Politics of Court Scandal*, p. 259).

The religious dimension of the poem is elucidated at its centre, where Drummond raises an anxiety which is familiar from other libels. Amidst the catalogue of temptations, James is briefly isolated as a religious subject, as the poet prays: 'From prick of Conscience such a sting / As staines the soule, heavens blesse my King' (lines 39–40). The contemporary religious doctrine outlined above posits the conscience as a critical link between the individual and God: 'It is (as it were) a little God sitting in the middle of mens hearts, arraigning them in this life as they shall be arraigned for their offences at the tribunall seat of the everlasting God in the day of judgement.'[124] Although strictly orthodox in these terms, the poem pointedly ignores theories that insisted on the unique status of a monarch. In medieval doctrine, it was held that the purity of the king's body politic 'wipes away every Imperfection of the other body'; and in early Stuart England, at a time when James was determined to preserve certain *arcana imperii* from the inquiry of parliament, such arguments attained a fresh urgency.[125] Significantly, in the light of contemporary discourse on the conscience, monarchical theorists at this time invoked Proverbs 25.3: 'the heart of a King is unsearchable'.[126] By contrast, the introduction of the concept of conscience in 'The Five Senses' suggests the disturbing possibility that the sins committed by the king's body natural may endanger at once his own soul and the health of the body politic. Hence there is an unavoidable imperative for the libeller to search the heart of the monarch; for while a king with physical desires is inevitable, a king with an infernally seared conscience would become a matter with ramifications for the entire Christian nation.

The final stanza of 'The Five Senses' ostensibly posits an orthodox solution to the dangers confronting the king. In a continuation of the poem's assault on Buckingham, the concluding suggestion is that the integrity of the monarch will be reasserted once the sources of corruption are 'found, and scourg'd for their offences' (line 77). On closer analysis, however, the conclusion is perhaps not quite as stable and conservative as this statement might suggest. The preceding lines pray not for the king's protection from danger, but rather for a harshly instructive exposure:

> Give him a *Taste* and tymely too
> Of what his Subjects undergoe
> Give him a *Feelinge* of there woes

---

[124] Perkins, *Works*, p. 621.
[125] Plowden, *Reports*, p. 238: quoted in Kantorowicz, *King's Two Bodies*, p. 11. James VI and I, 'His Majesties Declaration, Touching his Proceedings in the Late Assemblie and Convention of Parliament' (1622), in *Political Writings*, ed. Johann P. Sommerville (Cambridge, 1994), pp. 252–3.
[126] See, for example, Roger Maynwaring, *Religion and Alegiance: in two sermons* (1627), p. 17.

> And noe doubt his royall nose
> Will quickely *Smell* those rascalls forth
> Whose blacke deeds have ecclips't his worth.
>
> (lines 71–6)

The lines shift attention from the sinful splendour of the court to the 'woes' endured daily by lower members of the body politic. Subsequently, the apparent confidence of the statement, 'noe doubt his royall nose / Will quickely *Smell* those rascalls forth', is invested with a destabilizing note of irony. Given the poem's anxiety about James's corporeal fallibility, there is clearly good reason to 'doubt' his capacity to identify and punish the threatening 'rascalls'. Consequently, the final stanza assumes undertones of populist menace, juxtaposing the experiences of king and people, and positing the subjects' 'woes' as a source of authority. As much as any other early Stuart libel, therefore, this poem presents a powerful interrogation of founding myths of royal authority, and hints at radically new structures of political speech and action.

'The Five Senses' is particularly significant within the context of early Stuart political culture because of its assumption that the identity of the monarch, as well as those of his courtiers, might be fashioned and contested in libels. The king is thus drawn into processes of personal and political contestation, within which the manipulation of identities becomes a central technique of power. These struggles were at once pervasive and unavoidable. Posthumous libels contesting the identities of men such as Raleigh and Cecil contributed to ongoing factional struggles at court, while in the 1620s the virulent attacks on Buckingham helped to make his assassination at once conceivable and laudable. In some of the more impressive libels, as we have seen, attacks on individuals also provided occasions for some strikingly sophisticated analyses of the political system. By extension, libels reinforced demands among the populace for information about, and ultimately a sense of involvement in, political processes. As I will argue further in the following chapters, published poetry and prose pamphlets clarified these demands, and in turn offered to define emergent political alignments within the state. It is in this context that John Reynolds dedicated a pamphlet to James in 1624, archly conflating a rhetoric of counsel with a tradition of libel in his prayer: 'So blesse my Soveraign and all his sences in the reading therof.'[127]

---

[127] *Votivae Angliae* (1624); quoted in Taylor, 'Literary Presentation of James I and Charles I', p. 190.

PART II

Public politics

CHAPTER 3

Freeing the tongue and the heart: satire and the political subject

In the 1590s, Everard Guilpin claimed that the 'Decorum' of satire necessitates 'Bringing a foule-mouth Jester who might sing / To rogues, the story of a lousie king'.[1] Satire is thus figured as a mode that oscillates uneasily between the court and the people; the licensed voice of a courtly 'Jester' gathers an undeniably subversive edge when he is displaced from an elite milieu, adopting 'foule' speech and addressing an audience of 'rogues'. In the subsequent decades, political satirists sought to clarify the status of their mode, defining a place for satire within the state. Like Guilpin, they struggled with questions of audience and authority. A 'foule-mouthed Jester' might speak to the monarch, bearing harsh but necessary truths; however, he might equally speak to 'rogues', in an effort to initiate popular political action. They struggled also with the associated question of whether satire might function legitimately within existing courtly models of counsel, or whether it should break with these strictures and speak to a wider and less exclusive audience. Their struggles in turn helped to illuminate a fundamental tension within the English state, for the model of counsel was predicated on an assumption that all speech is directed towards and authorized by the monarch, whereas the alternative might suggest democratic or republican forms of political engagement. Fundamentally, the question is whether a satirist is speaking *to* a monarch or *with* his peers: whether he, or she, is a subject or a citizen.

This chapter, the first of two in the book's central part, is concerned with these interactions between a literary mode and emergent political discourses. After the opening chapters, this represents in some respects a turn backwards, to some fundamental questions about the nature of satire. Yet it equally moves forwards, towards an examination of the ways in which satire functioned in the period's public politics, as contemporaries sought

[1] *Skialetheia or A Shadowe of Truth, in Certaine Epigrams and Satyres* (1598), ed. D. Allen Carroll (Chapel Hill, 1974), p. 58.

85

to make sense of apparent tensions within their state. In Part II, then, the range of material expands from a focus on libels to embrace also printed poetry, prose pamphlets, and some drama. In these texts, writers extend the processes of inquiry observed already, in ways that are often more expansive and speculative than is possible within the context of a libellous attack on an individual. This chapter's sphere of inquiry is, of course, part of a much bigger picture; notably, intellectual and cultural historians have demonstrated the extent to which humanist and classical influences were transforming English political culture in this period.[2] Yet a study of satire highlights kinds of texts and textual practices which were utterly familiar to contemporary readers and writers, but which are often overlooked by forms of history that prioritize reason and clarity in political expression. By attending to such sources, we may come to see that satire valuably amplifies and elucidates debates over the limits of free speech and the role of the political subject, and helps contemporaries to imagine new models of political interaction.

A central purpose in this chapter is to examine the textual hinterlands between the authorized and the unauthorized: liberty and licence. According to one influential theory, satire enables writers to present criticism in an acceptable manner; its strategies of artful indirection depend on the codes of 'functional ambiguity' that Annabel Patterson identifies as 'a creative and necessary instrument' of the early modern censorship regime.[3] The texts to be considered here, however, evidence writers straining at the boundaries of this structure, and increasingly forging instead unauthorized and libellous forms of political commentary. This requires a broader model of political debate in the nation than many previous studies would admit. Significantly, although the texts often respond to parliamentary proceedings – especially in years such as 1614 and 1621, when the very existence of the sessions hung on debates over the limits of allowable speech – the chapter does not focus at length on conflicts between kings and parliaments.[4] Instead, it considers the achievements of satire as more interrogatory, speculative, and ongoing. When searching for the earliest signs of an early Stuart citizen breaking free from traditional constraints on speech and action, we can hardly expect perfect clarity or easily identifiable lines of progression. Writers at

[2] See esp. David Norbrook, *Writing the English Republic: Poetry, Rhetoric and Politics, 1627–1660* (Cambridge, 1999); Markku Peltonen, *Classical Humanism and Republicanism in English Political Thought 1570–1640* (Cambridge, 1995); and J. G. A. Pocock, *The Machiavellian Moment: Florentine Political Thought and the Atlantic Republican Tradition* (Princeton, 1975).

[3] *Censorship and Interpretation: The Conditions of Writing and Reading in Early Modern England* (Madison, 1984), pp. 18, 11.

[4] Cf. the approach adopted in Stephen Clucas and Rosalind Davies, eds., *1614: Year of Crisis: Studies in Jacobean History and Literature* (Aldershot, 2002).

this time were grappling with the strictures of censorship, and struggling further to conceive of novel discourses of politics, founded on radically new notions of individual freedom. Satire, with its resources of provocation and indirection, was a valuable tool for this project.

The chapter pivots on the year 1620, when James first issued his forceful proclamation on 'Lavish and Licentious Speech of matters of State'. The opening section focuses on the relation between satire and the court through the early and middle phases of James's reign, considering prevailing theories of satire as a form of counsel, and examining the ways in which some writers questioned the value of such approaches. George Wither, who thought more rigorously about the politics of satire than almost any of his contemporaries, is a critical figure in this context, and his *Satyre: Dedicated to His Most Excellent Majestie*, written from prison in 1614, demonstrates especially well the particular strains on satirists and their literary mode. The following section concentrates on developments in unauthorized writing of the 1620s: not because such writing did not exist before this decade, but rather because of the marked proliferation of illicit political satire, much of it in printed form, produced in the wake of James's proclamation. Such texts – many of which were published as pamphlets, and most of which evade or flaunt restraints of censorship – decisively break with both authorized forms of satire and courtly models of counsel. Finally, the third section looks across the period to consider the ways in which satiric texts represent the processes and contexts of popular political engagement. In their valorization of furtive exchanges and strategic insurgency, I argue, we might discern critical efforts towards the construction of an early modern public sphere.

BITTER AND WITTY KNAVES: SATIRISTS AT COURT

Writing in 1621, James Howell remembered an incident at the Jacobean court, which aptly demonstrates a predominant cultural ideal of satire's function within a monarchical state. Howell is reminded of the occasion by reading a pasquil in Rome against the Scots, which 'had some gaul in't, yet it had a great deal of wit . . . so that I think if K. *James* saw it, he would laugh at it'. This assessment of the king's taste is based upon his recollection that:

some years since there was a very abusive *Satire* in Verse brought to our King; and as the passages were a-reading before him he often said, That if there were no more Men in *England*, the Rogue should hang for it: At last being come to the Conclusion, which was (after all his Railing)—
  Now God preserve the King, the Queen, the Peers,
  And grant the Author long may wear his Ears;

this pleas'd his Majesty so well, that he broke into a laughter, and said, *By my sol, so thou shalt for me*: Thou art a bitter, but thou art a witty Knave.[5]

For the king, wit legitimizes transgression. Consequently, although the author of the poem is not elevated by his action, remaining fixed in the position of a 'knave', his text is nonetheless incorporated into a courtly structure of counsel. The mix of 'Railing' and humour first gains access to the monarch, and then wins a qualified approval. (As Donne had similarly asserted, the only truly effective libels are those 'which entertain us long with a delight, and love to the things themselves'.[6]) This model of interaction informed the work of satirists throughout the early Stuart period, even as they became disillusioned about the likelihood of avoiding punishment. It provided a potent ideal for satirists seeking to situate their art in relation to the state, and to project their grievances into the face of authority.

The political function of satire assumed a particular urgency in the context of widespread concern about practices of counsel. In the orthodox view articulated by Francis Bacon, the teachings and example of Solomon demonstrated that 'in counsel is stability', and underlined the need for open discussions between contemporary counsellors and their monarch.[7] Parliament was also incorporated into this model. Even some staunch defenders of parliamentary powers held that their institution did 'but advise' the king, rather than independently formulating law and contesting authority; and even at the height of parliamentary crises, according to recent scholars, most members of parliament remained committed to this goal.[8] At the same time, however, many commentators perceived that the channels of counsel had become polluted by corruption and faction. The works of Tacitus, in particular, reinforced such beliefs, through their delineation of political discord and their concern with the self-interested slipperiness of language within the court: an environment in which there is 'nothing

---

[5] *Epistolæ Ho-elianæ: The Familiar Letters of James Howell*, ed. Joseph Jacobs (2 vols., London, 1892), II.89. I am grateful to Debora Shuger for drawing this passage to my attention.

[6] *Letters to Severall Persons of Honour* (London, 1651), pp. 89–90; see above, p. 23.

[7] *The Essays*, ed. John Pitcher (London, 1985), p. 120; Bacon is adapting Proverbs 20.18 ('Every purpose is established by counsel: and with good advice make war').

[8] Walter Raleigh, *The Prerogative of Parlaments in England* (1628), p. 57; cf. Graham Parry's assessment of Robert Cotton ('Cotton's Counsels: The Contexts of *Cottoni Posthuma*', in C. J. Wright, ed., *Sir Robert Cotton as Collector: Essays on an Early Stuart Courtier and his Legacy* (London, 1997), pp. 88–9). David Colclough argues that members of the 1614 Parliament remained committed to the model of counsel ('"Better Becoming a Senate of Venice"? The "Addled Parliament" and Jacobean Debates on Freedom of Speech', in *1614: Clucas and Davies, eds., *Year of Crisis*, p. 56). For the general argument that a parliament was a body convened to counsel the monarch, see esp. Conrad Russell, *Unrevolutionary England, 1603–1642* (London, 1989), pp. 1–29.

simple and sincere, and no true Fidelity even amongst Friends'.[9] Consequently, the courtier's arts of dissimulation, which had been lauded in literature of the sixteenth century, were increasingly refigured as strategies of mere deception. In the words of one character sketch, the courtier is a 'vaine promiser, idle protester, servant of folly, and scholler of deceit . . . so that his oaths and words are like smoake and aire: and his deeds and actions meerly shadowes'.[10]

Within this context, those who continued to presume a capacity for independent judgement worked hard to fashion for themselves identities freed of such expectations. In rhetorical terms, their efforts typically invoked *parrhesia*, or the figure of frank speech. As David Colclough has shown, *parrhesia*, though recognized as an antidote to flattery, had been constrained in its impact during the course of the sixteenth century, transformed steadily into 'a figure of excusing for speaking boldly rather than the act of speaking boldly itself'.[11] According to Henry Peacham, it 'doth best beseeme a man of wisedome and gravitie, who is best able to moderate the forme of his speech, and to restrain it from that rude boldnesse which doth more hurt then good'.[12] Yet it appealed in its purer form to those who valued the supposed 'freedom' of the English man, and it always retained the more radical potential signalled in the translation adopted by 'the more conservative Romans', *licentia*.[13] As James himself feared, 'libertie of speeche' sprawls, as though by nature, 'into licence'.[14] Theoretically, the conventional royal grant of freedom of speech to a session of parliament acknowledged this potential, and Sir Walter Raleigh was thus entirely orthodox when he urged that, 'if any man of the commons house should speake more largely, then of duety hee ought to doe, all such offences [should] be pardoned'.[15] But a history of arrests of members and premature closures of parliaments, throughout the early Stuart era, amply demonstrates the limits of royal patience. Within the court, meanwhile,

---

[9] Degory Wheare (quoting the Tacitean scholar Justus Lipsius), *De Ratione et Methodo Legendi Historias Dissertatio* (Oxford, 1623), pp. 106–7: quoted in Alan T. Bradford, 'Stuart Absolutism and the "Utility" of Tacitus', *Huntington Library Quarterly*, 46 (1983), 128.

[10] [Thomas Gainsford], *The Rich Cabinet Furnished with Variety of Excellent Discriptions* (1616), fols. 18v–19r.

[11] '*Parrhesia*: The Rhetoric of Free Speech in Early Modern England', *Rhetorica*, 17 (1999), 207.

[12] *The Garden of Eloquence* (1593), sig. R2r: quoted in Colclough, '*Parrhesia*', 207.

[13] David Norbrook, '*Areopagitica*, Censorship, and the Early Modern Public Sphere', in Richard Burt, ed., *The Administration of Aesthetics: Censorship, Political Criticism, and the Public Sphere* (Minneapolis and London, 1994), p. 18. On the political valence of 'freedom', see David Underdown, *A Freeborn People: Politics and the Nation in Seventeenth-Century England* (Oxford, 1996), esp. p. 27.

[14] Quoted in Christopher Thompson, *The Debate on Freedom of Speech in the House of Commons in February 1621* (Orsett, Essex, 1985), p. 3.

[15] Raleigh, *Prerogative of Parliaments*, p. 55.

Sir Anthony Weldon relates an anecdote about a courtier who dared to inform Charles about the full magnitude of England's military losses at the Isle of Rhé. For Weldon, the courtier assumed the status of an 'honest Tell-truth'; Charles, however, deemed him worthy only of banishment, for it remained 'a strange boldnesse in a poore and private person, to advise Kings'.[16]

Despite the evident dangers of such actions, satirists founded their identities upon comparable stances. In the Renaissance traditions established in the latter decades of the sixteenth century, the typical satiric persona emerged as that of 'a blunt, honest man', while the pervasive influence of Juvenal injected a further level of outspokenness and moral indignation.[17] In this context, the 1599 Bishops' Ban marks one more effort by the early modern state to draw a line between liberty and licence.[18] Furthermore, as I argued in Chapter 1, while the Ban did not necessarily drive satire 'underground', it contributed to a dispersal or diffusion of the mode, which subsequently informed a wide range of texts, from manuscript libels to printed pamphlets. Concurrently, satiric styles were modified, as the Elizabethan vogue for Juvenalian railing converged with a widespread appreciation for a terse and sententious style, derived as much from Tacitus as from Martial.[19] But what unquestionably remained, and was consistently developed through the early Stuart decades, was a strong sense of the political value of satire. Crucially, in the Jacobean era we can observe writers anxiously negotiating a place for dissent, and struggling to resituate political satire within their culture in the wake of the Ban.

The most concerted effort to fashion a distinctly public form of political satire under James was made by the loose alignment of poets who have become known as the English Spenserians. These poets found in the work of Edmund Spenser examples of political satire informed by principles of moral and religious rectitude, yet contained by assumptions of loyalty to the reigning monarch. In particular, Spenser's *Prosopopoia: or Mother Hubberds Tale* (1591), a beast satire aimed at the influence of William Cecil, Lord Burghley, and his son, Robert Cecil, provided an instance of dissent grounded upon Elizabethan ideals of protestant militancy.[20] At the outset of James's reign, when there seemed reason to hope that the

[16] *The Court and Character of King James* (1651), pp. 185–6; Raleigh, *Prerogative of Parlaments*, p. 62.
[17] Alvin Kernan, *The Cankered Muse: Satire of the English Renaissance* (New Haven, CT, 1959), pp. 16, 64–79.
[18] On the political motivations behind the Bishops' Ban, see Cyndia Susan Clegg, *Press Censorship in Elizabethan England* (Cambridge, 1997), pp. 198–217.
[19] P. Burke, 'Tacitism', in T. A. Dorey, ed., *Tacitus* (London, 1969), p. 151.
[20] See Spenser, *Poetical Works*, ed. J. C. Smith and E. De Selincourt (Oxford, 1970), pp. 494–508.

new king would remove Robert Cecil from authority, Michael Drayton seized on both Spenser's model and his targets in *The Owle* (1604).[21] In the subsequent decade, *Mother Hubberds Tale* was reprinted (1612), and helped to galvanize a fresh wave of dissent.[22] This was the moment immediately after Cecil's death, when the issue of succession to his position was unclear and factional struggles were attracting considerable attention throughout the nation.[23] The work of the Spenserians thus coincided with the unprecedented flood of libels that greeted his death, and it seemed for a time to represent a truly public – even, albeit tenuously, authorized – form of political satire. Christopher Brooke's *Ghost of Richard III* (1614), to take one example, in many respects parallels libellous poems comparing Richard and Cecil, yet develops a more rigorous study of 'the failure of counsel' within a corrupt court. The codes of contemporary libels are here brought into conjunction with a 'humanist discourse of tyranny', as Brooke uses his historical framework to explore contemporary tensions between king, counsellors, and parliamentarians.[24] For Wither, Brooke had accurately 'character'd the *Condition* / . . . of a meere *Polititian*'.[25]

Brooke was also a member of the 'Addled' Parliament of 1614, and in this capacity he contributed to epochal debates concerning free speech and counsel. Crucially, these debates concentrated on the language of counsel; though many MPs ultimately adopted positions that might fairly be described as 'oppositional', the predominant mood throughout was to preserve an open forum which might best fulfil its duty to advise the king.[26] The debates were examined and expounded in a range of poetry, much of which was produced by the Spenserians. William Browne's *The Shepheards Pipe* (1614), and Wither's *The Shepherds Hunting* (1615), for example, pursue political critique through pastoral satire. In such works, the authors repeatedly dwell on the threat of arbitrary authority, drawing parallels between the abuse of counsel and the threat of censorship.[27] Hence the imprisonment of parliamentarians in 1614 – including the satiric poet Sir John Hoskyns – is represented as a clear threat to the free pursuit

[21] *Works*, ed. J. William Hebel (5 vols., Oxford, 1931–41), II.477–514. See David Norbrook, *Poetry and Politics in the English Renaissance*, revised edn (Oxford, 2002), p. 175.
[22] See Michelle O'Callaghan, *The 'shepheards nation': Jacobean Spenserians and Early Stuart Political Culture* (Oxford, 2000), p. 14.
[23] See esp. Alastair Bellany, *The Politics of Court Scandal in Early Modern England: News Culture and the Overbury Affair, 1603–1660* (Cambridge, 2002), pp. 44–50.
[24] O'Callaghan, *The 'shepheards nation'*, p. 67.
[25] Commendatory poem to Brooke, *Ghost of Richard III*, sig. A3v.
[26] Norbrook, *Poetry and Politics*, pp. 175–6; Colclough, '"Better Becoming a Senate of Venice"?', p. 56.
[27] Michelle O'Callaghan, '"Now thou may'st speak freely": Entering the Public Sphere in 1614', in Clucas and Davies, eds., *1614: Year of Crisis*, p. 63.

of political debate. For Sir Henry Wotton, defending the imprisonments, the men had transgressed 'the natural capacity of subjects', deploying a form of 'wit' which was rightly to be seen as 'licentiousness baptized freedom'.[28] The men themselves, however, fought to fashion themselves as truly loyal 'patriots', concerned to defend traditional liberties and oppose corruption at court.[29] Their vision, that is, was of a political culture within which parliamentarians and poets alike might speak openly, without fear of suppression.

These struggles were of vital interest to Wither, who was himself imprisoned in 1614 for his authorship of *Abuses Stript, and Whipt* (1613). Henry Howard, Earl of Northampton, interpreted passages in Wither's poem as libellous, and appears to have secured his imprisonment on grounds of *scandalum magnatum*.[30] Northampton was no supporter of free speech, either from poets or parliamentarians, and his reactionary positions appear to have only exacerbated tensions in 1614.[31] Faced with such a powerful and intransigent enemy, and from his imprisonment in the Marshalsea, the young Wither wrote a poem which considers not only his own fate, but also the very foundations of his poetics of dissent. *A Satyre: Dedicated to His Most Excellent Majestie* (1614) is therefore in part a satire about satire. From its outset, the poet self-consciously invokes satiric precedents, in an effort to set his work in the context of classical and native traditions:

> What once the POET said, I may avow,
> *'Tis a hard thing not to write Satyres*, now.
> Since what we speake, abuse raignes so in all,
> Spight of our hearts will be *Satyricall*.
>
> (sig. A6v)

The echo of Juvenal's famous title for his first satire ('*Difficile est Saturam non Scribere*'), which claims a need for satire within troubled times, is developed later in the poem, when Wither wonders why '*Seneca, Horace, Persius, Juvenall*. / And such as they', were not, like Wither himself, 'put ... in a *Cage*' (sig. E1r–v). The comparison is disingenuous, since classical satirists

---

[28] Quoted in Colclough, '"Better Becoming a Senate of Venice"?', pp. 52, 58.

[29] O'Callaghan, *The 'shepheards nation'*, p. 18. See also Thomas Cogswell, *The Blessed Revolution: English Politics and the Coming of War, 1621–1624* (Cambridge, 1989), pp. 84–99; and Ronald Knowles, '"The All-Attoning Name': The Word *Patriot* in Seventeenth-Century England', *Modern Languages Review*, 96 (2001), 624–43.

[30] Allan Pritchard, '*Abuses Stript and Whipt* and Wither's Imprisonment', *Review of English Studies*, n.s. 14 (1963), 337–45; Cyndia Susan Clegg, *Press Censorship in Jacobean England* (Cambridge, 2001), p. 113.

[31] Norbrook, *Poetry and Politics*, p. 194; Linda Levy Peck gives a measured assessment in *Northampton: Patronage and Policy at the Court of James I* (London, 1982), esp. pp. 185–212.

were hardly free from political pressures. In a literary context, however, the placement of Seneca (the only one of the four Romans who is not recognized as a satirist) at the head of the list signals Wither's desire to extend the practices of the Elizabethans, by incorporating into satire a neo-Stoic political philosophy. Significantly, Seneca and Tacitus were linked in Renaissance political thought, as writers 'who do not have masters or do not want to have them anymore'.[32]

But *A Satyre* is far from comfortable with the potential implications of this logic, and in general reverts to the model of political engagement used by the 'witty Knave' who won privileged access to James. Wither considers the reasons why he chooses 'rudely' to make a satire:

> And why? my friends and meanes in *Court* are scant,
> Knowledge of curious Phrase, and forme, I want.
> I cannot bear't to runne my selfe in debt,
> To hire the *Groome*, to bid the *Page* intreat
> Some *favour'd follower*, to vouchsafe his word,
> To get me a cold comfort from his *Lord*.
> I cannot sooth, though it my life might save,
> Each *favourite*, nor crouch to every *Knave*:
> I cannot brooke delayes as some men do,
> With scoffes, and scornes, and tak't in kindnesse to.
>
> (sig. A7r–v)

Satire is presented here as a conduit between the subject and the king, which enables the poet to avoid the circumlocutions of the court and its discourse. It is a vehicle through which the loyal subject might alert the king to problems within his realm; as Wither asks, recalling the Elizabethan fixation on the figure of the rough woodland satyr as satire's originating voice, 'Can my hopes (fixt in thee great KING) be dead? / Or thou those *Satyres* hate thy *Forrests* bred?' (sig. A8v).[33] Further, it is a mode for the outsider, detached from the court variously by a lack of resources, a proclaimed 'young *Rusticitie*', and a commitment to honesty and free expression (sig. E6r). Indeed Wither aims to harness the rhetorical force of *parrhesia*, binding it to a conventional view of the corrective powers of his chosen mode:

> He that will taxe these *Times*, must be more bitter,
> Tart lines of *Vinegar*, and *Gall* are fitter.
>
> . . .
>
> I'de have my *Pen* so paint it, where it traces,

---

[32] Andrew Shifflett, *Stoicism, Politics, and Literature in the Age of Milton* (Cambridge, 1998), p. 26.
[33] On the satyr theory, see Kernan, *Cankered Muse*, p. 55; and on the seventeenth-century challenges to it, see Dustin Griffin, *Satire: A Critical Reintroduction* (Lexington, KY, 1994), pp. 12–13.

> Each accent should draw blood into their faces.
> And make them, when their *villainies* are blazed,
> *Shudder*, and *startle*, as men halfe amazed,
> For feare my *verse* should make so loud a din,
> Heaven hearing, might raine vengeance on their sin.
>
> (sig. B3r–v)

Rather than back away from his alleged indiscretions in *Abuses Stript, and Whipt*, Wither asserts an authority which at once appeals to the king and reaches beyond his judgement. The barely subdued violence of the satirist's 'Pen' is thus mirrored only by the authority of 'Heaven', which rains divine 'vengeance on their sin'.

While satire aspires to this higher level of truth, and the satirist prays for 'such a straine' in order to lift his 'scourging numbers', the practices and discourse of the court are represented rather as obstacles and agents of corruption (sig. B3v). *A Satyre* is prefaced by a 'Satyre to the meere Courtiers', which brashly announces an intention to reach the ear of the king regardless of who may 'denie admittance' (sig. A4v). Within the court, Wither perceives a need 'to temporize': literally, to mould his speech to the times, producing perhaps '*Fidlers* Songs, or *Ballets*, like an Asse, / Or any thing almost indeed but this' (sig. D8r–v). The courtly milieu distorts and subverts the truth, not only by affecting what courtiers may say, but also by disrupting practices of textual interpretation. Nothing here will be allowed to pass 'for what [it] seem'd' (sig. B4v); instead, he argues, the corrupt reader misconstrues general satiric attacks on vice as particularized aspersions against 'some private person in the state' (sig. B5r). Such readers find 'strange farre-fetcht meanings' in what Wither 'intended universally':

> Whereat *some* with displeasure over-gone,
>
> . . .
>
> Maugre those caveats, on my *Satyres* brow,
> Their honest, and just passage disallow.
> And on their heads so many censures rake,
> That spight of *me*, themselves they'le guilty make.
>
> (sig. B7r–v)

Consequently, the laws of censorship are identified as the property of the corrupt; for Wither, 'evil counsellors took advantage of the corruption of the times to silence the faithful for their own ends'. And Wither, notably, was not alone in being disturbed by Howard's personal use of

charges of *scandalum magnatum,* which extended the royal prerogative
and appropriated for the earl 'the rhetoric of the divine right of kings'.[34]

In the face of such oppression, Wither's appeal to the king's justice
characteristically bristles with self-assurance:

> How is it like that I my peace can win me,
> When all the ayde I have, comes from within me?
> Therefore (*good King*) that mak'st thy bounty shine
> Sometime on those whose worths are small as mine;
> Oh save me now from Envies *dangerous shelfe,*
> Or make me able, and I'le save my selfe.
>
> (sig. E7r)

The final line, which overwrites the professions of submission with an
insistent suggestion of individual agency, epitomizes the political satirist's
quandary, and realizes the manifold political tensions that Wither otherwise tries so hard to hold at bay. On the one hand, it becomes increasingly
difficult for the poet in his political criticism to isolate the monarch as a
single source of reliable authority. On the other hand, the logic of satire
establishes the poet less as a subject than as a moral equal in the sight of
God; as Wither says, 'My *body's* subject unto many Powers, / But my *soule's*
free, as is the *Emperours*' (sig. D4v). These tensions are evident equally in
the form of satire that Wither chooses. As much as he is committed to a
public mode, authorized by the king and disseminated in print, the text
veers nonetheless into an illicit discourse of personal politics and libelling,
as it pointedly revives the image of 'a *Man-like Monster*' that had caused
offence in *Abuses Stript, and Whipt* (sig. B5r).[35] He suggests, in fact, that
only a self-protective 'reason' has to date prevented him from telling '*Truth*
enough to have undone me' (sig. B4v). At a time when Howard was widely
reviled in libels, Wither in fact experiences his own chosen mode as a
form of constraint, which might well appear inadequate for the task he
accepts.

Wither's *Satyre* highlights a nexus of contemporary anxieties surrounding the expression of dissent. Such concerns were only compounded in the
following months and years, as the scandal surrounding the marriage of
Frances Howard to Robert Carr seemed to many observers to materialize
in England familiar Tacitean representations of the court. As libels proliferated, other writers sought to fuse libellous discourse with more public
voices. In particular, Thomas Middleton almost certainly alludes to the

[34] O'Callaghan, '"Now thou may'st speak freely"', p. 70.
[35] Cf. O'Callaghan, *The 'shepheards nation'*, pp. 176–7.

notorious scandal in his play *The Witch* (c.1615–16), Mary Wroth includes
a veiled narrative of it in *The Countess of Montgomeries Urania* (1621), while
William Goddard turned to a continental printer in order to avoid the
censors when he published 'A Morall Satire intituled the Owles arayngne-
ment', a topical poem in the allegorical tradition of Spenser and Drayton.[36]
Moreover, the perception of an unbridgeable gulf between the reigns of
Elizabeth and James appears to have taken hold in these years, underscored
by a spate of Elizabethan texts republished around 1617–18.[37] Early in the
following decade, a popular series of libels was framed as a petitionary exchange between a deified Elizabeth and her former subjects, 'her now most
wretched and Most Contemptible Commons of England'.[38] The strategy
of appealing to the example of Elizabeth, which had been employed by the
Spenserians earlier in the century to urge James towards reform, was thus
translated into a neat satiric binary. James was simply condemned by the
comparison.

In these years, then, poets contributed to a renegotiation of prevailing notions of political subjectivity. At a time when parliamentarians were
struggling to define the limits of allowable political speech, and were increasingly prepared to question the doctrine that their institution should
operate merely within structures of counsel, poets similarly forged new
discourses of dissent. Interestingly, one of the few noteworthy alterations
Wither made to his *Satyre* for a new edition in 1622 was to delete an early
declaration that the author is 'a *subject* true', replacing the phrase with
an assurance that he is rather 'loyall . . . and true'.[39] John Reynolds shifted
even more decisively, as documented in his two pamphlets of 1624: the
first of which (he claims) was offered in manuscript form as a New Year's
gift to James before being published with a dedication to 'Great Brittaynes
Hoape', Prince Charles; and the second of which decisively turns away
from the monarchy, dedicated rather to the 'illustrious and grave assembly' of parliament, 'and no other'.[40] As these examples demonstrate, in
the 1620s writers worked with new rigour to construct discursive strategies
that appropriated and subverted existing models of counsel. Within these

---

[36] Josephine A. Roberts, 'Lady Mary Wroth's *Urania*: A Response to Jacobean Censorship', in W. Speed
Hill, ed., *New Ways of Looking at Old Texts* (Binghamton, 1993), pp. 125–9. Goddard, *A Satyricall
Dialogue* (Dort, 1616?), sigs. F2r–F3v; cf. Thomas Scot, *Philomythie or Philomythologie* (1616). On
Goddard, see further Norbrook, *Poetry and Politics*, p. 196.

[37] Kevin Sharpe, *Politics and Ideas in Early Stuart England: Essays and Studies* (London and New York,
1989), p. 37.

[38] See 'Poems from a Seventeenth-Century Manuscript', 147–71.

[39] (1614), sig. A5v (my italics); cf. *Juvenilia* (1622), sig. A1r.

[40] *Votivae Angliae* (1624), t.p., *2r; *Vox Coeli* (1624), sig. A3r.

years, as I consider in the following section, the equivocations of Wither's *Satyre* gave way to more forthright representations of the inquisitive and politically informed citizen, newly freed to participate in the operation of the state.

TURBULENT HEADS AND FACTIOUS SPIRITS: UNAUTHORIZED SATIRE IN THE 1620S

The status of political satire at the outset of the 1620s was at once clarified and heightened by contemporary arguments over freedom of speech. The 1620 royal 'Proclamation against excesse of Lavish and Licentious Speech of matters of State', drafted by Bacon, established the parameters of this debate, with its equivocation over the borderline separating an allowable 'convenient freedome of speech' from overly 'bold Censure'.[41] In the Parliament of 1621 the House of Commons pressed the king on the issue, prompting him at one point to make an uneasy assurance that he had not intended to restrict parliamentary freedoms.[42] But beyond the parliament, James remained adamant about the dangers of 'excesse and presumption': the very qualities of textual and social and transgression, respectively, that underpinned Renaissance satire.[43] He concentrated on these threats in a poem written in response to libellers, at a moment when, according to the French ambassador, it was 'a strange thing the hatred in which this king is held, in free speaking, cartoons, [and] defamatory libels'.[44] The poem sets the powerful sight of kings, who can 'kill even by theire sharpe aspect', against the limited capacities of the people:

> Wherefore againe meere seeing people
> Strive not to see soe high A steeple
> Like to the ground whereon you goe
> Hig[h]e aspects will bring yow woe.

The representation of an act of 'meere seeing' underlines the folly of assuming a position beyond one's station, and justifies a reiteration of an earlier threat about the power of 'Hig[h]e aspects'. James's logical conclusion is

[41] James issued two proclamations under this title, in December 1620 and July 1621 (*Stuart Royal Proclamations. Volume One: Royal Proclamations of King James I, 1603–1625*, ed. James F. Larkin and Paul L. Hughes [Oxford, 1973], pp. 495–6, 519–21 [quotes at p. 495]).
[42] Thompson, *Debate on Freedom of Speech*, p. 15.
[43] *Stuart Royal Proclamations*, p. 496.
[44] Bodleian MS Add. D. 111, fol. 91r; quoted in Joseph A. Taylor, 'The Literary Presentation of James I and Charles I, With Special Reference to the Period c.1614–1630' (unpublished DPhil. dissertation, University of Oxford, 1985), p. 162.

a reminder of the laws of censorship, as he exhorts libellers to 'hold your
pratling spare your penn / Bee honest and obedient men'.[45]

But such directives were hardly likely to quell an insurgent subject such as
Wither, and indeed it is arguable that James's attempts to control legitimate
speech may actually have contributed to a proliferation of unauthorized
texts. Whereas Wither in 1614 still clung to a hope that political satire
might be accorded a legitimate place in the state, in the early years of the
1620s James effectively defined such efforts of commentary and counsel
as illicit.[46] Furthermore, his rhetoric appears to have been paralleled by a
newly rigorous imposition of licensing laws at this time. As a consequence,
political libels and pamphlets increasingly abandon any residual interest in
monarchical authorization, as they fashion freshly transgressive strategies
of expression and publication.[47] The relative lack of published satiric verse
at this time, therefore, should not be taken as evidence that satire was in any
way dormant.[48] On the contrary, these were years in which, according to the
anonymous author of *The Life of a Satyrical Puppy, Called Nim*, satire held a
unique potential for anatomizing a turbulent state.[49] When he describes his
fellow satirists, this pamphleteer gives priority to the political intent of their
respective works. The 'ambitious Pen' of one, he writes, '*soar'd* to reach the
actions of great States-Men'; another is notable for his 'factious Spirit'; while
a third (possibly Thomas Scott) lives in Holland, from whence he sends
'little *Pamphlets*: which are *new-years-guifts*, for all those turbulent Heads,
who pry into the old yeares actions in hope of alteration' (pp. 61, 67).[50] This

---

[45] *The Poems of King James VI of Scotland*, ed. James Craigie (2 vols., Scottish Text Society, Edinburgh
and London, 1955–8), II.184, 186, 190.

[46] Clegg, *Press Censorship in Jacobean England*, pp. 58–9.

[47] Notably, Clegg identifies a boom in the continental publishing of illicit English texts at this time
(*Press Censorship in Jacobean England*, pp. 183–4).

[48] Most formal studies of satire in this period are restricted to verse: hence Raman Selden's *English
Verse Satire 1590–1765* (London, 1978) leaps from Elizabethan to Commonwealth and Restoration
texts; Doris C. Powers's *English Formal Satire: Elizabethan to Augustan* (The Hague, 1971) is more
exhaustive, and considers Jacobean poems by writers such as Richard Corbett, George Wither and
George Chapman. John Peter's *Complaint and Satire in Early English Literature* (Oxford, 1956)
provides a model for a history of the genre not restricted by formal concerns; however, he does
not look much beyond 1600. Within this context, Leonie J. Gibson is notable for her argument
that 'Formal satire, even when it concerns topical issues, is ratiocinative, and to a certain degree,
reflective. In the 1620s, when political feeling among all sections of the people ran high, the natural
means of expressing these feelings would not be the formal satire, but the pamphlet, the ballad and
the play' ('Formal Satire in the First Half of the Seventeenth Century, 1600–1650' [unpublished
DPhil. dissertation, University of Oxford, 1952], p. 275).

[49] T. M. (1657), p. 49; on the authorship and dating of this text, see above, p. 30n.

[50] Gibson suggests that the first two men to whom T. M. refers may be William Goddard and George
Wither; however, she does not attempt to identify the pamphleteer based in Holland ('Formal Satire
in the First Half of the Seventeenth Century', pp. 300–2).

text thus assumes that satire in the 1620s was most prominent in libellous poetry and prose pamphlets, rather than in printed verse. Satire has in fact always been adept at assuming evasive and fugitive forms under conditions of political repression, and may be especially pertinent on occasions when it fails to announce itself.[51] The most effective political satire in a decade such as the 1620s, then, may assume forms very different to that of Wither's *Satyre*.

The direct address to James adopted by Wither in *A Satyre* gives way in such works to more provocative and ironic representations of the monarch and his relation to the people. For instance, at the end of *Vox Dei*, one of several semi-factual pamphlets of protestant activism published early in the 1620s by Scott, the king is shown summoning a parliament, in which:

he unmasketh all the mysteryes, hid before in the cloudes of concealement, dealing faithfully with his people, as a Prince that had found, and expected, to finde faith in them againe towards him, and his. He restores unto them their wonted lawfull libertyes, and freedome of speech; knowing that *where there is not liberty, there can be no fidelity*, and *where there is freedome of the tongue, there can be no danger of the heart, or hand*.[52]

Written in the heady aftermath of the failed Spanish Match negotiations, the passage functions partly as news, partly as wish-fulfilment, and partly as satire directed against a king who was widely believed to care little for his subjects' 'lawfull libertyes'. Crucially, Scott seizes upon two of the definitive debates which shaped the successive parliaments of the 1620s, as he yokes together the aspirations for 'lawfull libertyes' and 'freedome of speech'. Yet it is equally significant that this vision of reform should be framed in a discourse that is generically evasive, resisting the respective conventions of news and fiction. Like Scott's entire publishing career, the pamphlet thus highlights the significance of texts which either flouted or artfully evaded the strictures of early Stuart censorship, helping in the process to construct new concepts of discursive truth and individual freedom.

The political discourse of this decade is perhaps most notably informed by satiric traditions in its distinctive attention to the revelation of hidden

---

[51] See especially Brian A. Connery and Kirk Combe, 'Theorizing Satire: A Retrospective and Introduction', in Connery and Combe, eds., *Theorizing Satire: Essays in Literary Criticism* (Basingstoke and London, 1995), p. 5.

[52] (Holland, 1623?), pp. 70–1. (Like a number of Scott's other early pamphlets, this text was republished, in identical form and with identical pagination, in his *Works* [Utrecht, 1624]; facsimile edn [Amsterdam, 1973]). On the work of Scott, see especially Peter Lake, 'Constitutional Consensus and Puritan Opposition in the 1620s: Thomas Scott and the Spanish Match', *Historical Journal*, 25 (1982), 805–25; and Markku Peltonen, *Classical Humanism and Republicanism in English Political Thought 1570–1640* (Cambridge, 1995), pp. 229–70.

truths and exposure of hypocrisy. The Elizabethan satirist John Marston was entirely in accord with his age when he wrote confidently about his mode's capacity to 'unmaske the worlds detested sinnes'.[53] Yet satire was also always in excess of mere factual revelation, shaped further by wit and ridicule. Horace, who consistently stressed the importance of humour and 'play' (*ludo*) in his own work, thus defined the role of satire as being 'to tell the truth, laughing'.[54] Turning to the late Jacobean years, the plethora of anti-Catholic pamphlets published around 1624 relentlessly employ the trope of revelation, yet equally embrace satiric arts of ridicule.[55] John Gee, for example, while writing with the bold aim of 'unmasking the vailed fraud of the Jesuits & Priests', self-consciously adopts for the task a 'light and Ironicall' style. 'I jest but at their jesting,' he writes, 'that have made a jest of God, and of his blessed Saints in heaven, by casting upon their most pure and glorious faces, the cloud, nay, the dirt and dung of ugly, unsavory, ridiculous Fables.'[56] Similarly, Scott regularly draws his reader's attention to the curious mix of fact and fiction, folly and wisdom in his texts. In one, he defends his willingness '*to play the foole* (as wise men say) *in print*'; another is teasingly framed as a description of secret passages of state in Spain which has fallen into the hands of 'T. S.', and whether it is 'really acted, or poetically faigned I knowe not'.[57] Within the context of this fictionalizing trope he proclaims, with a self-conscious theatricality, that 'heerein you shall perceive the Curtaine (though not fully) drawne, from before the *Spaniard*' (sig. A2r).

While these strategies distance satire from the expectations of news, they equally create the potential for writers to lay claim to a more subtle category of truth, which may not be visible to a mere newsmonger. Scott posits such a distinction at the beginning of *Sir Walter Rawleighs Ghost*:

Although the liberty of these times (wherein your *Currants, Gazettas, Pasquils*, and the like, swarme too too abundantly) hath made all Newes (how serious or substantiall soever) lyable to the jealous imputation of falshood, yet this relation I assure you (although in some circumstances it may leane too neare the florish of invention, yet for the pith or marrowe thereof, it is as justly allyed and knit to truth, as the light is to the day, or night to darknesse.[58]

[53] *Poems*, ed. Arnold Davenport (Liverpool, 1961), p. 76.
[54] Quoted in Gilbert Highet, *The Anatomy of Satire* (Princeton, 1962), p. 234; see further Griffin, *Satire*, p. 85.
[55] On these pamphlets, see Cogswell, *Blessed Revolution*, p. 281.
[56] *The Foot out of the Snare* (1624), sig. Aa2r.
[57] *Vox Dei*, sig. π 4v; *The Second Part of Vox Populi* (1624), sig. A1v.
[58] (London?, 1626), sig. A2r.

The statement sets Scott's pamphlet against the dubious and ephemeral truths of news, as he claims that the more profound truth resides paradoxically in the text which leans towards 'the florish of invention'. In the process, he gestures towards some significant implications of the satiric goal of discrimination. Unlike a writer who merely relates facts, the satirist self-consciously exploits the shadowy realm between fact and fiction, simultaneously defining and stigmatizing. In Chapter 2 I explored the potency of such satiric practices in the context of individual reputations and identities; here I want to suggest their potential impact within a political structure that was ostensibly based on consensus ideology but was in fact fraught with tensions, as contemporaries were constructing new notions of political subjectivity.

More specifically, unlike a courtier or member of parliament, the anonymous critic of state could exploit his or her freedom from political alliances. For example, the speaker in the pamphlet *Tom Tell Troath or A free discourse touching the manners of the tyme* presents himself to the king as 'a poore unknowne subject, who never had the happiness to come neare your Majestye' (p. 1).[59] He figures himself sardonically as no more than a spokesman for the common people, who actually speaks in accordance with the Jacobean censorship regime:

I perswade my selfe I am not altogether without warrant for what I doe: for it was my duty not long since to take notice of two Proclamations, come out in your Majesties name, against immoderate talkings; Wherein, it is your gracious pleasure to make all your loving subjects of what condition soever instruments of state, by giving them, *not a bare voluntary power, but a subpoena charge and commission*, to informe against all those that shall at any time hereafter offend in that kinde. Now your Majestie shall know that I am one of the greatest company keepers in this towne, and therefore cannot but be guilty of hearing many thinges that I am bound to reveal in obedience to the royall command. (p. 1)

For all the wit of his equivocating sidesteps around the government's decrees, the speaker makes a significant claim to a position of subversive authority. Rhetorical commentaries commonly cited Diogenes as an exemplum of *parrhesia*, since he 'regarded harsh admonition as the obligation of the truth-telling philosopher speaking from the margins' of authority and patronage relations.[60] In early seventeenth-century pamphlet satire,

---

[59] The date of this text is uncertain. Although it refers to events in 1626, and the *STC* dates it 1630?, its opening references to 'proclamations' on speech strongly suggest an author engaging with Jacobean proclamations.

[60] Colclough, '*Parrhesia*', 182.

Diogenes assumed a similar status, in a manner that merged classical narratives with popular English traditions. Although more conservative commentators tried to align the Greek cynic with the 'faithfull and frequent guests of Duke HUMPHRAY', speculating idly on matters of state in the aisles of St Paul's, others proclaimed him a man of true virtue and integrity, who scorned to be 'pollitick wise' like the courtier.[61] A text such as *Tom Tell Troath* derives much of its authority from such discursive models. Significantly, certain theories of parliamentary authority figured members of the House of Commons as 'the general inquisitors of the realm'; for 'Tom Tell Troath', however, their inquisition was insufficiently incisive.[62] At a time, then, when many people were becoming sceptical about the capacity for courtiers or parliamentarians to speak openly and honestly within circles of power, the voice of an evasive outsider could gather a considerable force.

Within this context, even those who remained sensitive to the distinction between satire and libel were prompted to modify their authorial stances. Notably, Wither's relations with James in the early 1620s are far from straightforward, and the poet definitely benefited from royal patronage when he was granted a patent to have his *Hymnes and Songs of the Church* printed with all metrical psalm-books.[63] Yet he also continued his provocative development of a theory of godly citizenship, which would potentially authorize the poet to speak against a monarch.[64] In *Wither's Motto* (1622), written in part as a response to James's proclamations on speech, the author seeks to define his credo, at characteristic length. After the direct address to the king in *A Satyre*, this poem is published without a dedication, prefaced instead with an address 'To any body' (sig. A2r). As Michelle O'Callaghan has argued, Wither here becomes ever more concerned to reach beyond the king and his court, thereby transforming entirely traditional models of

---

[61] John Melton, *A Sixe-Folde Politician* (1609), pp. 8–9; Goddard, *A Satyricall Dialogue* (Dort, 1616?), sig. B3v. See further Samuel Rowlands, *Diogines Lanthorne* (1607), in *Complete Works* (3 vols., Hunterian Club, Glasgow, 1880), vol. I; Rowlands, *The Letting of Humours Blood in the Head-Vaine. With a new Morisco, daunced by seaven Satyres, upon the bottome of Diogines Tubbe* (1600), in *Complete Works*, vol. I; Anthony Stafford, *Staffords Heavenly Dogge* (1615); and Peltonen's comments in *Classical Humanism and Republicanism*, p. 131.

[62] Edward Coke; quoted in David Harris Sacks, 'Parliament, Liberty, and the Commonweal', in J. H. Hexter, ed., *Parliament and Liberty from the Reign of Elizabeth to the English Civil War* (Stanford, 1992), p. 92.

[63] Norbrook, *Poetry and Politics*, p. 216; Joseph Loewenstein, 'Wither and Professional Work', in Arthur F. Marotti and Michael D. Bristol, eds., *Print, Manuscript, and Performance: The Changing Relations of the Media in Early Modern England* (Columbus, 2000), pp. 103–23; Clegg, *Press Censorship in Jacobean England*, pp. 45–50. On Wither's imprisonment for his *Motto*, see Clegg, *Press Censorship in Jacobean England*, p. 62.

[64] Cf. O'Callaghan, *The 'shepheards nation'*, p. 157.

counsel.[65] Consequently, he explicitly contrasts the arts of 'The Parasite, and smooth tongu'd Flatterer' to his own 'bold truth-speaking *Lines*' (sig. c8v). His own poetic is grounded upon 'Raptures, which are free, and nobly borne': a definition which conflates a radical protestant concept of inspiration with a notion of freedom that deftly inverts social hierarchies (sig. B2r). Having established this position, his satire assumes a fresh stridency, especially when he turns to the relationships between kings and their favourites. Princes, he argues,

> By those they love, have greatly wronged been.
> Their too much trust, doth often danger breed,
> And Serpents in their Royall bosoms feed.
> . . .
> And (which is yet a greater wickednesse)
> When these the loyall Subjects doe oppresse,
> And grind the faces of the poore, alive;
> They'le doe it, by the Kings Prerogative.
>
> (sig. D5r)

Despite the apparent concentration on the conventional target of evil counsellors, the lines contain the seed of a more comprehensive, systemic critique. Notably, the closing line, while explicitly targeting corrupt courtiers who cloak themselves in royal authority, never quite erases the possibility that the 'Prerogative' itself is faulty. The poem thus allows a reading which sets the interests of the oppressed 'poore' against king and courtiers alike, and implies that the king's 'loyall Subjects' may have limited patience in the face of such conditions.

Interestingly, after the publication of *Wither's Motto* the poet's rivals scrutinized his professions of loyalty to the Jacobean regime, and highlighted the tensions at the heart of his project. The author of *An Answer to Withers Motto*, T. G. (probably Thomas Gainsford) thus renders Wither's claims to freedom and honesty as 'diffused cunning', and challenges him to be more direct:

> Therefore when that
> At such a point your shaft is aimed at,
> Either desist from shooting wide at all,
> Or hit the man, that you so sinfull call.
> For he that dare say this, sure doth not feare
> Though of *Magnatum scandulum* he heare.[66]

---

[65] *The 'shepheards nation'*, p. 162.
[66] T. G., *An Answer to Withers Motto* (Oxford, 1625), sigs. C3v–C4.

T. G. figures Wither as a mere libeller, evading the Star Chamber through brash claims and sly innuendo. Similarly, Ben Jonson's coded representation of Wither as 'Chronomastix' in his 1623 masque *Time Vindicated to Himselfe and to His Honors*, focuses on the definition of discursive liberty.[67] When the debased figures of Eyes, Ears and Nose foresee the dawning of Time's 'Saturnalia' – a world in which 'freedom' involves having 'the giddy world turned the heels upward' – they are duly lectured by Fame:

> A comely license! They that censure those
> They ought to reverence, meet they that old curse,
> To beg their bread and feel eternal winter.
> There's difference 'twixt liberty and license.
>
> (lines 28, 182–3, 177–80)

Suitably, the consequence of licence is poverty. By comparison, those who recognize the boundaries of liberty, and accept the hierarchies of 'reverence', may pass from the antimasque into the masque, and from the world of the popular press to the milieu of an idealized court.

While Wither continued to negotiate positions for himself in the hinterland between liberty and licence – which would produce, in response to the turmoil of the latter 1620s, a sprawling epic of political anxiety, *Britains Remembrancer* (1628) – other writers openly embraced a timely fusion of libel and satire. John Russell, for example, presents a highly personalized assault on George Villiers, Duke of Buckingham, in a text introduced under the authority of a modified Juvenalian epigraph: 'Possibile est Satyras non scribere?' For Russell, poetry is necessary for the expression of dissent:

> Must I turne mad, like *Solon* and write rimes,
> When *Philippicks* would better fit the times?
> Yes, Yes, I must. For what soe're they be
> In presse, or pulpit, dare of speech be free
> In truth's behalfe; and vent their grieved minde
> In phrase more serious, or some graver kinde,
> (Though, at the common good, they onely ayme,
> And be as strictly Carefull to shun blame
> As wisdome can devise): they cannot scape
> The malice of the age.

Russell suggests that, in comparison with prose invective delivered from the press or pulpit, the arts of the satiric poet, shaded with rhetorical excess,

---

[67] Jonson, *The Complete Masques*, ed. Stephen Orgel (New Haven, CT and London, 1969), pp. 390–408.

offer the author a chance of escaping 'The malice of the age'. Though he perhaps stretches his readers' credulity in doing so, he thus proclaims a loyal 'hope' that his 'rimes . . . shall not be censur'd'.[68]

Such representations of poetic authority were commonly based on appeals to the conscience. In Chapter 2 I considered the potency of libellous representations of the conscience, which was understood in puritan theology as a 'book' within each Christian, 'that shall be opened at the last day, & to which men shall bee put to, and by which they shall be judged'.[69] Although the pre-Reformation doctrine, which assumed that conscience and casuistry were founded on an objective basis, retained a stronghold over much of the English population, the emergent teachings asserted a divergent and unstable individualistic logic.[70] Fused with a commitment to free speech, appeals to the conscience might thereby underpin manifold expressions of dissent, in numerous relationships of power.[71] Indeed, as Linda Levy Peck has perceptively demonstrated, discourses of law, politics and religion converged around the notion of conscience:

Both Luther and Calvin had emphasized the separation of the individual and office in their attack on the proprietary church, a separation similar to the legal language of [Sir Edward] Coke who stressed that the official should not be influenced by private concerns either of blood or money, family or friends. Conscience was important to both. The separate scripts overlapped, providing a language in which both the secular and the divine resonated.[72]

As a consequence of this intertwining of discourses, numerous writers figured the court as an environment which by nature corrupts the conscience. According to the Stoic wisdom of Thomas Gainsford, 'positions of state break through the wall of our consciences'.[73] In particular, flattery

[68] I[ohn] R[ussell?], *The Spy* (Strasburg, 1628), sig. A1r.

[69] See above, pp. 65–8; Jeremiah Dyke, *Good Conscience: Or A Treatise Shewing the Nature, Meanes, Benefit, and Necessity Thereof* (1624), sig. B2v.

[70] Keith Thomas ably demonstrates the continuing dominance of objective notions of conscience, but arguably fails to pursue the contradictory potential of the new theories ('Cases of Conscience in Seventeenth-Century England', in John Morrill, Paul Slack and Daniel Woolf eds., *Public Duty and Private Conscience in Seventeenth-Century England: Essays Presented to G. E. Aylmer* [Oxford, 1993], pp. 29–56).

[71] Interestingly, Clegg documents the 1621 censorship of William Whately's popular marriage manual, *A bride-bush* (1617), and traces the state's concern about his use of a discourse of conscience to justify arguments for divorce. In the early 1620s, she suggests, such arguments were too sensitive to be allowed (*Press Censorship in Jacobean England*, pp. 190–6).

[72] *Court Patronage and Corruption in Early Stuart England* (London, 1993), p. 168.

[73] *Observations of State and Military Affairs, for the most part collected out of Cornelius Tacitus* (1612), p. 16: quoted in J. H. M. Salmon, 'Stoicism and the Roman Example: Seneca and Tacitus in Jacobean England', *Journal of the History of Ideas*, 50 (1989), 218.

was believed to mitigate against the activity of the conscience, distorting the pure expression which should emanate from the redeemed Christian.

The language of conscience shaped expressions of dissent in parliament and pamphlets alike. In the Commons, although a discourse of common law had traditionally belittled the claims of conscience, a succession of early Stuart speakers reassessed the significance of this internalized site.[74] In the free speech debates of 1621, Sir Edwin Sandys figured the parliamentarian's conscience as the only true authority; later in the decade, in consideration of the forced loan, Sir John Eliot insisted that 'it is no factious humour nor disaffection', but only his 'conscience', that set him in opposition to the Crown.[75] Such claims were echoed, with greater satiric edge, in the period's unauthorized texts. For Wither, his truly 'free' poetry emanates from 'the quiet of my conscience'; indeed his sole professed goal in *Wither's Motto* is 'to draw the true Picture of mine own heart'.[76] Similarly, 'Tom Tell Troath' claims to speak out of a 'good conscience', and contrasts this to the man who rather 'seekes reward' (p. 19), while a 1622 attack on the figure of a religious 'formalist' represents him as a man who, in his hunt for 'honour, wealth, or fame', 'Makes all religion and all conscience void'.[77] In Russell's vision, the threats to England are resonantly centred on this site of protestant subjectivity; the Jesuits, he claims, aim 'not only to enthrall / Mens consciences, but liberty and all' (sig. B2v). Within such texts, then, it is only the independent critic of state who can truly claim to be free of the constraints of flattery: speaking from 'the Puritye of my heart & Conscience'.[78]

Moreover, since the theology of conscience potentially authorized the views of people from all social levels, voices of outsiders might in fact appear more authoritative the more closely they are identified with the great mass of the English people. This is how Scott commonly situates himself in print. Markku Peltonen argues convincingly that Scott developed throughout his career some cogent arguments in favour of an 'extended system of counsel'.[79] Yet his satiric manipulation of the language of counsel on occasion stretches its bounds in such a way that he in fact interrogates its very

---

74 Alan Cromartie, 'The Constitutionalist Revolution: The Transformation of Political Culture in Early Stuart England', *Past and Present*, 163 (1999), 83.

75 Thompson, *Debate on Freedom of Speech*, pp. 11–12; Eliot, quoted in Anna R. Beer, *Sir Walter Ralegh and his Readers in the Seventeenth Century* (London, 1997), p. 113.

76 *A Satyre*, sig. EE1v; *Wither's Motto*, sig. A2v.

77 [Alexander Leighton?], *The Interpreter. Wherein three principal Terms of State, much mistaken by the vulgar, are clearly understood* (1622); reprinted in *An English Garner: Stuart Tracts, 1603–1693*, ed. C. H. Firth (London, 1903), pp. 243, 239. I will discuss this text further at pp. 130–32, below.

78 BL Add MS 24201, fol. 3r; quoted in Taylor, 'The Literary Presentation of James I and Charles I', p. 251.

79 On Scott's commitment to counsel, see Peltonen, *Classical Humanism and Republicanism*, pp. 267–9.

premises of subjecthood and obedience, valorizing instead an independent 'voice of the people' (as signalled in the title of his influential pamphlet *Vox Populi*).[80] Further, many critics of the government, especially the authors of anonymous and manuscript texts, appear to have self-consciously fashioned for themselves socially coded identities. The use of a figure such as 'Tom Tell Troath' for instance, pointedly situates unfettered political judgement among the commoners; Tom speaks not only as 'a poore unknown subject' (p. 1), but also as a persona with a history in pamphlet satire. In John Lane's *Tom Tel-Troths Message, and His Pens Complaint* (1600), for example, the speaker admits at the outset that 'the plot of my Pamphlet is rude, though true, the matter meane, the manner meaner'.[81] In fact this was an established satiric convention, and one that was invoked with increasing regularity in the decades after the 1590s, as the initial elitism of neoclassical satire gave way to a new populism. By the 1620s, it was entirely appropriate for political satire.

Such textual strategies illuminate the ways – complex, hesitant, yet insistent – in which radical new notions of citizenship were forged in this period. Involved in some of the defining early Stuart political debates, writers such as Scott and Wither were critically reassessing constructions of political subjectivity. Their work was informed by a makeshift amalgam of theological and classical sources, but also sharpened by satiric strategies of provocation and sceptical interrogation. Indeed it might well be argued that the intervention into political discourse made by the anonymous and insistently popular figure of 'Tom Tell Troath' was at least as insightful as that of any contemporary parliamentarian. The discursive achievements of such texts therefore created a context within which radical political ideas could be formulated and entertained. As such, while they may not overtly expound republican or democratic ideas, they help to make radicalism thinkable. For, in the political conditions of early Stuart England, the teasing and the illogical statement could be at least as effective as the reasonable and logical.

IMAGINING A PUBLIC SPHERE

These various acts of discursive enfranchisement required the further imaginative construction of contexts within which free debate might take place.

---

[80] *Vox Populi: or newes from Spaine* (London?, 1620).
[81] Lane, P. S. The figure returned with new force in the 1640s, when the earlier *Tom Tell Troth* was republished (1642), along with tracts such as *Tom Tel Troths come to towne againe* (1643).

Indeed, as a number of recent studies have argued, England was developing in these years what would later become recognizable, in the terms of Jürgen Habermas, as a public sphere. For Habermas, the public sphere is a socially inclusive space in which ideas may be freely exchanged, in a manner governed by reason. He identifies its emergence in the coffee-houses of late seventeenth-century London; however, other scholars have argued that his model overlooks the significance earlier in the century of news networks, print culture and tavern societies.[82] But it is undeniable that any effort to construct a public sphere was at this time heavily constrained by the state, which maintained a regime – however unreliable and unpredictable it may have been – of surveillance and censorship. Within this context, I suggest that it is again worth attending to the period's unauthorized texts, in which the subtle and speculative resources of satire provide ways for writers to think themselves beyond these constraints. Their efforts repeatedly reveal a sophisticated awareness at once of the pressures and the possibilities.

The critical initial steps in this process may be identified in the era of Wither's *Satyre*, a moment when certain poets and parliamentarians were united in a desire for a space within which free debate might take place. The 1614 imprisonment of parliamentarians and poets alike provided ample evidence for some commentators that parliament could be relied upon as neither representative nor free. The Spenserian poets, like many of the outspoken parliamentarians, were steeped in an Inns of Court tradition of free speech, and were creating an associated tavern culture characterized by discursive license. The circulation of texts, meanwhile, offered a mechanism for the expansion of such a culture. For example, a poem principally written by John Hoskyns within a context of tavern sociability, 'The Parliament Fart', a witty though relatively benign commentary on members of the House of Commons, achieved an extraordinary manuscript circulation after its composition around 1610.[83] Moreover, as we have already seen, the Spenserians, including Hoskyns's fellow parliamentarian Brooke, seized on the capacity of print to pursue an even broader conversation. Not surprisingly, the spectre of unrestrained political discussion spreading across the

---

82 Habermas, *The Structural Transformation of the Public Sphere: An Inquiry into a Category of Bourgeois Society*, trans. Thomas Burger (Cambridge, MA, 1991). See also Love, *Culture and Commerce of Texts*, pp. 203–7; O'Callaghan, *The 'shepheards nation'*, pp. 5–8; O'Callaghan, '"Now thou may'st speak freely"'; Peter Lake and Steven Pincus, eds., *The Public Sphere in Early Modern England* (Manchester, forthcoming); and David Zaret, *Origins of Democratic Culture: Printing, Petitions, and the Public Sphere in Early Modern England* (Princeton, 2000).

83 On Hoskyns and 'The Parliament Fart', see Baird W. Whitlock, *John Hoskyns, Serjeant-at-Law* (Washington, DC, 1982), esp. ch. 10.

country was an acute source of anxiety for King James. His spokesman in the 1621 Parliament maintained that the proclamation on licentious speech applied particularly 'to discussions of state matters in alehouses': sites which typically drew together those of lowly degree.[84]

In the following decade, licensed and unlicensed print was increasingly exploited as a mechanism for taking unauthorized political comment to the alehouses. The government had feared the potential of print ever since the time of the Marprelate tracts in the late 1580s, when clandestine presses had facilitated the spread of notoriously transgressive clerical satire. Jonson plays upon this anxiety for his stigmatization of Wither in *Time Vindicated*, figuring the outspoken poet's printer as a 'ragged rascal', who

> keeps
> His press in a hollow tree where to conceal him;
> He works by glowworm light, the moon's too open.
>
> (lines 133, 135–7)

The satiric vignette was calculated to vex Wither, who in fact resisted forms of publication that would have undermined his public persona; other writers, however, accepted unauthorized printing as a logical consequence of censorship. As studies of Jacobean censorship have demonstrated, it was often possible for writers to evade or manipulate the mechanisms of censorship, or else to exploit other methods of dissemination. Notably, there is strong evidence that some works, such as Scott's pamphlets, were reproduced in manuscript form by commercial scribes.[85] Other texts (also including many of Scott's) were printed on the continent and smuggled back into England.[86] The subsequent dissemination was fraught with risk, and many such texts probably circulated only within relatively small circles of readers. Nonetheless, the mere possibilities of scribal publication and continental printing informed and reshaped conceptions of political discourse, creating a new cultural space for the self-consciously transgressive voice.[87]

Numerous texts accentuate an antagonistic relationship between author and authority, drawing attention through the resources of print to

[84] Thompson, *Debate on Freedom of Speech*, p. 9.

[85] On Scott's *Vox Populi*, see H. R. Woudhuysen, *Sir Philip Sidney and the Circulation of Manuscripts* (Oxford, 1996), p. 52. Copies of *The Interpreter* (1622), probably written by Alexander Leighton, were also prominent in manuscript miscellanies (see, for example: Bodleian MS Eng. poet. c.50, fols. 16v–20v; BL Harley MS 6383, fols. 50v–59v; Beinecke, Osborn b.197, pp. 192–201; Huntington MS HM 198, pp. 180–4).

[86] Clegg, *Press Censorship in Jacobean England* (on continental printing, pp. 183–4).

[87] Stephen Foster, *Notes from the Caroline Underground: Alexander Leighton, the Puritan Triumvirate, and the Laudian Reaction to Nonconformity* (Hamden, CT, 1978), pp. 59–60.

an uncontainable sphere of political discourse. By contrast with the government's efforts to police particular sites, such as alehouses or St Paul's, many pamphlets suggest instead an interaction that is both anonymous and placeless, connected purely by myriad national networks of exchange. 'Tom Tell Troath', as we have seen, alludes vaguely to his extensive 'company keep[ing]' in London, which he merely translates into print. Scott's pamphlets, by comparison, repeatedly foreground their very lack of any identifiable physical context. Both parts of *Vox Populi* are presented as Spanish news tracts that had fallen into his hands; *Newes from Parnassus. The Political Touchstone* (Holland, 1622) is prefaced by a possibly spurious letter to an unnamed 'lord', in which the equally anonymous author expresses a wish that the text should be kept 'from the Presse, as from the fire' (sig. A2r–v); and *Robert Earle of Essex His Ghost* (1624) employs the satiric convention of a judgement on contemporary times issued from a former hero now in heaven. Printing conventions could equally be manipulated to underline a text's unauthorized satiric intent. For instance, Scott's *Newes from Parnassus* is declared on the title-page to have been 'Printed at Helicon', while *Robert Earle of Essex His Ghost* was 'Printed in Paradise'. More topically, the imprint on Alexander Leighton's *An Appeal to the Parliament, Or Sions Plea Against the Prelacie* declares that the work was printed 'in the year and month wherein Rochelle was lost'. This was, however, 'a deliberate misdating', designed 'to remind readers of the precarious state of the Protestant cause', and thereby galvanize opinion against the foreign policy of Buckingham and Charles.[88]

Print also has the potential to transform an authorized document of counsel into an unauthorized expression of dissent. Hence the works of writers who perceived themselves as operating within courtly coteries, and perhaps even vying for the ear of the monarch, might be refigured for a wider audience. As Anna Beer has shown, Raleigh's *Dialogue betweene a Counsellor of State and a Justice of peace*, a text conceived as 'manuscript advice to the King', created a significantly different impact when printed in 1628, 'using first the false imprint of "Hamburg" and then "Middelburg"'. In its printed form the text was retitled *The Prerogative of Parliaments*, a change which packaged an arguably moderate text as 'a case study of the powers of parliament'. In fact, according to the title-page, 'the prerogative of Parliament is actually "proued" by the text'.[89] Similarly, when Sir Robert Cotton was examined after the publication in 1627 of *A Short*

---

[88] (Amsterdam, 1628); Foster, *Notes from the Caroline Underground*, p. 25.
[89] Beer, *Sir Walter Ralegh and his Readers*, pp. 2, 115.

View of the Long Life and Raigne of Henry the Third, he claimed that he had written it as a private work of advice for James fifteen years earlier, and it had now been published without his consent. Although the veracity of this defence remains a matter of conjecture, in the latter 1620s the text's narrative of a king who re-establishes his authority after being undermined by corrupt counsellors and 'Lawlesse Minions' was inevitably assimilated into the wealth of unauthorized discourse surrounding Buckingham (p. 18).[90] 'These vapours did ever and easily vanish', Cotton comments, in a characteristically sententious assessment that might look to either the past or the present, 'so long as the helme was guided by temperate spirrits, and the King tied his actions to the rule of good Councell, and not to young passionate or single advise' (p. 5). Within a culture shaped as much by libels as by 'good Councell', such statements would obviously accrue fresh, and quite possibly unintended, venom.

Yet it is crucial to appreciate that, as much as many people desired free and open discourse, they were equally aware of the ways in which their efforts were frustrated. Under such conditions, some of the most insightful visions of public politics depended less on Habermasian reason than on satiric strategies of indirection and provocation. For Scott, the only honest debate is that conducted beyond the grasp of authority, in 'flying Pamphlets', and 'Songs and Ballads Sung up and downe the Streetes'.[91] The brother-in-law of the puritan pamphleteer John Bastwick sought to situate such interaction in a physical space, and employed 'some pevish intelligencer in London' to acquire unauthorized texts, 'which he usually reades in the street evry markett daye att Colchester about whom the zealants thronge as people use where Ballads are sunge'.[92] Such actions, however, remained equally unusual and unadvisable. By comparison, the uneasy juxtaposition of ideals of free speech against the realities of constraint are epitomized in a libellous poem that represents a prison as a site of political exchange:

> Heere A perpetuall parliament doth sitt
> Which I doe not comend for speach or witt,
> Att this wee all are speakers, and each bringes
> Affaries of state to light. Closett of kings.[93]

[90] See D. R. Woolf, *The Idea of History in Early Stuart England: Erudition, Ideology, and 'The Light of Truth' from the Accession of James I to the Civil War* (Toronto, 1990), pp. 159–60; and Kevin Sharpe, *Sir Robert Cotton 1586–1631: History and Politics in Early Modern England* (Oxford, 1979).
[91] *Second Part of Vox Populi*, pp. 7, 5.
[92] SPD 16/276, 29 October 1634; quoted in Foster, *Notes from the Caroline Underground*, p. 47.
[93] 'In reading these my Lord youll see I've gott' (Bodleian MS Malone 23, pp. 59–60).

There may in fact be some truth in this image; Thomas Cogswell cites a letter from this period which describes the Fleet as a source of 'good intelligence of state occurrences'.[94] Yet the poem is more suggestive than a mere relation of fact, as it implicitly contrasts the 'perpetuall parliament' of the prisoners to the notoriously irregular parliaments called by the king, in a manner that simultaneously alludes to the various parliamentarians and poets who had been imprisoned for transgressing restrictions on political comment. Moreover, while contemporary members of parliament struggled under the weight of royal surveillance, the mock-parliament in prison truly searches into the 'Closett of kings'.[95] Paradoxically, it is only under the constraints of prison that an unconstrained political discussion becomes possible; and this discourse, as contemporary usages of the word 'Closett' might suggest, is capable not only of scrutinizing the monarch's inmost counsel, but also, perhaps, of anatomizing his own mind or conscience.[96]

This poem's representation of freedom realized in the very teeth of authority typifies the uncertain yet insistent emergence of new political ideals in early Stuart England. As I have been arguing, however, it also suggests that in order to appreciate the achievements of political writers in this period we should set aside Habermasian assumptions about social inclusion and principles of reason. In particular, as David Norbrook has argued, Habermas's 'highly rationalistic portrait of the bourgeoisie fails to acknowledge the strong religious motivations behind the emergence of the public sphere in England'.[97] Hence the conscience only becomes significant for Habermas when Thomas Hobbes identifies it with 'opinion', and thereby effects the separation of an individual's religious identity from the practices of politics.[98] By contrast, as I have tried to show, when considering the early Stuart decades the politicization of this religious site of identity is a process which helps to explain much wider political transformations. Moreover, Habermas's reification of a single and tangible sphere of free engagement effaces the achievements of earlier writers, who struggled to conceive of such spaces in the face of political repression. While they may not have created a public sphere precisely in Habermas's terms, their powers of argument

---

[94] 'Underground Political Verse and the Transformation of English Political Culture', in Susan D. Amussen and Mark A. Kishlansky, eds., *Political Culture and Cultural Politics in Early Modern England: Essays Presented to David Underdown* (Manchester, 1995), p. 285.

[95] Mark Kishlansky, 'The Emergence of Adversary Politics in the Long Parliament', *Journal of Modern History*, 49 (1977), 619.

[96] Cf. Richard Rambuss, *Closet Devotions* (Durham and London, 1998), pp. 103–35; in the 1620s, Wither is one writer who employed the metaphor of 'the closet of my minde' (*Wither's Motto*, sig. B4r).

[97] Norbrook, '*Areopagitica*, Censorship, and the Early Modern Public Sphere', p. 5.

[98] *Structural Transformation of the Public Sphere*, pp. 90–1.

and imagination helped to remould models of political engagement in England. Consequently, we might do well to modify Habermas's definition when considering this period. The early Stuart public sphere might then take shape as by necessity plural, contingent, ephemeral and tactical: a forum shaped as much by Scott's placeless pamphlets as by the intellectual discourses of the Inns of Court.[99]

Satire, as we have seen, assumed a particular significance within this context. Its interventions into political discourse tested the boundaries of free speech, and lent shape to emergent constructions of political subjectivity. The voice of an evasive and anonymous commoner informed only by the light of a redeemed conscience might thus accrue greater authority than that of a member of parliament or courtier, who were seen to be constricted by ties of faction and patronage. Moreover, satire's strategies of indirection and discrimination, as I consider further in the following chapter, facilitated fresh and enlightening attempts to delineate the shifting alignments and interactions of an unstable era. These qualities did not necessarily encode this literary mode as politically transgressive; indeed, as Chapter 5 demonstrates, satire was equally important to a developing royalist tradition, which required its own discourses of exclusion and stigmatization. Yet many commentators at the time agreed nonetheless that satire's characteristics of excess and presumption threatened authority, and that practices of detraction were more appropriate to democracies or 'popular states', in which 'the liberty of evil tongues hath been more tolerated then now it is'.[100] Therefore, while it is fair to say that only few of the satirists of early modern England wanted democracy, and perhaps only a minority would have understood what this might involve, they helped to imagine democratic conditions. Through their provocative and evasive writings, we might glimpse a model of politics in which citizens vigorously debate the government of their state.

---

[99] Cf. O'Callaghan, *The 'shepheards nation'*, pp. 5–6.
[100] [William Cavendish], *Horæ Subsecivæ: Observations and Discourses* (1620), pp. 56–7. The term 'popular estate' is used as a synonym for a democracy in the only contemporary English translation of Aristotle's *Politics* (*Politica*, trans. from French by I. D.? [1598], p. 191); however, in Raleigh's *Prerogative of Parliaments*, the term is rather equated with 'an *Aristocratia*' (p. 30).

CHAPTER 4

Discourses of discrimination: political satire in the 1620s

When Francis Osborne looked back on the political censorship of the early Stuart era, he commented: 'Nor did they scape who were any way Satyricall, a thing not to be avoided by the lovers of truth'.[1] Like many of the writers considered in the previous chapter, Osborne suggests that satire is inevitable, and even necessary, under a repressive regime. Under such conditions, quite simply, this literary mode becomes an invaluable vehicle of 'truth'. With Osborne's perception in mind, this chapter aims to examine some of the ways in which satire helped to define the unstable truths of early Stuart England. It argues that satire contributed to rapid and vital changes in English political discourse. In particular, English men and women at this time were reconceiving political alliances and identities, as well as concepts of conflict and contestation. Osborne was hardly alone in recognizing the value of unauthorized texts within such a context; John Selden, for instance, commented that 'More solid things do not shew the Complexion of the Times, so well as Ballads and Libells.'[2] Consequently, in order to appreciate these changes it is worth attending to the textual strategies employed in such material, as it struggles to delineate the complexion of its unsettled times.

Although many of the developments to be considered here may be traced through earlier decades, my analysis concentrates on the sustained outpouring of political writing in the 1620s. As seen in Chapter 3, this decade began with debates over freedom of speech, prompted particularly by James's 'Proclamation against excess of Lavish and Licentious Speech of matters of State', and pursued at once within parliament and in pamphlet literature. Over the following ten years, critical political faultlines emerged in the state. At court, the failed Spanish Match negotiations, the seemingly inexorable

---

[1] *Traditionall Memoryes on the Raigne of King James* (1658), p. 63.
[2] *Table Talk*, ed. S. H. Reynolds (Oxford, 1892), p. 105: quoted in Adam Fox, *Oral and Literate Culture in England 1500–1700* (Oxford, 2000), p. 299.

rise of George Villiers, Duke of Buckingham, the Caroline succession, ongoing problems with corruption and factional struggles, and equivocation
over England's contribution to the Thirty Years' War, all contributed to
conditions of heightened instability. A series of tense parliaments exacerbated these tensions, especially by demanding at once more involvement
in issues of international relations, and greater restrictions on the Crown's
arbitrary authority. As a result, this decade has also become significant for
historiographical reasons, since it has been the focus of debates instigated
by revisionist historians concerning the nature of political opposition before the 1640s. If the origins of oppositional politics can be traced from the
early Stuart decades, as a number of important post-revisionist studies have
argued, the 1620s seems without question to have been a pivotal decade.[3]
Here, I will suggest that while opposition movements in the 1620s may
not have been organized and coherent, a range of discursive strategies were
taking shape which enabled new appreciations and expressions of political
conflict.

The resultant practices of representation were informed by converg-
ing strands of political thought, derived in large part from classical and
continental sources. Consequently, while the texts to be considered in this
chapter amply demonstrate the capacity of English writers to forge new discourses for new circumstances, it is also important to acknowledge other
intellectual influences. In particular, the works of Tacitus coloured perceptions of the court, offering a sophisticated model of corruption and
tyranny. The influence of Machiavelli was even more traumatic for the
English, since his arguments threatened to undermine orthodox assumptions of consensual politics grounded on moral and religious foundations.
Arguably, he 'articulated existing tensions that the normative conventions
and discourse had kept in delicate control'; unquestionably, he offered critics of the early Stuart regime powerful new ideas of political contestation.[4]
Moreover, in a period before the first English translations of Machiavelli's
works were allowed, perceptions of Tacitus and Machiavelli appear loosely

[3] See esp. the arguments of Thomas Cogswell, in *The Blessed Revolution: English Politics and the Coming of War, 1621–1624* (Cambridge, 1989), and 'Politics and Propaganda: Charles I and the People in the 1620s', *Journal of British Studies*, 29 (1990), 187–215; Richard Cust, in *The Forced Loan and English Politics 1626–1628* (Oxford, 1987), and 'Politics and the Electorate in the 1620s', in Richard Cust and Ann Hughes, eds., *Conflict in Early Stuart England* (London, 1989), pp. 134–67; and Derek Hirst, in 'Revisionism Revised: The Place of Principle', *Past and Present*, 92 (1981), 79–99.
[4] Kevin Sharpe, *Politics and Ideas in Early Stuart England: Essays and Studies* (London and New York, 1989), p. 26. Sharpe demonstrates the impact of Machiavelli on the thinking of one early Stuart reader in *Reading Revolutions: The Politics of Reading in Early Modern England* (New Haven, CT and London, 2000).

to have merged, linked under the umbrella of 'reason of state' theory.[5] Though originally coined in an attack on Machiavelli, this term rapidly attained wider resonance; according to an anti-Tacitean text translated into English in 1626, 'Reason of State' had 'infected Europe like a contagious disease'.[6] In turn, these shifts in political theory also affected the writing of history, which itself was often undertaken as a form of counsel. 'Politic' historians in the early seventeenth century rejected providential explanations of causation.[7] In their works, it is 'not surprising to discover . . . that Machiavelli's view of the past as a guide to making tough decisions tends to drown out the older, Ciceronian tradition of history as a general source of wisdom and moral behaviour'.[8]

The development of Renaissance satire in England was intertwined with this pervasive interest in 'politic' forms of statecraft. Like Tacitus, the Roman satirists whose works were adopted as models by poets in the 1590s had been concerned with the representation of a corrupt and decadent age. Juvenal, in particular, was a direct contemporary of Tacitus, and his scathing satiric vision of his political milieu complements the more terse and sceptical prose of the historian. In the final years of Elizabeth's reign, these influences informed not only a rash of formal verse satires, but also John Hayward's Tacitean history-play, *Henry IIII* (1599), which marked a break from the more comfortably providential approaches to history in earlier plays.[9] Significantly, both the satires and the play incurred the wrath of the authorities, in the years of agitation that preceded the failed rising of Robert Devereux, Earl of Essex.[10] At the outset of James's reign, Ben Jonson's *Sejanus* brought political satire to the stage, and established a dramatic concern with Roman history that would continue throughout the early Stuart decades.[11] By 1640, at least fifty-seven such plays had been produced in England, for audiences trained to draw parallels between Roman circumstances and their own

---

[5] See P. Burke, 'Tacitism', in T. A. Dorey, ed., *Tacitus* (London, 1969), p. 165; and J. G. A. Pocock, *The Machiavellian Moment: Florentine Political Thought and the Atlantic Republican Tradition* (Princeton, 1975), pp. 351–2.

[6] Alan T. Bradford, 'Stuart Absolutism and the "Utility" of Tacitus', *Huntington Library Quarterly*, 46 (1983), 136. (Bradford is first quoting, then paraphrasing, *The New-found Politicke* (1626), a translation of Traiano Boccalini's *Ragguagli di Parnaso*.)

[7] Bradford, 'Stuart Absolutism and the "Utility" of Tacitus', 132.

[8] D. R. Woolf, *The Idea of History in Early Stuart England: Erudition, Ideology, and 'The Light of Truth' from the Accession of James I to the Civil War* (Toronto, 1990), p. 144.

[9] Malcolm Smuts, 'Court-Centred Politics and the Uses of Roman Historians, c.1590–1630', in Kevin Sharpe and Peter Lake, eds., *Culture and Politics in Early Stuart England* (London, 1994), p. 30.

[10] Cyndia Susan Clegg, *Press Censorship in Elizabethan England* (Cambridge, 1997), pp. 198–217; on Hayward's history, see Woolf, *The Idea of History*, pp. 107–15.

[11] On Jonson's Tacitism, see esp. Blair Worden, 'Ben Jonson Among the Historians', in Sharpe and Lake, eds., *Culture and Politics in Early Stuart England*, pp. 67–89.

context, and increasingly intrigued by classical conflicts between monarchism and republicanism.[12] A wealth of tragedies for the stage, many of which were steeped in satiric traditions and studded with topical allusions, powerfully extended such appreciations of politics.

In accordance with the premise of *Literature, Satire and the Early Stuart State*, this chapter focuses on texts written within this context, but which were more openly transgressive in their approaches. These include the libels I considered in Chapters 1 and 2, the pamphlets and printed poetry which formed the basis of my analysis in Chapter 3, and also Thomas Middleton's notorious political play, *A Game at Chess*. Such texts consistently combine sophisticated ideas with wit and scurrility, and look at once to elite and popular audiences. While much of the material may seem naive or simplistic, in some cases apparently conventional forms and discourses provide a context for surprisingly subtle political analysis. Indeed the period's unauthorized texts were involved in fundamental debates about the nature of politics, and often focus with striking clarity on emergent structures of identity and conflict. For instance, I argue that they help to give shape to concerns about court favouritism and corruption, and to explore new ideas about popular participation in political processes. Many also bring predominantly religious concerns to bear upon the politics of the decade, and I suggest that religious discourse enables new conceptions of political polarization, especially once certain writers accept and embrace the hitherto stigmatizing label of 'puritan'. The religious language of the conscience, already considered in the previous two chapters, also undersets contrasts between the court and commons, and in turn shapes Middleton's representation of diplomacy and courtly intrigue in *A Game at Chess*.

The chapter's first section examines representations of the court, and suggests that Tacitism helped writers to clarify images of the period's dominant politicians, and to conceive new discourses of anti-court radicalism. The second section considers ways in which satire contributed to contemporary efforts to define political groupings and identities, and suggests that its resources of artful indirection informed strategies for confronting the power of the monarchy, and for conceiving of 'the people' as a political force. And the final section analyses satiric representations of political process and conflict, and considers ways in which traditional models were refashioned in accordance with contemporary demands: as may be observed, most notably, in *A Game at Chess*.

---

[12] Woolf, *The Idea of History*, p. 172.

THE COURT: POLITICIANS AND FAVOURITES

In 1619, one A. D. B. published a manual for courtiers, *The Court of the Most Illustrious and most Magnificent James, the first*, which aims to lay down 'certaine rules and precepts of a Courtly and Politicall life' (sig. A1r). Compared to the great books of courtiership published in the sixteenth century, this text curiously foregrounds its status as belated, and even beleaguered. In fact, the dedication to Buckingham sets the volume in direct confrontation to 'the perverse petulance of many Poets, which laid so many odious aspersions upon Courts, as if no vertue had in them any residence' (sig. π3r). Moreover, it betrays throughout an anxious awareness of the negative images of the court presented by such poets. Hence the existence of overreaching courtiers is warily acknowledged, and the phenomenon of 'counterfeiting or colourable dissembling' is touched upon. The author, however, identifies no apparent problems at James's court, and recoils from Elizabethan celebrations of dissimulation, valorizing instead 'Truth or good councell' (pp. 38, 29). Yet this attempt to restore dignity to the court merely underscores the impact of the poems and 'divers Pamphlets' that the author had seen published under James: 'composed, in the disgrace of Princes' (p. 3). While such writing was hardly a new phenomenon, A. D. B. was right to perceive an intensification in illicit political commentary in his time, and right also to feel sensitive on account of his patron. Such discourse, in fact, was helping to transform contemporary perceptions of courts and princes.

From the end of Elizabeth's reign, commentators on the court had focused on factional struggles. Moreover, as Malcolm Smuts has noted, their observations were freshly filtered in the 1590s through 'Tacitean attitudes', which took hold especially among the circle of the Earl of Essex.[13] Such perceptions informed numerous libels produced at the time – most notably, the exchange initiated by Walter Raleigh's 'The Lie', and probably including a virulent piece by Essex himself – and also established a pattern that continued into the reign of James.[14] Factional networks of patrons and clients could be remarkably complex and fluid; however, as a consideration of libels demonstrates, their significance may depend almost as much on how they were perceived as on how they actually functioned.[15] For instance, the libels on Robert Cecil, and the flurry initiated by the scandal surrounding the

---

[13] 'Court-Centred Politics', p. 29.
[14] 'The Poems of Edward DeVere, Seventeenth Earl of Oxford and of Robert Devereux, Second Earl of Essex', ed. Steven W. May, *Studies in Philology*, 77 (1980), 'Texts and Studies' supplement, 106–8. See above, pp. 56–7.
[15] Cf. Linda Levy Peck's definition: 'Factions, portrayed pejoratively by classical political theorists, Roman historians such as Tacitus, and contemporary European observers, were networks of patrons

marriage of Robert Carr and Frances Howard, and the subsequent murder of Sir Thomas Overbury, consistently impose Tacitean models upon the English court.[16] Cecil is thus inscribed as the corrupt counsellor, promoting a faction at the expense of the nation. In one poem written after his death, Cecil and 'these lecherous wretches all / Which plotted worthy Essex fall', are figured as having been purged, so that 'the king, & state [shall] be blest, / And subjects all shall live in rest'.[17] The challenges facing the Howard faction prompted similar notes of celebration:

> The howse of the Howards
> Is now growing towards
>   Theire wonted declining
> For that generation
> Nere had moderation
>   In theire sunne shining
>
> For when they are greate
> They imprison and beate
>   To make themselves awfull
> Yet ever and anone
> Fate drives them upon
>   Some instance unlawfull
>
> From whence itt doth arise
> That we see with oure eyes
>   Theire quick revolution
> They waxe and they wayne
> And that is the payne
>   Of theire absolution.[18]

The speaker here strikes a detached and weary pose, observing a 'revolution' that aligns not only with Tacitean narratives, but also with medieval theories of fortune and 'Fate'. This model, however, does not prevent the inclusion of more topical points. The reference to the family's practices of 'imprison[ment]', for instance, alludes to Henry Howard, Earl of Northampton's controversial use of the Star Chamber to pursue libellers and satirists, including George Wither.[19] The final lines, with their image

and clients who, at the least, were viewed by others as connecting and co-ordinating their political behavior' (*Court Patronage and Corruption in Early Stuart England* [London, 1993], p. 53).
[16] Cf. Alastair Bellany, *The Politics of Court Scandal in Early Modern England: News Culture and the Overbury Affair, 1603–1660* (Cambridge, 2002), pp. 97–111.
[17] 'O Ladies, ladies, howle & cry' (Bodleian MS Tanner 299, fol. 12r).
[18] BL MS Egerton 2230, fol. 70r.
[19] Linda Levy Peck, *Northampton: Patronage and Policy at the Court of James I* (London, 1982), pp. 81–3; Allan Pritchard, '*Abuses Stript and Whipt* and Wither's Imprisonment', *Review of English Studies*, n.s. 14 (1963), 337–45.

of a painful absolution, combine delight in the eradication of the Howards with a sly allusion to the family's reputation as crypto-Catholics. Their 'absolution' is their downfall.

The fall of the Howards, as considered in Chapter 2, was also linked in libellous discourse to sexual immorality, in a manner that seemed to typify within the English court a Tacitean nexus between sexuality and court politics. In one poem, for instance, Frances Howard is figured as a leaky 'pinke' (a boat, though also a whore), which threatens all who trust it: 'her will commandes what ere shee please, / Without controule, even o're all the seas'.[20] Similar tactics were deployed in libels on Buckingham. Although neither Buckingham's rise nor his subsequent manipulation of patronage were entirely driven by factional allegiances, his relatively lowly background and indeterminate sexuality provided easy targets. Libellers do not commonly focus their attention on the sexuality of the Duke's relationship with James; however, one libel, as James Knowles has shown, deploys a language of sodomy more indiscriminately, to represent 'the whole Villiers clan . . . sodomising the nation'.[21] It begins:

> Heaven blesse King James our joy,
>   And Charles his baby
> Great George our brave viceroy
>   And his fayre Lady
> Old Beldame buckinghame
>   With her lord Keeper
> Shee loves the fucking game
>   Hee's her cunt creeper.
>   Thes be they goe so gay
>   In court and citty
>   Yett no man cares for them,
>   Is not this pitty.
>
>   . . .
>
> Old Abbott Anthony,[22]
>   I think hath well done,
> Since he left sodomy,
>   To marry Sheldon.
> Shee hath a buttock plumpe,
>   Keepe but thy tarse whole,

---

[20] 'From Katterin's dock there launcht a pinke' ('Poems from a Seventeenth-Century Manuscript', 74–5).

[21] 'To "scourge the arse / Jove's marrow so had wasted": Scurrility and the Subversion of Sodomy', in Dermot Cavanagh and Tim Kirk, eds., *Subversion and Scurrility: Popular Discourse in Europe from 1500 to the Present* (Aldershot, 2000), p. 77.

[22] Identified in a marginal note as Sir Anthony Ashley.

> And shee'le hold up her rumpe,
>> With her black arse hole.
>>> These bee they, goe so gay,
>>>> In court & citty,
>>> Yett the next springe, ye must singe,
>>>> Thee cockoes ditty.[23]

Whatever personal motivation might have prompted this poem, it functions as an exercise in the creation of faction, as it connects a series of statesmen to the Villiers family through bonds of debased sexuality. In the first stanza, the Lord Keeper and Bishop of Lincoln, John Williams (identified in a marginal note in the manuscript), is figured as being seduced as much by the patronage of the son as the sexual allure of the mother. In a poem that intertwines allusions of witchcraft with the 'porno-political' discourse of sodomy, the courtiers are figured respectively as a 'cunt creeper' to an 'Old Beldame', and a sodomite drawn to an ambiguously sexualized 'black arse hole'.[24] The images of gender and sexual inversion thereby underscore the poem's driving argument of political malaise.

Texts more closely concerned with the personalities of courtiers typically equate men such as Buckingham and Williams with the stigmatized figure of the 'politician'. A range of classical and continental sources contributed to the construction of this type; what is remarkable about the unauthorized political literature of the period, however, is the way in which such influences are naturalized and popularized, as they are mixed with arguments from biblical sources and English history. Debate about the role of 'policy' in government was particularly urgent in the decades around the turn of the century, fuelled especially by a growing awareness of the work of Machiavelli. For Joseph Wybarne, early in the Jacobean era, policy and morality are essentially incompatible:

for policie sheweth what can be done, moralitie what should be done; the Moralist saith, men should be good and not mutinous, the Polititian answereth, that men commonly neither are nor will be good, except they be constrained or deceived.[25]

More specifically, the politician was represented as someone who corrupts the language of counsel; the vice of flattery, according to one observer, 'hath quite lost his auncient attribute cousenage, and hath gotten it selfe graced with the name of Policie'.[26] Within this context, libellous poems

---

[23] Beinecke MS Osborn b.197, p. 187.
[24] Cf. Knowles, 'To "scourge the arse"', p. 77.
[25] *The New Age of Old Names* (1609), p. 18.
[26] [William Cavendish], *A Discourse Against Flatterie* (1611), sig. A4r–v.

follow a predictable pattern. One libel directed against enemies of Essex at the Elizabethan court alleges that amongst them, 'pryde spight & pollicie taketh place / in steade of conscience honor & grace'. It continues:

> There may you see walk hand in hand
> the polititians of our land
> that wrong arts glorie with a tongue
> dipt in *Water* from Limbo spronge.[27]

The poem pursues a simple strategy of discrimination, as the methods of the politician – associated specifically in the final line with 'Wa[l]ter' Raleigh – are set against not only the moral absolutes of honour, grace and 'arts glorie', but also the religious touchstone of conscience. The image of 'a tongue / dipt in *Water* from Limbo spronge' typifies the charge of courtly dissimulation, an art which separates language from truth.

While the basic outline of this character-type survives throughout the early Stuart era, it is valuably substantiated in the religious and political discourse of the 1620s. For Alexander Leighton, good counsel, by definition, could only come from a good man: 'The counsell is as the counsellor; witnesse *Salomon, Prov.* 12.5, *The counsels of the wicked are deceit*; the words are very emphaticall in the originall; *the craftie counsels of the ungodly are deceit*'.[28] Other writers similarly look to the Bible for authority. Henry Burton, writing on Joshua 7, posits Achan as an archetype of courtly division, since he divided '*God* from *Israel*' and '*Israel* from themselves'. He prays in 1628 that members of parliament should 'Let not the *Achan* faction, by their privie whisperings, divide them, by working disaffections.'[29] The preacher Robert Jenison was a little more cautious, and appears to have withheld the publication of three 1628 sermons on Achan due to the urgings of censors; Samuel Austin, however, continued the coded assault after Buckingham's death, alluding to him as 'this cursed Achan'.[30] Meanwhile, Nathanael Carpenter's *Achitophel, Or, The Picture of a Wicked Politician* (1629),[31] which anticipates John Dryden's application of the Absolom and Achitophel narrative to English politics, filters a representation of the politician at once through Old Testament morality and protestant doctrine concerning the

---

[27] 'Admir-all weaknes wronges the right' (Bodleian MS Rawlinson poet. 26, fol. 20v).

[28] *Speculum Belli sacri: Or The Lookingglasse of the Holy War* (Amsterdam, 1624), p. 93.

[29] *Israels Fast. Or, a Meditation Upon the Seventh Chapter of Joshuah; A faire Precedent for these Times* (1628), sigs. A3v–A4r. Cf. James Holstun, *Ehud's Dagger: Class Struggle in the English Revolution* (London, 2000), p. 161.

[30] Anthony Milton, 'Licensing, Censorship, and Religious Orthodoxy in Early Stuart England, *Historical Journal*, 41 (1998), 632–3; *Austins Urania* (1629), sig. A6v.

[31] First published before Buckingham's death, in Dublin, 1627.

conscience. Referring to Achitophel, he writes:

Behold here the first and chiefest character of a worldly wise Politician, who cares little how great a rupture he make through Gods sacred lawes and common equitie to meet with his own advantage, choosing rather to lose his soule than his wicked purpose; as one by Patent allowed to dispence with any obligation of conscience and religion. (p. 5)

Though Carpenter avoids specific criticism of any contemporary courtiers and statesmen, the contrast between the respective powers of God and the monarch is sustained throughout, satirically reinforced in the closing reference to the authority of 'Patent'. The definition of such corruption might suggest a range of different remedies. Carpenter, however, recommends merely a neo-Stoic rejection of the court; 'An upright and honest man', he writes, 'would rather find himselfe at home in his owne conscience, than seeke himselfe abroad in other mens opinions' (p. 7).

By far the most controversial manifestation of the politician, at the Jacobean court as in the world of Tacitus, was the court favourite. If courtiers were all 'like *Counters*, which sometime goe for a Thousand pound, and presently before the Court be past but for a Single pennie', the favourite was the counter of greatest value.[32] In Robert Cotton's image of satiric inversion, the king himself stands 'but as a cypher' alongside the favourite, 'set to adde to this figure, the more of number'.[33] Yet his position was also precarious. For satirists, the quintessential exemplar of the favourite was Sejanus, whose rise and fall under Tiberius provided an historical narrative which had been a staple of neoclassical satire (as evidenced most notably in Juvenal's famous tenth satire, 'The Vanity of Human Wishes'). Sir Edwin Sandys quoted lines from Juvenal's poem in the Parliament of 1614, to support a point about the extremes of royal authority.[34] Three years later, William Barkstead's translation of the satire, under the title *That Which Seemes Best Is Worst* (1617), underlined the value of the figure for a wider range of contemporary satirists. The pivotal text in the application of the Sejanus figure

---

[32] Richard Brathwaite, *The English Gentleman* (1630), pp. 37–8: quoted in Ruth Marion Little, 'Perpetual Metaphors: The Configuration of the Courtier as Favourite in Jacobean and Caroline Literature' (unpublished Ph.D dissertation, University of Cambridge, 1993), p. 15.

[33] *A Short View of the Long Life and Raigne of Henry the Third* (1627), p. 15.

[34] He quoted lines 112–13: 'Ad generum Ceceris sine caede et vulnere pauci / Descenderunt reges, et sicca morte tyranni' ('Few indeed are the kings who go down to Ceres' son-in-law save by sword and slaughter – few the tyrants that perish by a bloodless death!': *Juvenal and Persius*, trans. G. C. Ramsay [Loeb Classical Library, Cambridge, MA, 1918], p. 201). The incident is reported in Theodore Rabb, 'Revisionism Revised: The Role of the Commons', *Past and Present*, 92 (1981), 69–70.

to England, however, was Jonson's *Sejanus*. As Ruth Little has argued:

> Through Jonson, the recently rediscovered Tacitean image of the court favourite was standardised and publicised, and his attributes fixed as inevitably corrupting of monarchy and the common weal. These attributes include homosexuality, ambition, spiritual perversion, and power to encroach upon the boundaries of sovereignty and femininity.[35]

Hence an identifiable role existed from the very outset of James's reign, which subsequently could be applied to the king's court favourites. Even at moments when there were no obvious candidates for attack, libellers might still, in the words of Cecil, 'look for a Tiberius or Sejanus'.[36]

In the 1620s the Duke of Buckingham emerged as an apparently clear match for this role, and he was consequently 'conscripted into a tradition which then redefined itself in relation to him'.[37] This process is evident not only in the libellous poetry devoted to him, but also in pamphlets and political speeches. Even at a moment when Leighton found himself in agreement with Buckingham, after the collapse of the Spanish Match negotiations in 1624, he nonetheless wrote pointedly against any ruler placing his trust in only one counsellor, who would become like Sejanus to Tiberius.[38] In 1628, Pierre Matthieu's Tacitean *The Powerfull Favorite, Or, The Life of Ælius Sejanus* was published under a 'Paris' imprint (though probably from London) in two separate English translations. Although it makes no explicit comparisons to Buckingham, the implicit analogy could hardly have been missed by readers at the time. Nor was the comparison lost on the Duke's opponents in parliament. Sir John Eliot declared that:

> Of all the precedents I can find none so near resembles him as does Sejanus, and him Tacitus describes thus: That he was *[animus] audax, sui obtegens in alios criminator juxta adulator et superbia*. And if your Lordships please to measure him by this, pray see in what they vary. He is bold. We had the experience lately and such a boldness, I dare boldly say, as is seldom heard of. He is secret in his purposes and more, that we have showed already. Is he a slanderer? Is he an accuser? I wish this parliament had not felt it nor that that was before. And for his pride and flattery, what man can judge the greater?[39]

---

[35] 'Perpetual Metaphors', p. 179.

[36] *Proceedings in Parliament 1610*, ed. Elizabeth Read Foster (2 vols., New Haven, CT and London, 1966), II.168; also quoted in David Underdown, *A Freeborn People: Politics and the Nation in Seventeenth-Century England* (Oxford, 1996), p. 20.

[37] Little, 'Perpetual Metaphors', p. 161.

[38] *Speculum Belli Sacri*, sig. PIV; discussed in Joseph A. Taylor, 'The Literary Presentation of James I and Charles I, With Special Reference to the Period c.1614–1630' (unpublished DPhil. dissertation, University of Oxford, 1985), p. 137.

[39] *Proceedings in Parliament, 1626*, ed. William B. Bidwell and Maija Jansson (4 vols., New Haven, CT and London, 1991–6), I.223.

The statement exemplifies both a desire to identify one cause for the state's ills, and a belief that Sejanus presents a precedent for understanding Buckingham. Unsurprisingly, given his wilful public adoption of an unauthorized discourse – and the unflattering conclusion drawn by Charles that 'He must intend me for Tiberius' – Eliot was sent to the Tower.[40]

The history of the English court furnished further examples of corrupted power dynamics between a king and his favourite, which could equally be conflated with Tacitean models and applied to contemporary circumstances. Cotton, in *A Short View of the Long Life and Raigne of Henry the Third*, was careful to distinguish between the king and his counsellors, selecting as his historical analogy 'an inherently good prince, who simply needed good advice'.[41] This text, in which Cotton presents 'a collection of Tacitean maxims' as an exercise in counsel, describes Henry's achievements in banishing corrupt courtiers, and thereby purifying his rule.[42] Other analogies carried more subversive potential. Sir Henry Yelverton was imprisoned in 1621 for comparing Buckingham to Hugh Spencer, whose career as the favourite of Edward II was well known from the chronicle history of Raphael Holinshed, and from Christopher Marlowe's subsequent play, *Edward II*.[43] Later in the decade, Sir Francis Hubert's poem, *The Historie of Edward the Second*, published in two pirated editions in 1628 and an authorized one in 1629, rehearsed the narrative of relations between Edward and his favourites. Moreover, while such discourse contributed to the stigmatization of Buckingham around the time of his assassination, it could potentially be turned against the king himself, thereby reviving long-standing arguments about the legitimacy of deposing corrupt monarchs. Debates on this question shaped numerous Elizabethan history plays, and remained alive in political discourse over the following decades. When Michael Drayton published a miscellaneous volume of poems, *The Battaile of Agincourt*, in 1627, Jonson offered a cryptic commendatory poem, praising the author for 'instruct[ing] these times, / That Rebells actions, are but valiant crimes!' Curiously, the great court poet of his age proceeds to invoke Lucan, the great classical poet of republicanism, to support a tenuous – and, in the context, arguably seditious – notion of 'authoriz'd wickednesse'.[44]

---

[40] Quoted in Burke, 'Tacitism', p. 162.
[41] Woolf, *The Idea of History*, p. 160. On the dating of this text, see above, pp. 110–11.
[42] J. H. M. Salmon, 'Stoicism and the Roman Example: Seneca and Tacitus in Jacobean England', *Journal of the History of Ideas*, 50 (1989), 213.
[43] Robert Zaller, *The Parliament of 1621: A Study in Constitutional Conflict* (Berkeley, 1971), p. 120.
[44] 'The Vision of Ben. Jonson, On the Muses of his Friend M. Drayton', in Drayton, *Works*, ed. J. William Hebel (5 vols., Oxford, 1931–41), III.4. On the status of Lucan in this period, see David

The suggestion that a political discourse concerned with courtly corruption might threaten the monarch, or even the very structure he represents, is clarified by a closer consideration of certain libellous attacks on Buckingham. A number of texts focus purely on the personal relationships between Buckingham and his successive royal patrons, and identify the Duke as the single source of corruption. In the words of one, considered above in Chapter 2, the Duke sought 'To gett possession of my soveraignes heart'.[45] Elsewhere, however, there is evidence of greater sophistication, which indicates that Buckingham provided an occasion for the articulation of new conceptions of political confrontation. Indeed criticism of a favourite was by nature difficult to contain, and many writers and readers were complicit in the translation of such statements into coded attacks on the monarch. Francis Bacon warned Buckingham of this, when he advised that 'the King himself is above the reach of his people, but cannot be above their censures, and you are his shaddow'.[46] Consequently, although parliamentary discourse was typically cautious in this regard, Hugh Pyne was merely giving voice to a sensitive yet apparent point when he commented of charges against Buckingham in 1628 that 'to name a particular would reflect upon a higher than he'.[47]

In just this spirit, some libels on Buckingham are infused with unmistakable notes of anti-royalist menace. As I argued in Chapter 2, 'The Five Senses' (probably by William Drummond) glances meaningfully towards a populace suffering under the weight of courtly oppression.[48] Another poem develops the metaphor of a buck which is destroying its forest:

> The forresters say, while hee's alive
> The tender thicketts nere can thrive,
> Hee doth soe barke and pill the trees;
> That wee for game our profitt leese.[49]

The introduction of first-person plural pronouns is telling, as it identifies a loose alliance of the population, whose 'profitt' is affected by the strength

---

Norbrook, *Writing the English Republic: Poetry, Rhetoric and Politics, 1627–1660* (Cambridge, 1999), pp. 23–62. Cf. Thomas Cogswell's more benign reading of this intriguing poem ('The Path to Elizium "Lately Discovered": Drayton and the Early Stuart Court', *Huntington Library Quarterly*, 54 [1991], 215).

[45] 'The argument is cold and sencelesse clay' (*Poems and Songs*, p. 38); see above, p. 67.

[46] *A Letter of Advice Written by Sir Francis Bacon to the Duke of Buckingham, When he became Favourite to King James* (1661), p. 2.

[47] *Proceedings in Parliament: Commons Debates, 1628*, ed. Mary Frear Keeler, et al. (6 vols., New Haven, CT and London, 1977–83), VI.128; quoted in Underdown, *A Freeborn People*, p. 40.

[48] See above, pp. 75–82.

[49] 'Of Brittish beasts the Buck is king' (*Poems and Songs*, p. 6).

of the buck. The poem's close expands its focus, deftly touching on the monarch himself:

> A *Buck*'s a beast; a *King* is but a man,
> A *Game*'s a pleasure shorter then a span;
> A beast shall perish; but a man shall dye,
> As pleasures fade. This bee thy destinie.
>
> (p. 6)

Calls for the assassination of Buckingham were not unusual in the year or two before his death. What sets this poem apart is the careful allusiveness of the prophecy, which slides from a prediction of the Duke's death, through (perhaps) a sly suggestion of sexual 'pleasure shorter than a span', towards a treasonous implication of the monarch (a mere 'man') in the projected purge.[50] The confrontation, clearly delineated by the end, is between a king steeped in lasciviousness and a collective 'wee' who are suffering as a result.[51]

Court satire is not necessarily founded on ideological opposition to the court as an institution. In fact, for satirists who subscribed to the predominant view of their mode as curative or purgative, an adherence to the values of monarchy might underpin attacks on immorality and corruption at court. Similarly, Tacitism, which provided a discourse that could so easily be turned against the court, was itself ambiguous politically. While Tacitus might well be held to demonstrate the inherent corruption of monarchical structures, James was committed to a variant interpretation, and patronized Edmund Bolton's history of the reign of Nero, which was intended 'to demonstrate that the worst ruler was better than the anarchy of revolt'.[52] As I have argued, however, the unauthorized texts of the early Stuart era, though not consistent in their politics, on occasion assert with stunning clarity satire's more radical potential: as becomes evident in their pointed suggestions of systemic corruption, and strategic assumptions of a court fundamentally opposed to the interests of the populace. These texts, therefore, help to construct potent discourses of corruption, defining new images of the dynamics of power in their nation.

---

[50] Cf. Holstun, *Ehud's Dagger*, p. 160.

[51] Cf. Alastair Bellany's discussion of libels which 'dared to implicate the king in Buckingham's offences' ('"Raylinge Rymes and Vaunting Verse": Libellous Politics in Early Stuart England, 1603–1628', in Sharpe and Lake, eds., *Culture and Politics in Early Stuart England*, pp. 304–5).

[52] *Nero Caesar or Monarchy Depraved* (1623); see Salmon, 'Stoicism and the Roman Example', 224.

POLITICAL IDENTITIES: DEFINITIONS OF DIFFERENCE

Political confrontations depend on a language to define them. This point was at the foundation of the revisionist assault on the notion of opposing political 'parties': a term revealed as anachronistic when applied to early Stuart England.[53] Yet some of the more sophisticated post-revisionist work has focused afresh on particular instances of opposition, and has initiated 'an analysis of political rhetoric and the relationships of political discourse to political tension and conflict'.[54] Resultant models of conflict are notably dynamic and contingent; conflicting discourses, in the words of one scholar, 'were not mutually exclusive', but 'could and did coexist in individual minds'.[55] In the present context, given satire's commitment to practices of discrimination, it is reasonable to ask what influence this literary mode may have had on emergent definitions of division. I begin to answer this question in this section by considering the ways in which the satire of this period politicizes religious categories, in the process creating a potential for new conceptions of opposition. Subsequently, I consider a language of 'liberty', which increasingly underpins representations of confrontations between parliament and court. And finally, I turn to the relation between parliament and 'the people', and argue that satiric texts helped to construct a simple yet potentially subversive conception of the power of the English populace.

The connection between politics and religion in the 1620s remains a matter of conjecture. According to some historians, the categories were inextricably confused; in the words of Thomas Cogswell, 'most contemporaries were intellectually unable to separate politics and religion'.[56] As others have demonstrated, however, this proposition does not fully account for the political impact of religious discourse. Peter Lake, for example, has examined ways in which the prejudice of 'anti-popery' could be exploited to influence domestic and foreign policy.[57] While this indicates to Lake the predominance of religious thought in political life, it might equally be

---

[53] See, for example, Mark Kishlansky, 'The Emergence of Adversary Politics in the Long Parliament', *Journal of Modern History*, 49 (1977), 624–5.

[54] Kevin Sharpe reviews these historiographical developments in *Remapping Early Modern England: The Culture of Seventeenth-Century Politics* (Cambridge, 2000), pp. 3–37 (quote p. 10), and in the following chapter in the same volume, 'A Commonwealth of Meanings: Languages, Analogues, Ideas and Politics', which itself attends to political discourse (pp. 38–123).

[55] Timothy Raylor, *Cavaliers, Clubs, and Literary Culture: Sir John Mennes, James Smith, and the Order of the Fancy* (Newark, 1994), p. 108.

[56] Thomas Cogswell, 'England and the Spanish Match', in Cust and Hughes, eds., *Conflict in Early Stuart England*, p. 109.

[57] 'Anti-Popery: The Structure of a Prejudice', in Cust and Hughes, eds., *Conflict in Early Stuart England*, pp. 72–106.

suggested that such religious categories could be manipulated for political ends. If Thomas Scott consistently assimilates 'various faults and corrupt tendencies to the influence of popery', it becomes fair to ask whether a 'prejudice' is driving a political programme, or a political programme is emerging out of the vocabulary of religion.[58] A sophisticated appreciation of the political value of religious discourse is also apparent in texts which suggest that religion is being used as little more than a cloak for political and materialistic goals. This is the underlying argument of a poem about the Thirty Years' War, dated 1623 in one manuscript. It addresses 'Religion thou most sacred power on earth', and questions 'Why . . . these wars' should 'Terme thee the Author of their Civill Jarres'. It then addresses itself directly to secular rulers:

> O princes leave to use these wicked Artes
> Religion's in your eyes not in your harts
> Yet your high purpled bid you proceede
> Tis meritorious for the Church to bleede
> What though ten thousand perish, soe you winn
> A stinkinge hole to thrust your doctrine Inn.[59]

Though it does not explicitly criticize any protestant ruler, the poem pointedly locates pure religion with 'the labouringe plowe' rather than in any of Europe's 'greate princes Courtes' (fol. 143r). Power, it suggests, invariably harnesses religion for its own ends.

A crucial discursive strategy through which the weight of religion could be brought to bear more particularly upon political life was satire's technique of stigmatization. Within political discourse, practices of labelling perceived transgressors were commonplace, and contributed to the ongoing project of defining categories of political allegiance. For instance, Lake suggests that Northampton's 'known crypto-popery fitted him all too well' for the 'role of evil counsellor', and that it was largely as a result of this that he was blamed for the failure of the Addled Parliament of 1614.[60] At the other extreme, accusations of puritanism could carry similar weight. As Patrick Collinson has argued, 'puritan' originated as a term of abuse, 'a gibe hurled . . . at all too evidently religious persons, Protestants, by their less obviously religious

[58] See Peter Lake, 'Constitutional Consensus and Puritan Opposition in the 1620s: Thomas Scott and the Spanish Match', *Historical Journal*, 25 (1982), 811.
[59] 'Religion thou most sacred power on earth' (BL MS Stowe 962, fol. 142v). It is dated 1623 in this source, while another (Bodleian MS Eng. poet. c.50, fol. 29r) states that it was 'Writen after the beginning of the Bohemian war'.
[60] 'Anti-Popery', 88.

or crypto-Catholic neighbors'.[61] By the 1620s, such accusations had become a valuable tool of political interaction. Lucy Hutchinson reflected that at the time of the Spanish Match negotiations, those who preached against it 'were hated' at court, 'and in scorn had the name of Puritan fixed upon them'.[62] Scott makes a similar point within the fictional structure of *Vox Populi*, when the Spanish ambassador, Count Gondomar, boasts that, if any opponents of the Match 'be found longer tongued then his fellowes, we still have meanes to charme their sawciness, to silence them, and expell them the Court, to disgrace them and crosse their preferments, with the imputation pragmaticke Puritanisme'.[63] Such 'imputations' had their origin in the Theophrastan character literature that flourished in the early seventeenth century, and were clarified and consolidated through a wealth of scurrilous writing.[64] One poem, 'In Puritans', is loaded with politicized accusations:

> If lyes; if slanders; if debate
> Private Malice; perfect hate;
> Contumelious bribes; check-mate
> To Government of church and state;
> True tokens bee, of sanctitie
> The Puritan a saint must bee.[65]

The category of 'puritan' is here aligned with sedition and rebellion. Through the circular logic of the poem – a logic clearly familiar to Hutchinson and Scott in the 1620s – a puritan is a rebel and a rebel is a puritan.

Within this context, attempts to reclaim and refashion the category of 'the puritan', in the process redirecting the resources of satire onto those claiming a position of orthodoxy, assume a critical position in the development of oppositional identities. Wither moved cautiously in this direction in 1613, asking rhetorically, 'Who are so much tearm'd *Puritans* as they / That feare God most?'.[66] A more important text in this respect, however, is a pamphlet-length poem probably written by Leighton, *The Interpreter.*

[61] *The Puritan Character: Polemics and Polarities in Early Seventeenth-Century English Culture* (Los Angeles, 1989), p. 20; see also 'Ecclesiastical Vitriol: Religious Satire in the 1590s and the Invention of Puritanism', in John Guy, ed., *The Reign of Elizabeth I: Court and Culture in the Last Decade* (Cambridge, 1995), p. 155.
[62] Quoted in R. Malcolm Smuts, *Court Culture and the Origins of a Royalist Tradition in Early Stuart England* (Philadelphia, 1987), p. 35.
[63] *Vox Populi: or newes from Spaine* (London?, 1620), sig. C3r.
[64] On the influence of character literature, see Collinson, *Puritan Character*, pp. 3–6.
[65] Beinecke MS Osborn b.197, p. 144.
[66] *Abuses Stript, and Whipt* (1613), in *Juvenilia* (1626), p. 276: quoted in David Norbrook, *Poetry and Politics in the English Renaissance*, revised edn (Oxford, 2002), p. 188.

Wherein three principal Terms of State, much mistaken by the vulgar, are clearly understood (1622), which presents extended character sketches of 'A Puritan', 'A Protestant' and 'A Papist'. The description of the papist is considerably the shortest of the three, a fact which highlights the relative lack of controversy surrounding this widely vilified category. By comparison, the other pieces are motivated by a commitment to redefine the puritan, and are characterized by a subtle awareness of the capacity of language to shape reality. 'A Puritan', then, is 'So nicknamed, but indeed the sound Protestant' (p. 235). He is truly loyal, but demonstrates his loyalty by a commitment to 'Laws and Truth':

> He neither sides with that man nor with this,
> But gives his voice just as the reason is,
> And yet, if Policy would work a fraction
> To cross Religion by a foreign faction
> Pretending public good; he'll join with those
> Who dare speak Truth.
>
> (p. 237)

While interests of 'Religion' are situated at the foundation of the puritan's identity, he is defined further as a man concerned with abstract notions of 'reason' and 'truth'. In accordance with the discursive developments traced above in Chapter 3, the author polemically redefines the identity of a truly honest counsellor, who emerges stripped of a courtier's personal ties and material interests.

The Interpreter's sketch of the protestant is perhaps even more significant, as it satirically defines a type of corrupt statesman who is not stigmatized simply as a papist. 'Protestant', the author declares at the outset, is merely a name that 'the Formalist' chooses for himself; the genuine protestants, as he has already argued, are those called puritans. This formalist, or false protestant, is figured rather as the true hypocrite:

> A Protestant is an indifferent man,
> That with all faiths, or none, hold quarter can;
> So moderate and temperate his passion
> As he to all times can his conscience fashion.
>
> (p. 243)

This malleability of 'conscience' is directly related to a susceptibility to corruption:

> Briefly, whatsoe'er he be, except alone
> Directly honest (of which few or none
> Remain alive) a Statist, ways can find,

> By policy to work him to his mind.
> And thus the Common wealth may conquered be,
> The Church deflowered, beslaved our Liberty,
> Without all bloodshed; under the pretence
> Of Peace, Religion, Love, and Innocence.
>
>   (p. 243)

Again the text returns, in a manner characteristic of Renaissance verse satire, to an argument that abstract values are being appropriated and reshaped for sinister ends. The 'protestant', without a sufficient strength of conscience, may easily be swayed from paths of truth and reason by a deceitful 'statist', or politician. The alleged quality of malleability is usefully reflected in A. D. B.'s manual for courtiers, which advises against 'meddl[ing] . . . with too nice inquisition after unprofitable and unnecessary things'. Citing examples of religious changes initiated by governments across Europe from the early sixteenth century, the author states: 'I would not (good Courtier) that thou shouldst bee too strictly bound with this indissoluble bond of Religion, from which thou maist easily untie and unlose thy selfe.'[67] What becomes evident from this conjunction of an unauthorized poem and a determinedly orthodox manual, therefore, is the way in which satiric strategies enable a writer to drive a wedge between differing attitudes towards government and counsel. Making such a distinction, through a struggle over certain key terms of categorization, helps to establish a basis for political confrontation.

Further, the claim in *The Interpreter* that the statist's policy has 'beslaved our Liberty' isolates a term with conjoined religious and political connotations, that would become a catchcry of dissent in the course of the decade. Assumptions that the subject possessed liberty, or right in property, underset both the natural law tradition and theories of the ancient constitution.[68] In religious discourse, the term was common in anti-Catholic propaganda, with its spectre of an international conspiracy to overwhelm the English Church, while it also became associated with the notion of the free conscience as a source of unfettered individual judgement. Consequently, recurrent arguments in parliament about the liberty of the subject, which emerged at the end of the sixteenth century and culminated in the 1628 Petition of Right, provided a focus for interlinked anxieties concerning an individual's participation in the commonwealth and rights in the face of

---

[67] *The Court of the most Illustrious and most Magnificent James, the First*, p. 121.
[68] Markku Peltonen, *Classical Humanism and Republicanism in English Political Thought 1570–1640* (Cambridge, 1995), p. 122.

state authority.[69] As others have recognized, Scott, in particular, echoed these arguments in his pamphlets. For instance, in *The Second Part of Vox Populi* he 'quoted William Verheyden *in extenso* to demonstrate the crucial importance of liberty', while in *The Belgicke Pismire* 'the third necessary measure to stave off corruption was "to restore libertie"'.[70] Similarly, as seen above in Chapter 3, nascent notions of citizenship relied heavily on ideals of 'freedom', or liberty.

Libellous poems written after the death of Buckingham elucidate the nature and potential consequences of these developments. One piece, written by James Smith, directly situates the assassination of the favourite in relation to debates on liberty, as it addresses 'You auntient lawes of right', and asks them how they can condemn to death John Felton, Buckingham's assassin:

> Can you (I say) speake death in your decrees
> To one whose life procur'd your liberties?
> Or you, late tongue-ty'd judges of the land,
> Passe sentence on his act, whose valiant hand
> Wrencht off your muzzells, and infranchiz'd all
> Your shakl'd consciences from one mans thrall?[71]

The poem is steeped in legal discourse. Hence the appeal to the 'auntient lawes', with its allusion to ongoing debates over the authority of the ancient constitution, gives way to a pointed comment on the corrupting power of one who has 'muzzled' justice and suppressed individual 'liberties'. The final suggestion that Felton 'infranchiz'd all / Your shakl'd consciences' appeals to the source of a Christian's integrity, while simultaneously alluding to the nature of a subject's liberty within the nation. To 'enfranchise', at this time, could mean to set free (as a slave or serf), to release from confinement, and also 'to admit to municipal or political privileges' (*OED*). Moreover,

---

[69] *The Constitutional Documents of the Puritan Revolution*, ed. Samuel Rawson Gardiner, 3rd edn (Oxford, 1906), pp. 66–70. On ideas of liberty, see esp. J. P. Sommerville, *Royalists and Patriots: Politics and Ideology in England 1603–1640*, 2nd edn (London and New York, 1999), pp. 134–75. David Harris Sacks traces the development of a discourse surrounding the term 'liberty of the subject' ('Parliament, Liberty, and the Commonweal', in J. H. Hexter, ed., *Parliament and Liberty from the Reign of Elizabeth to the English Civil War* [Stanford, 1992], p. 94); and Linda Levy Peck argues the significance of the Petition of Right in this regard ('Kingship, Counsel and Law in Early Stuart Britain', in J. G. A. Pocock, ed., *The Varieties of British Political Thought, 1500–1800* [Cambridge, 1993], pp. 104–6).

[70] Peltonen, *Classical Humanism and Republicanism*, p. 240 (citing *The Second Part of Vox Populi: or Gondomar appearing in the likenes of Machiavell in a Spanish parliament* [1624], sig. D2v–D3r; and *The Belgicke Pismire* [Holland, 1622], p. 39).

[71] 'You auntient lawes of right, can you, for shame' (*Poems and Songs*, p. 70); on Smith, see Raylor, *Cavaliers*, pp. 50–70.

as David Harris Sacks has argued, the noun 'franchise' was itself the centre of ideological debate, and was gradually being redefined in accordance with newly inclusive theories of parliamentary election. 'The franchise was ceasing to be a matter of privilege,' Sacks writes, 'and becoming one of liberty, to be defended in the interests of the commonwealth as a whole.'[72]

Zouch Townley's widely disseminated poem, 'To his Confined Friend Mr. Felton', from its opening lines deploys almost identical language:

> Enjoy thy bondage; make thy prison know
> Thou hast a libertie thou canst not owe
> To those base punishments; keep't entire, since
> Noething but guilt shackles the conscience.[73]

The poem works satirically around the contrast between the 'libertie' of the Christian whose actions are directed by his conscience, and the state's corrupted definitions of imprisonment and liberty. Its implicit argument is that only by confronting tyranny, at whatever level, may the nation's subjects truly achieve liberty. Consequently, Felton takes both the punishment and the glory for an act that was collectively willed by the nation as a whole:

> Let the dukes name solace and crowne thy thrall:
> All wee by him did suffer, thou for all.
> And I dare boldlie write, as thou dar'st dye,
> Stout Felton, Englands ransome, heere doth lye.
>   (pp. 75–6)

Again, a poem written against the court favourite gestures towards a fundamental division within the state, between a corrupted court and the 'wee' who suffer at its hands. Pointedly, Townley appropriates for the people's hero a monarchical verb; the name of the dead duke, he proclaims, should '*crowne* thy thrall'.

The perceived challenges to the people's liberties posed by a corrupt counsellor also prompted commentators to focus their attentions on the powers of parliament. Indeed the period's emergent perception of power struggles is epitomized in Cotton's sententious observation, that a polity is always subject to the 'distempers' attendant upon a conflict of interests between 'the Commons greedy of liberty, and the Nobilitie of Rule'.[74] Significantly, members of parliament in the 1620s were themselves finding new ways to target court policies – and members of the nobility – by

---

[72] 'Parliament, Liberty, and the Commonweal', pp. 109–10.
[73] *Poems and Songs*, p. 74.
[74] *A Short View of the Long Life and Raigne of Henry the Third*, p. 4

experimenting with impeachment, a strategy 'which served to project the
stigma of disloyalty onto others'.[75] While Conrad Russell argues that im-
peachments were principally the result of struggles between rival courtiers
and factions at court, the practice itself unquestionably marked a departure
from the theory that parliament was merely a body of counsel, and therefore
attracted considerable attention in contemporary political discourse.[76] In
Raleigh's *The Prerogative of Parliaments in England*, the legitimate 'remov-
ing of Councellors', more than anything else, problematizes easy hierarchies
between king and subject. For this reason, Raleigh suggests, the king has
'cause . . . to feare a Parliament'.[77]

By the time Raleigh's text was posthumously published, in 1628, his
comments seemed to underscore efforts to turn this weapon against Buckingham. Satiric writing of this time was more polemical in intent, and
commonly emphasized the value of liberty by representing the nobility's
desire for 'Rule' as overbearing and exploitative. One of the best poems in
manuscript circulation in the 1620s was in fact satirically presented as the
work of Buckingham himself, and titled 'The Copie of His Grace's Most
Excellent Rotomontados, sent by his servant the Lord Grimes, in answere to
the lower house of parliament, 1628'.[78] The poem's calculated haughtiness
of tone (a 'rodomontade' is an extravagantly boastful or arrogant speech)
is in fact close to that actually adopted by James in his poem written in response to libellers earlier in the decade; however, it slides unmistakably into
satire by virtue of its excessive denigration of the Commons.[79] It begins:

> Avaunt, you giddie-headed multitude,
> And doe your worst of spight: I never sued
> To gaine your votes, though well I know your ends
> To ruine me, my fortunes, and my friends;
> Which had I fear'd, how easie had it been
> By quick prevention to avoyde your teene,

---

[75] Robert Zaller, 'The Concept of Opposition in Early Stuart England', *Albion*, 12 (1980), 233.
[76] *Parliaments and English Politics 1621–1629* (Oxford, 1979), p. 15. Alan Cromartie quotes John Pym,
who described MPs, in the light of impeachment debates, as 'law-makers, as counsellors, and as
judges' ('The Constitutionalist Revolution: The Transformation of Political Culture in Early Stuart
England', *Past and Present*, 163 [1999], 104).
[77] (1628), pp. 30, 61.
[78] A copy in Bodleian MS Ashmole 36, 37, fol. 57r, attributes this poem to 'I. S.'. Since 'You ancient
laws of right' is in the same volume attributed to 'Ja[mes] Smith' (fol. 31r), it would be reasonable to
suggest Smith as the author of this piece as well. (I will quote from the version of the poem printed in
Poems and Songs, pp. 28–31.) For a brief discussion of the poem in the context of parliamentary debates
concerning Buckingham in 1628, see Samuel R. Gardiner, *History of England from the Accession of
James to the Outbreak of the Civil War, 1603–1642*, reprint edn (10 vols., New York, 1965), VI.321.
[79] On James's poem, see above, p. 34.

> And eas'd your tedious journies, speeches, witts,
> At first, by once prohibiting the writts
> That call'd you hither to a good intent,
> Not causing a brabling confus'd parliament?
> For in my power it was (maugre each foe)
> To say it should, or it should not be soe.
>
>   (pp. 28–9)

The early reference to 'votes' implicitly contrasts the respective foundations of the power of the Duke and the parliament. Subsequently, the poem highlights the arbitrary nature of Buckingham's authority, which alone threatens to forestall the combined 'speeches' and 'witts' of the elected representatives of those denigrated, socially and intellectually, as a 'giddie-headed multitude'. The application of an exaggerated patrician disdain towards the Commons is continued later, when 'Buckingham' urges them to 'Meddle' only 'with common matters, common wrongs', since 'Coblers their latchetts ought not to transcend' (p. 30). While it remains disputable whether the conflicts of the seventeenth century might usefully be understood in terms of class struggle, this poem's representation of the contest between parliament and court almost demands such terminology. It makes, implicitly, a powerful case for the political involvement of the 'multitude'.

Earlier in the decade, conflicting responses to the impeachment of Bacon focused similarly on the status and functions of parliament. One widely circulated poem in support of Bacon, probably written by William Lewis, provost of Oriel College, Oxford, mobilizes the same rhetoric that was later turned satirically against Buckingham.[80] It upbraids the 'Bould Plebeans' of the Commons for their 'rashnes' and 'hate':

> for in a senceles fury yow have slayne
> a man as far beyond the spongy brayne
> of common knowledge as is Heaven from Hell,
> & yet tryumphinge thinke yow have don well.
> O that the monster multitude should sitt
> in place of justice, reason, conscience, witt
> nay in the throane & spheare above them all,
> for tis a supreame power that can call
> all these to the Barre & with a frowninge Brow
> make Senators nay mighty Counsells bowe.[81]

---

[80] The attribution is made in several sources, including: Bodleian MS Eng. poet. f. 10, fol. 104r; BL MS Stowe 962, fol. 55v; and BL Add. MS 25303, fol. 83r. See also *First-Line Index of English Poetry 1500–1800 in Manuscripts of the Bodleian Library Oxford*, ed. Margaret Crum (2 vols., Oxford, 1969), w1641.

[81] 'When yee awake dull Bryttaines & beholde' (BL Add MS 25303, fol. 83r).

For Lewis, the Commons is a place of 'common knowledge', which threatens to undermine the courtly system of counsel. The satire rests on the author's claim to the abstract values of 'justice, reason, conscience, witt', which he sets against the populist mentality of the 'monster multitude'. The House is thus figured as grotesquely representative of the people, in lines that mobilize a fear of democracy and anarchy. In the words of an earlier satirist, it may become merely 'The Abstract of our Mobb'.[82] A poem written in response to Lewis, however, reclaims the vocabulary of corruption, arguing that Bacon himself sold 'right & wrong & conscience too'. The parliament is here figured as 'a Sennate whose grave Doome can fright / the most out daring insolence!'; it is 'no monster multitude', but rather a 'state' which 'verry hardly parraleld may be / for wisedome Courage & Integrety'.[83] Implicit in this defence is a potentially radical claim for parliamentary power, as the poem first associates the 'Sennate' with the quality of 'grave' judgement commonly located in the Crown, and then levels the socially coded charge of 'insolence' against the court and its dependants. A strain of populist satire is continued in a suggestion that Bacon's punishment might well have been harsher, given the example set by 'Count Holland, who for one Cowe / condemnd his bailife to the fatall Bough' (p. 136).[84]

As much as James continued to insist that parliament's function was 'merely advisory', this discourse posited instead a body freed of courtly, and even monarchical, structures of authority.[85] Although such arguments are rarely well developed, the unauthorized political discourse of the 1620s, founded upon ideals of godly citizenship, thereby contributed to a reassessment of parliament's position in relation to the king.[86] For several writers, parliament was at this time assuming a coherent and enduring institutional identity, as opposed to being merely an irregular event called by the monarch.[87] Hence in Scott's pamphlets, as Lake notes, 'parliament had an almost mystical significance as the ultimate source of unity and concord',

---

[82] Elizabeth Grymeston, *Miscelanea. Meditations. Memoratives* (1604), p. 11.

[83] 'What hatfull fury dipt thy raging Quill' (Huntington MS HM 198, pp. 134–5).

[84] Possibly a reference to the courtier Henry Rich, first Earl of Holland; however, he was not granted this title until 1624, and I have not traced the incident to which the poem refers.

[85] Johann P. Sommerville, 'Parliament, Privilege, and the Liberties of the Subject', in Hexter, ed., *Parliament and Liberty*, p. 78.

[86] On arguments in 1620s' parliaments over the powers of the institution, see Peck, 'Kingship, Counsel and Law in Early Stuart Britain', pp. 94–8. On godly citizenship, see Michelle O'Callaghan, *The 'shepheards nation': Jacobean Spenserians and Early Stuart Political Culture* (Oxford, 2000), pp. 156–7.

[87] Russell argues that parliaments throughout this period were primarily perceived as events (*Parliaments and English Politics*, p. 3).

while for Burton, later in the century, it was simply 'this Sacred Senate'.[88]
Leighton followed the example of other pamphleteers when he dedicated
one of his most strident publications to the 'cure-all court of Parliament'.
The text itself focuses anxiously on the power of the monarch to close a
parliament, claiming that 'everie dissolution . . . without reall reformation
is against *right, reason, & record*'. According to the ancient constitution, he
argues, a parliament could rightfully remain in session 'so long, as there were
any matters . . . to be determined', despite advice to the contrary proffered
by 'the common adversaries'.[89] The latter allusion to corrupt counsellors
unites the king and his people against a 'common' foe; the balance of power
in this relationship, however, slides decisively away from the Crown.

Certain texts also work to refashion prevailing assumptions of parliamentary representation. The relation between the Commons and the
commons – the parliament and the people – was a contentious matter
among contemporary commentators, and has remained so with historians.
Elizabethan observers famously dismissed a huge mass of the population
from the political nation, as people who 'have neither voice nor authority
in the commonwealth, but are to be ruled and not to rule other'.[90] Even by
the early Stuart decades, Christopher Hill has argued, 'the people' generally
had a heavily restricted meaning in political discourse, denoting upper yeo-
manry, rising tradesmen and artificers.[91] Yet consideration of the period's
unauthorized political writing indicates that markedly broader notions of
political involvement were becoming thinkable. Once again, the work of
Scott is exemplary. In particular, Scott believed passionately in the process
of election, which he claimed to be in accord with 'the law of nature'.[92]
Like many of his contemporaries, he perceived voting as a godly duty,
which binds the public and spiritual dimensions of the commonwealth.[93]
Consequently, he attacked parliamentary elections that were dominated by
'faction', in which 'the countrey people themselves will every one stand for
the great man their Lord or neighbour, or master, without regard of his
honesty, wisedome, or religion'.[94] He exhorted electors rather to be 'wary'

[88] 'Constitutional Consensus', 818; Burton, *Babel no Bethel* (1629), sig. **IV.
[89] *An Appeal to the Parliament, Or Sions Plea Against the Prelacie* (Amsterdam, 1628), pp. 337–8; cf.
Stephen Foster, *Notes from the Caroline Underground: Alexander Leighton, the Puritan Triumvirate,
and the Laudian Reaction to Nonconformity* (Hamden, CT, 1978), p. 38.
[90] William Harrison, *The Description of England*, ed. Georges Edelen (Ithaca, 1968), p. 118.
[91] 'Parliament and People in Seventeenth-Century England', *Past and Present*, 92 (1981), 120.
[92] *Aphorisms of State* (1624), sig. C4v.
[93] See further Sacks, 'Parliament, Liberty, and the Commonweal', pp. 111–12.
[94] *Vox Populi*, sig. B3v.

and to make their choices 'for conscience sake'.[95] Such decisions, borne out of individual wisdom and directed towards the interests of the nation, help to define for Scott the concept of 'a good Citizen'.[96]

Moreover, representations of political action in satiric texts occasionally glance beyond the parliament and its electors. In Scott's *Second Part of Vox Populi*, for example, Gondomar boasts about the gullibility of those of higher degree, but confesses anxiously that 'the Common people . . . beare generally an inbred spleene towards us'. He says, 'we cannot passe (though no violence I confesse is offered) but we have the bans and revilings of the multitude, I meane the baser sort' (pp. 12, 34). The parenthetical remark is crucial, since Scott is not about to promote violent rebellion. Nonetheless, through the text's satiric representation of the Spanish courtiers, he claims a significant place for popular forms of political action, detached from the operation of parliament and identified specifically with the 'bans and re-vilings' which are so characteristic of libellous dissent. Later in the decade, while Buckingham's assassin was typically lauded in manuscript culture as a noble hero, the murder in the London streets of Buckingham's servant and physician, Dr John Lambe, was figured in very different terms.[97] Before his association with Buckingham, Lambe had been convicted of rape and imprisoned for witchcraft. Subsequently, he was depicted as a quintessential manifestation of moral and political disorder at court; in the words of one pamphlet, he 'was an absolute Witch, a Sorcerer and Jugling person absolutely given over to lewd wicked and diabolicall courses'.[98] News reports of his death were equally clear about the murderers and their justification. William Whiteway noted that 'Dr Lambe the witch was beaten to death in London streetes by the boyes and apprentices'; for John Rous, the 'devill' was returning home from a play, 'and being houted and wondered at by prentises and watermen, was at length battered with stones and otherwise, and so slaine'.[99] Libels seized on the instance of popular action:

> Here Doctor Lambe the Conjurer lies,
> Who 'gainst his will untimely dies:
> The Div'll did shew himselfe a glutton,

---

[95] *The High-Waies of God and the King* (Holland, 1623), p. 86; see further Cust, 'Politics and the Electorate', pp. 138–9.

[96] *Belgicke Pismire*, pp. 36–7; see further Peltonen, *Classical Humanism and Republicanism*, pp. 247–8.

[97] For a good example of the heroic representation of Felton, see 'Immortall man of glorie, whose brave hand' (*Poems and Songs*, pp. 69–72); cf. Norbrook, *Writing the English Republic*, pp. 53–8.

[98] *A Briefe Description of the Notorious Life of John Lambe* (Amsterdam, 1628), p. 6.

[99] William Whiteway of Dorchester, *His Diary 1618 to 1635* (Dorset Record Society, vol. XII, 1991), p. 97; *Diary of John Rous*, ed. Mary Anne Everett Green (Camden Society, 1861; reprint edn, New York and London, 1968), p. 17.

> To take him, yer he was a mutton
> The Div'll in hell will rost him there,
> Whom London Prentises basted here.
> In hell they wondred when he came,
> Amongst the goats to see a lambe.[100]

The resounding endorsement of the London apprentices, whose actions are seen to prefigure Lambe's eternal judgement, is echoed in another epigram that glances meaningfully beyond this incident, to the king and his favourite. It warns: 'Let C. & G. doe what they canne, / Yett G. shall dy like Doctor Lambe'.[101]

These pieces occupy one extreme of the political spectrum; even Rous, despite his evident disgust for Lambe and his increasing anxiety about court corruption, described the latter prophecy as 'foolish and dangerous'.[102] Nonetheless, as I have argued throughout this section, satire contributed in this period to some striking revisions of political identities. In part, the origins of this process might be located in defences of a 'puritan' identity, opposed at once to papists and hypocritical 'formalists'. In part, also, it derived force from contemporary discourses of liberty. As we have seen, one eventual result, which would have vital consequences for English political culture, is a location of political rectitude outside established centres of power, among the common people.

OUR STATE'S A GAME AT CARDS: REPRESENTING
THE POLITICAL PROCESS

Yet satirists and political commentators of the 1620s were faced not only with the challenge of identifying competing political interests, but also with that of representing the interaction of various forces in the nation. The processes of interaction were at once unprecedented and mystifying; as Hill comments, 'it is of the essence of the situation that no one really understood what was happening'.[103] Crucially, the political developments of the decade also stretched the causative models previously dominant in English satire. Both medieval and classical precedents were in various ways inadequate

---

[100] BL Add. MS 44963, fol. 37r.

[101] Bodleian MS Tanner 465, fol. 100r.

[102] Rous has a variant version: 'J. and C. have done what they can, / And G. must die as did Doctor Lambe' (*Diary*, p. 26). On the development of Rous's thinking in the course of 1628, see Cogswell, 'Politics and Propaganda', 188.

[103] 'Parliament and People', 108.

to encompass the emergent conflicts, while even Tacitean discourse might seem clumsy when trying to comprehend the interconnected diplomatic, religious, social and ideological determinants of England's political situation. Within this context, Abraham Holland attacked the simple-mindedness of many contemporary satirists:

> Others that ne're search'd new borne Vice at all,
> But the *seven deadly Sinnes* in generall,
> Drawne from the Tractate of some cloyster'd Frier,
> Will needs write Satyrs, and in raging fire
> Exasperate their sharpe Poeticke straine,
> And thinke they have toucht it, if they raile at Spaine,
> The Pope and Devill.[104]

Railing at an external force such as Spain is as inadequate a response to the times as a rehearsal of medieval condemnations of the seven deadly sins. If satirists are truly to 'touch' contemporary political practices and problems, he implies, they must develop entirely new strategies of representation. In the light of this critique, I want to consider in this section the ways in which satire struggles to reassess and refashion traditional conceptions of political interaction. Although certain classical and medieval models maintain a powerful influence, we might identify some significant developments, as certain writers grapple with the circumstances of their turbulent era. Most significantly, in Middleton's *A Game at Chess* a satirist of considerable perception freshly manipulates traditional satiric resources, to produce a subtle and penetrating assessment of English politics.

The residual influence of medieval satire is apparent throughout early Stuart political discourse. One of the longest political poems of the decade, for example, is titled 'Fortunes wheele', and attempts to set a wide range of tensions and conflicts apparent during the reign of James into one of the most traditional of all explanatory models.[105] The poem certainly strains at the bounds of this model, as it presents a considerable array of detail and offers a trenchant defence of parliament. Its description of the 1624 session, for instance, notes that 'A manie fould enormities is righted / and blinded Justice is made nowe quicke sighted' (fol. 5v). But the close of each stanza rehearses afresh the causative model of 'fortunes wheele' – which 'is quicklie turnde about' – and gestures further towards supernatural powers directing the wheel's revolutions. 'The heavens doe three sunnes at one time

[104] 'A Continued Inquisition Against Paper-Persecutors' (1625); published in John Davies of Hereford, *The Scourge of Folly*, ed. Alexander Grosart (London, 1878), p. 80.
[105] 'Some would complaine of Fortune and blinde chance' (Bodleian MS Eng. poet. c.50, fols. 1r–7r).

showe', it concludes, 'yet who the secretts of the heavens knowe?' (fol. 7r).
At a time when some people were recognizing 'that time could change
not only dynasties but societies, not only individuals but institutions', this
profoundly traditional model thus offers a certain reassurance, despite its
increasingly obvious limitations.[106] A more specific commitment to providentialism underpins recurrent representations of Buckingham as a comet.
In Sir Dudley Digges's extended development of this metaphor for his 1626
speech in the Buckingham impeachment debate, the king is figured as a
'glorious Sun', which 'by his powerfull beames of grace and favour shall
draw from the bowels of this earth an exhalation that shal take fire and
burne and shine out like a starre'.[107] The star, as numerous other commentators suggest, might influence the people and disturb the nation, but it is
inevitably subject to universal forces beyond its control, whether they are
identified with the king or God. An assumption that a comet will burn 'out',
while the sun will remain 'glorious', is at least implicit in almost all such
representations.[108]

The ship of state was another image with medieval roots, yet one that
might be appropriated for the circumstances of the 1620s. One poem is
specifically related, in one manuscript, to the year 1628:

> When onely one doth rule and guide the shipp,
> Who neither card nor compasse knew before,
> The master pilot and the rest asleepe,
> The stately shipp is splitt upon the shore,
> But they awaking, start up, stare, and crye,
> 'Who did this fault?' – 'Not I!' – 'Nor I! – 'Nor I!'
> Soe fares it with a great and wealthie state,
> Not govern'd by the master, but the mate.[109]

Unlike an image such as the wheel of fortune, the ship of state may be removed from a universe governed by fate or providentialism, and set rather
alone and fragile upon the ocean. In 1628 it also invited topical allusion.
Buckingham's command of the naval expedition to the Isle of Rhé is thus
touched on in the opening lines, which conflate the Duke's failed military
leadership with his allegedly disastrous control over the state. The subsequent lines target Charles for his failure to act against Buckingham; his
indolence, like that of all others on the ship, is aptly figured in the condition of sleep. Finally, the poem's most potent barb lies in the closing
word, with its suggestion that Buckingham stands in relation to Charles as

---

[106] Woolf, *The Idea of History*, p. 25.
[107] *A Speech Delivered in Parliament* (1643), p. 5.
[108] See further Little's discussion of this metaphor ('Perpetual Metaphors', pp. 165–9).
[109] *Poems and Songs*, pp. 33–4; it is dated in Bodleian MS Malone 23, p. 120.

a wife or sexual partner. Although Buckingham's relationship with James was unquestionably eroticized, and consistently framed by the pair in a discourse of marital or familial love, there are in fact no indications at all that he had a sexual relationship with Charles. Yet sodomy, as recent scholars have argued, was at this time a generalized category of disorder, which yoked together anxieties about sexual, gender, social and political hierarchies.[110] Hence a discourse of sodomy applied to Buckingham in James's reign might reasonably be revived under Charles, to underline the poet's point about moral and political (if not necessarily sexual) subversion.

Forms of beast satire afforded slightly more flexible models for the representation of power relations. Edmund Spenser's *Prosopopoia: or Mother Hubberds Tale* (1591), a coded attack on William and Robert Cecil, established the political potential of the medieval mode; and the republication of his text in 1612, as noted in Chapter 3, reinforced its significance for a new generation.[111] In 1622, Thomas Scot published *Philomythie or Philomythologie. wherin Outlandish Birds, Beasts, and Fishes, are taught to speake true English plainely*, while John Hepwith's *The Calidonian Forest* circulated in manuscript form at the end of the decade.[112] Another text, which amply demonstrates the resources of the mode, is Richard Niccols's *The Beggers Ape* (1627). Niccols had attacked the early Jacobean court in *The Cuckow* (1607); his later work, by comparison, focuses more rigorously on a context of corruption and favouritism in the 1620s. The ape, probably representative of Buckingham, appreciates that at court, 'Onely they rise that can by guilefull wit / Serve their owne turne with gainefull benefit' (sig. B2v). But after enjoying great success, the climactic scene brings him into direct confrontation with the ox and the sheep, who boldly argue for the honest values of the country in opposition to the illusory delights of the court. Significantly, the sheep and ox are duly brought before 'the *Lyons* Councell' and arraigned 'for lewd Speech us'd 'mongst the vulgar sort / Seeking thereby to defame the Court' (sig. E1r). The forces of the country, the poem suggests, lack the legal clout of the court, and thus honest

---

[110] As Jonathan Goldberg argues, acts of sodomy in the Renaissance 'emerge into visibility only when those who are said to have done them also can be called traitors, heretics, or the like' (*Sodometries: Renaissance Texts, Modern Sexualities* (Stanford, 1992), p. 19. Comparable arguments have been made in Gregory W. Bredbeck, *Sodomy and Interpretation: Marlowe to Milton* (Ithaca and London, 1991); and Bruce R. Smith, *Homosexual Desire in Shakespeare's England: A Cultural Poetics* (Chicago and London, 1991).

[111] See Spenser, *Poetical Works*, ed. J. C. Smith and E. De Selincourt (Oxford, 1970), pp. 494–508; O'Callaghan, *The 'shepheards nation'*, p. 14.

[112] *The Calidonian Forest* was published in 1641; manuscript copies exist in Bodleian MS Malone 23, pp. 67–102, Folger MS v.a.275, pp. 63–86, and BL MS Harley 6920, pp. 1–22.

criticism is falsely translated into vulgar lewdness. Yet once the poem has developed this narrative of courtiers undermining loyal subjects, it reverts to a narrative closure entirely in accord with medieval traditions, as 'Eternall Jove' interrupts the proceedings to purge the court of corruption (sig. E2r–v). However much the poem may stretch the boundaries of its form, it ultimately imposes a neat providential model on the vicissitudes of politics.[113]

Such attempts to account for political conflict demonstrate at once the difficulty of breaking with inherited models and the urgent need for new ones, which might adequately represent their 'rowlinge tumblinge age'.[114] One poem, for example, struggles to incorporate a discussion of the decade's manifold tensions within the metaphorical framework of the king and parliament as husband and wife. The couple have 'parted in discontent' after 'Englands wanton Duke' attempted to rape the wife; she, however, 'ne're turnde up her tayle, / to him unless to kisse'.[115] More sophisticated models are afforded by certain games of chance and skill, which afford a secular logic that may break free from the prevailing moralism and providentialism of other texts. For example, one of the most widely distributed poems in early Stuart manuscript culture, which one manuscript dates as having been 'writt 2 monethes before [Buckingham's] death', is constructed around the metaphor of a game of cards.[116] If the dating is correct, the poem should be situated in the context of heated parliamentary debates over the Petition of Right, perhaps in the wake of Charles's decision to close the session early, on June 26. A further source gives it the suggestive (though possibly incomplete) title 'subject People'.[117] It reads:

> Our state's a Game at cards, the councell deale
> The Lawyers shuffle & the clergie cutt
> The King wynnes, from the loosing publique weale
> The duke keepes stakes, the courtiers plott & putt
> The Game i'th stock, & thus the citty Jumpes
> Still crosse, for why? Prerogative is trumpe.[118]

[113] See further Kathryn Perry, 'Political Animals: Spenserian Beast Satire 1591–1628' (unpublished Ph.D dissertation, University of Reading, 2000).
[114] 'Our worthy Chancellour rendred up his place' (Bodleian MS Eng. poet. c.50, fol. 13r).
[115] 'The Kinge and his wyfe the Parliament' (Bodleian MS Eng. poet. c.50, fol. 14r).
[116] Bodleian MS Ashmole 36, 37, fol. 174v. It is also dated, or titled, '1628', in Bodleian MS Rawlinson poet. 26, fol. 6v; and Bodleian MS Malone 23, p. 119.
[117] BL Add. MS 29492, fol. 56r; the top of this page may have been cropped, thus deleting words preceding these in the poem's title.
[118] Even by the standards of early Stuart manuscript circulation, this text is remarkably unstable, and an examination of over a dozen copies affords numerous variants. I will note variations from my chosen version (Bodleian MS Ashmole 36, 36, fol. 174v) where appropriate.

The poem is concerned with the subject's liberty; however, it considers that issue without a single use of the contentious term. Instead, the satiric device of a game at cards is employed to demonstrate the impotence of the subject in the face of the competing forces of the dominant powers in the state. The central confrontation is highlighted in the third line, with its stark assertion that the 'publique weale' simply lose to the king. Beyond that confrontation, the author makes a series of neat comments about the interests of the respective groups and individuals involved in the 'game'. Hence the lawyers pursue an amoral 'shuff[ling]', the clergy are associated with a random process of division, while the Duke's actions appear to serve his own interests at least as much as those of his monarch. To put 'The Game i'th stock' refers literally to the action of returning a bunch of cards to the pack after a hand has been played and won.[119] The subterfuge and finality of the action, coupled with the poem's concluding line, however, suggests an allusion to the early close of the parliamentary session. 'Prerogative', in this state, retains an authority beyond all others.[120]

The period's most sustained and successful use of games imagery for satiric purposes is contained in Thomas Middleton's play, *A Game at Chess*, which enjoyed an infamous run of nine consecutive days at the Globe Theatre in August 1624. The play represents the tensions between England and Spain around the time of the Spanish Match negotiations by using the allegorical structure of a game at chess. It thereby sets the white 'players' of English protestantism against the black of Spanish Catholicism, and focuses most pointedly on the machinations of the Black Knight, a figure clearly recognizable as Gondomar. As more than one critic has noted, *A Game at Chess* was presented at a fortuitous moment in Anglo-Spanish relations, when the dominant attitudes within government circles roughly aligned with those of outspoken protestant pamphleteers such as Thomas Scott.[121] Nevertheless, it took definite risks. Its brief season was closed on the order of the king after pleas from the Spanish ambassador, and while the official treatment of those involved appears to have been surprisingly lenient,

---

[119] One variant has 'gaines' for 'Game', which would reinforce the sense of polarization, with the king and courtiers set against the 'publique weale' (Bodleian MS Malone 23, p. 119).

[120] The positioning of the city ('thus the citty Jumpes / Still crosse') is unclear, and perhaps also baffled contemporary readers, as some scribes substituted 'all' (Bodleian MS Malone 23, p. 119) or 'the silly' (Rosenbach MS 239/27, p. 46).

[121] Thomas Cogswell, 'Thomas Middleton and the Court, 1624: *A Game at Chess* in Context', *Huntington Library Quarterly*, 47 (1984), 273–88; T. H. Howard-Hill, *Middleton's 'Vulgar Pasquin': Essays on 'A Game at Chess'* (Newark, 1995), pp. 86–7, 90.

it is possible that Middleton was imprisoned for a time.[122] Consequently, while numerous plays of the early Stuart era contain elements of political satire, *A Game at Chess* alone demands extended consideration in the present context, as a singularly notorious example of unauthorized political commentary presented on the public stage.[123]

Critics of the play have disagreed about its relative commitments to moral allegory and topical satire. From one perspective, it is predominantly an allegorical representation of the struggle between good and evil, rooted in the morality tradition which was the dominant theatrical form through to the late sixteenth century.[124] Such criticism rightly points to the fact that the play's treatment of the Spanish Match negotiations is condensed into a couple of late scenes, while the principal action centres on attempts by those from the black house to seduce the White Queen's Pawn, who stands as a central figure of protestant purity. From another perspective, however, the play is claimed as fundamentally topical, and allusions to the Spanish Match and other controversies are uncovered throughout.[125] My aim is not necessarily to enter the debate on either side, but rather to consider the way in which Middleton appropriates traditional dramatic strategies, and refashions them in accordance with the concerns of contemporary political satire. His audiences certainly appear to have recognized the play's satiric resonance. The Florentine ambassador wrote that 'it is a very satirical thing, and gives great enjoyment', while John Holles made a connection to libelling when he described it as a 'vulgar pasquin'.[126] Such comments highlight at once the play's qualities of satiric discernment and its appeal to what Holles called 'popular opinion'.[127] Like the contemporary pamphlets and libels on which Middleton drew, *A Game at Chess* was perceived to have combined populism and discrimination, in a manner that promised new insight into the machinations of politics and diplomacy.

The basic structure of *A Game at Chess* suggests a relatively conservative perception of political process. Middleton's clear identification of the black house with Spain and Catholicism locates corruption outside England, and

---

[122] T. H. Howard-Hill, 'Introduction' to *A Game at Chess* (The Revels Plays, Manchester, 1993), p. 22.
[123] On the political drama of the period, see especially: Albert H. Tricomi, *Anticourt Drama in England 1603–1642* (Charlottesville, 1987); Jerzy Limon, *Dangerous Matter: English Drama and Politics in 1623/24* (Cambridge, 1986); and Martin Butler, *Theatre and Crisis 1632–1642* (Cambridge, 1984). On the links between the play and contemporary pamphlets, see especially Howard-Hill, *Middleton's 'Vulgar Pasquin'*, pp. 237–65.
[124] See, for example, Howard-Hill, *Middleton's 'Vulgar Pasquin'*, p. 72.
[125] See, for example, Jane Sherman, 'The Pawns' Allegory in Middleton's *A Game at Chess*', *Review of English Studies*, n.s., 29 (1978), 147–59.
[126] Documents reprinted in Revels edition, pp. 201, 198.
[127] Revels edition, p. 198.

draws strict lines of demarcation between good and evil. By extension, the play's drama is based not on any particularly complex interaction between the houses, but rather on the process of 'discovery', as the white players relentlessly expose their opponents' corruption. In fact the play ends with a 'checkmate by discovery', when the White Knight and White Duke (respectively figures of Charles and Buckingham) trick the Black Knight into revealing his Machiavellian political manoeuvres. Comparable strategies govern Middleton's representation of Gondomar as the Black Knight. As Dorothy M. Farr has argued, Middleton took 'certain risks' when he revived the stage Machiavel, since by 1624 'the bogey politician . . . with his tortuous brain and his schemes veiled in the mystery of a superhuman intelligence, had had his day'.[128] Yet the Black Knight is simultaneously imaged in the terms of popular discourse, developed in libels and memorably directed against Gondomar in Scott's pamphlets. Contemporary reports make it clear that he was carried onto the stage in a sedan chair, identical to that used by Gondomar, with a hole cut in the seat to accommodate his anal fistula. In the play, as in popular discourse, this physical inconvenience provides a focus for richly scatological imagery of corruption, seen to infect both the Spanish body and the English body politic. The Black Knight thus admits to 'a foul flaw in the bottom of my drum', and calls for 'my chair of ease, my chair of cozenage' (IV ii 7, 3). Another character, describing him as 'the fistula of Europe', claims that 'once I undertook to cure [his disease] / With a High Holborn halter' (II ii 46–8). In a strategy familiar from the libels considered in Chapter 2, the corporeal affliction is associated with failures in political relations, and the only 'cure' is that reserved for the moral turpitude of the felon.

Other aspects of Middleton's satiric practice, meanwhile, complicate the neat polarization between black and white. As other critics have suggested, the satire of *A Game at Chess* might be seen to glance in more than one direction, raising questions about the English as well as the Spanish.[129] This degree of complexity is in part a function of the play's conception of characterization. 'In contrast to its archaic form,' Paul Yachnin argues, 'the language of *A Game at Chess* is remarkably modern – complex, flexible, and expressive of characters' inward lives as well as of their outward roles in the play's *psychomachia*.'[130] Moreover, the concern with inwardness is derived

---

[128] *Thomas Middleton and the Drama of Realism: A Study of Some Representative Plays* (Edinburgh, 1973), p. III.

[129] See especially Paul Yachnin, '*A Game at Chess*: Thomas Middleton's "Praise of Folly"', *Modern Language Quarterly*, 48 (1987), 107–23; and Richard A. Davies and Alan R. Young, '"Strange Cunning" in Thomas Middleton's *A Game at Chess*', *University of Toronto Quarterly*, 45 (1976), 236–45.

[130] '*A Game at Chess*', 121.

largely from Middleton's use of a protestant discourse of conscience, familiar from the political satire examined above.[131] Suitably, while the Black Knight admits that his conscience is 'becalmed', and thus senseless to the stirrings of sin (IV ii 39), the conscience of the protestant is a more active agent, which frustrates the Catholics' attempts to uncover its workings. Within this framework, the Black Bishop's Pawn's pursuit of the White Queen's Pawn, which is the play's central intrigue, is represented as a projected spiritual as well as physical violation. He says:

> Resolve you thus far, lady,
> The privat'st thought that runs to hide itself
> In the most secret corner of your heart now
> Must be of my acquaintance, so familiarly
> Never she-friend of your night-counsel nearer.
>   (I i 122–6)

The White Queen's Pawn is vulnerable to this assault because she struggles to reconcile her independence of judgement, under the eyes of God, with a commitment to 'obedience', which is 'a virtue / I have ever thought on with especial reverence' (I i 191–2). The challenge she is posed is to disentangle, and correctly prioritize, competing forms of obedience.

While the White Queen's Pawn survives the attempts made upon her, Middleton further explores the potential for the individual conscience to set a person apart from a group through the character of the Black Knight's Pawn. This Pawn has previously castrated the White Bishop's Pawn, and as a result engages in an agonized process of self-scrutiny. 'The sting of conscience', he declares, 'takes away / My joy, my rest' (II i 227–30). He later tells the Jesuit Black Bishop's Pawn:

> I have a worm
> Follows me so that I can follow no game;
> The most faint-hearted pawn, if he could see his play,
> Might snap me up at pleasure. I desire, sir,
> To be absolved; my conscience being at ease,
> I could then with more courage ply my game.
>   (IV i 19–24)

The joke underpinning this debilitating remorse is that, while the Jesuits' casuistic 'book of general pardons of all prices' (IV ii 83) stipulates monetary sums that will buy absolution for virtually any conceivable sin, it says

---

[131] Farr acknowledges that the 'theme of conscience', which 'has its interest for Middleton in other connections', is especially prominent in this play; however, she does not pursue the point (*Thomas Middleton*, p. 101). See my discussion above, pp. 66–8, and pp. 105–6.

nothing about castration. Yet the play's satire also reaches further than this straightforward anti-Catholic barb might suggest. The Black Knight's Pawn's examination of his conscience in fact challenges the very premise of absolution, and suggests further the uselessness within the 'game' of the man stricken by a disturbed conscience. He does not abandon his side, but nor does he further its ends.

On the other side, the White King's Pawn is specifically revealed as a traitor, and this too is represented in terms of a contrast between outward appearances and inner realities. Adopting a corporeal term commonly associated with the conscience, he tells the Black Knight: 'You see my outside, but you know my heart, Knight, / Great difference in the colour' (1 i 313–14).[132] This archetypal representation of treachery is used by Middleton as the basis for topical satire, with the White King's Pawn almost certainly fashioned as a figure of Lionel Cranfield, Earl of Middlesex, who was an opponent of a Spanish war, and was impeached shortly before Middleton's play was produced.[133] Moreover, the scene in which his deceit is revealed directs attention from the basic contrast between external and internal allegiances, towards processes of courtly fashioning within the white house:

> BLACK KNIGHT. See what sure piece you lock your confidence in.
> I made this pawn here by corruption ours,
> As soon as honour by creation yours;
> This whiteness upon him is but the leprosy
> Of pure dissimulation. View him now:
> His heart and his intents are of our colour.
>   . . .
> WHITE KING.   Has my goodness,
> Clemency, love, and favour gracious raised thee
> From a condition next to popular labour,
> Took thee from all the dubitable hazards
> Of fortune, her most unsecure adventures,
> And grafted thee into a branch of honour,
> And dost thou fall from the top-bough by the rottenness
> Of thy alone corruption, like a fruit
> That's over-ripened by the beams of favour?
> Let thy own weight reward thee, I have forgot thee;
> Integrity of life is so dear to me

---

[132] On the heart, see above, pp. 65–6.
[133] The identification was first made by R. C. Bald, in his 1929 Cambridge edition of the play (pp. 11–12). Howard-Hill discusses, from an analysis of variant sources, the way in which Middleton infused this topical satire into the play (*Middleton's 'Vulgar Pasquin'*, pp. 63–5).

Where I find falsehood or a crying trespass,
Be it in any whom our grace shines most on,
I'd tear 'em from my heart.

(III i 256–76)

The White King's Pawn's corruption is represented in conventionally physical terms. For the White King, he is 'like a fruit . . . over-ripened by the
beams of favour', and rotting within; for the Black Knight, the whiteness
is rather analogous to a physical disease, as he coins the metaphor of his
white dress as 'the leprosy / Of pure dissimulation'. Yet each man is equally
concerned with the fact that the White King's Pawn has been shaped by
'honour' as much as by 'corruption'. In his expansion of the fruit metaphor,
the White King states that the pawn was 'grafted . . . into a branch of honour'
(probably a reference to the marriage of Cranfield to Anne Brett, a relative
of Buckingham). Hence the extent to which this Pawn has flourished within
the white house not only suggests the gullibility of its rulers, but also poses
important challenges to the very principles upon which white and black
are distinguished in the play. Middleton's strikingly modern attention to
the construction of subjectivity – which considers both 'conscience' and
'honour', subjective and social forces – thus threatens to deconstruct the
play's otherwise neat polarities between good and evil. The White King's
final image for the purging of corruption, when he declares that he will
'tear' corruption 'from my heart', is entirely appropriate. It suggests a need
for a form of self-mutilation which will affect both body politic and body
natural. Given the play's consistent attention to the conscience and the
'heart', it visualizes a process of probing to the very core of his own being.

The possibility of corruption within the white house must therefore
be acknowledged as a fundamental premise of the play. This is a world
in which the fixed identities of the morality give way to the more com-
plexly subjective, and potentially satiric, vision of the Jacobean stage. As
one White Pawn comments casually, 'white quickly soils' (III ii 12). Richard
A. Davies and Alan R. Young argue that the unmasking of the White King's
Pawn reveals the 'true nature' of the white house, and that the play as a
whole works to 'destroy any sense of distinction between the two houses'.[134]
While their interpretation seems to me overstated, and gives too much cre-
dence to the words of the black players, it certainly directs attention to
Middleton's problematization of the distinctions between good and evil
in the arena of political action. Consequently, as other critics have recognized, the play can embrace some sharp notes of satire directed against

[134] '"Strange Cunning"', 240.

the English court. The Black Knight, for example, boasts that 'The [white] court has held the city by the horns / Whilst I have milked her' (III i 108–9): a claim that directly echoes charges laid against the court by contemporary pamphleteers, and thus invites the London audience to question the purity of their white house.[135] While the conflict between the court and city may here be attributed to an external source of evil, the power and the integrity of the court is distinctly impugned.

Within this context, the most sensitive task Middleton faced was the representation of the White Knight and the White Duke. While the majority of critics have argued, with Trevor Howard-Hill, that Charles and Buckingham could not have 'read the play without gratification at the manner in which they were depicted', others have identified evidence that the key white players are not entirely free of taints. Crucially, in the climactic scene of 'checkmate by discovery', the White Knight and White Duke elicit the Black Knight's confession of moral enormities after first pretending to vices of their own. Among other things, the White Duke hints at sexual indiscretions:

> WHITE DUKE. Some that are pleased to make a wanton on't
> Call it infirmity of blood, flesh-frailty,
> But certain there's a worse name in your books for't.
> BLACK KNIGHT. The trifle of all vices, the mere innocent,
> The very novice of this house of clay: venery!
> If I but hug thee hard I show the worst on't.
>
> (v iii 121–6)

This confession aligns unmistakably with Buckingham's popular reputation for lasciviousness, which had been shaped in part by libellous poems and pamphlets.[136] Further, as Margot Heinemann has suggested, the Black Knight's response, perhaps accompanied by a 'hard' hug (possibly even from behind), carries 'more than a hint of homosexual lechery'.[137] The specificity and topicality of these lines thereby inject a destabilizing note of satire, despite the fact that they are presented merely as mock-confessions.

More fundamentally, this scene indicates the white house's commitment to courtly arts of dissimulation. Throughout the play, Middleton represents the Black Knight as the archetypal dissembler, thereby associating

[135] Cf. Margot Heinemann, *Puritanism and Theatre: Thomas Middleton and Opposition Drama under the Early Stuarts* (Cambridge, 1980), pp. 160–1.
[136] See esp. Knowles, 'To "scourge the arse"', p. 78.
[137] *Puritanism and Theatre*, p. 164. 'Hug' is accepted contemporary slang for a coital embrace (Gordon Williams, *A Dictionary of Sexual Language and Imagery in Shakespearean and Stuart Literature*, [3 vols., London and Atlantic Highlands, 1994], II.697–8).

the capacity for deception with Catholicism and immorality. As the Black Knight declares to the White Knight, in a *tour de force* of dissembling:

> I will change
> To any shape to please you, and my aim
> Has been to win your love in all this game.
>   (IV iv 42–4)

The manifold ironies of this statement, as the Black Knight invokes an established courtly rhetoric of 'love' in his attempt to win the favour and hence cause the overthrow of his counterpart, are multiplied at the play's conclusion when precisely the opposite result occurs. The White Knight's final mock-confession is that he is 'an arch-dissembler', and has never yet 'spoke / What my heart meant' (v iii 145–8). This prompts the Black Knight's admission that 'what we have done / Has been dissemblance ever', and that in turn causes the White Knight to proclaim 'checkmate by / Discovery' (v iii 158–61). In fact, therefore, the White Knight's skill in dissimulation is exactly what wins the game. The side of protestant virtue triumphs as a result of its greater abilities in manipulating 'the "games" that politicians play'.[138]

A Game at Chess, with its apparent location of evil in a stigmatized and externalized other, but its nagging sense of shadowy forces of corruption within England, to a considerable extent typifies the political satire of the 1620s. As I have argued throughout this part of the book, writers in this decade sought new strategies for the representation of tensions within the state, and the literary resources of satire proved instrumental to their project. The satiric writing that proliferated in the early Stuart era marked a radical break with orthodox models of counsel and subjecthood. Instead, satiric writing posited an articulate and outspoken citizen, with an identity grounded in a protestant conscience rather than any relation to secular power. Upon this basis, numerous texts struggled to comprehend the unprecedented political upheavals of the decade, and their achievements encoded important new discourses of conflict. The writers to be considered in the final chapters, though their work overlaps with much of the material considered here, grasped still more clearly and surely the significance of these emergent confrontations. In their writings, therefore, we might trace further the insistent emergence of an early Stuart politics and poetics of division.

---

[138] Limon, *Dangerous Matter*, p. 103.

PART III

The politics of division

CHAPTER 5

Satire and sycophancy: Richard Corbett and early Stuart royalism

Richard Corbett (1582–1635) was one of the most popular poets in manuscript circulation in the first half of the seventeenth century. Although his work has rarely attracted the attention of modern readers, in Corbett's lifetime only the poetry of John Donne was more prevalent in manuscript verse miscellanies. [1] Indeed much of the appeal of Corbett may be attributed to the fact that he situated himself at the heart of the period's flourishing culture of manuscript composition and compilation. For the first thirty years of the century he was associated with the most important centre of manuscript culture, Christ Church, Oxford: as an undergraduate, Student (i.e., fellow), Dean, and finally as the Bishop of Oxford. Within this time he not only wrote poems and encouraged other poets, but also involved himself unashamedly in controversy and debate, over issues of local and national concern. In the 1620s, his close ties with George Villiers, Duke of Buckingham, marked him as a spokesman for the politics of the early Stuart court, and in turn invited responses that dismissed him as a signal example of sycophancy. But while Corbett's poetry may expose itself to charges of self-interest and naivety, I intend to consider it more seriously, within the context of a literary culture in which the modes of satire and panegyric were equally under strain, as writers were forced to reassess the assumptions of community upon which each was typically founded. Corbett's existence and activities within this culture, I argue, helped to define a new politics and poetics of controversy.

Corbett was a man who wrote poetry when he felt that occasion required him to do so, rather than a poet who chose to write occasional verse. Consequently his output is at once slight (covering less than a hundred pages in the modern edition) and historically specific. [2] Although this

---

[1] Mary Hobbs, *Early Seventeenth-Century Verse Miscellany Manuscripts* (Aldershot, 1992), p. 3. (Hobbs links Corbett and his friend William Strode in this respect.)

[2] *The Poems of Richard Corbett*, ed. J. A. W. Bennet and H. R. Trevor-Roper (Oxford, 1955). Unless stated otherwise, all references are to this edition.

approach to poetry has undoubtedly deterred modern readers, it binds him tightly to a context of court patronage, and consequently thrusts him to the forefront of a study concerned with the politics of early Stuart poetry. His engagement with politics is evident in his two favoured modes of poetry: on the one hand, patronage poems, which identify the poet with the values and aspirations of his addressee; and on the other hand, satiric assaults on political and religious opponents. Indeed Corbett's combination of satire and panegyric situates him within a literary culture which was, as demonstrated in the previous chapters, becoming increasingly concerned with manifestations of political division. In Chapter 2 I considered the ways in which traditions of epideictic rhetoric – the rhetoric of praise and blame – were appropriated for unauthorized poems of stigmatization. As I argued in that chapter, however, the culture of libelling, especially in the early part of our period, was violently contestatory without being clearly polarized. By comparison, Corbett was a man utterly committed to the prevailing structures of power, who appreciated as well as anyone the political logic of a poetics of discrimination. I argue here that Corbett's work cannot simply be dismissed as lazy and sycophantic. Rather, a contextual reading of Corbett demonstrates the emergence of a trenchant conservative response to the insistent early Stuart expressions of political dissent. The substance of this response, I suggest, helps to delineate the contours of Caroline royalism.

This chapter, which is concerned at once with Corbett himself and the culture he helped to shape, begins by considering the relationship between patronage and praise in Renaissance verse: discussing the rhetorical and political context, then looking briefly at the work of Ben Jonson, before examining Corbett's own distinctive poetics of flattery. In Corbett's work, I suggest, rhetorical excess and unashamed self-interest may be seen as logical responses to a milieu in which assumptions of common values were fracturing under the weight of political dissension. The subsequent section focuses on Corbett's satire. While his anti-puritan satires pursue apparently conventional strategies of stigmatization, they are underpinned by consistent efforts to translate religious categories into political terms, a project which is powerfully extended in his poem 'Against the Opposing of the Duke in Parliament, 1628'. As considered above in Chapter 4 – and as becomes more sharply apparent in Chapter 6 – this represents one side of a process of polarization, which would have widespread and ultimately violent consequences. Finally, I turn to the political culture of the early 1630s, a time when Corbett's own relative inactivity was paralleled by the apparent reluctance of other poets to tackle political issues.

A brief comparison of Corbett with Jonson and Thomas Carew, how-ever, reveals a subdued though deeply entrenched acceptance of political division.

THE POLITICS AND POETICS OF PRAISE

Panegyric leans uneasily against satire, the two modes bound together as positive and negative statements of discrimination, equally reliant upon assumptions of common moral and ideological values. For the Elizabethan George Puttenham, this relationship was relatively straightforward; he claimed that the act of discrimination underpins all poetry, which is con-cerned with either 'the laud honour & glory of the immortall gods' or 'the praise of vertue & reproofe of vice'.[3] In this respect poetry assumed a distinctly public function, since only the poet (in the words of Jonson) 'can faine a *Common-wealth* . . . can governe it with *Counsels*, strengthen it with *Lawes*, correct it with *Judgements*, informe it with *Religion*, and *Morals*'.[4] Yet this function was problematized by growing appreciations of the manipulations involved in both rhetoric and poetry, and there-fore of the inherent difficulty of determining fixed and clear grounds for acts of discrimination. I outlined these issues in Chapter 2; here, though, it is worth considering more closely the tensions inherent within panegyric, and the ways in which the conditions of early Stuart England exacerbated them. As I have been arguing throughout, this was a culture intensely scep-tical about the relation between language and power. Hence, while Francis Bacon could state boldly that 'Praise is the reflection of virtue', he appreci-ated as well as anybody the extent to which the position and motivation of the praiser would inform statements of panegyric.[5] Discrimination might thus be subordinated to personal prejudice or political interest; and within such a context, notwithstanding the sanguine views of Puttenham, the composition of 'stately *Panegyricks*' may not necessarily serve the interests of a unified state.[6]

This problem of panegyric was embedded in traditions of epideictic rhetoric. Although the rhetoric of praise and blame was based on as-sumptions of factual content, the relation between truth and language was

[3] *The Arte of English Poesie*, ed. Gladys Doidge Willcock and Alice Walker (Cambridge, 1936), p. 24.
[4] *Ben Jonson*, ed. C. H. Herford, Percy Simpson and Evelyn Simpson (11 vols., Oxford, 1925–52), VIII.595. All subsequent references are to this text.
[5] *The Essays*, ed. John Pitcher (London, 1985), p. 215.
[6] Roger Tisdale, *Pax Vobis* (1623), p. 1.

notoriously problematic.[7] Aristotle had taught that personal qualities could be manipulated rhetorically; hence 'an irascible and excitable person' may be praised as '"straightforward" and an arrogant person "high-minded" and "imposing"'.[8] The analysis of such acts of 'moral redescription' was developed further by Quintilian, and subsequently became a commonplace of Renaissance rhetorical theory, which classified the manipulation illustrated by Aristotle as *paradiastole*.[9] It was argued that, since certain vices and virtues were closely related, a skilful rhetorician may on the one hand 'go some way towards excusing or extenuating an evil action by imposing upon it the name of an adjoining virtue'; or, on the other hand, 'he can ... denigrate or depreciate a good action by imposing upon it the name of some bordering vice'.[10] According to one conventional statement, a flatterer might thus call 'anger severity: fury: zeale, rashnesse: boldnesse: pride, fortitude: pusillanimitie, humilitie: covetousnesse, parcimony, or the like'.[11] (In a subsequent tract, the same writer worried over the way that a detractor might simply reverse these translations: 'if a man be liberall, hee is prodigall: if parsimonious, covetous'; and so on.)[12] Certain Tudor rhetoricians even concluded 'that the figure of paradiastole can actually be *defined* as a method of excusing the vices by redescribing them as virtues'.[13] Other commentators identified the potential for epideictic discrimination to be translated into the arts of flattery and defamation, and argued that 'flatterers and sclaunderous reproches' equally depart from a goal of honest counsel.[14] Each act, that is, simultaneously destabilizes structures of linguistic and political order; as another wrote, flattery is 'a base merchandise of words, a plausible discord of the heart, and lips'.[15]

For poets, an appreciation of such strategies brought a sense of power, but also instilled anxiety. Puttenham speaks with pride about the way that *paradiastole* can 'excuse a fault' or 'make an offence seeme lesse then it is'; and even Sir Philip Sidney, despite his eagerness to confute the claim that poets are 'the principal liars' of the commonwealth, concludes *A Defence of*

---

[7] Brian Vickers, 'Epideictic and Epic in the Renaissance', *New Literary History*, 14 (1983), 513.

[8] *Aristotle on Rhetoric*, trans. George A. Kennedy (Oxford, 1991), p. 83.

[9] See Quentin Skinner, *Reason and Rhetoric in the Philosophy of Thomas Hobbes* (Cambridge, 1996), pp. 138–80.

[10] Skinner, *Reason and Rhetoric*, p. 156.

[11] [William Cavendish], *A Discourse Against Flatterie* (1611), pp. 36–7. On the authorship of this tract, see Skinner, *Reason and Rhetoric*, p. 169.

[12] [William Cavendish], *Horæ Subsecivæ: Observations and Discourses* (1620), p. 54.

[13] Skinner, *Reason and Rhetoric*, p. 163.

[14] *A Plaine description of the Auntient Petigree of Dame Slaunder* (1573), sig. B2v.

[15] [Cavendish], *Discourse Against Flatterie*, p. 4.

Poesy by boasting of the power of his art to shape reputations.[16] Subsequent
writers, however, were more troubled, as they perceived at once that moral
categories could be made to seem merely arbitrary, and that definitions
of virtue might then be appropriated to serve personal or political causes.
Jonson, whose career within the milieu of the early Stuart court was founded
on poetry of praise and blame, and whose work will warrant close attention
in the present context, thus commented that the writer 'that malignes
all' is equally culpable as the one 'that praises all' (VIII.613). As one of the
leading panegyrists of the era, Jonson struggled continually to justify his art
against charges of flattery, and appealed repeatedly to abstract values which
might stabilize otherwise slippery claims. In one statement, for example,
he claimed that 'It cannot be Flatterie, in me . . . and lesse then Love, and
Truth it is not, where it is done out of *Knowledge*' (VII.232): the apparently
disinterested purity of 'knowledge' thereby grounding the poet's mysterious
fusion of 'Love, and Truth'.[17] At a time when others were appreciating just
how malleable ideas of 'love' and 'truth' could be, Jonson tries desperately
to found his very poetic identity upon them.

   Patronage relations, as suggested in earlier chapters, further worked to
politicize the work of poets, implicating them within factional disputes and
ideological struggles. Structures of patronage, which were an accepted fact
of life for the vast majority of poets, were indebted to the Senecan theory
that society was based on the exchange of mutual benefits.[18] A client's praise
of a patron, however, was always liable to be perceived rather as flattery:
'the earewig of the mightie'.[19] The experience of Jonson in this respect is
again exemplary. The 'laureate' identity that Jonson attempted to maintain
depended on a reputation for integrity and discrimination, and for this
reason he aimed throughout his career to reconcile praise and honesty.[20]
Jonathan Goldberg draws attention to the 'fantasy of power' that Jonson
admitted to William Drummond: 'he heth a minde to be a churchman, &
so he might have favour to make one Sermon to the King, he careth not
what y'after sould befall him, for he would not flatter though he saw Death'
(I.141). This is a fantasy of independent counsel (rather than 'rebellion', as

---

[16] *Arte of English Poesie*, p. 220; *Sir Philip Sidney*, ed. Katherine Duncan-Jones (Oxford, 1989), pp. 235,
   249–50. (Cf. Jonathan Goldberg, *James I and the Politics of Literature: Jonson, Shakespeare, Donne,
   and Their Contemporaries* [Baltimore and London, 1983], p. 227.)
[17] See further Jean Le Drew Metcalfe, 'Subjecting the King: Ben Jonson's Praise of James I', *English
   Studies in Canada*, 17 (1991), 135.
[18] Linda Levy Peck, *Court Patronage and Corruption in Early Stuart England* (London, 1993), pp. 10–12.
[19] [Cavendish], *Discourse Against Flatterie*, p. 42.
[20] Richard Helgerson, *Self-Crowned Laureates: Spenser, Jonson, Milton and the Literary System* (Berkeley
   and London, 1983), p. 172; Metcalfe, 'Subjecting the King', 135.

Goldberg contends), but one predicated on a source of authority unavailable to the fundamentally secular poet.[21] Within the competitive literary culture he inhabited, it is in fact hardly surprising that the most notorious literary attack on Jonson, Thomas Dekker's representation of Horace in *Satiromastix*, presents him as a flatterer and literary opportunist, whose attitude towards his patrons is consciously cynical.[22] As Jonson himself 'confess[ed]' in a verse epistle to John Selden, he had indeed on occasion 'too oft preferr'd / Men past their termes, and prais'd some names too much' (VIII.159; lines 19–21).

Precariously situated thus between flattery and praise, sycophancy and a qualified autonomy, Jonson's patronage poetry recurrently meditates on the nature of its project. As several critics have argued, this produces anxious and paradoxically self-negating poetry, which consistently asserts the failures of poetic representation in the face of true virtue.[23] The especially fraught position of the poet in relation to political authority is evident in one of three epigrams Jonson wrote to Robert Cecil, James's secretary of state, probably around 1605. Cecil, as Jonson commented to Drummond, 'never cared for any man longer nor he could make use of him'; however, in the first decade of James's reign, a time when Jonson's own career at court oscillated between ostracism and endorsement, his patronage was crucial.[24] But rather than openly praise his subject, Jonson dwells on the function of the poet:

What need hast thou of me? or of my *Muse?*
    Whose actions so themselves doe celebrate;
Which should thy countries love to speake refuse,
    Her foes enough would fame thee, in their hate.
'Tofore, great men were glad of *Poets:* Now,
    I, not the worst, am covetous of thee.
Yet dare not, to my thought, lest hope allow
    Of adding to thy fame; thine may to me,
When, in my booke, men reade but CECILL's name,

[21] *James I and the Politics of Literature*, p. 221.
[22] Printed in *'Poetaster' by Ben Jonson and 'Satiromastix' by Thomas Dekker*, ed. Josiah H. Penniman (Boston and London, 1913). See Robert C. Evans, *Ben Jonson and the Poetics of Patronage* (Lewisburg, 1989), p. 148.
[23] See esp. Stanley Fish, 'Author-Readers: Jonson's Community of the Same', *Representations*, 7 (1984), 26–58; Helgerson, *Self-Crowned Laureates*, pp. 101–84; Evans, *Ben Jonson and the Poetics of Patronage*.
[24] *Ben Jonson*, 1.142; quoted in Robert Wiltenburg, '"What need hast thou of me? or of my *Muse?*": Jonson and Cecil, Politician and Poet', in Claude J. Summers and Ted-Larry Pebworth, eds., *'The Muses Common-Weale': Poetry and Politics in the Seventeenth Century* (Columbia, 1988), p. 37.

> And what I write thereof find farre, and free
> From servile flatterie (common *Poets* shame)
> As thou stand'st cleere of the necessitie.
>
> (VIII.40–1)

There are some tensions here, borne out of the poet's struggle to reconcile himself with his subordinate position. While it is perhaps an overstatement to claim that the poem is 'full of suppressed violence', there is definitely a subtext of edgy constraint, evident especially in the isolated and 'covetous' Jonsonian 'I', a central note of self-assertion on which the piece hinges.[25] Jonson is aware that the lines of a patronage poet can never simply be 'free', in the manner claimed by the determinedly independent George Wither; rather, in a careful qualification underscored by enjambment, they are 'free / From servile flatterie'.[26] As much as it may draw attention to this context, however, the poem functions nonetheless as an artful statement of praise, established on the familiar conceit of the poet's inability to augment Cecil's 'fame'. Indeed, in another typical Jonsonian gesture, the poem ultimately rests on 'CECILL's name'. As Stanley Fish has argued, this strategy resists the politically troublesome labour of representation, and appears on the surface to render the poem superfluous.[27] But what it does achieve is an assumption of 'a circle of admiration, sympathy, obligation, and common effort', which aligns the poet with his patron – lifting them both above the level of the 'servile' and the 'common' – even as it ostensibly denies the efficacy of panegyric.[28]

The Cecil epigram thus asserts virtue by implying a community founded on its acceptance, and in this way seeks to resolve the nagging question of how the poet can authorize his claims and avoid charges of flattery. Significantly, the statesman's 'foes' are situated unproblematically beyond his 'country', and the poem insists on the integrity of a nation united in 'love'. Yet this reification of nationhood and apparent suppression of politics might just as well function, especially for a politicized readership, as an implicit reminder of the existence of dissent *within* the state.[29] Such problematic manoeuvres, which almost unavoidably engage in politics while attempting to transcend the political, typify Jonson's panegyrics on statesmen and

---

[25] Cf. Wiltenburg, '"What need hast thou of me? or of my *Muse*?"', p. 42.
[26] On Wither, see above, esp. pp. 103–4.
[27] Fish, 'Author-Readers', 34.
[28] Wiltenburg, '"What need hast thou of me? or of my *Muse*?"', p. 40.
[29] Cf. Curtis Perry, *The Making of Jacobean Culture: James I and the Renegotiation of Elizabethan Literary Practice* (Cambridge, 1997), pp. 37–8; and Evans, *Ben Jonson and the Poetics of Patronage*, p. 99.

courtiers. An epigram 'To Thomas, Earl of Suffolk', for instance, situates
its subject equally 'high' in fame and deed. It concludes:

> And thou design'd to be the same thou art,
>   Before thou wert it, in each good mans heart.
> Which, by no lesse confirm'd, then thy kings choice,
>   Proves, that it is gods, which was the peoples voice.

(VIII.49)

Goldberg has persuasively argued that the king functions in Jonson's poetry
as a figure of ultimate authority, legitimating praise and valorizing desires;
hence 'Salisbury, Suffolk, and their ilk are representative men because they
represent the king'.[30] But such an interpretation seems inadequate for this
poem, which curiously mystifies relations between the constituent loci of
authority in the state. The conflation of king and god is of course hardly
unconventional, and it seems appropriate that the 'designer' of Suffolk's
greatness should remain syntactically ambiguous. Yet the focus, in the same
sentence, on 'each good mans heart' invokes a model of political subjectivity that is apparently contained though theoretically autonomous; and
the closing couplet, with its resonant rhyme on 'kings choice' and 'peoples
voice', suggests a delicate coalition of interests. While the poem is sustained
by Jonson's imperious ability to position himself at the centre of this polity,
his informing myth of unity and cohesion is both syntactically and ideolog-
ically tenuous, and stands in danger of rupture under the political strains
of the era.

   In fact, for all the artistic and political labours of Jonson's patronage
poetry, it is arguable that his strategies were in the process of becoming
outmoded by the time that Corbett rose to prominence. This is one consequence of the processes I am concerned to trace throughout this book.
Significantly, in the course of James's reign the government restructured the
patronage system, demonstrating an escalating preparedness to sell honours,
titles and offices in order to maximize its own income. As Linda Levy Peck
has demonstrated, this fuelled increasing court corruption, which in turn
led to a reassessment of 'the boundaries between legitimate and corrupt
transactions'.[31] In the preceding chapters of this book I have argued that
such developments stimulated new practices and discourses of dissent; not
surprisingly, however, they also appear to have affected discourses of praise.
Jonson himself perceived a troubling inflation of flattery in his lifetime.
He claimed in *Discoveries* that 'it is come to that extreme folly, or rather

---

[30] Goldberg, *James I and the Politics of Literature*, p. 224.
[31] Peck, *Court Patronage and Corruption*, p. 5.

madnesse, with some: that he that flatters them modestly, or sparingly, is thought to maligne them' (VIII.597). By implication, a poet will achieve greater success within this system through an approach that is at once openly sycophantic and unashamedly political, identifying with a patron in direct opposition to that person's acknowledged opponents. In the words of a contemporary court manual, 'wee must sometimes permit our selves to flatter, thereby to worke and skrew our selves into our *Princes* favour'.[32] While such writing seemed to many poets a kind of 'base servile fawning', it is worth considering it within its context, as a successful approach that contributed to significant modifications of political discourse.[33]

Corbett emerges as a pivotal figure in a study of these processes. Far from mystifying political contestation, in the professedly detached and au-tonomous Jonsonian manner, Corbett's patronage poetry self-consciously embraces a culture of confrontation. Crucially, at a time when libelling was appreciated within manuscript culture as a pre-eminent demonstration of wit, Corbett developed for the same sphere a form of anti-libels, 'offering rival interpretations of controversial events or attacking those whom the libellers criticised'.[34] Hence an early Corbett poem, written on the death in 1615 of Lord William Howard, directs its attention specifically to a culture of news and popular political discourse (pp. 20–3). Corbett claims to find a remarkable dearth of libels on the occasion of Howard's death, and glances in the process towards established practices of dissent:

> Nor was it modest in thee to depart
> To thy eternall home, where now thou art,
> Ere thy reproach was ready: or to die
> Ere custome had prepard thy calumny.
> Eight daies have past since thou hast paid thy debt
> To sinne, and not a libell stirring yet:
> Courtiers that scoffe by Patent, silent sit,
> And have no use of Slander or of wit:
> But (which is monstrous) though against the tyde,
> The Water-men have neither rayld nor lide.
>
> (lines 57–66)

---

[32] Eustache Du Refuge, *A Treatise of the Court or Instructions for Courtiers*, trans. John Reynolds (1622), p. 22.

[33] Henry Reynolds, 'Mythomystes', in *Critical Essays of the Seventeenth Century*, ed. J. E. Spingarn (3 vols., Oxford, 1908–9), 1.155: quoted in David Norbrook, *Poetry and Politics in the English Renaissance*, revised edn (Oxford, 2002), p. 178.

[34] Alastair Bellany, 'The Poisoning of Legitimacy? Court Scandal, News Culture, and Politics in England 1603–1660' (unpublished Ph.D dissertation, Princeton University, 1995), p. 115.

Though couched as a statement of Howard's spotless reputation, the passage
is in fact based on a curious logic, which prefigures Corbett's work of the
1620s. To be involved perforce in a world of 'sinne', the poem suggests, is
to be exposed to the universal 'custome' of 'calumny'; and to be involved
successfully in the realm of politics is to incite scoffs and libels. While
Corbett in this poem does little more than scold the writers of such poetry,
his later poetry is by comparison far more willing to engage directly with
them, in a determinedly political manner.

Indeed Corbett's most significant patronage poetry, produced over the
following fifteen years, was written for a man far more deeply embroiled
in political and personal controversy, the Duke of Buckingham. Corbett
attached himself to the rising favourite very soon after the Howards fell
from power in the wake of the Overbury murder trial.[35] This was an as-
tute decision. During the latter reign of James, Buckingham assumed a
virtual 'monopoly of patronage'; as his critics claimed, the Duke gained
influence over every 'place . . . of justice . . . office of the crowne [and] degree of honor in the kingdome'.[36] Within the Church his overriding influence over preferments prompted the satiric comment that he was 'ad-
mirall of our bishops' seas, / As well as of the straites'.[37] Concurrently,
the unique position and personality of the Duke appear to have impelled
the development of a new mode of panegyric, which Corbett would do
more than any other poet to define. Though unquestionably and unflinch-
ingly sycophantic, such poetry fundamentally rejects the standards of poets
who were more independent in outlook. Consequently, to dismiss such
poetry as tending 'towards blandness', and evidencing 'a polish that excluded serious commitment', may be to overlook the very different codes
within which it is framed.[38] In contrast to the work of a writer such as
Jonson, this poetry effectively isolates the relationship between poet and
patron, commits itself unashamedly to the task of representing the patron's interests and values, and seeks judgement purely in terms of tangible
reward.[39]

This approach is evident in a poem written by Corbett early in the 1620s,
presumably to thank Buckingham for the poet's advancement in June 1620

---

[35] Bennett and Trevor-Roper, 'Introduction', *Poems of Richard Corbett*, p. xix.

[36] Peck, *Court Patronage and Corruption*, p. 4; George Eglisham, *The Forerunner of Revenge* (Frankfort?, 1626), p. 10.

[37] 'Rejoyce, brave English gallants' (*Poems and Songs*, p. 17).

[38] Norbrook, *Poetry and Politics*, p. 209.

[39] Cf. Joseph A. Taylor's arguments about the impact of Buckingham on styles of panegyric ('The Literary Presentation of James I and Charles I, With Special Reference to the Period *c.*1614–1630' [unpublished DPhil. dissertation, University of Oxford, 1985], pp. 145–51).

to the position of Dean of Christ Church. 'A New-Yeares Gift, To my
Lorde Duke of Buckingham' begins with an audacious effort to define the
significance of the patronage relationship:[40]

> When I can pay my Parents, or my King,
> For life, or peace, or any dearer thing:
> Then, *Dearest Lord*, expect my due to you
> Shall bee as truly paid, as it is due.
>
> (pp. 71–2; lines 1–4)

The lines establish immediately the poem's dominant and intertwined
themes of intimacy and exchange. Unlike patronage poems in the tradition of Jonson, however, 'A New-Yeares Gift' does not resist its status
as an inadequate token within a system more dependent upon financial interactions. Instead, the poem is replete with mercantile imagery.
Corbett asserts that his 'conscience bindes not to restore but owe', and
offers 'Thankes *Sterling*' to a patron who knows 'a true *Diamond* from
a *Bristow stone*' (lines 10, 19, 22). In the logic of the poem, such unre-
quitable bonds serve to establish the patron–client relationship as comparable to that of a parent and child: or, as the opening line almost casually adds, that of a king and subject. While Jonson relies on the king
as the keystone of a patronage system which promises to unify the nation, it is significant that Corbett raises his relationship with Buckingham
at least to a comparable level. In the process, he reassesses conventional
ideas of familial bonds within the polity, positing a quality of exclusivity
founded upon political loyalty. Buckingham, after all, recognizes 'a *true*
Diamond'.

The poem's close elucidates the terms of exclusion:

> You know those men alwaies are not the best
> In their intent, that lowdest can protest;
> But that a *Prayer* from the Convocation
> Is better then the Commons *Protestation*.
> Trust those that at your feet their lives will lay,
> And know no Arts, but to *Deserve*, and *Pray*;
> Whilst they, that buy preferment without praying,
> Begin with bribes, and finish with *betraying*.
>
> (lines 23–30)

---

[40] The title was given to the poem in the first printed volume of Corbett's work, *Poetica Stromata*
(1648). It has been retained by Corbett's modern editors, despite the fact that Buckingham was not
elevated to a dukedom until 18 May 1623, probably over a year after the poem was written (*Poems of
Richard Corbett*, p. 143).

Like so much of Corbett's work, the lines bring the weight of clerical and biblical authority to bear upon political confrontations. Suitably, given Corbett's clerical position, 'pay' is translated by the final lines into 'pray'. (Although, as Gerald Hammond has noted, Corbett 'is not attacking the offering of bribes, merely the offering of them without accompanying prayers for Buckingham's welfare'.)[41] Despite their resort to an urbane religiosity, the lines also contain an important political barb, centred on the allusion to the controversial 1621 Protestation of the House of Commons, which asserted the right of parliament freely to discuss national affairs. On closer inspection, then, this marks an audacious strategy of division. On the one hand, by aligning his own prayers with those of the (ecclesiastical) 'Convocation', and suggesting a form of martyrdom in the image of a client prepared to lay his life at the feet of a patron, Corbett idealizes and mystifies the structures of patronage which have underpinned his career within the Church. On the other hand, he excludes and stigmatizes the 'Commons', effectively accusing the institution of an ungodly and self-serving mode of action: underlined by a muted allusion to Judas embedded in the closing attack on those who 'Begin with bribes, and finish with *betraying*'.

Such arguments wilfully courted controversy. In fact Corbett appears at least to have been complicit in the process through which he emerged within manuscript culture as a figure whose mere existence clarified debates concerning patronage and corruption. His position in the Church, which he was so willing to exploit in 'A New-Yeares Gift', became a particular focus of attention. To those whom Corbett helped to define as 'puritans', the Dean of Christ Church was a definitive example of the early Stuart Church subordinating religious principle to supine careerism. Such fundamentally compromised ministers, it was argued, 'will hould themselves bound in duty' to praise even the most dissolute monarch: 'and laying aside divinitie make the pulpitt a stage of flattery where you shall have them indue him in a most Poeticall manner with more then all the vertues'.[42] Manuscript poets addressed more pointedly the 'mad, vayneglorious deane', questioning what even 'Rome and Spaine' may 'thinke of other mens devotion / when deanes dare thus profane to gett promotion'.[43] One of the most popular manuscript poems on Corbett related an occasion when he was invited to preach before King James at Woodstock, but lost his concentration

---

[41] *Fleeting Things: English Poets and Poems 1616–1660* (Cambridge, MA, 1990), p. 16.
[42] *Tom Tell Troath or A free discourse touching the manners of the tyme* (Holland, 1630?), p. 26.
[43] 'Tell me for Gods sake Christchurch what you meane' BL Add. MS 61481, fol. 64r.

because he was preoccupied with a ring given to him by the king. The poem survived into the latter half of the century, when John Aubrey recited a version:

> A reverend Deane,
> With his Ruffe starch't cleane,
>   Did preach before the King:
> In his Band-string was spied
> A Ring that was tyed,
>   Was not that a pritty thing?
> The Ring without doubt
> Was the thing putt him out,
>   So oft hee forgot what was next;
> For all that were there,
> On my conscience dare sweare
>   That he handled it more than his Text.[44]

The satiric inversion of monarchical patronage and biblical authority makes a charge found elsewhere in a clearer language of invective; Corbett, as 'a Parasite' and 'a Cicophant', makes his patron his 'god'.[45]

Yet Corbett was apparently undeterred by such notoriety, and continued to propound his vision of a familial circle of royal patronage, hedged from criticism by the lines of a loyal poet. His poem on the Spanish Match negotiations, 'A Letter to the Duke of Buckingham, being with the Prince in Spaine', draws towards a conclusion with an image of Buckingham and Charles returning to sit 'At either hand of *James*': '*Hee* on the right, *you* on the left, the King / Safe in the mid'st, you both invironing' (pp. 76–9; lines 80–2). Here, as much as anywhere in his work, Corbett's poetics of patronage are fraught with religious tensions, since the image of the three men evokes the request made to Jesus by James and John, 'that we may sit, one on thy right hand, and the other on thy left hand, in thy glory' (Mark 10.37). Jesus seizes on the request as an opportunity to speak against earthly hierarchies, stating that 'to sit on my right hand and on my left hand is not mine to give; but it shall be given to them for whom it is prepared' (Mark 10.40). For Corbett, by contrast, the vision of king, prince and duke rather epitomizes a principle of hierarchy, which in the final lines is stretched further to include the poet himself:

> In this I have a part, In this I see
> Some new addition smiling upon mee:

---

[44] *Aubrey's Brief Lives*, ed. Oliver Lawson Dick (London, 1987), p. 167.
[45] 'Tell me for Gods sake *Christchurch* what you meane' (BL Add. MS 61481, fol. 64r).

> Who, in an humble distance, claime a share
> In all your greatnesse, what soe ere you are.
>
> (lines 89–92)

Although this outright profession of self-interest risks (if not openly invites) charges of servility, it is important to the poem that Corbett should situate himself as poet and political commentator, legitimized by his proximity to his patron.[46] At a moment of heightened national controversy, Corbett invokes a patronage relationship as a stamp of authority, and fashions a forthrightly political voice for his statement of panegyric.

As though speaking throughout from the safety of this enclosed and self-sustaining realm, Corbett develops in the poem extended passages of satire on the fervid exchanges of politicized news on the Spanish Match. He targets in particular the 'Poets of *Paules*', who 'feede on nought but graves, and emptinesse' (lines 53–4), and the wealth of unauthorized pamphlets:

> First *written*, then *translated out of Dutch*:
> *Corantoes, Diets, Packets, Newes, more Newes*,
> Which soe much innocent whitenesse doth abuse;
> If first the *Belgicke Pismire* must be seene,
> Before the Spanish *Lady* be our *Queene*;
> With such successe, and such an end at last,
> All's welcome, pleasant, gratefull, that is past.
>
> (lines 70–6)

The attack represents a bold effort to stigmatize those who were in fact creating for themselves identities as truly loyal 'patriots' through their opposition to the match.[47] Erected around a patronizingly neat providential model, Corbett combines a specific allusion to the pamphlets of Thomas Scott (whose *Belgicke Pismire* was published in 1622), with the emblematic image of black printer's ink abusing the innocence of the common people. Patriotism is thereby fashioned instead within the terms of James's own theories of relations between king and subject, determined by his favoured doctrine of *arcana imperii*. The 'faithfull hearts' of such subjects, in the comparable conception of Corbett's fellow Stuart panegyrist Sir John Beaumont, are paradoxically liberated through the constraints imposed by 'our Countries Father'; 'we . . . could not live so free', Beaumont writes, 'Were we not under him'.[48]

---

[46] Cf. Hammond's comment that it is 'puzzling' that 'Corbett could have let his mask slip so obviously' (*Fleeting Things*, p. 17).

[47] See Thomas Cogswell, *The Blessed Revolution: English Politics and the Coming of War, 1621–1624* (Cambridge, 1989), pp. 84–99.

[48] 'A Panegyrick at the Coronation of our Soveraigne Lord King Charles', in *Bosworth-field* (1629), p. 119.

A widely circulated poem written in response to Corbett's 'Letter' highlights the relation between satire and sycophancy within this context. It presents the facetious argument that Corbett could not possibly have written such self-interested work, and seizes from the outset on the indignant exclamation at the heart of his poem ('False, on my *Deanery!*'), which characteristically leans the weight of his office against the purveyors of news. The respondent retorts:

> False on his Deanrye? false nay more, Ile lay
> As many poundes, as he, or-s freinds did pay
> great Phœbus dearling for his dignity,
> that noe such thought abusd his braine, that he
> is growne in witt, as well as beard and place.[49]

While the attack on Corbett concentrates, predictably enough, on his sycophancy, it goes on to suggest more particularly that 'some Satyrick quill' may have written the poem, then 'coynd a Deanry to steele credit to it' (fol. 53v). And, despite the teasingly personalized satire, the comment is subtly perceptive. For the author's implicit argument is that excessively sycophantic poetry can undermine itself, revealing the extent to which personal reputation and political values are discursively constructed, and thus rendering the poet and his politics subject to ridicule and rebuke. Such work exposes politics as shaped through contestation rather than consensus; however, that does not necessarily make Corbett's poetry bad, as the contemporary critic posits, because it seems that this was precisely the task that Corbett embraced when writing patronage poetry for the 1620s.

The distinction between satire and sycophancy was also partly a matter of interpretation, within a readership rapidly developing a taste for political poetry. I considered in Chapter 1 the ways in which contemporary readers of manuscript verse collected political poetry, often transcribing in the same volume poems representing diametrically opposed positions. Within this context, Corbett's reputation was enhanced by virtue of his personal prominence and his overtly controversial stance. Consequently, as readers were faced with a confusing mass of otherwise anonymous material, it is hardly surprising that Corbett's corpus should include a number of works of uncertain authorship. In some cases, he may have allowed pieces to pass into circulation without clear attribution; in others, readers may have been all too eager to attach a well-known name to an anonymous poem. Yet instances of misattribution that are based on apparent misinterpretations of the politics of a poem are especially interesting, as they highlight the extent

---

[49] Bodleian MS Rawlinson D 1048, fol. 53r.

to which satire and panegyric were at this time so closely intertwined as to become in some instances virtually indistinguishable. I will consider below John Rous's belief that Corbett's poem on the birth of Prince Charles must be the satiric work of a 'puritan'; another reader, however, was prepared to attribute an archly satiric epigram on Buckingham to the hand of Corbett. The compiler of Bodleian MS Eng. Poet. e.97, a collection closely related to Christ Church circles in the 1630s, ascribes to Corbett the following:

> 'To the Duke'
> The king loves you, you him,
> Both love the same.
> You love the king, hee you,
> Both Buck-in-game.
> Of you the king loves game,
> Of Game the Buck.
> Of all you. why you?
> Why he the Lucke.[50]

The attribution is by no means incomprehensible. Like Corbett's poems of the early 1620s, this piece defines a close and reciprocally nurturing relationship between the Duke and one of the Stuart kings, which the poet himself views with envy. Yet the two notes of almost incontrovertible satire are contained in the hint of sodomy ('Both Buck-in-game'), and the conclusion that mere luck sets Buckingham apart from the poet as a recipient of royal favour. A skilful patronage poet such as Corbett would be careful to avoid such suggestions.

Other versions of this poem clarify its status as satire. One changes the final four lines:

> Of sports the king loves games,
> Of games the duke;
> Of all men you; and you
> Solely, for your looke.[51]

Another, perhaps modified after Buckingham's death in order to comment sardonically on his fate, concludes: 'Of all men, you; why you? / Why? See the Luck'.[52] But while such variations provide valuable evidence of readers interacting with poems, and perhaps altering texts out of an uneasy

[50] Bodleian MS Eng. poet. e. 97, p. 92. My analysis of this poem has benefited from discussions with Alastair Bellany and Bradin Cormack.
[51] *Poems and Songs*, p. 5 (transcribed from Bodleian MS Ashmole 47, part 94, p. 53).
[52] Folger MS v.a.170, p. 248. The poem was transmitted into the latter half of the seventeenth century in very similar form, printed in the midst of several other Buckingham libels in the anthology *Wit Restor'd In severall Select Poems* (1658), p. 58.

realization that satire may in some instances be indistinguishable as such, the version ascribed to Corbett is in many respects the most interesting, precisely because of its slipperiness. Since satire and sycophancy are crafted out of the same discourses of power, they perform comparable and often overlapping functions. Moreover, as I have argued, this generic convergence and confusion was heightened in the 1620s because of the period's increasingly open and divisive political debates. Consequently, while James had functioned in Jonson's patronage poems as an unchallengeable signifier of authority, by the 1620s the judgement of the monarch was freshly exposed to question. And once the king's 'love' could be interpreted as a sign of corruption rather than a reward for virtue, and the poet no longer concerned himself with the distinction between disinterested praise and self-serving flattery, political poetry could become a freshly potent vehicle of division. Corbett, perhaps more than any of his contemporaries, committed himself to constructing this newly politicized poetics of praise.

THE REBELLIOUS PURITAN: SATIRE OF DIVISION

Corbett's explicitly satiric poetry attends even more rigorously to the perceived forces dividing the state. Like so much satire, Corbett's seeks to police the boundaries of his political position, and to stigmatize those who seem to pose a threat to him. He is perhaps best known for his anti-puritan satires, which are in many respects unremarkable, but are significant for the way that they politicize puritanism, positing deviant religious attitudes as a threat to hierarchy and monarchy. At a time when, as we have already seen, discourses of politics and religion were almost inseparably intertwined, Corbett therefore does much to define the political threat posed by puritanism. Further, in one of his later works, concerned with the conflict between court and parliament in 1628, he powerfully clarifies his vision of confrontation, producing a pointed and prescient satiric epigram that not only influenced his contemporaries but also helped to establish a vital new direction for political satire.

As considered in Chapter 4, by the 1620s the identity of 'the puritan' was a matter of heightened contestation. Although it had emerged 'as a term of more or less vulgar abuse, and continued as a weapon of increasingly sophisticated stigmatisation', certain people were increasingly prepared to embrace the label and engage themselves in a struggle over representation.[53]

[53] Patrick Collinson, 'A Comment: Concerning the Name Puritan', *Journal of Ecclesiastical History*, 31 (1980), 486.

Corbett's satire situates itself firmly within this culture of controversy and invective. While he can be identified definitely as the author of only a handful of anti-puritan poems, their significance was magnified by virtue of his reputation and office. As Dean of Christ Church, and later Bishop of Oxford, Corbett wielded influence at once over literary activity and religious practice. He surrounded himself with men who were both poets and clerics, such as William Strode, Jeramiel Terrent and Thomas Lushington, and his poetry served to commemorate and consolidate their community. 'Iter Boreale', for example, his longest and one of his most frequently transcribed poems, narrates a summer journey into the Midlands undertaken by Corbett, Leonard Hutton and two other Oxford men (pp. 31–49). Its popularity may be attributed largely to the way that it affirms the values of Corbett's circle, through its satiric excursions and prevailing mood of jocular conviviality. For instance, the notoriously puritanical town of Banbury (noticed also by Jonson as the home of the hypocritical puritans of *Bartholomew Fair*) offends in its utter disregard of Corbett's own protocols of revelry and ceremony:

> *In th' name of God Amen*, first to begin,
> The *Altar* was translated to an *Inne*;
> Wee lodged in a Chappell by the signe,
> But in a banquerupt Taverne by the Wine:
>   . . .
> Now yee beleeve the *Church* hath good varietye
> Of Monuments, when *Inns* have such satiety;
> But nothing lesse: ther's no *Inscription* there,
> But the *Church-wardens names* of the last yeare:
> Instead of Saints in Windowes and on Walls,
> Here Bucketts hang, and there a Cobweb falls.
>   (lines 447–60)

He returned to the issue of church furnishings on another trip to view the stained glass in the church at the Gloucestershire village of Fairford. On this occasion Strode and Terrant also wrote poems; however, only Corbett's piece, 'Upon Faireford Windowes', seizes an opportunity for satire, as it turns on the allegedly hypocritical 'Anti-Saintes' who would dismiss such decoration (p. 87).[54] They are troubled by stained glass, Corbett suggests, because of its unsettling resemblance to themselves: 'So py'de, soe seeming'; 'The Inside drosse, the Outside Saint' (lines 11, 20). Corbett's own community, characterized by tradition and hierarchy, is thus threatened in such

---

[54] See further James Loxley, *Royalism and Poetry in the English Civil Wars: The Drawn Sword* (London, 1997), p. 105.

poems by hypocritical forces of novelty and disorder. Increasingly, that threat would be defined in more clearly political terms.

Corbett also became known as a man associated with the political and clerical elite who employed a popular and scurrilous mode of satire. Basically an act of cultural appropriation, though with established roots in the universities, this strategy intimated a conjunction of popular and elite voices in an assault on an aberrant group, and thereby provided a model that would be adopted by royalist poets over subsequent decades.[55] In 'The Distracted Puritane', for example, he constructs an image of separatist fervour out of a series of mock-heroic stanzas, probably intended to be sung (pp. 56–9). The puritanical speaker, trained 'In the howse of pure Emanuel [College, Cambridge]' and steeped in 'The black Lines of Damnation' to be found in '[William] Perkins Tables', dreams of ending his life as 'One of Foxes Martyrs' (lines 10, 50–1, 18).[56] The refrain proclaims:

> Boldly I preach, hate a Crosse, hate a Surplice,
> 　Miters, Copes, and Rotchets:
> Come heare mee pray nine times a day,
> 　And fill your heads with Crotchets.
>
> 　　　　　　　　(lines 6–9)

The poem's construction of a puritan's voice, a strategy indebted to theatrical traditions, underlines the representation of a form of deviance that is social as well as religious. For Corbett, the puritan is characterized not only by a misinterpretation of imagery, but also by 'a zealous misuse of language': a point underscored in the suggestion that excessive prayer destabilizes meaning, producing instead unorthodox or perverse conceits ('crotchets').[57]

He extends this perception in another anti-puritan dramatic monologue, 'An Exhortation To Mr. John Hammon minister in the parish of Bewdly, for the battering downe of the Vanityes of the Gentiles, which are comprehended in a May-pole; written by a Zealous Brother from the Black-fryers' (pp. 52–6). The poem is concerned immediately with the controversy over rural sports: a matter which Corbett evidently took very seriously indeed, since one report from the 1630s claims that he said 'That those that refused to read the booke for Sports, were it not for a point in the Common

[55] Cf. Hobbs, *Early Seventeenth-Century Verse Miscellany Manuscripts*, p. 34; Timothy Raylor, *Cavaliers, Clubs, and Literary Culture: Sir John Mennes, James Smith, and the Order of the Fancy* (Newark, 1994), pp. 53–4.
[56] Perkins's tables of election and reprobation were published in *A Golden Chaine* (1591); reprinted in *Works* (1603), pp. 1–130.
[57] Loxley, *Royalism and Poetry*, p. 108.

law, deserved to be hang'd, drawne & quartered'.[58] Predictably, then, 'An Exhortation' follows the imperatives of Stuart policy, suggesting that an attack on such customs represents an assault on the very foundations of English life.[59] Consequently, whereas puritan criticism of sports typically focused on issues of sexual immorality, Corbett draws on an equally well-established counter-tradition, which figured puritans themselves as secretly licentious.[60] The speaker presents puritan recreations as thoroughly in accord with their biblical fundamentalism:

> If the times sweete entising, and the blood
> That now begins to boyle, have thought it good
> To challenge Liberty and Recreation,
> Let it be done in *Holy contemplation*:
> *Brothers* and *Sisters* in the feilds may walke,
> Beginning of the *holy worde* to talke,
> Of *David* and *Uriahs* lovely wife,
> Of *Thamar*, and her lustfull Brothers strife;
> Then, underneath the hedge that woes them next,
> They may *sitt downe*, and there *Act* out the *Text*.
>
> (lines 63–72)

Yet there is also a latent political point mixed with the populist scurrility here, since the debate over sports, like so much of the political conflict of the early Stuart period, centred on the very definition of lawful 'Liberty'. The puritans' 'challenge' to state policy is underlined elsewhere in the poem, as the speaker states that "tis a *Spirituall* thing / To raile against a *Bishopp*, or the *King*' (lines 15–16). Liberty, as so many conservative commentators feared, is here translated into licentiousness. There is consequently an urgent political charge in the puritan's claim that 'wee do hope these times will on, and breed / A Faction *mighty* for us' (lines 97–8). While the only '*Idoll*' to be 'overthrow[n]' immediately may be a mere maypole, the exhortation's overtly political diction introduces suggestions of more fundamental forms of rebellion.

This understated ascription of political aspirations helps to fix the puritan for Corbett's readers as a figure intrinsically representative of dissent and disorder. In this respect Corbett's work outlines one side of a process of polarization evident throughout the 1620s, in the course of which 'two

---

[58] Bodleian MS Tanner 299, fol. 158r.
[59] On the controversy, see further Leah S. Marcus, *The Politics of Mirth: Jonson, Herrick, Milton, Marvell, and the Defense of Old Holiday Pastimes* (Chicago and London, 1986).
[60] See esp. Kristen Poole, *Radical Religion from Shakespeare to Milton: Figures of Nonconformity in Early Modern England* (Cambridge, 2000).

structurally similar but mutually exclusive conspiracy theories' emerged, 'both of which purported to explain the political difficulties of the period'. In the words of Peter Lake, 'one was centred on a populist Puritan plot to undermine monarchy, the other on a popish plot to overthrow English religion and law'.[61] But the lines of confrontation were by no means obvious, and writers from across a spectrum of positions, as we have seen numerous times already, desperately sought to give definition to times perceived by William Prynne as 'ambiguous and wavering'.[62] A poem Corbett wrote at the end of the 1620s, in response to attacks on Buckingham in the 1628 Parliament, valuably furthers this process of definition, in a freshly taut and lucid mode of satire.[63] 'Against the Opposing of the Duke in Parliament, 1628' survives in numerous manuscript sources, often transcribed alongside an anonymous rejoinder, 'An Answere to the Same, Lyne for Lyne'. Moreover, whereas all of Corbett's other poems circulated principally within verse miscellanies, 'Against the Opposing of the Duke' appears also to have been particularly prominent in news reports, since it appears in each of the news diaries kept in different parts of the country by Walter Yonge, William Whiteway and John Rous.[64] Here, then, in one of his later poems, written shortly before the death of his patron and his own move to the see of Norwich, where he lapsed into semi-retirement as a poet, Corbett reaches a wide audience and forges an influential new satiric voice.

Compared to Corbett's earlier work, it is striking that in this poem his patron is never actually named; instead, the poem merely invokes Buckingham in its (usual) title, thereby offering a pointed reminder of the figure who provided a cynosure for religious and political controversy in the late 1620s.[65] The poem combines throughout the topicality of news with Corbett's

---

[61] 'Anti-Popery: The Structure of a Prejudice', in Richard Cust and Ann Hughes, eds., *Conflict in Early Stuart England* (London and New York, 1989), p. 91.
[62] *A Briefe Survay and Censure of Mr Cozens His Couzening Devotions* (1628), p. 88.
[63] Cf. Leonie J. Gibson, who finds in this poem and the response to it 'a genuine desire to comment on political affairs, couched in a language which has lost [the satirist's] conventional exhibitions of rage and exhortation ('Formal Satire in the First Half of the Seventeenth Century, 1600–1650' [unpublished DPhil. dissertation, University of Oxford, 1952], pp. 294–5).
[64] 'Richard Corbett's "Against the Opposing of the Duke in Parliament, 1628" and the Anonymous Rejoinder, "An Answere to the Same, Lyne for Lyne": The Earliest Dated Manuscript Copies', ed. V. L. Pearl and M. L. Pearl, *Review of English Studies*, 42 (1991), 32–9.
[65] It is not clear whether Corbett named the poem himself. The version transcribed by Walter Yonge and edited by Pearl and Pearl has a variant title, 'An episcopall libell against the Lougher House', while more dubious scribal efforts to situate the poem include 'On the Parliament 1627' (BL Add. 22118, fol. 36v), and 'A Libell found at the Court, and presented to the King by the Bishop of London, Dr. Lawde. 8th March 1628' (CUL Dd.xi.73, fol. 102v).

familiar spectre of socio-political inversion:

> The wisest King did wonder when hee spy'd
> The Nobles march on foot, their Vassalls ride;
> His Majestie may wonder more to see
> Some that will neede bee Kinge as well as hee.
> A sad presage of dainger to this land,
> When lower strive to gett the upper hand:
> When Prince and Peeres to Peysants must obey,
> When Lay-men must their Teachers teach the way:
> When Pym and Prinn and Jourdan must define
> What Lords are het'rodox and what divine.
> Good brother Brough, Elder of Amsterdam,
> Shutt up at home your wilde Arminian Ram.
> If heere he comes, these men will cutt his throat;
> Blest Buchanan sings them a sweeter note.
> Hee teacheth how to curbe the power of Kings,
> And shews us how to clipp the Eagles Winges.
> It is a Paritie must sett all right:
> Then shall the Gospell shine like Phœbus bright.
> Our Consistorian Fabrick is the thing
> We must reare up in spight of Church and King.
> Against the Papists we have gott the day:
> Blinde Bishops onely now stand in our way.
> But wee will have a trick to tame their pride,–
> Tonnage and poundage ells shall bee deny'd.
>
> (pp. 82–3)

Though framed in a traditional manner, the poem develops a remarkably subtle commentary on the intertwined ideological issues that dominated the early Caroline parliaments. The opening lines allude to the vision of disorder in Ecclesiastes 10.7,[66] while the subsequent catalogue of prophetic clauses employs a rhetorical trope familiar from a literature of social and religious complaint. Yet the naming of the parliamentarians John Pym and Ignatius Jordan, and the controversialist Prynne, lends substance to the generalized vision of 'Peysants' overturning an established order. More particularly, the lines allude to struggles between the houses of Lords and Commons, and the appointment by the 'Lay-men' of the Commons of a Committee on Religion, which 'must their Teachers teach the way'.

The depiction of confrontation between puritans and Arminians is somewhat obscure, but represents a significant development on Corbett's earlier religious satire. Thus, while the identity of 'brother Brough' is unclear, the

---

[66] 'I have seen servants upon horses, and princes walking as servants upon the earth.'

image of the 'wilde Arminian Ram', with its probable allusion to Peter Ramus and its possible suggestion of the issue of free will (a variant version has 'will-Arminian Rame'),[67] aptly denotes the challenge of Arminianism, in a tone marked by anxiety in the face of religious extremism of any kind. (Corbett, though he inevitably gravitated towards Arminianism, appears to have had little desire to engage in theological controversy. And, as I will demonstrate in the following chapter, Arminianism only really took shape as a political threat in the 1630s.) After a reference to George Buchanan, the Scottish Calvinist whose resistance theories did so much to politicize puritanism, the poem then slides into Corbett's characteristic ventriloquization of a debased puritan voice. In its latter half, then, the parliamentarians' concern for liberty is translated into a more sinister 'Paritie', while the 'Blinde Bishops' are proclaimed as ideological obstacles to be brushed from the true 'way'. The final couplet highlights a signal issue in the emergent struggle between arbitrary power and the liberty of the subject. The subsidy of tonnage and poundage, though customarily voted by parliament to a monarch for life, had initially been granted to Charles only for a year; and his refusal to acknowledge this limitation prompted the commons to list it as 'a great Grievance, under which the subject suffereth'.[68]

The 'Answere' to Corbett's poem adopts a presbyterian perspective, and turns the satire against the episcopate:

> The warlike king was troubl'd when hee spi'd
> His darling Absolons aspiring pride.
> His majestie may more Disdaine to see
> Some Priest that would be king as well as hee.
> A sadd presage of danger to the Land,
> When Prelats strive to gett the upper hand
> Where Prince and Peare the Clergie must obey,
> Where Laymen may those teachers teach the way,
> Where Pym and Prinn, even Jordan, may define
> What Prelat's orthodox, and what devine.
> Pelagian Broude, Elder then Amsterdam,
> Garland your Bull, court your Arminian Ram.
> The Commons, if they cann, will clense their throats,
> And make them with Buchanan sing clearer notes;
> And teach them how that Parliament and Kings
> Can crush their pride and clipp their Eagles wings.
> It is a paritie must sett all right,

---

[67] Pearl and Pearl, eds., 'Richard Corbett's "Against the Opposing of the Duke in Parliament, 1628"', 37.
[68] Quoted in J. P. Sommerville, *Royalists and Patriots: Politics and Ideology in England 1603–1640*, 2nd edn (London and New York, 1999), p. 145.

> Then shall the Gospell shine like Phœbus bright.
> True Protestant Religion is the thinge
> Wee must reare upp to honor Church and Kinge.
> Against the Papists wee should have the day,
> If some blinde Bishops stood not in the way:
> But they will finde A tricke to hold their pride,
> Though Tonnage, Poundage, never be deny'd.

Although this poem lacks the argumentative rigour and vocal subtlety of the original, and seems at times constrained by the need to follow its structure, it nonetheless fashions a cogent counter-argument out of Corbett's charges. The opening replaces Corbett's Old Testament topos of social inversion with that of a court-centred rebellion led by an archetypal flatterer (drawing on 2 Samuel 15).[69] Thereafter, attention is focused on the aspirations of priests and bishops, with 'Parliament and Kings' united against the 'pride' of prelates. Significantly, the author willingly repeats two lines that Corbett gives his puritan: 'It is a paritie must sett all right, / Then shall the Gospell shine like Phœbus bright'. Providing yet another instance of the slipperiness of satire, the lines pivot on a single word, 'paritie', for which each poem invites a divergent interpretation.[70] Whereas Corbett raises the spectre of what a contemporary described as 'Anabaptistical paritie', suggesting the undermining of civil authority, his respondent invokes rather what the same man called 'puritan parity', meaning a reduction simply in the power of bishops.[71] Consequently, with 'True Protestant Religion' liberated from the cankered stranglehold of the Church, tensions between the court and Commons evaporate. 'Tonnage, Poundage', therefore, need 'never be deny'd'.

This satiric exchange, with its sophisticated examination of the relation between politics and religion, underscores the significance of the late 1620s in the history of English political literature. These years of early Caroline parliaments were dominated by debates over the role of English protestantism on the continent and the power of the king arbitrarily to impose taxes, while the fervent opposition to Buckingham highlighted issues of court patronage and corruption. Within this milieu, as seen already in Chapter 4, contemporaries were prompted to abandon the dominant model of consensual relations between the king and parliament, and to

---

[69] On Absolon as flatterer, see [Cavendish], *Discourse Against Flatterie*, p. 74.

[70] A variant reading is 'puritie' (Pearl and Pearl, eds., 'Richard Corbett's "Against the Opposing of the Duke in Parliament, 1628"', 39).

[71] The words are those of Thomas Scott of Canterbury, trying to define his own form of puritanism: quoted in David Underdown, *A Freeborn People: Politics and the Nation in Seventeenth-Century England* (Oxford, 1996), p. 46.

consider other explanations for the operation of power. While Corbett's work highlights the value of satire in this process, it equally demonstrates that new approaches to the mode were required for the changing context. Whereas early Renaissance theorists agreed that the role of satire was to cure vice and discomfit the vicious, the uncertain political circumstances of the 1620s demanded that the forensic powers of satire be politicized. As Corbett appreciated, the satiric confrontation of vice and virtue was thus giving way to a contestation between crystallizing political forces and ideologies.[72]

THE 1630S: CONSTRUCTING CAROLINE ROYALISM

After 1628 Corbett steadily withdrew from both literary culture and political controversy. He spent the following four years as bishop of Oxford, and was then translated to Norwich, where he died in 1635. For one anonymous poet, writing to admonish his contemporaries for their apparent failure to mark the death of the Swedish military hero Gustavus Adolphus, Corbett's poetic quiescence was directly related to his episcopal duties. The poem concludes that 'tis a thing / Rarely performed, at once to preach and sing'.[73] In fact the critic was wrong on this point, since Corbett did mark the death of Gustavus; however, he was never likely to have endorsed the mood of protestant militancy that surrounded the Swede, and 'A small Remembrance of the great King of Sweden' is a pointedly perfunctory elegy (pp. 89–90). It ends with a rhetorical question aimed directly at those so determined to eulogize Gustavus:

> 'Twas said of John, that he should never dye,
> And th'envious mates were checkt for reasoning why.
> If this disciple also be as hee,
> And tarry till Christ comes, what's that to thee?
>
> (lines 11–14)

The final line capably bears the weight of the poet's scepticism in the face of populist fame and fervour, and by implication situates Corbett in a beleaguered and marginal position within his culture. In the light of this telling glimpse of cultural disjunction, I want in this final section to look more closely at Corbett and his milieu in the early years of the 1630s.

---

[72] Cf. T. O. Calhoun's arguments about Abraham Cowley's satires of the early 1640s, based on formal analysis of his use of classical models ('Cowley's Verse Satire, 1642–43, and the Beginnings of Party Politics', *Yearbook of English Studies*, 21 [1991], 197–206).

[73] Folger MS v.a.170, p. 348.

Despite a veneer of ease and retirement, we might identify in the poetry of this last decade of peace a stubbornly residual undercurrent of antagonism and confrontation. In a process that can be traced through Corbett's work, then observed further in that of Jonson and Carew, satire and sycophancy become virtually inseparable elements within a consolidating royalist literary tradition.

Three of Corbett's only poems directed towards the court after the death of Buckingham engage in a new wave of Caroline panegyric focused on the expanding royal family. The succession of royal births that punctuated the 1630s provided recurrent stimuli to poets in a great 'age of panegyric'.[74] The resultant volumes of panegyric, emanating especially from the universities, helped to consolidate a dominant Caroline iconography, structured around values of chaste love and sexual fertility.[75] All of Corbett's contributions to this literary outpouring were written to mark the birth of the future Charles II in 1630 (pp. 84–6); of the two most accomplished pieces, one was composed for a printed collection, while the epigram 'On the Birth of the Young Prince Charles' passed into Corbett's more familiar context of manuscript circulation.[76] It is, however, an extraordinarily prickly piece of praise:

> When private men get sonnes they gette a spoone,
> Without eclipse, or any Starre at noone;
> When kings get sonnes, they get withall supplies
> And succours, farr beyond five Subsidies.
> Welcome, Gods Loane, greate tribute of the state,
> Thou mony new come in, rich fleete of plate:
> Welcome, blest babe, whom God thy father sent
> To make him rich without a Parliament.
>
> (p. 86)

The governing conceit of a self-generating and self-sufficient royal family is consistent with Corbett's depiction of a familial relationship uniting Buckingham with his king and prince in the early 1620s. Yet the notes of satire which invaded his earlier encomia now become entirely pervasive, as he circles obsessively around the contrast between the ease of godly procreation and the difficulties Charles was experiencing obtaining supply. The

---

[74] Raymond A. Anselment, 'The Oxford University Poets and Caroline Panegyric', *John Donne Journal*, 3 (1984), 181.

[75] Ann Baynes Coiro, '"A ball of strife": Caroline Poetry and Royal Marriage', in Thomas N. Corns, ed., *The Royal Image: Representations of Charles I* (Cambridge, 1999), pp. 26–46.

[76] The other poem, 'On the Birth of Prince Charles', was published in *Britanniæ Natalis* (1630).

explicit glance towards parliament in the final line thus underscores a poem motivated more by embittered resentment than joyous triumphalism. As we have seen, however, such an approach creates an increasingly unstable dynamic between sycophancy and satire, which at least creates the possibility of an ironic reading. Interpreted from the view of a 'private man', as Hammond has suggested, the poem might even become a comment on the use of increased taxes to support royal ostentation.[77] John Rous was one contemporary who appears to have read the poem in this way. He suspected a misattribution, and speculated that it was written not by Corbett but rather by 'such an one as is . . . termed Puritan'.[78]

This poem underlines the difficulty of writing panegyric in the 1630s. By this time, recognition of a fundamental antagonism between two political forces – whether articulated as 'court' and 'country', 'king' and 'people', or in any other terms – was increasingly accepted as a premise of political poetry. Jonson perceived this better than anybody, and he appreciated also the consequences for the modes of satire and panegyric. Jonson had once rested these modes on a supposed community of shared assumptions; by contrast, in his final years, as Martin Butler has also recognized, 'a climate of dissolving consensus . . . profoundly impacted on the established co-ordinates of his early Jacobean poetry'.[79] Consequently, in his posthumous verse collection, *Under-wood*, although he continues to contrast 'Freedome, and Truth' to the constrained discourse of 'the flatterer' (VIII.241; lines 5–6), his verse is in fact informed by an appreciation of unavoidable political pressures. Easy distinctions between flattery and praise here become untenable, and a commitment to personal integrity is replaced by a more anxious voice and contingent selfhood. Whereas earlier poems had veiled their requests for patronage, he now solicits favours more openly; and where once he had fashioned a laureate's 'publike voyce', he now perceives an environment in which 'whisper'd Counsells . . . only thrive' (VIII.234; line 6). As Annabel Patterson has argued, he constructed in this volume 'a voice that whispered

---

[77] Hammond, *Fleeting Things*, pp. 19–20.
[78] *The Diary of John Rous*, ed. Mary Anne Everett Green (Camden Society, 1861; reprint edn, New York and London, 1968), p. 55. Some modern readers find cause to favour Rous's interpretation; however, the poem is attributed to Corbett in contemporary manuscripts (e.g., Bodleian MS Eng. poet. e.97, p. 96; Rawlinson poet. 26, fol. 12v; BL Sloane 1446, fol. 9r), and included in one of the first published volumes of Corbett's work (*Poetica Stromata* [1648], p. 69). Cf. Gerald M. MacLean's analysis of similar notes of 'anxiety' in Corbett's other poem written on the occasion of this birth (*Time's Witness: Historical Representation in English Poetry, 1603–1660* [Madison, 1990], pp. 49–50).
[79] '"Servant, but not Slave": Ben Jonson at the Jacobean Court', *Proceedings of the British Academy*, 90 (1995), 85.

of careerism, of the limits of idealism, of necessity, of the impossibility of independence'.[80]

Under these conditions, Jonson produced a style of panegyric that converges with that developed over the preceding decade by Corbett. Interestingly, there has been some critical disagreement about the nature of Jonson's politics under Charles; just as Rous read Corbett's panegyric ironically, so some critics have identified an 'ironic economy' which dismantles from within the royalist panegyric of *Under-wood*.[81] It is not my purpose to engage directly with such debates, but rather to consider further the interaction between literary mode and political context. For Jonson, like Corbett, is drawn almost unavoidably into political discourses of confrontation and division. This is apparent in the terse opening to 'An Epigram. To our Great and Good K. Charles on his Anniversary Day', which turns immediately from the monarch to his obstinate people: 'How happy were the Subject, if he knew, / Most pious King, but his owne good in you!' (VIII.236; lines 1–2). While Jonson had consistently sought to align his own poetic identity with the authority of the monarch, the extent to which this relationship is now represented as besieged by popular forces is striking, and shifts Jonson towards the strategies developed by Corbett. (Further, as Jean Le Drew Metcalfe has perceived, Jonson employs a comparable model of power relations in his grumpy 'Ode to Himselfe', which responds to unappreciative theatre audiences by constructing the analogy between the 'political disenfranchising of the king's subjects' and an imagined 'disempowering of Jonson's readers'.)[82]

The virtues of the king are at issue on a more urgently personal level in 'An Epigram. To K. Charles for a 100. pounds he sent me in my sicknesse', which compares Charles's apparent capacity to cure the '*Kings Evill*' and his willingness to patronize loyal but indigent poets. It concludes:

> O pietie! so to weigh the poores estates!
> O bountie! so to difference the rates!
> What can the *Poët* wish his *King* may doe,
> But, that he cure the Peoples Evill too?
> (VIII.235; lines 11–14)

---

[80] *Censorship and Interpretation: The Conditions of Writing and Reading in Early Modern England* (Madison, 1984), pp. 134, 139.

[81] Patterson, *Censorship and Interpretation*, p. 135; Martin Butler, in an essay concerned principally with Jonson's Caroline drama, reaches a contrary conclusion, arguing that his basic 'ideological assumptions ... remain the same' ('Late Jonson', in Gordon McMullan and Jonathan Hope, eds., *The Politics of Tragicomedy: Shakespeare and After* ([London, 1992], p. 172).

[82] Metcalfe, 'Subjecting the King', 137.

The poem is one of several in the collection that speaks openly of Jonson's financial problems, and his immediate need for the most tangible forms of patronage. Yet, despite the poem's undeniable premise of servility, and Jonson's apparent willingness to rail at the king's enemies, it is surprisingly ambiguous. The potential for irony, in the first year of the personal rule, lies in the closing description of the national predicament; indeed 'Peoples Evill' resonates uneasily against '*Kings Evill*', and consequently hovers between a condemnation of an evil populace and a concern for evil perpetrated against the people.[83] Moreover, the irony might well have been compounded for some readers, in the knowledge that Charles was in fact famously reluctant to engage himself in the traditional practice of 'curing' the king's evil.[84] As a result, the sympathies of the 'Poët', situated in his familiar position between 'people' and 'King', seem strangely inscrutable. Although he embraces both satire and sycophancy as conditions of Caroline panegyric, the relation between the two is even more radically unstable than it had been in the hands of Corbett.[85]

A similar, if less pervasive, pattern is evident in the poetry of Thomas Carew. Although he was active as a poet at the same time as Corbett, and was read within the same circles, the bulk of Carew's corpus explicitly dissociates itself from the self-consciously public poetry so evident in the 1620s. It is also notable that his readers within the period's manuscript culture appeared far more interested in his often explicitly erotic love poetry than his few clear statements on court figures and political issues. Even his two elegies on Buckingham received a relatively limited circulation, each surviving in only three known manuscript sources.[86] As Kevin Sharpe has shown, however, the appearance of political disengagement may be deceptive; in Carew's hands the 'poetry of love and nature' might become 'a discourse through which he examined political relationships and offered counsel and criticism to the court and king'.[87] And even in his poetry commemorating literary friendships, it has been argued, a pervasive politicized discourse, familiar from the late work of Jonson, sets true authors alongside kings

---

[83] Cf. Patterson, *Censorship and Interpretation*, pp. 135–6.

[84] Judith Richards, '"His nowe Majestie" and the English Monarchy: The Kingship of Charles I before 1640', *Past and Present*, 113 (1986), 88–93.

[85] See further my 'The Poetics of Sycophancy: Ben Jonson and the Caroline Court', in David Brooks and Brian Kiernan, eds., *Running Wild: Essays, Fictions and Memoirs Presented to Michael Wilding* (Sydney, 2003), pp. 29–42.

[86] Scott Nixon's essay, 'The Manuscript Sources of Thomas Carew's Poetry' (*English Manuscript Studies, 1100–1700*, 8 [2000], 186–224), includes a useful appendix documenting the number of extant manuscript versions of particular poems (214–16).

[87] *Criticism and Compliment: The Politics of Literature in the England of Charles I* (Cambridge, 1987), p. 135.

for their wisdom and taste, and rejects the rest of the populace as unworthy of independent judgement. A concept of 'unsafe libertie' is thus
imported from contemporary political controversies, in order to condemn
an audience willing 'To use their Judgements as their tastes . . . / Without
controule'.[88]

In his overtly political poems, Carew attempts more consistently to situate the Caroline monarchy within a pastoral vision of peace and prosperity.
These efforts, however, are repeatedly undone – as though against the force
of the poet's considerable will – by intimations of discord. This pattern
is evident from a poem on the death of Buckingham, which is structured
around a hypnotic repetition of the word 'safe':

> so high, so great
> His growth was, yet so safe his seate.
> Safe in the circle of his Friends:
> Safe in his Loyall heart, and ends:
> Safe in his native valiant spirit:
> By favour safe, and safe by merit;
> Safe by the stampe of Nature, which
> Did strength, with shape and Grace enrich:
> Safe in the cheerefull Curtesies
> Of flowing gestures, speach, and eyes:
> Safe in his Bounties, which were more
> Proportion'd to his mind then store;
> Yet, though for vertue he becomes
> Involv'd Himselfe in borrowed summes,
> Safe in his care, he leaves betray'd
> No friend engag'd, no debt unpay'd.[89]

For all its assertiveness, the poem is informed by a neurotic desire to repress
the brutal fact of the favourite's assassination, and thereby secure a form of
safety in the very face of violence. Carew's dilemma is evident in the barely
suppressed paradoxes that shape the poem. In the line, 'By favour safe,
and safe by merit', for instance, Carew yokes together two explanations for
Buckingham's greatness, which contemporary libellers were determined to
separate. (For Buckingham's critics, the monarch's 'favour' had all too little
to do with his subject's 'merit'.) The sense of a poet holding paradox at
bay is continued throughout the poem to a final rhetorical question, which

---

[88] 'To the Reader of Master William Davenant's Play', in *The Poems of Thomas Carew*, ed. Rhodes
Dunlap (Oxford, 1949), p. 97; Diana Benet, 'Carew's Monarchy of Wit', in Claude J. Summers and
Ted-Larry Pebworth, eds., *'The Muses Common-Weale': Poetry and Politics in the Seventeenth Century*
(Columbia, 1988), pp. 80–91.

[89] *Poems of Thomas Carew*, pp. 58–9, lines 11–26.

reflects uncertainly on the nature of justice in the face of 'vicious thoughts, [and] a Murderers knife': 'who can be happy then, if Nature must / To make one Happy man, make all men just?'

A poem written a couple of years after the death of Buckingham, 'A New-yeares gift To the King', expands upon the mythologized iconography of Caroline safety that was assuming a dominant place in contemporary culture. Formed as a prayer addressed to Janus, it assiduously represents the nation's 'great continued festivall', in an age 'crown'd' with 'Lawrell wreathes'. Yet it concludes arrestingly in paradox and decapitation:[90]

> Let his strong vertues overcome,
> And bring him bloodlesse Trophies home:
> Strew all the pavements, where he treads
> With loyall hearts, or Rebels heads;
> But *Byfront*, open thou no more,
> In his blest raigne the Temple dore.
>
> (lines 29–34)

If the image of 'loyall hearts' trodden under the royal foot seems unnervingly servile, that of 'Rebels heads' strikes the reader as menacingly divisive. (And the fact that the lines should have been borrowed for a piece of royal panegyric written in 1640, when their violence bore a greater topical resonance, is hardly surprising.)[91] With just two words, then, Carew prompts the reader to re-examine the 'bloodlesse Trophies' of Caroline peace, and perhaps even to consider the suitability of Janus as the poet's deity. Although appropriate as the 'two-faced god of the year', he might equally epitomize duplicity, and his temple door which opens in wartime suggests at least the omnipresent potential for conflict.[92]

Politics invades a pastoral idyll similarly in another poem, which prays that the people of England may sit in 'secure shades', and

> use the benefit
> Of peace and plenty, which the blessed hand
> Of our good King gives this obdurate Land.[93]

'Obdurate' is a notorious crux. For Thomas Corns, it is merely a literal description of those who disagree with the king's pacifist foreign policies;

[90] *Poems of Thomas Carew*, pp. 89–90, line 14.
[91] John Talbot(?), 'Greate Blessings create wonder: Joyes that be', in *Horti Carolini Oxoniensum pro serenissima Regina Maria* (1640), sig. a4v: quoted in Anselment, 'The Oxford University Poets and Caroline Panegyric', 193.
[92] *Poems of Thomas Carew*, p. 258.
[93] 'In answer of an elegiacall Letter upon the death of the King of Sweden from Aurelian Townsend, inviting me to write on that subject', pp. 74–7; lines 46–8.

for Hammond, by contrast, the word 'sinks shafts of discontent into the poem'.[94] Yet such indeterminacy, as we have seen, is entirely characteristic of a politicized early Stuart poetry of praise and blame, and Carew is here acutely aware of his context. Indeed the poem as a whole responds to Aurelian Townshend's verse letter, urging him to mark the death of Gustavus Adolphus.[95] Like the anonymous poet who lamented Corbett's apparent silence on this occasion, and like numerous other participants in contemporary manuscript culture, Townshend appears to have perceived this as a moment which might unite England in an elegiac expression of common values. But Carew, like Corbett, is all too aware of underlying division. At a time when some were concerned that the death of Gustavus was overshadowing celebrations to mark Charles's recovery from smallpox, and when corantoes celebrating the Swede were officially banned, Carew tries judiciously to assert the values of England's own 'good king'.[96] He does so, in the course of the poem, by setting a factual rehearsal of Gustavus's achievements against an exhaustive celebration of England's pastoralized 'calme securitie' (line 102). Oddly, he argues that only the latter is a fit subject for poetry; Gustavus's 'actions', by comparison, 'were too mighty to be rais'd / Higher by Verse', and should instead 'in prose be prays'd' (lines 15–16). But as much as the poem may struggle to extricate itself from a milieu of political poetry, it remains perforce entrenched in discourses of confrontation. Charles is unavoidably compared to Gustavus; and perhaps those who read the poem in manuscript circulation may have identified irony in the terms of that comparison.

This final example demonstrates once again the extent to which the literary techniques of praise and blame had been transformed within the early Stuart political context. Rhetorically inflated praise of the monarch is thus almost inevitably balanced by comments which seek out that monarch's enemies, just as Carew's famous line sets a 'good King' against his 'obdurate Land'. Corbett, as we have seen, built a considerable poetic reputation on these strategies. For him, as he sought to insinuate himself into the factional politics and patronage systems of the 1620s, satire became inseparable from sycophancy, and poetry was accepted as a valuable tool for the delineation of ideological difference. Consequently, while his work might initially

[94] 'Thomas Carew, Sir John Suckling, and Richard Lovelace', in *The Cambridge Companion to English Poetry: Donne to Marvell*, ed. Thomas N. Corns (Cambridge, 1993), p. 204; *Fleeting Things*, p. 24.
[95] 'Elegy on the death of the King of Sweden: sent to Thomas Carew', in Townshend, *Poems and Masques*, ed. Cedric C. Brown (Reading, 1983), pp. 48–9.
[96] Loxley, *Royalism and Poetry*, p. 26; Sharpe, *The Personal Rule of Charles I* (New Haven, CT and London, 1992), p. 609n.

seem naive and guileless in comparison with the early patronage poetry of Jonson, it should nonetheless be recognized as a central and definitive product of his culture. At a time when the predominant form of manuscript political poetry was the libel, Corbett provided a powerful voice of orthodoxy and conservatism, prepared to manipulate the libellers' discourses and techniques for his own divergent ends. By extension, at a time when political alliances could seem muddled and makeshift, his significance is magnified due to the simple fact that he stood boldly as a figure against which a poetry of 'opposition' could be refined.

What Corbett helps to construct, and what the late Jonson and Carew take for granted, is royalism. For the early Jonson, royalism was a universal assumption. He could write about the king, address the king, and even counsel and cajole the king, but always within a comfortable ideological framework which rested on the presence of the king. But the definitive royalism of the 1630s and 1640s was constructed, like Corbett's poetry, on contrary assumptions, of subversion and division. Indeed, both panegyric and satire were for Corbett founded on an acceptance of ideological difference, and an acknowledgement that the decisions of monarchs are intrinsically contestable. This understanding informed poetry more widely in the 1630s, producing fraught and unnerving references to 'people's evil' and 'Rebels heads' set amidst otherwise tranquil and seamlessly celebratory poems. Consequently, while the culture of the 1630s seems unquestionably more subdued and less contestatory than that of the 1620s, a recognition of at least the potential for division was by now deeply embedded. Writers in both these decades could not know that their country would soon descend into civil war, nor could they appreciate how their work would be appropriated within that context.[97] But for such people the discourses of division and rebellion were entirely familiar; they, in fact, had helped to write them.

---

[97] Cf. Corns's comments about interpretations of Carew and Suckling ('Thomas Carew, Sir John Suckling, and Richard Lovelace', pp. 201–3).

CHAPTER 6

Stigmatizing Prynne: puritanism and politics in the 1630s

At the close of the 1637 Star Chamber trial of John Bastwick, Henry Burton and William Prynne, the judges conceived an elaborate display of authority:

> *The Lord Cottingtons Censure.*
> I Condemne these three men to loose their eares in the Pallaceyard at *Westminster*, to be fined five thousand pounds a man to his Majestie: And to perpetuall prisonment in three remote places of the Kingdome, namely, the Castles of *Carnarvon*, *Cornwall*, and *Lancaster*.
> *The Lord Finch added to this Censure.*
> Mr. Prynne to be stigmatized in the Cheekes with two Letters (*S & L*) for a Seditious Libeller. To which all the Lord agreed.[1]

Prynne was perhaps singled out for stigmatization because he had been before the Star Chamber three years earlier, for the publication of *Histriomastix*. On that occasion he had been sentenced 'to stand on the pillorye att Westminster and Cheape side, to loose an eare att eyther place', and to wear 'a paper placed in his hatt', identifying him 'as a sedicious person'.[2] The subsequent judgement thus sought not only to complete the state's apparently unfinished business with his ears, but also to render onto the face of the offender an identification previously inscribed only on paper. Prynne, however, pointedly resisted the state's meaning, reinterpreting the letters 'S. L.' as 'Stigmata Laudis', or 'Lauds Scars'. In a poem circulated after the punishment, he proclaimed:

> Triumphant I returne, my face discryes
> Laud's scorching Scarrs,
> God's gratefull sacrifice.[3]

---

[1] [John Bastwick], *A Briefe Relation of Certaine speciall and most materiall passages, and speeches in the Starre-Chamber* (1638), p. 17.

[2] *Documents Relating to the Proceedings against William Prynne in 1634 and 1637*, ed. Samuel Rawson Gardiner (Camden Society, London, 1877), p. 17; Bodleian MS Douce 173, fol. 7v.

[3] *Documents Relating to the Proceedings*, p. 90. The verse, however, may have been written by a supporter of Prynne rather than by the man himself ([Prynne], *A New Discovery of the Prelates Tyranny* (1641), pp. 65–6).

An exercise of inversion, which typifies the actions of the men and their supporters, the poem translates authorized marks of sedition into unauthorized signs of salvation. It claims for Prynne the status of a martyr, while instead isolating William Laud, Archbishop of Canterbury, as the principal agent of tyranny in the nation. Hence, like so many other details from the careers of these three men, it evidences a state losing control of the semiotics of loyalty and criminality. As Thomas Fuller recalled, 'so various were men's fancies in reading the same letters, imprinted in his face, that some made them to spell the guiltiness of the sufferer, but others the cruelty of the imposer'.[4]

Bastwick, Burton and Prynne published a range of tracts attacking the structure of episcopacy and the policies of the Caroline Church. They came from different backgrounds – Bastwick was a physician, Burton a minister and former courtier, Prynne a lawyer – and there is little evidence of contact between them until their trial in 1637. They never saw themselves as forming a coherent 'party', and their arguments and styles of writing differed widely: at the extremes, from Prynne's tendency towards a prolix and legalistic construction of argument, to Bastwick's populism and scurrility. They were united, however, in a commitment to forms of writing and levels of criticism that would stretch the boundaries of the acceptable and the authorized. Moreover, after the failure of Prynne's defence of *Histriomastix* on the grounds that it had been properly licensed, they were increasingly united also by their rejection of the licensing system and their adoption of clandestine methods of publication. (By 1637 links between puritan authors and Dutch printers, in particular, were well established.[5]) Consequently, it was becoming commonplace, even before the trial, for commentators to link the three men as a 'puritan triumvirate'.[6] Their eventual punishment, which received wide publicity, thus aimed to identify them incontrovertibly as figures of illicit opposition: seditious libellers.

Yet this label was never self-evident, and depended ultimately on a particular definition of 'sedition'. The men themselves began their careers insistently proclaiming loyalty to the king; and, compared to many of the libellous poems circulated in the previous decades, some of their publications can seem turgid and unremarkable. They were bitterly opposed to

---

[4] *The Church History of Britain* (1655), book II, 153–4: quoted in David Cressy, *Travesties and Transgressions in Tudor and Stuart England: Tales of Discord and Dissension* (Oxford, 2000), p. 224.

[5] See Stephen Foster, *Notes from the Caroline Underground: Alexander Leighton, the Puritan Triumvirate, and the Laudian Reaction to Nonconformity* (Hamden, CT, 1978), esp. pp. 58–61.

[6] Alexander Leighton was occasionally added to their number, despite having been more prominent in the 1620s (see, for example, Peter Heylyn, *A Briefe and Moderate Answer* [1636], sig. a3r).

certain of the policies of the Caroline Church, to the existing system of
Church government, and increasingly to Archbishop Laud himself. Such a
position was always going to be dangerous, and always going to verge upon
libel, but the fact that it was rendered seditious says much about the cultural
conditions of the 1630s: and, specifically, about the relation between religion and politics in these years. After the ferment of the preceding decade,
in the early years of the 1630s there were 'no burning issues' in the political
sphere, and no parliaments which might serve to galvanize ideological confrontations.[7] Instead, people across the country were troubled by changes
in church furnishings, puzzled over alterations to ceremony and liturgy,
and disturbed most profoundly by a sense that the boundaries of religious
orthodoxy were shifting. Though historians continue to argue over the extent to which religion might be appreciated as a cause of the Civil War,
recent work has usefully explored the passion underlying religious disputes,
and demonstrated the ways in which religious discourse fostered a powerfully binary world view.[8] Within this particularly fraught context, there
is a value in attending to the language of religious polemic. For Bastwick,
Burton and Prynne, whatever their original intentions, were incorporated
into a culture of political controversy, and their treatment at the hands of
the state duly took its place in a mythology of Caroline tyranny.[9]

The satiric strategies employed by Bastwick, Burton and Prynne, I want
to suggest, are critical in this regard. Despite their stylistic differences,
all three were concerned with the ways in which language constructed
meaning, and could thereby underpin conflict. Even before Prynne's literal
stigmatization, Burton was expressing concern at how his enemies 'stigmatizeth' puritans, and he was similarly troubled that his sermons would
be 'branded with sedition'.[10] Equally, they were determined to redefine

<hr />

[7] Thomas Cogswell, 'Politics and Propaganda: Charles I and the People in the 1620s', *Journal of British
Studies*, 29 (1990), 214.

[8] For an argument that only religious issues stirred the requisite passion to drive people to fight, see
John Morrill, 'The Religious Context of the English Civil War', *Transactions of the Royal Historical
Society*, 5th series 34 (1984), 155–78; on the binary world view of early Stuart protestantism, see esp.
Peter Lake, 'Anti-Popery: The Structure of a Prejudice', in Richard Cust and Ann Hughes, eds.,
Conflict in Early Stuart England (London, 1989), pp. 72–106; on the political values of religious
debates, see esp. J. P. Sommerville, *Royalists and Patriots: Politics and Ideology in England 1603–1640*,
2nd edn (London and New York, 1999), pp. 176–214.

[9] Cf. two recent analyses of Bastwick, Burton and Prynne, which have similarly situated the events and
discourse surrounding them as pivotal in the emergence of political conflict (Alastair Bellany, 'Libels
in Action: Ritual, Subversion and the English Literary Underground, 1603–42', in Tim Harris, ed.,
The Politics of the Excluded, c.1500–1850 [Basingstoke, 2001], pp. 99–124; and Cressy, *Travesties and
Transgressions*, pp. 213–33).

[10] *A Brief Answer to a Late Treatise of the Sabbath Day* (1635), p. 3; *For God, and the King* (1636),
sig. (a)4v.

categories such as popery and Arminianism, and ultimately to contest categories of orthodoxy and loyalty. Satire, as Prynne demonstrated in his verse on the letters 'S. L.', can be a potent tool for subverting authorized meanings, and positing rival versions of the truth. In the sections of this chapter, then, I consider the construction of opposition in two contexts: first, in the texts written by the three men; and second, in discourse surrounding their trial and punishment. After early efforts to speak as loyal subjects, the chapter argues, the puritan triumvirate ultimately did more than anybody in these late Caroline years to define the terms of political conflict.

CONSTRUCTING OPPOSITION: THE WORKS OF BASTWICK, BURTON AND PRYNNE

By the mid-1630s, all three of the puritan writers had experienced surveillance and suppression at the hands of the Church and State, and the strains were increasingly informing their works. For Bastwick, writing from imprisonment in the Gatehouse in the months preceding the Star Chamber trial, the pressure was palpable; Laud, he commented, 'hath a long time beene nibling at my eares'.[11] Crucially, the three men were struggling at this time to reconcile their habitual professions of loyalty with a sense that whatever they said would be construed as dissent. Burton's *An Apology of an Appeale* (Amsterdam, 1636), for example, is framed as a direct complaint to Charles. He argues, however, that the collapse of a system of counsel at court has severed any line of contact between subjects and their king, so he has been forced to 'give forth [printed] copies' of his text, in the hope that 'some well minded man' will 'dare to doe you so much worthie service, in bringing a Copie to your Majesties hand' (sig. (a)3v). And, however disingenuous the statement may seem, it underpins a subtle perception about the construction of opposition:

Againe, what censures may I expect of them, who cannot indure to have their deeds brought to the open light? They will be readie to charge me with Popularity, Faction, Sedition, and what not, and all for thus bringing their actions upon the open stage. (sig. (a)4r)

For Burton, under conditions of constraint the voice of a loyal critic, bringing 'actions upon the open stage' becomes perforce the voice of seditious libel. In the year before he would lose his ears and his liberty, embracing

---

[11] *The Letany of John Bastwick* (Leiden, 1637), p. 5.

his fate with the passion of a martyr, he uneasily accommodates himself to the inevitability of this role.

As evidenced by the teasing play of humility and insurgency in Burton's address to the king, the resources of satire were instrumental to the process through which opposition was created. Satire offered the puritans a model for authorized criticism, a vehicle for unauthorized confrontation, and strategies for evading clear lines of demarcation between the licit and illicit. From native traditions of satire they adopted, when appropriate, the persona of a 'plain-dealing English-man', or 'poore Outcast' observer.[12] If his style seemed 'sharper then usuall', this could be attributed to an excess of passion: 'Zeale and Fidelitie for God and for Your Majestie', as Burton would have it. Like many writers of the 1620s, Burton further invoked the rhetorical figure of *parrhesia*: 'this liberty, and freedome of speech', which 'Sometimes . . . showes it selfe in meeknesse and mildnesse, sometimes in a greater measure of zeale, and roughnesse'.[13] *Parrhesia* offered an antidote to 'the cowardise of our times', and legitimized the intrusion of 'the meanest subjects hand' into the business of state.[14] Moreover, as discussed above in Chapter 3, under conditions of censorship it might also justify illicit pamphlets, such as Bastwick's successive parts of his *Letany*, written in prison and printed on the continent, or *Newes from Ipswich*, which may have been written by any or all of the triumvirate.[15] As the *Newes* proclaims in its opening paragraph, the 'presses formerly open only to *Trueth* and *Piety*, are closed up against them both of late, and patent for the most part, to nought but *errour superstition, and profanenesse*'. The true news, therefore, must be disseminated perforce in an unauthorized 'Coranto'.[16]

The verbal dexterity exhibited in such texts underpins a sophisticated attention to the powers and trickeries of language itself. Prynne, though typically dry and methodical, occasionally quotes classical satirists, and also seeks models in the Bible. The title-page of a tract designed to refute the arguments of Giles Widdowes, for example, invokes the Proverbs alongside Horace: 'Answer a Foole according to his folly, lest he be wise in his

---

[12] Prynne, *A Quench-Coale. Or A Briefe Disquisition and Inquirie, in what place of the Church or Chancell the Lords-Table ought to be situated* (Amsterdam, 1637), p. 1; Burton, *The Baiting of the Popes Bull* (1627), sig. ¶1v.

[13] *For God, and the King*, sig. (a)4r, p. 27; on *parrhesia*, see above, p. 89.

[14] Burton, *For God, and the King*, p. 27; Bastwick, *A More Full Answer* (Leiden, 1637), p. 4.

[15] On the authorship and printing of *Newes from Ipswich*, which is usually attributed to Prynne, and which was probably first printed in Edinburgh, see Foster, *Notes from the Caroline Underground*, pp. 73–4; and William M. Lamont, *Marginal Prynne 1600–1669* (London, 1963), pp. 38–9.

[16] *Newes from Ipswich* (1636), sigs. A2r, B1v.

owne conceit ... O major tandem parcus insane minori' (Proverbs 26.35; *Satires*, II iii 326).[17] Bastwick was still more insistent in his commitment to invention and subversion. He described his *Letany* pamphlets as 'Limbo Rhetorick', vindicating his 'liberty' and freedom of speech in the face of the evident constraints of 'my Schoole in Limbo Patrum'.[18] In one passage, he claims:

> there is no just cause why any should blame mee for mingling *ioca seriis et seria iocis*; all scurrility and prophanesse being avoyded. For there wants not presidents of this kind in sacred writ: that in the most grave and waightiest matters it pleased the Prophets of old to use ironicall speeches, yea the holy Scriptures are full of them.[19]

Moreover, he argues, variety of style suits 'this age, where there is such plurality of mutations in all things'. A text which sets forth the truth 'something merrily' is thus not only more likely to 'please mens phantasies', but may also prove more skilful in identifying the verbal ploys of the enemies of truth. For Bastwick's project, perhaps more clearly than that of either Burton or Prynne, is the demystification of the episcopal authorities' discourse.

At stake in these pamphlets, therefore, is the very definition of orthodoxy, and the weapons in the battle were the names used to identify the threat of forces and ideas perceived as dangerous. As noted in earlier chapters, labels such as 'puritan', 'papist', 'Calvinist', 'Arminian' and 'Laudian', which could be so useful in a discourse of religious and political polemic, were all coined as terms of abuse. Many observers were justifiably anxious about this practice. At the end of the 1620s, George Wither surveyed a religious culture fracturing into, among other categories, '*Papists*', '*Semi-puritans*', '*Anabaptists*', 'Some ... term'd *Arminians*', others 'termed *Puritans*', 'And some, that no man can tell what they be'.[20] The puritans of the 1630s, though expressing similar concerns, committed themselves nonetheless to the controversy. All three men focused especially on the ways in which they were being 'turned into puritans', arguing that positions considered orthodox in the 1620s were increasingly being labelled as aberrant by the Laudian establishment.[21] Yet while they regularly interrogated the term,

---

[17] *Lame Giles His Haultings* (1630). ('O greater one, spare, I pray, the lesser madman.')

[18] *Letany*, p. 10.

[19] *The Letany of John Bastwick [the second part]* (Leiden, 1637), sig. A2r.

[20] *Britain's Remembrancer* (1628); facsimile edn. (New York, 1967), fols. 246v–247r. Cf. Kevin Sharpe, *The Personal Rule of Charles I* (New Haven, CT and London 1992), p. 362.

[21] Patrick Collinson, *The Puritan Character: Polemics and Polarities in Early Seventeenth-Century English Culture* (Los Angeles, 1989), pp. 14–15; cf. Nicholas Tyacke's argument that Arminianism

they also came to embrace it, just as Leighton had done in the reign of James.[22] Bastwick thus narrates being '*bred*' in his youth '*in as great hatred of Puritans*, as any tender yeares was capable of'; it was only years later that he realized '*that those that were comonly branded with the name of Puritans*, were the happiest, and that if any were eternally blessed, they were such of them as squared there lives in sincerity according to their profession'. He claims that the label is wielded by papists in an effort to marginalize the only forces who oppose their dominance in the English Church: 'and therefore they so hate them they stigmatize them with the name of *Puritans*'.[23] Prynne, more earnestly though with the same intent to reclaim and refashion a term of abuse, devotes a considerable slab of one tract to the definition of true puritanism.[24]

If puritanism was to be aligned with protestant orthodoxy, the policies and theology espoused by Laud had to be positioned by contrast as innovative. Hence 'novelist' became a word on which the confrontation hinged. This label could inflict considerable damage within a church anxious about its roots, and had been deployed with effect in earlier ecclesiastical controversy.[25] By the 1630s, in the heat of debate over the Book of Sports, Burton was rebutting claims that those who opposed this contentious Caroline policy were 'factious Sabbatarian Novellists', and claiming instead a sabbatarian tradition which included such pillars of orthodoxy as Richard Hooker and Lancelot Andrewes.[26] In a subsequent text he relentlessly turns the label on his enemies, cataloguing 'innovations' in the Church and arguing that:

these novellers . . . are in fact the most dangerous enemies of the King, who under a pretence of honor and love, doe machinate the overthrow of his Kingdome and State, as by altering the State of religion, and by that meanes alienating and unsettling the hearts of his Subjects.[27]

Similarly, Prynne rounded upon 'pur-blinde, squint-eyed, ideal Arminian Novellists', and argued that parliament should 'Strike . . . at the roots, as

---

'almost overnight . . . rechristened' Calvinism as puritanism in the early 1630s, in an effort to redraw the boundaries of orthodoxy (*Anti-Calvinists: The Rise of English Arminianism* [Oxford, 1987], p. 81).

[22] See above, pp. 130–1.

[23] *Letany of John Bastwick [the second part]*, sigs. A3v–A4, C3r.

[24] *The Perpetuitie of a Regenerate Mans Estate* (1627), sigs. **1v–**6v.

[25] See, for example, Sir John Harington's early seventeenth-century attack on 'fantasticall Novellists' (*A Briefe View of the State of the Church of England* [1653], p. 13).

[26] *A Brief Answer*, p. 13.

[27] *For God, and the King*, p. 99.

well as the branches of these prevailing Factions'.[28] Both men, steeped as they were in a commitment to an ideal of a godly commonwealth, articulated so passionately in the 1620s by writers such as Wither, wilfully conflate religious and political threats. Obviously enough, for a parliament to purge the realm of 'faction' (a term itself derived from courtly intrigue), the structures of personal rule must first be collapsed.

These strategies evidence the puritans' own skills in the arts of stigmatization, as they insistently suggest the interrelated religious and political dangers associated with the spectre of Arminianism. In the 1620s, and especially in the wake of the failed Spanish Match negotiations, anti-papist discourse served to define and unite the early Stuart Church. Popery was constructed as 'an anti-religion, a perfectly symmetrical negative image of true Christianity'.[29] In the subsequent decade, by comparison, puritan writers turned the structures and conventions of anti-popery on their opponents *within* the English Church. While Corbett admitted anxiety about the term 'Arminianism' in 1628, and Laud himself referred to the 'great bugbear called Arminianism', those stigmatized as puritans were increasingly willing to label Laud and the episcopate as Arminians, and to dismiss the doctrine as 'in truth meere Popery'.[30] This was an act of opportunism – as John Selden commented, 'Wee charge the prelaticall Clergie with popery to make them odious though wee know they are guilty of no such thing' – but it was unquestionably effective.[31] The vague yet compelling equations of Laudian innovation with Arminianism, and Arminianism with popery, underpinned easy suppositions about threats posed not only to the Church but to the subject's liberties.[32] Bastwick thus identified a political threat when he described Arminians as 'spaniolized', and 'affect[ing] Romanality'.[33] In another tract, he commented wryly that it had in fact become impossible to write traditional anti-papist tracts, since 'such correspondency there is now between the Pope and the *Prelats*, that one cannot write against [the pope], but the *Prelats* say by and by that they are meant by it'.[34]

The political charge carried by such attacks was underlined by the extent to which the writers interwove strands of anti-court discourse with their

---

[28] *Anti-Arminianisme* (1630), sigs. a3r, b2v.

[29] Lake, 'Anti-Popery', p. 73.

[30] See above, p. 177; Laud quoted in Collinson, *The Puritan Character*, p. 26; Prynne, *Anti-Arminianisme*, sig. 2π3r (cf. Sommerville, *Royalists and Patriots*, p. 211).

[31] *Table talk of John Selden*, ed. Sir Frederick Pollock (London, 1927), p. 99: quoted in Sommerville, *Royalists and Patriots*, p. 181.

[32] Lake, 'Anti-Popery', p. 90.

[33] *The Vanity and Mischeife of the Old Letany [the third part of the Letany]* (Leiden, 1637), p. 19.

[34] *Letany [second part]*, sig. B1r.

ecclesiastical polemic. In Jacobean England, popery was consistently associated with a nexus of courtly sins, including 'the notion of evil counsel'.[35]
By the 1630s, in the absence of a feared and dominant statesman such as
Robert Cecil or the Duke of Buckingham, and at a time when parliaments
were an aspiration rather than an actuality, Arminian prelates were newly
figured as the greatest threat to a stable relationship between the king and
his subjects. Burton even offered a character sketch, adapting a literary
model used countless times against the puritans. The Arminian, he writes,

is no lesse ambitious of head-ship over men, then his Religion is of copartnership
(at least) with God, in His glory. Secondly, as his Religion flatters him, so he men;
very officious in soothlesse soothings, the Spaniels, that finde his ambition game.[36]

Arminianism, that is, becomes the doctrine of the courtier. The representation of the man's ambition, and his discourse of 'soothlesse soothings',
simply appropriates an existing model from anti-court discourse. Moreover,
according to Prynne the 'chiefe practise' of the prelates has

allwayes beene to alienate subjects affections from their Kings, by putting them
upon unjust Taxes, exaction, Projects, Monopolies, oppressions, Innovations; by
giving them evill counsell, by stopping the course of lawes, of common Right
and Justice, of the preaching power and progresse of the Gospell, by advancing
Idolatry, Popery, Superstition, with their owne intollerable Hierarchie and Lordly
jurisdiction, by fathering all their unjust proceedings upon Kings, &c. and on
the contrary to estrange the Kings hearts from their Subjects, by false Calumnies,
by sedicious Court-Sermons and by infusing jealousies and discontents into their
heads and hearts against their best and loyallest Subjects without a cause.[37]

Characteristically exhaustive, the statement declares a notional loyalty while
nonetheless challenging a swathe of Caroline secular and ecclesiastical policies. Although the most extensive study of Prynne argues that in the 1630s he
avoided constitutional issues and resisted a forthrightly oppositional stance,
Laud could hardly be blamed for perceiving such attacks on prelates as politically inflected.[38] The image of corrupt prelates 'fathering all their unjust
proceedings upon Kings' (used similarly by Burton),[39] with its underlying
assumption that at least the name of the king may be unreliable, lurches
towards a justification of popular dissent.

---

[35] Alastair Bellany, *The Politics of Court Scandal in Early Modern England: News Culture and the Overbury
Affair, 1603–1660* (Cambridge, 2002), pp. 141–3; Lake, 'Anti-Popery', p. 88.
[36] *A Plea to an Appeale* (1626), sig. a1v.
[37] *A Looking-Glasse for all Lordly Prelates* (London?, 1636), p. 25.
[38] Lamont, *Marginal Prynne*; cf. Sommerville's critique of this argument (*Royalists and Patriots*, p. 205).
[39] *For God, and the King*, p. 72.

The pre-eminent target of such attacks was Laud himself, who was raised in libellous discourse almost to the status achieved by Buckingham in the 1620s. He was figured as the great 'Politician' of the decade, and was besieged by what he saw as '*the undeserved* Calumny *of those men,* whose mouthes are speares and arrowes, and their Tongues a sharpe sword'.[40] Bastwick, more than any other, approached this calumny in the tradition of the scurrilous verse libelling of previous decades. He repeatedly draws attention to the archbishop's body, setting the splendour of his office against an alleged corruption within:

if you should meet him, coming dayly from the starchamber, and see what pompe grandeur and magnificence he goeth in; the whole multitude standing bare where ever he passeth, having also a great number of Gentlemen, and other servants waiting on him, al uncovered, some of them cariyng up his tayle, for the better breaking and venting of his wind & easing of his holy body (for it is full of holes).[41]

Subsequently, he ironically writes Laud into a letter requesting that his jailer approach the archbishop on the author's behalf, since his wife is on the point of giving birth and has been left devoid of friends. 'I say she desirs', Bastwick writes, that Laud and William Juxon, Bishop of London, should act as godfathers to the child:

And if you can obtaine this favour at their hands, in her behalfe, that as they *ex officio* ruined her poor husbend; so they would likewise *ex officio mero* do this good as to gratify here in yeelding to, and granting her supplication, (by which, she shall pretily well be provided for of GODFATHERS) *I am most confident I shall procure the* WHORE OF BABILON, *their old Mistris, to be* GODMOTHER, *with whom they have so long committed fornication.*[42]

Like a further suggestion that Laud might consider inviting Bastwick to live with him, the passage juxtaposes assumptions of Christian charity against a reality of discord and oppression.[43] It seeks to demolish, through the resources of satiric wit, the elaborate edifices of authority which Laud, and indeed the entire episcopal structure, had created.

Such assaults carry a serious intent, and it is no surprise that this passage should have been pinpointed in the Star Chamber document of information against Bastwick, Burton and Prynne.[44] Crucially, these strategies signify that, to the extent that the writers' professions of loyalty may

---

[40] [Prynne], *A New Discovery*, p. 4; Laud, *A Speech Delivered in the Starre-Chamber* (1637), sig. A2v (invoking Psalm 57.4).

[41] *Letany*, p. 6.

[42] *Letany*, p. 11.

[43] *Letany*, p. 13.

[44] Bodleian MS Tanner 299, fol. 147r.

be believed, they are at the same time fashioning a different concept of the Christian nation from that upheld by Laud, or even Charles. In a barbed letter to Laud, Prynne produced an anagram on his name, 'I made Will Lau', in which the elevation of 'will' above 'law' typifies a perception of individual desires undermining established liberties.[45] Similarly, Burton revises images of the body politic, asking, 'are not the lawes of the Kingdome the ligaments, which fasten and unite the Head and members, the King & his people together?'[46] Elsewhere, like Bastwick and Prynne, he focuses more specifically on the Petition of Right, which is perceived as a definitive statement of the relation between 'the Kings Prerogative, his just lawes, & the Peoples liberties'.[47] The potential for a reader to dwell on the adjective 'just' invokes ongoing debates which 'brought to centre stage claims that a fundamental law, guaranteeing to each free man security and due process of law in his lands and goods, shaped the polity of which the king was only a part'.[48] The call for the protection of 'liberties' thus sprawls pointedly outward from a religious context, and into a more fundamentally political debate. Moreover, it may remind the reader of the suppression of parliament; as Burton claimed later, the true culprits of this era were those who 'divided the King from the Parliament'.[49]

The king himself, for all the puritans' claims to be defending the royal prerogative from the unconstitutional incursions of the episcopacy, is represented at telling moments as remarkably fallible. Burton, in a passage that one of his critics found to be so 'execrably scandalous' that he could 'not so much as mention it', hints that James I's publication of the Book of Sports may have been influenced by his personal circumstances.[50] Indeed he was, on his progress into Scotland in 1617, 'more then ordinarily merily disposed'.[51] Helpfully unpacking the satire, a more forthright critic asks Burton: 'Good Sir, your meaning. Dare you conceive a base and disloyall thought, and not speake it out, for all that *Parrhesia* which you so commend against Kings and Princes'.[52] For Burton, however, the contemplation of a tipsy monarch was not necessarily an act of disloyalty. As he seeks to demonstrate in *A Divine Tragedie Lately Acted*, the higher 'judgements' of

[45] *Documents Relating to the Proceedings*, p. 55.
[46] *An Apology of an Appeale*, p. 29.
[47] *An Apology of an Appeale*, p. 28.
[48] Linda Levy Peck, 'Kingship, Counsel and Law in Early Stuart Britain', in J. G. A. Pocock, ed., *The Varieties of British Political Thought, 1500–1800* (Cambridge, 1993), p. 105.
[49] *A Narration of the Life of Mr. Henry Burton* (1643), p. 8.
[50] Christopher Dow, *Innovations Unjustly Charged upon the Present Church and State* (1637), p. 74.
[51] *For God, and the King*, p. 58.
[52] Heylyn, *A Briefe and Moderate Answer*, pp. 51–2.

God 'upon Sabbath-breakers and other like libertines, in their unlawfull Sports' may be observed in a pattern of providential punishment evident throughout the realm.[53] By comparison, the king is bound 'in Conscience' (that critical site of identity in protestant theology) to enforce 'his just Lawes'.[54] A pointed analogy demonstrates this duty:

If any will take upon him to coyne money, by counterfeting the Kings stampe and name: his act is treason: how then shall they escape, if presume to coyne what time they please for Gods solemne worship, though they set the counterfeit stampe of God upon it. Now the Sabbath day is of the Lords owne making and stamping, and therefore called the Lords day.[55]

As his readers would have been well aware, the Book of Sports was issued in the form of a royal proclamation in 1618 and 1633, clearly bearing 'the Kings stampe and name'.[56] The effect of Burton's analogy is thus no less than to suggest that the royal prerogative may itself project an illegal affront to both God and the subject. It may, therefore, perform an unholy act of 'counterfeit'.

Burton was unquestionably the most politically engaged of the puritan triumvirate in the 1630s. Nonetheless, even he would not necessarily have become an overtly oppositional figure if the state had not determined to confront him, in print as well as in the courts. Annabel Patterson has argued that the (first) trial of William Prynne marks a signal instance of a rupture in 'a highly sophisticated system of oblique communication, of unwritten rules whereby writers could communicate with readers or audiences . . . without producing a direct confrontation'.[57] This phenomenon, however, is equally evident in a series of tracts published against the puritans, concerned to mark a clear boundary between authorized and unauthorized discourse. Most notably, Peter Heylyn, Christopher Dow and Francis White wrote in response to Burton, all evidently mobilized by the hierarchies of Church and State: '*commanded* by *authority*', in the words of Heylyn, to rebut a 'Lawlesse, and unlicensed Pamphlet'.[58] Heylyn admitted a legitimate concern that, 'should the State thinke fit, that every libell of yours . . . should have a solemne Answer to it, you would advance your heads too high, and

---

[53] (Amsterdam, 1636), title-page.
[54] *For God, and the King*, p. 39; on the conscience, see above, pp. 66–8.
[55] *A Brief Answer*, p. 11.
[56] *The Kings Majesties Declaration to His Subjects, Concerning Lawfull Sports to be Used* (1618, 1633).
[57] *Censorship and Interpretation: The Conditions of Writing and Reading in Early Modern England* (Madison, 1984), p. 45.
[58] Heylyn, *A Briefe and Moderate Answer*, sig. d1v; Francis White, *An Examination and Confutation of a Lawless Pamphlet* (1637), sig. A2v.

thinke you had done something more then ordinary'.[59] Equally, such acts of controversialism served to clarify emergent polarities in the nation, prefiguring the Star Chamber trial in their relentless translation of religious invective into a position of coherent political opposition.

Burton's critics performed this act of interpretation by employing similar strategies to those used by the puritans themselves. Hence, while the texts examined above repeatedly charge that the episcopacy is misrepresenting puritanism, White claims similarly that if anyone challenges Burton, 'Hee forth-with stigmatizeth them in print'.[60] More significantly, while the puritan writers argue that the bishops are appropriating and subverting the name of the king, Heylyn charges that Burton's choice of title, *For God, and the King*, is employed 'as *Rebells* doe most commonly in their *insurrections* [pretending] the safety of the King, and the preservation of Religion, when as they doe intend to destroy them both'.[61] Criticism of the bishops might thus be interpreted as veiled attacks on the king himself: 'If men may, at their liberty, Father the *Kings* acts upon whom they favour not, and then rayle at them at their pleasure . . . his Majesty will ere long be faine to stand to his subjects courtesie for obedience to his royall commands.'[62] As seen above, the same image of 'fathering' was employed by Prynne, to represent the prelates' abuse of the king's name. Like any satiric tactic, however, this was always potentially reversible. Consequently, whatever the intentions of Bastwick, Burton and Prynne, and despite their often quite genuine attempts to separate religious and political discourse, their works are rendered oppositional. For White, their goal is 'to usher in rebellion and sedition, in the Church and State'.[63] The outcome of their trial, therefore, was virtually inevitable.

CONSTRUCTING SEDITIOUS LIBEL: THE 1637 TRIAL AND
ITS AFTERMATH

None of the three controversialists was new to the legal system. Bastwick wrote his *Letany* pamphlets from the Gatehouse, where he was being kept until such time as he should 'recant his errors'; Burton had a history of

---

[59] *A Briefe and Moderate Answer*, p. 191.
[60] White, *An Examination and Confutation*, p. 25.
[61] *A Briefe and Moderate Answer*, p. 24. Indeed it is entirely possible that Burton intended a measure of irony in his choice of title, since a text titled *God and the King*, containing an exposition on the Oath of Allegiance, was published by the Jacobean state for circulation to all schools (Cyndia Susan Clegg, *Press Censorship in Jacobean England* [Cambridge, 2001], p. 42).
[62] Dow, *Innovations Unjustly Charged*, pp. 38–9.
[63] *An Examination and Confutation*, p. 133.

examination dating back to the late 1620s; while what remained of Prynne's ears after his visit to the Star Chamber in 1634 inspired jokes of recognition from his judges three years later.[64] The 1637 trial, however, exponentially raised the profiles of the men and their texts. Even Kevin Sharpe, despite arguing that the judges went to great lengths to ensure fairness, concludes that the hearing and subsequent punishment marked a turning point in relations between the state and its subjects.[65] In this final section, then, I want to consider how the trial crystallized lines of division in the nation, and reinforced connections in the popular imagination between religious and political confrontations. The trial and punishment took three outspoken yet relatively powerless individuals, and constructed around them a coherent and threatening opposition movement.

The trial itself was characterized by a complete lack of engagement between the defendants and their judges. Eventually the court proceeded *pro confesso*, since none of the men demonstrated any willingness to answer the charges in a legitimate manner. Instead, Bastwick, Burton and Prynne concentrated their attention on procedural matters, in an effort to undermine the authority claimed by the Star Chamber. Prynne focused immediately on the confusion between secular and ecclesiastical authority in the Chamber, arguing that no bishops should be involved in judging the trial: it 'being no way agreeable with equity or reason that they, who are our Adversaries, should bee our Judges'. The predictable failure of his plea – dismissed as 'libellous' – merely served to reinforce a perception that the prelates were appropriating to themselves the machinery of state.[66] All three also argued that a lack of proper access to legal counsel, and the censorship of their prepared statements, had eroded the 'free liberties of speech' to which a defendant is entitled.[67] Hence what may appear to historians as a wilfully obstructive approach was presented to the public as a denial of natural justice.[68] As a sympathetic account of the case stated:

the sole charge against them, and the ground of their censures was a supposed *contemptuous refusall to answer*, when as the Offence, and contempt was on the contrary side, in refusing to accept of their answers tendred, and ordering Counsell not to signe their answers.[69]

---

[64] *Personal Rule of Charles I*, p. 758; DNB, *sub.* Bastwick; [Bastwick], *A Briefe Relation*, p. 3.
[65] *Personal Rule of Charles I*, pp. 758–65.
[66] [Bastwick], *A Briefe Relation*, p. 4.
[67] [Bastwick], *A Briefe Relation*, p. 9; see further DNB, *sub.* Burton.
[68] Cf. Sharpe, *Personal Rule of Charles I*, p. 760.
[69] [Prynne], *A New Discovery*, p. 40.

Their principal response was in fact presented in the form of a cross bill against the prelates. Though dismissed by a newswriter as 'a bold presumption of wretched men', the significance of the cross bill lay in its provocative effort to imagine the process of justice being inverted.[70] The cross bill rehearses and expands upon many of the anti-episcopal arguments the men had previously published, and turns against the bishops the exact charges that they were facing themselves. It is thus the bishops who are of 'schismaticall ambition, & seditious humor', and it is Laud whose actions and speeches 'are of very dangerous consequence contrary to the common lawes, customes, & statutes of this kingdome . . . & deserve due, & exemplary punishment'.[71] As fanciful as it may be within a legal context, the document projects to the nation a deft act of polarization: setting charge against counter-charge, and one identifiable group against another.

The men's judges effectively endorsed this plot. Laud, whose speech was published soon after the trial and who made perhaps the most concerted effort to refute the alleged libels, denies at the outset the puritans' claims to be concerned only with the sphere of religion. For Laud, 'of all *Libels*, they are most *odious* which pretend *Religion*'. Instead, he categorically translates attacks on bishops into political terms, arguing that 'no man can *Libell* against our *Calling* (as these men doe) bee it in *Pulpit*, *Print*, or otherwise, but he *Libels* against the *King* and the *State*, by whose *Lawes* wee are established'.[72] The relation between monarchy and episcopacy was one of the great debates of the early seventeenth century. The traditional declaration, 'No bishops, no king', which James I was held to have invoked at the 1604 Hampton Court conference, was duly echoed by Heylyn in his exchange with Burton, and in turn underpins Laud's own assertion.[73] His speech equally echoes claims made in the 1620s in response to Buckingham libels, as he warns Charles: "tis not Wee onely, that is; the *Bishops*, that are strucke at, but through our sides, *Your Majesty*, *Your Honor*, *Your Safety*, *Your Religion*, is impeached'.[74] An attack on episcopacy is thus rendered an attack on the very constitution of the state. Laud, like his fellow judges in 1637, underscores the fear expressed by Sir Thomas Edmondes in the Star

[70] Quoted in Sharpe, *Personal Rule of Charles I*, p. 761.
[71] Bodleian MS Tanner 299, fols. 149r, 161r.
[72] *A Speech Delivered in the Starre-Chamber*, pp. 1, 4.
[73] *A Briefe and Moderate Answer*, p. 106. On the debate, see esp. Anthony Milton, *Catholic and Reformed: The Roman and Protestant Churches in English Protestant Thought 1600–1640* (Cambridge, 1995), pp. 454–75; and Sommerville, *Royalists and Patriots*, pp. 196–9.
[74] *A Speech Delivered in the Starre-Chamber*, sig. A2v.

Chamber three years earlier; Prynne, Edmondes declared, 'taketh uppon him to forme a new kinde of governmente'.[75]

The courtroom polarization between the puritan writers and their judges spilled over into the theatre of punishment. The sentences, as we have seen, were by no means unanticipated, and it is fair to say that the defendants 'actually sought "puritanical martyrdom" for their cause'.[76] Predictably, the execution of the sentences attracted a large crowd, and the men's performances at the pillory were carefully scrutinized and widely reported. According to one report, Bastwick was characteristically 'witty and pleasant all the tyme', punning that 'they had coller daies in the King's Court, and this was his coller daye in the King's Pallace'.[77] As Alastair Bellany suggests, this is probably an 'allusion to the royal ceremonial surrounding the Order of the Garter', and thus turns 'the wooden collar of the pillory . . . into his Garter badge'.[78] Burton, meanwhile, seized the moment by sustaining what amounted to an extended commentary on the action, calculated to subvert the state's penal semiotics. In particular, he drew a series of comparisons between the present punishments and the suffering of Christ. On his first sight of the pillories he is said to have proclaimed:

Me thinkes . . . I see Mount Calvery, where the three Crosses (one for Christ and the other two for the two theeves) were pitched: And if Christ were numbred among theeves, shall a Christian (for Christs cause) thinke much to be numbred among Rogues, such as wee are condemned to be? Surely, if I be a Rogue, I am Christs Rogue, and no mans.[79]

Although his sense of self-importance verges upon blasphemy, Burton deftly reminds his audience of the state's audacious efforts to degrade the three men. Heylyn observed subsequently that it 'was a very great trouble to the spirits of many very moderate and well-meaning men, to see the three most eminent professions . . . to be so wretchedly dishonoured'.[80] Burton simply offered such observers an alternative interpretation.

The state's imposition of marks on the bodies of the transgressors was similarly reinterpreted. One judge in 1634, when Prynne ultimately escaped

---

[75] *Documents Relating to the Proceedings*, p. 23.
[76] Sharpe, *Personal Rule of Charles I*, p. 761.
[77] *Documents Relating to the Proceedings*, p. 87.
[78] 'Libels in Action', p. 112.
[79] [Bastwick], *A Briefe Relation*, p. 24.
[80] *Cyprianus Anglicus or the History of the Life and Death of William Laud* (1668), part 2, p. 313: quoted in Sharpe, *Personal Rule of Charles I*, p. 764.

with at least some of his ears intact, mockingly contemplated marking his crime in other ways as well:

I cannott tell whether I should censure him to be branded like Cain with a visible marke, to have his nose slitt, or a brand on his forehead, & to have his ears cutt. but then it may be he may weare a periwigg to hide his forehead or a couple of lovelocks, which he hath soe much inveighed against to hide his ears.[81]

But this comment fails to grasp the potential significance of such marks to the stigmatized puritan. For men trained in a Calvinist tradition, to seek 'the severall markes and characters whereby [Christians] may infallibly know' whether they are numbered among the elect, the marks imposed by a corrupt court might easily be claimed as signs of a godly triumph.[82] For Burton, they were 'glorious marks of the Lord Jesus', and thus no cause for shame.[83] For Prynne, although his critics felt that he 'should have covered his face like the Leper, and cryed, I am uncleane, I am uncleane', the marks defined his identity of opposition.[84] Curiously, in the months after the punishment the authorities in Chester expended considerable efforts tracing freshly painted portraits of Prynne, which presumably traded in part on the subject's earless and stigmatized state. In a futile gesture of control, the authorities then proceeded to 'deface' the portraits afresh — and when they found themselves short of portraits for a public burning, they burned the picture-frames instead.[85]

As this anecdote indicates, in the aftermath of the trial the state fought a desperate and overwhelmingly unsuccessful battle to reassert its stigmatization of the puritan triumvirate. The judges presumably believed that by banishing the men to prisons in distant corners of the land they would efface their threat at the centre of the nation. In fact, though, the men's respective journeys away from the capital were transformed into wondrous parodies of a royal progress, as the marked miscreants were followed by crowds and richly entertained by supporters. Laud, already troubled by the performance at the pillory, wondered aloud why 'there were thousands suffered to be upon the way to take their Leave, and God knows what else'.[86] He worried also about a flood of libellous poems and performances

[81] Bodleian MS Tanner 299, fol. 131r.
[82] Prynne, *The Perpetuitie of a Regenerate Mans Estate* (1627), title-page.
[83] Burton, *A Narration of the Life*, p. 45.
[84] [Prynne], *A New Discovery*, p. 102.
[85] Cressy, *Travesties and Transgressions*, p. 228.
[86] Thomas Wentworth, Earl of Strafford, *The Earl of Strafforde's Letters and Dispatches*, ed. William Knowler (2 vols., Dublin, 1740), II.99.

rgeted him in the months after the case.[87] Although only a few of
ms survive, it is evident that some of the more pointedly success-
sought visually to invert the structures of justice and authority
ch the state had relied in the Star Chamber. In one case, the Lord
sent Laud:

> a board hung upon the Standard in Cheap, and taken by the watch (the thing, I
> mean, not the man), a narrow board with my speech in the Star Chamber nailed at
> one end of it, and singed with fire, the corners cut off instead of the ears, a pillory
> of ink with my name to look through it, a writing by – 'The man that put the
> saints of God into a pillory of wood, stands here in a pillory of ink'.[88]

Laud's speech, printed at the 'commaund' of the king, is pilloried.[89] The
libellers, whose only weapon was 'ink', asserted in opposition to Laud
an unauthorized yet culturally influential version of the trial and punishment. As Thomas Wentworth, Earl of Strafford, commented darkly to
Laud (as one future royalist martyr to another): 'a Prince that loseth the
Force and Example of his Punishments, loseth withal the greatest Part of his
Dominion'.[90]

   The release of the men three years later marked a triumph for the unauthorized interpretation of the trial, and no doubt underscored for Laud
and Strafford the prescience of the latter's Machiavellian aphorism. In the
early weeks of the Long Parliament, the Commons reviewed the trials, set
aside the convictions and sentences, and awarded the men damages against
their persecutors.[91] Imprisoned by now on the Channel Islands, they returned to London in another procession through the country, affirming
in the process a national community of the godly. Yet this time they were
authorized; for the puritans, the will of God was finally coming into alignment with the lesser political authority of the state. As Burton declared to a
woman who welcomed him at Charing Cross, 'my suffering on the pilory
was made glorious by an inward spiritual power, and hand of heaven upon
my soule', whereas 'this my return from captivity was attended with an ex-
ternall glory shining forth from humane favour'.[92] They duly exploited this

---

[87] See Thomas Cogswell, 'Underground Political Verse and the Transformation of English Political
Culture', in Susan D. Amussen and Mark A. Kishlansky, eds., *Political Culture and Cultural Politics
in Early Modern England: Essays Presented to David Underdown* (Manchester, 1995), p. 277.
[88] *The Works of William Laud*, ed. W. Scott and J. Bliss (7 vols., Oxford, 1847–60), VII.371.
[89] Laud, *A Speech Delivered in the Starre-Chamber*, sig. A2r.
[90] *The Earl of Strafforde's Letters and Dispatches*, II.119.
[91] Morrill, 'The Religious Context of the English Civil War', 166.
[92] Burton, *A Narration of the Life*, p. 42.

favour by returning to the press, presenting new accounts of their lives, trials and punishments, along with freshly radical political arguments. Notably, Prynne marked the occasion by publishing his first overtly constitutional tract – a piece on Ship Money, written but left unpublished in 1637 – in what would be a long and unnervingly prolific career in this sphere.[93] By comparison, Laud was troubled at this time by a fresh wave of libels, 'threatening death and hell', which he now felt unable to stop.[94] At the time of his trial in 1644, he would lament in that 'never man hath . . . been made so notorious a subject for ridiculous pamphlets and ballads'.[95] Like Buckingham before him, Laud had lost control of the fashioning of his own identity, and was executed in due course as a scapegoat for the perceived failures of the Caroline regime.

By the 1640s, then, the trial and punishment of Bastwick, Burton and Prynne had been incontrovertibly politicized. While the men's aims had initially been religious, their writings through the 1630s increasingly assumed political significance, and their trial and its aftermath clarified their status as figures of opposition. The resistant stance they adopted in the Star Chamber resonated through the following years, and helped to fashion the myth of this court as an agent of oppression. The Star Chamber was in fact abolished by parliament in 1641, an act perhaps 'steamrollered through by a minority in the frenzied politics of 1641'.[96] For Burton, in his 1643 autobiography, the role of parliament in these years was crucial; describing the experience of receiving news of his own imminent release, he comments, 'Blessed tidings indeed, and the more, because it came from a Parliament'.[97] Although he does not call directly for the overthrow of the monarch, Burton is nonetheless decisive in his political sympathies. In an image that pointedly undercuts the authority of monarchical insignia, he declares that he will bear 'what wounds I receive from the adversaries . . . as *crownes* upon me, whose weight the greater it is, the more sensible thereof is my weaknesse and unworthinesse to bear it'.[98]

Analysis of the works and experiences of these three men in turn helps to elucidate the interconnections between religion and politics on the eve of the Civil War. In the 1630s, as John Fielding has argued, many anxious observers had been trained by religious discourse to view politics as 'a conflict

---

[93] *An Humble Remonstrance to his Majesty* (1641); see Lamont, *Marginal Prynne 1600–1669*, p. 23.

[94] Quoted in Benne Klaas Faber, 'The Poetics of Subversion and Conservatism: Popular Satire, c.1640–c.1649' (unpublished DPhil. dissertation, University of Oxford, 1992), p. 101.

[95] Quoted in Cogswell, 'Underground Political Verse', p. 293.

[96] Sharpe, *Personal Rule of Charles I*, p. 680.

[97] *A Narration of the Life*, p. 38.

[98] *A Narration of the Life*, p. 46; my italics.

between two opposing ideals of the commonwealth, which corresponded to the familiar dichotomy between Christ and Antichrist'.[99] Thomas Scott's vision of a corrupt court beset by a papal threat thus translates neatly into Burton's model of monarchical authority undermined by Arminian bishops and counsellors, and this in turn provides the framework of a model for reform in Church and State which would be adopted in parliaments of the 1640s. In many respects it is futile to try to separate religion and politics; the discourses of each were too closely intertwined, and contemporaries too adept at manipulating their relationship. Close attention to language and texts, however, helps nonetheless to identify vital shifts. Therefore, while it is perhaps an overstatement to argue that 'religious resistance *was* constitutional resistance', an analysis of the careers of Bastwick, Burton and Prynne certainly demonstrates the ways in which religious resistance could be *translated into* constitutional resistance.[100] As we have seen, this construction of opposition was achieved partly through the men's writing, with its artful strategies of subversion and confrontation, and partly also through the state's own miscalculated efforts at stigmatization.

---

[99] 'Opposition to the Personal Rule of Charles I: The Diary of Robert Woodford, 1637–1641', *Historical Journal*, 31 (1988), 778.

[100] Sommerville, *Royalists and Patriots*, p. 214.

Epilogue
Early Stuart satire and the Civil War

The publication in 1641 of Richard Overton's *A New Play Called Canterburie his Change of Diot* typifies the cultural gulf separating the early 1640s from the late 1630s. This pamphlet-play opens with Archbishop William Laud feasting on the ears of John Bastwick, Henry Burton and William Prynne, then sketches a carnivalesque fantasy of his decline into imprisonment and humiliation. In a central scene of socio-political inversion, a carpenter holds Laud's nose to a grindstone, while his boy turns the wheel. Although aimed at a different audience to that which Overton presumably reached, John Milton's contemporaneous pamphlets against the structures of episcopacy similarly assert the satirist's right to deploy a full range of invective. A 'Satyr', Milton claims, should 'strike high, and adventure dangerously at the most eminent vices among the greatest persons, and not to creepe into every blinde Taphouse that fears a Constable more then a Satyr'.[1] Like the libellers of the preceding decades, then, Milton and Overton both perceived satire as a weapon to be wielded against the 'greatest' men and women in the state. But satire in these years was more prevalent and public than it had ever been before. And increasingly, satirists of the 1640s disseminated their visions in signed and printed pamphlets: a move which signalled not only a collapse in the tenuous boundaries between libel and satire, but also a parallel disintegration of borders between authorized and unauthorized discourse.

This cultural rupture has been examined by numerous critics of the literature and politics of the 1640s and 1650s. Nigel Smith, for example, argues that the literature of these decades 'underwent a series of revolutions in genre and form' as 'a response to the crises of the 1640s'.[2] Others, including James Loxley, Lois Potter and Steven Zwicker, have focused attention on

---

[1] *The Complete Prose Works of John Milton*, ed. Don M. Wolfe *et al.* (8 vols., New Haven, CT and London, 1953–82), I.916.
[2] *Literature and Revolution in England, 1640–1660* (New Haven and London, 1994), p. 1.

the ways in which literature was conscripted into the polemics of warfare.[3] As 'tangible, collective and partisan identities' assumed distinct shapes, the discursive conditions of polemic 'engulfed the literary and tempered all the idioms of culture'.[4] Yet these developments, as I hope the preceding chapters have made clear, were not without roots. In this epilogue, then, I want to consider the ways in which the practices of the preceding decades informed fresh outbursts of satire, and were in turn transformed by the altered imperatives of the revolutionary moment. My position is that the extraordinary textual production of the mid-century can better be appreciated in the context of earlier traditions, albeit traditions which are often obscured from the view of literary history.[5] Given the constraints of space, I can hardly pretend to a comprehensive discussion. Instead, the epilogue will begin by considering the ways in which polemical discourse bursts so forcefully into public in the early 1640s, and will then consider three examples of how political satire functioned under these conditions.

THE 1640S: WRITING WITHOUT AUTHORITY

The crisis of royal authority in the early 1640s was precipitated by a series of struggles in the preceding years, culminating in the efforts of Charles and Laud to impose a new prayer-book on the Scots. Resistance to this move, documented in a wealth of libels from north of the border, led to the Scots war, which concluded for Charles in ignominious defeat.[6] Crucially, the economic demands of war then forced the king to recall parliament for the first time in eleven years: an act which produced consequences he could never have foreseen. Functioning under the shadow of intense negotiations between the king, the Scottish army and leading parliamentarians, and pressured by popular unrest in London and beyond, the Long Parliament, from its opening in November 1640, tackled a range of controversial issues, and dismantled many key edifices of the Caroline and Laudian regime. In particular, the courts of High Commission and Star Chamber were abolished, the king's powers to arbitrarily impose taxes were restrained, and

---

[3] Loxley, *Royalism and Poetry in the English Civil Wars: The Drawn Sword* (London, 1997); Potter, *Secret Rites and Secret Writing: Royalist Literature, 1640–1660* (Cambridge, 1989); Zwicker, *Lines of Authority: Politics and English Literary Culture, 1649–1689* (Ithaca and London, 1993).

[4] Loxley, *Royalism and Poetry*, p. 3; Zwicker, *Lines of Authority*, p. 7.

[5] Cf. David Norbrook's approach in *Writing the English Republic: Poetry, Rhetoric and Politics, 1627–1660* (Cambridge, 1999).

[6] For a fine collection of Scottish libels from these years, see National Library of Scotland, Advocate's Library MS 19.3.8.

the despised statesman, Thomas Wentworth, Earl of Strafford, was hurried to his execution.[7] Meanwhile, as the parliament stretched from months into years, its debates were translated and transfigured for people across the country, in an extraordinary boom in topical and polemical publishing.

While censorship was never officially abolished, and parliament in fact strived to assert a fresh regime of control, the old order was unquestionably collapsing, even before the closure of the Star Chamber in July 1641.[8] The consequent effects on political discourse in the nation were, to say the least, remarkable. The pre-eminent textual form in these years was the pamphlet: short and cheap productions issued from an increasing number of presses, which ensured what Smith has described as 'a democratising' in the 'availability' of printed matter.[9] One function of such texts was simply the dissemination of information. As the ban on reporting anything other than international events gave way, the reporting of news proliferated, and the debates of the Long Parliament were documented through the publication of speeches and (from November 1641) weekly news reports.[10] Yet news, as we have seen before in this study, has a way of transmuting into allegation and stigmatization, and the newsbooks thus amplified the voices of a divided nation. Moreover, the period's pamphlet literature was steeped in satiric traditions. Libels on Laud and Strafford, for instance, reached the press, while other printers affirmed a native heritage of political satire by publishing a number of the Marprelate tracts, provocative early Stuart pamphlets, outspoken Jacobean and Caroline parliamentary speeches, and some libels on Buckingham.[11] Authors branded as seditious by the Caroline regime, meanwhile, returned to the press in a fury of pamphlets. Most notably, William Prynne established himself as perhaps the most prolific writer of a prolific age. According to one antagonist in 1645, Prynne had 'of late so inconsiderately bespatter'd so many Pamphlets, which

[7] Conrad Russell, *The Crisis of Parliaments: English History 1509–1660* (Oxford, 1971), pp. 329–41.
[8] See esp. Michael Mendle, 'De Facto Freedom, De Facto Authority: Press and Parliament, 1640–1643', *Historical Journal*, 38 (1995), 307–332; and, on parliament's efforts to redefine censorship on its own terms, Dagmar Freist, *Governed by Opinion: Politics, Religion and the Dynamics of Communication in Stuart London 1637–1645* (London and New York, 1997), pp. 72–3.
[9] *Literature and Revolution*, p. 24.
[10] Norbrook, *Writing the English Republic*, p. 99; see further Joad Raymond, *The Invention of the Newspaper: English Newsbooks, 1641–1649* (Oxford, 1996).
[11] N. Smith, *Literature and Revolution*, pp. 28, 297; and Thomas Cogswell, 'Underground Political Verse and the Transformation of English Political Culture', in Susan D. Amussen and Mark A. Kishlansky, eds., *Political Culture and Cultural Politics in Early Modern England: Essays Presented to David Underdown* (Manchester, 1995), p. 288. For an example of a republished pamphlet, see *Tom Tell-Troth, or a Free Discourse Touching the Murmurs of the Times* (1642); for parliamentary speeches, Sir Dudley Digges, *A Speech Delivered in Parliament* (1643), and William Hakewill, *The Libertie of the Subject* (1641); for libels in print, *Hell's Hurlie-Burlie* (1644).

have infected the very aire, far worse than any most malignant epidemicall contagion'.[12]

The exuberance of pamphleteering in this period stretched the already capacious category of satire. My argument in Chapter 1, that the libel emerged in the early Stuart decades as the most pertinent form of satire, might be modified for the 1640s, since few writers now even attempted to distinguish between the two categories. John Bond, one man who sought in vain to control the phenomenon of scurrilous pamphleteering, catalogued in 1642 'the Names of every lying Lybel that was printed last year', expressing his fear of the 'lying and Non-sense' issuing from 'Satyricall quills'.[13] For him, satire is dangerous: an instrument of division, and ultimately a weapon of warfare. By the end of the Commonwealth era, the boundaries between textual forms such as 'libel', 'pamphlet' and 'satire' had virtually collapsed under the sheer weight of pamphleteering. Joshua Poole, compiling synonyms of 'libel', lists 'seditious', 'calumnious', 'injurious', 'licentious', and 'loose'; for 'pamphlet', he has 'loose', 'seditious', 'libellous', 'calumnious', 'licentious' and 'injurious'; and for 'satire' he gives 'libellous', 'defaming' and 'calumnious'.[14] Such evidence suggests that strategies of personalized invective, previously restricted to unauthorized texts, had now moved decisively into the public sphere. Satire, in all of its unseemly breadth, was offering a new generation resources for reflecting upon, and engaging with, unprecedented realities of conflict.

The liberation of censorship in the early 1640s did not last; indeed by 1644 Milton felt the need to protest, in *Areopagitica*, at the parliament's new regime of constraint. Over the two decades between the assembly of the Long Parliament and the restoration of monarchy, it is fair to say that censorship was flexible and uncertain, subject always to negotiation and interpretation. Nonetheless, the conditions of the decades before 1640, which produced the unauthorized texts which have been the subject of the present study, had been decisively shattered. Writers consequently faced a new set of challenges when confronting political issues, and took fresh approaches to the writing of satire. While the texts to which I now wish to turn are often approached as examples of pre-Restoration satire, they might more profitably be viewed as transitional: linking unauthorized writing

---

[12] Henry Robinson, *The Falsehood of Mr. William Pryn's Truth Triumphing* (1645), sig. A2r: quoted in N. Smith, *Literature and Revolution*, p. 27.
[13] *The Poets Knavery Discovered, in all their lying Pamphlets* (1642), title-page, sig. A2r.
[14] *The English Parnassus* (1657); quoted in Benne Klaas Faber, 'The Poetics of Subversion and Conservatism: Popular Satire, *c.*1640–*c.*1649' (unpublished DPhil. dissertation, University of Oxford, 1992), p. 109.

of the reigns of James and Charles with political satire – authorized and unauthorized – in the era of John Dryden.[15] In relation to the material which has provided the foundation for this book, my choice of examples at this stage may seem incongruous, since the texts lean rather towards royalism than opposition. In part this may be justified by the fact that, under conditions of civil war, the concept of 'opposition' loses its earlier, more stable, signification. In part, also, it typifies a context in which 'there is no style or form which will not be capable of being used by the enemy'.[16] Satire belonged alike to all combatants.

LIBELLING IN PRINT: JOHN TAYLOR AND HENRY WALKER

A period of intense and polemical pamphleteering, freed from the constraints of censorship, creates its own personalities and rivalries.[17] To take one example, in a series of pamphlets published in 1641, John Taylor and Henry Walker mixed populist debate on matters of religious and political principle, with bitter and lively personal invective. The exchange was initiated by Taylor's *A Swarme of Sectaries, and Schismatiques*, which presented a series of revelatory sketches of mechanic preachers. Walker responded with *An Answer to a Foolish Pamphlet Entituled A swarme of Sectaries and Schismaticks*; however, this succeeded only in rousing Taylor to produce the undoubted masterpiece of the controversy, *A Reply as true as Steele, To a Rusty, Rayling, Ridiculous, Lying Libell*. The tone of this exuberantly vitriolic text is established from the title-page woodcut, depicting Walker emerging from the arse of the devil, who is 'hard bound . . . / To shit a libeller'. While Walker attempted to raise the stakes in *Taylors Physicke has purged the Divel* – complete with a woodcut of a loosened devil defecating into Taylor's mouth – he could not match his adversary's skills, and the exchange petered out.

In the context of arguments developed in the course of this book, what is perhaps most remarkable about this spat is the way in which men from the middling and lower ranks of society so boldly asserted themselves as political agents. Indeed, as much as the royalist Taylor fulminates against the phenomenon of mechanic preachers, he typifies as well as anyone the expansion of popular engagement in religious and political controversy.

---

[15] See esp. *Poems on Affairs of State: Augustan Satirical Verse, 1660–1714*, ed. George de F. Lord (7 vols., New Haven, CT and London, 1963–75). The title 'poems on affairs of state' was also used for several anthologies published in the late seventeenth and early eighteenth centuries.

[16] Margaret Anne Doody, *The Daring Muse: Augustan Poetry Reconsidered* (Cambridge, 1985), p. 32.

[17] Cf. Mendle, 'De Facto Freedom', 324.

Walker, in the course of his exchange with Taylor, boasts that the latter's 'pedegree' is 'farre inferiour to mine', and invites his antagonist to 'search the Heralds office for my Predecessors'.[18] His touchiness on the matter of degree, however, rather misses the point, since Taylor himself had long founded his authorial identity on a rejection of elitist pretension. Taylor was the 'water poet', a Thames waterman who produced pamphlets of prose and verse for an audience which stretched across social and cultural divides.[19] Moreover, although he had been accused earlier in the century of writing anonymous manuscript libels, he was committed rather to public displays of self-assertion within the marketplace of print.[20] In particular, after the humiliating collapse of a planned public performance with William Fennor in 1614, Taylor engaged in a spiteful pamphlet exchange, in the manner of a flyting, which served at once to defend his name and raise his profile.[21] Throughout his career he also identified strongly with Thomas Nashe, whose own work as a struggling author in the late-Elizabethan print marketplace offered influential models of verbal play, personalized satire, and religious conservatism. In the 1640s, Taylor strategically recalled Nashe's role in confronting the Marprelate tracts, invoking his predecessor as a satiric persona for the purpose of an attack on Prynne, titled *Crop-Eare Curried, Or, Tom Nash His Ghost* (1644).[22]

Rather than concerning himself with issues of social degree, Taylor labours hard in his exchange with Walker to establish his credentials as a writer. Like Donne, who had claimed earlier in the century that libels are only effective if they 'entertain us long with a delight, and love to the things themselves',[23] Taylor posits in one passage an aesthetic of invective:

> Thou hat'st the muses, yet dost love to muse
> In railing tearmes thy betters to abuse,
> Verse must have method, measure, order, feet,
> Proportion, cadence, weight and number, sweet
> But thou that hat'st good verse, and libels make
> Dost with the Devills cloven foot thy measure take.[24]

While the charge that only Walker may be classified a libeller seems obviously disingenuous, it highlights a residual anxiety about the literary merits

---

[18] *Taylors Physicke*, sig. A2v.
[19] On Taylor, see Bernard Capp, *The World of John Taylor the Water-Poet 1578–1653* (Oxford, 1994).
[20] Capp, *The World of John Taylor*, p. 14.
[21] Capp, *The World of John Taylor*, pp. 14–15.
[22] Cf. the anonymous pamphlet, *Tom Nash his Ghost* (1642).
[23] *Letters to Severall Persons of Honour* (London, 1651), pp. 89–90; see above, p. 23.
[24] *A Reply as true as Steele* (1641), pp. 6–7.

of the mode. Taylor implies that libels are defined less by content than by quality, and he situates himself as one of Walker's 'betters' because he is a better poet. Elsewhere in the text he boasts of his speed of composition, and correctly attacks Walker for having borrowed at length from the work of Fennor, now three decades old.[25] He is thus concerned with a notion of literary decorum, albeit of a peculiarly demotic kind. Consequently, for all the effort devoted by each man to representing his opponent as infernally inspired, it would be a mistake to overlook their respective assertions of independence and integrity.[26] The poet who understands the mysteries of 'method, measure, order, feet' – which, for Taylor, are by no means restricted to a cultural elite – might legitimately commit himself to the emergent contestation in his country. He has, quite simply, learned how to speak in the public sphere. Assured of his status as a professional writer, Taylor aligns himself with the cause of the king; the logic of his writing, however, posits this as the free choice of a political agent, rather than the unthinking allegiance of a subject.

An edgy combination of defamation and self-assertion is sustained throughout the pamphlets. Each man proffers anagrams of the other's name: Walker derives 'ART THOU IN HEL, O POET' from 'John Talour the Poet', while Taylor in turn translates 'HENRIE WALLKER' into 'KNAV, REVILER, HEL'.[27] As seen above in Chapter 2, the anagram serves a complex function, comically collapsing identity in a play of wit, yet simultaneously hinting at hidden truths. Crucially, it is 'an exercise of power over the object named', and Walker for one was uneasy about its effects, as he quibbled in his second pamphlet about Taylor's misspelling of his name.[28] Taylor seeks a similar effect in his attention to his adversary's body, in a manner that again recalls the practices of libellers earlier in the century:

> I could write lines, (thou fowle ill looking elfe)
> Should make thee (in Iambicks) hang thy selfe,
> Th'art fowle within, and my sharp lancing quill
> Can make Incision, and with Art and skill

---

[25] *A Reply as true as Steele*, p. 2.

[26] Cf. Faber, 'Poetics of Subversion and Conservatism', pp. 181–2, 194.

[27] *Taylors Physicke*, sig. A2v; *A Reply as true as Steele*, p. 1.

[28] Faber, 'Poetics of Subversion and Conservatism', p. 193; *Taylors Physicke*, sig. A4v. In the late 1640s Walker idiosyncratically extended his use of the anagram in his parliamentary newsbooks, which regularly enlisted the Hebrew language to 'do the work of providing divine assurance by taking English names, spelling them in Hebrew characters, and then translating the "meaning" of them back into English' (Nigel Smith, 'The Uses of Hebrew in the English Revolution', in Peter Burke and Roy Porter, eds., *Language, Self, and Society: A Social History of Language* [Cambridge, 1991], p. 62).

> Search deep for dead flesh and Coroded Cores
> And from corruptions cleare and clense thy sores.
> Th'art almost Gangren'd, and I surely think
> No Ballsums better then a Poets Inke.[29]

Elizabethan verse satirists conventionally compared their art to that of the barber-surgeon, for its beneficial though often violent qualities of revelation and purgation.[30] In accordance with the aims of his pamphlet, Taylor translates such claims into a carnivalesque register, inviting his reader to visualize the 'Coroded Cores' within Walker's 'fowle ill looking' self. The image of poetry as 'Ballsum' is no more than an afterthought; the poet, here, is defined through the act of destruction.

And it is critical to the respective projects of the two men that the destruction of an individual is inextricably linked to the stigmatization of a religious or political position. Taylor, in particular, deploys satiric excess to refine stereotypes of the puritan. The likes of Walker, he alleges, must perforce 'raile':

> And like unmannag'd wild untoward Jades
> Lay by their laudable and lawfull Trades,
> And sawcily to preach, prate, rore, and lie
> Against all order rule and descencie;
> And all such as are not seditious
> To call them Papists, and idollatrous.[31]

The imagery of disorder wilfully fuses religious and political dissent, as unlicensed preaching is translated into an affront to 'all order' and 'rule'. Significantly, Taylor thus accepts not only the evident polarization in the state, but also the power of language to define its parameters. Hence all who are not, in Taylor's perception, 'seditious', are in the eyes of their opponents 'Papists, and idollatrous'. In the lines following this passage, the charge of sedition assumes a physical form, as Taylor states that 'though unhappy *Strafford* be struck dead / They mount him up a cock-horse sans a head'. This vision of grotesque celebration surrounding the highly divisive event of Strafford's death – for one side a legitimate execution, for the other an unlawful assassination – was calculated to sting. Walker duly responded in the accepted language of puritan dissent, claiming that, 'My allegiance to my royall King; my sincerity and reall submission to that honourable

[29] *A Reply as true as Steele*, p. 7.
[30] Mary Claire Randolph, 'The Medical Concept in English Renaissance Satiric Theory', *Studies in Philology*, 38 (1941), 127–59.
[31] *A Reply as true as Steele*, p. 5.

Assembly, to the godly Lawes of this Land, and my love to the Church and State, is well knowne to those that know me.'[32] Taylor, however, took one last shot at his target, claiming in a prose biography of Walker – needless to say, unauthorized – that his publishing business was sustained purely by 'such people as . . . loved contention, or were willing to beleeve any thing that tended to rend or shake the piece of either Church or State'.[33] For the moment, at least, the royalist was still able to lay claim to a position of orthodoxy.

JOHN CLEVELAND: SATIRE OF THE BATTLEFIELD

John Cleveland was a poet raised into traditions of manuscript circulation among a cultural elite, but whose significance was radically altered when he turned to print. Unlike a practised pamphleteer such as Taylor, Cleveland never affected a popular voice, and his satires are frequently obscure and intellectually demanding, indebted in part to the famously crabbed style of Persius.[34] His success and influence in the nation, however, are documented by the simple fact that twenty editions of his poems were published between 1647 and 1660, and a further seven over the following twenty-seven years.[35] In Smith's terms, while Cleveland did not necessarily write 'popular verse', his work nonetheless 'occupied the public space in which the definition of "popular" consists'.[36] As a satirist, Cleveland thus emerges as a pivotal figure in literary history, since he combines practices of formal verse satire derived from classical and Elizabethan writers, with the topical and libellous imperatives of early Stuart manuscript culture. In 'The Rebell Scot' he pauses to summon his satiric powers:

> Come keen *Iambicks*, with your Badgers feet,
> And Badger-like, bite till your teeth do meet.
> Help ye tart Satyrists, to imp my rage,
> With all the Scorpions that should whip this age.[37]

Despite a nagging sense of belatedness, which lends the passage a burlesque edge, the invocation typifies Cleveland's combination of earnest savagery

---

[32] *Taylors Physicke*, sig. A4v.
[33] *The Whole Life and Progresse of Henry Walker the Ironmonger* (1642), sig. AIv.
[34] Loxley, *Royalism and Poetry*, p. 103.
[35] Loxley, *Royalism and Poetry*, p. 98.
[36] Smith, *Literature and Revolution*, p. 306.
[37] *The Poems of John Cleveland*, ed. Brian Morris and Eleanor Withington (Oxford, 1967), p. 29 (lines 27–30). All references are to this edition.

with an 'aggressive humor of despair'.[38] Indeed, throughout his satiric work the vitriolic force is typically tempered by a certain anxious self-awareness and intellectual rigour, which prompts him to reassess traditional satiric strategies. For all his verbal energy, Cleveland is a poet of his age, fundamentally sceptical about the foundations of authority and order in the nation.

'To P. Rupert', the poem around which I want to structure my discussion of Cleveland, is not only an exercise in the poetry of warfare, but also an exploration of the very functions of language within a state of conflict. Ostensibly, it is a panegyric on King Charles's young nephew, who was one of the most successful royalist commanders in the early years of war. Yet, as in so much of the poetry examined in Chapter 5, conditions of political stress demand that panegyric embrace satire; in Cleveland's words, his 'Muse', as though against the poet's will, 'Feed'st . . . on coales and dirt' (lines 49–50).[39] Moreover, from the outset the poem raises the question of the poet's authority to discriminate between the praiseworthy and blameworthy. For Ben Jonson, as we have seen, poetic authority was derived directly from the king.[40] In the 1640s, as the monarch's power becomes the very issue of military contention, Cleveland teases with the implications of the conflict for a poet: 'O that I could but vote my selfe a Poet! / Or had the Legislative knacke to do it!' (lines 1–2). Like the mechanic preachers who so infuriated Taylor, poets in this age may elect themselves, or appeal instead to the authority of parliament. It is a satiric vision, yet one that troubles the poem, as it notably avoids any reference to the king, and clings throughout to the miraculously successful soldier. Cleveland draws to a conclusion in a conventionally Jonsonian manner, by invoking Rupert's name as a signifier of authority; however, the poem's tendency towards scepticism and irony introduces even here a note of destabilizing hyperbole. 'Your name', he asserts, 'can scare an Atheist to his prayers'; and, 'In fine, the name of *Rupert* thunders so, / *Kimbolton's* but a rumbling Wheel-barrow' (lines 173, 179–80).

The poem's concern with the nature of poetic truth is developed in a substantial passage reflecting on the language of a nation at war:

> Could I but write a-squint; then (Sir) long since
> You had been sung, *A Great and Glorious Prince*.

---

[38] Doris C. Powers, *English Formal Satire: Elizabethan to Augustan* (The Hague, 1971), p. 145; cf. Raman Selden, *English Verse Satire 1590–1765* (London, 1978), p. 82; and *Poems*, p. lviii.
[39] Cf. Loxley, *Royalism and Poetry*, p. 100.
[40] See above, pp. 161–2.

> I had observ'd the Language of the dayes;
> Blasphem'd you; and then Periwigg'd the Phrase
> With Humble Service, and such other Fustian,
> Bels which ring backward in this great Combustion.
> I had revil'd you; and without offence,
> *The Literall* and *Equitable Sence*
> Would make it good: when all failes, that will do't:
> Sure that distinction cleft the Devill's Foot.
> This were my Dialect, would your Highnesse please
> To read mee but with Hebrew Spectacles;
> Interpret Counter, what is Crosse rehears'd:
> Libells are commendations, when revers'd.
>
> (lines 13–26)

Cleveland perceives that the subversion of authority initiates a parallel crisis within the order of language. As James Loxley argues, 'The reversed peal of bells, a signifier of alarm or crisis in deliberate contrast to its festive opposite, is here to be understood as an inversion of the entire vocabulary of Stuart panegyric.' The image of 'Hebrew Spectacles', with its suggestion of 'reading backwards', involves the reader in the struggle over meaning. 'Libells', crucially, 'are commendations, when revers'd'.[41] But while the poem clings to a commitment to truth – just as it clings to its own conception of Charles as *'a Great and Glorious Prince'* – it is aware that meaning in this context becomes a product of politics. As a result, the poet is permitted neither the lofty authoritativeness of Jonson, nor even the self-absorbed disengagement of Thomas Carew. Instead, the art of the poet, and particularly that of the satirist, is rendered uncomfortably contingent upon the imperatives of conflict.

Cleveland subsequently warms to his polemical task, fashioning rival images of the conflict's opposing sides. A central index of discrimination in the poem, which he develops out of discourse we have encountered in preceding decades, is sexuality. Puritans and parliamentarians are associated here with a dysfunctional and hypocritical sexuality: evident, for example, in 'the zeale-twanging Nose' of a man ravaged by pox, which 'Snuffl[es] devoutly' but requires the support of a 'silver bridge' (lines 81–2). By contrast, Cavalier sexuality is represented as the assertion of proper, patriarchal authority. A passage alluding to Rupert's sexual appetite gently titillates with its references to 'the *Bonny Besses*', whose 'every arrow / Had launc'd your noble breast and drunk the marrow' (lines 35, 37–8). While parliamentary propagandists may claim that Rupert 'kill[s] women' (line 43),

---

[41] Loxley, *Royalism and Poetry*, p. 89.

Cleveland suggests rather a mutuality of desire, analogous to that uniting royalist leaders with the people. The strand of imagery centres ultimately on contrasting images of King Charles and the parliamentary leader, the Earl of Essex:

> Impotent *Essex*! is it not a shame
> Our Commonwealth, like to a *Turkish Dame*,
> Should have an *Eunuch*-Guardian? may she bee
> Ravish'd by *Charles*, rather then sav'd by thee.
>
> (lines 45–8)

Essex, who had been divorced by Frances Howard on grounds of impotence earlier in the century, and was by this time estranged from his second wife, offers an appropriate index of sterility.[42] By contrast, the image of royal ravishment signifies that the Caroline discourse of love must now assume a more forceful character, thoroughly in accord with the times.

The mock-trial of Rupert's dog, 'that four-legg'd *Cavalier*', develops the poem's satire in burlesque mode (line 122). The dog is in every way a loyalist:

> Who name but *Charles*, hee comes aloft for him,
> But holds up his Malignant leg at *Pym*.
> 'Gainst whom they've severall Articles in souse;
> First, that he barks against the sense o'th House:
> *Resolv'd Delinquent*, to the Tower straight;
> Either to th' Lions, or the Bishops Grate.
> Next, for his ceremonious wag o'th taile:
> But there the Sisterhood will be his Baile,
> At least the Countesse will, *Lusts's Amsterdam*,
> That lets in all religious of the game.
>
> (lines 125–34)

The dog's barking 'against the sense o' th House' parodies not only the process of opinion formation in parliament but also its very understanding of 'sense' – which the reader is invited to weigh against the normative '*Literall* and *Equitable Sence*' invoked at the beginning of the poem (line 20). Further, its 'ceremonious wag o'th taile' mocks the puritan preoccupation with ceremony, while also reintroducing sexual undertones. For, like its master, the dog has a vigorous masculinity, pissing at the name of Pym yet

---

[42] Alastair Bellany documents further examples of satire on Essex's sexuality, in *The Politics of Court Scandal in Early Modern England: News Culture and the Overbury Affair, 1603–1660* (Cambridge, 2002), pp. 271–2.

rising – somewhat ambiguously – at that of Charles. The subsequent gesture towards the grotesque sexual desire of the 'Countesse' (probably Lucy,
Countess of Carlisle) compounds the poem's representation of debased puritan sexuality.[43] Throughout, puritan sexuality is encoded as uncontrolled
feminized lust; the Cavalier equivalent as a correct, masculine self-assertion.

Yet, for all the snide arrogance of this satire, there remains an undeniable
anxiety at the heart of the poem. This registers in a passing mention of
'the glorious *Strafford*', and recurs in an injunction that Rupert 'Scatter th'
accumulative King': an allusion to the assumption of quasi-regal authority
by the 'Five Members' (lines 154, 167).[44] Within a nation at war, the name of
the king is no longer a reliable signifier of authority (for all of its mysterious
effects on the actions of a loyal dog), while the name of Rupert is ultimately
no more than that of one combatant in an uneasily balanced struggle.
This note of unease resonates throughout Cleveland's work, providing the
foundation most notably for 'The Kings Disguise', a poem which meditates
on the significance of Charles's infamous act of obscuring the external
markers of his authority in order to avoid capture. Therefore, as much
as he situates himself in relation to existing traditions of satire, Cleveland
adapts himself perforce to a startlingly new context, in which distinctions
between the authorized and unauthorized refuse to hold.

ANDREW MARVELL, 'TOM MAY'S DEATH'

'Tom May's Death' was written anonymously, but almost certainly by
Andrew Marvell, and probably soon after May's death in November 1650.[45]
May had a long and turbulent history in the political and literary culture
of the seventeenth century, stretching back to his translation of Lucan's
republican epic, the *Pharsalia*, in 1627, through a period as a court poet in
the 1630s, and finally to his authorship of *The History of Parliament* (1647).
He was buried in Westminster Abbey, a hero of the revolutionary cause.
In retrospect, it is fitting that a man whose public identity was so steeped
in a literature of political controversy should have been challenged after
his death in a manuscript libel; the only thing that remains surprising is
that the parliamentarian Marvell should have written that libel. Yet the
poem, which follows a Lucianic narrative of judgement in the underworld,

---

[43] *Poems*, p. 129.
[44] *Poems*, p. 130.
[45] *Marvell: The Poems of Andrew Marvell*, ed. Nigel Smith (Harlow, 2003); all references are to this
edition.

provides a space for Marvell to reflect not only on May's unstable political allegiances, but also on his evidently opportunistic approach to literature. It is thus, in part, a poem about the relation between poetry and politics.

Like the vast majority of early Stuart libels, 'Tom May's Death' sets out to dismantle the identity its subject fashioned so carefully in his lifetime. May did not exactly help his cause, apparently choking to death in his sleep after drinking heavily. For the libeller, this provides an easy pretext for farce:

> As one put drunk into the packet-boat,
> Tom May was hurried hence and did not know't.
> But was amazed on the Elysian side,
> And with an eye uncertain, gazing wide,
> Could not determine in what place he was,
> (For whence, in Stephen's Alley, trees or grass?)
> Nor where *The Pope's Head*, nor *The Mitre* lay,
> Signs by which still he found and lost his way.
>
> (lines 1–8)

The image of drunken disorientation as the poet stumbles into Elysium, Howard Erskine-Hill comments, 'becomes a derisive summary of his political career, first so loyal to . . . Charles I, then so staunch for Parliament, now quite confused'.[46] It also establishes an appropriate mood for the journey on which May is embarked. In accordance with libellous traditions, the poem takes delight in a culture of controversy, as it at once translates Christian concerns with judgement into the discourse of the carnivalesque, and deploys an exuberant satire to reflect on the nature of political engagement. Hence May's 'eye uncertain' assumes an emblematic quality, in a libel tailored to Marvell's uncertain age.

'Tom May's Death' consistently sets qualities of order and integrity, in poetry and politics, against May's notorious uncertainty. In particular, it alleges that May abandoned the royalist cause because of 'malice fixed and understood', prompted by being passed over for the laureateship when Jonson died in 1637 (line 56). More importantly, his judge in the underworld, who ultimately consigns his soul to hell, is Jonson himself. As critics have recognized, Jonson is employed in the poem partly as 'an exemplar of moral integrity', but partly also as a dramatic voice which is to some degree inseparable from Marvell's own.[47] Given the figure's willingness to denounce Roman republicans, this is clearly Jonson the court

---

[46] *The Augustan Idea in English Literature* (London, 1983), p. 191.
[47] Christine Rees, '"Tom May's Death" and Ben Jonson's Ghost: A Study of Marvell's Satiric Method', *Modern Language Review*, 71 (1976), 482–3. Cf. Erskine-Hill, *The Augustan Idea in English Literature*,

poet rather than the Jonson who wrote some politically provocative Roman plays early in his career.[48] Indeed Marvell's representation of Jonson
specifically echoes loyalist discourse of the 1630s, as he is first discovered to
the reader, 'Sounding of ancient heroes, such as were / The subject's safety,
and the rebel's fear' (lines 15–16). The encoding of monarchy as 'safety',
which was a common strategy in Civil War controversy, recalls Carew's
relentless repetition of the word in his elegy on Buckingham, examined
in Chapter 5.[49] Jonson subsequently ridicules an established oppositionist
discourse of 'liberty', as he sarcastically urges May to:

> Go seek the novice statesmen, and obtrude
> On them some Roman-cast similitude,
> Tell them of liberty, the stories fine,
> Until you all grow consuls in your wine.
>
> (lines 43–6)

Whereas Jonson founded his poetic career on addressing the king, May is
figured rather as speaking to 'novice statesmen', ill-equipped to assert control. Further, mobilizing a conservative trope that can be traced throughout
the early Stuart period, in the absence of clear authority 'liberty' shades inevitably into licence. May's dreams of liberty and republicanism are figured
satirically as the idle fantasies of a pompous drunkard: the 'Dictator of the
glass' (line 47).

Yet the trajectory of Jonson's diatribe ultimately privileges poetry over
politics, as Marvell shifts subtly away from the absolutist rhetoric of the en-
raged laureate. May's error is not so much his particular choice of allegiance
as his self-interested opportunism. The vehemence of Jonson's denuncia-
tion of May thus accords with the Jonson observed in Chapter 5, trying
so hard to repress elements of mindless sycophancy from the patronage
relationship. Jonson's life as a court poet was indeed a constant struggle to
distinguish his own praise from the sort of 'servile flatterie' which is the
'common *Poets* shame'.[50] It is in this mood that Marvell's Jonson rounds
on May, stigmatizing him as: 'Most servile wit, and mercenary pen. / . . .
Malignant poet and historian both' (lines 40–2). While Jonson in his life
had praised May's translation of Lucan, his charge now is that poetry has
been subordinated to the demands of partisan politics. In a statement at

---

pp. 192–3; and Elsie Duncan-Jones, 'Marvell: A Great Master of Words', *Proceedings of the British
   Academy*, 61 (1975), 283.
[48] Cf. Rees, '"Tom May's Death"', 483.
[49] *Marvell*, "Tom May's Death", note to line 16; see above, p. 184.
[50] *Ben Jonson*, ed. C. H. Herford, Percy Simpson and Evelyn Simpson (11 vols., Oxford, 1925–52),
   VIII.40–1; see above, pp. 159–62.

the heart of the poem, which is also 'a reversal of the real Jonson's commendatory poem to May's translation of Lucan', he defines the poet's true
duty:[51]

> When the sword glitters o're the judge's head,
> And fear has coward churchmen silencéd,
> Then is the poet's time, 'tis then he draws,
> And single fights forsaken Virtue's cause.
> He, when the wheel of empire whirleth back,
> And though the world's disjointed axle crack,
> Sings still of ancient rights and better times,
> Seeks wretched good, arraigns successful crimes.
>
> (lines 63–70)

Characteristically, Jonson isolates the cause of 'Virtue', which he at least
attempts to raise above the vicissitudes of political change. The commendatory poem had employed the conventional image of 'fortunes wheel'; significantly, however, that is now translated by Marvell into an image of political revolution, as 'the wheel of empire', somewhat ambiguously, 'whirleth
back'. In contrast to this pervasive flux, virtue is embodied in tradition and
integrity, as the poet proclaims a particularly Jonsonian fixity, singing '*still*
of ancient rights and better times' (my emphasis). Yet what has perhaps
not been adequately acknowledged in criticism of the poem is the way that
these lines modify the outspoken royalism that Marvell's Jonson had pronounced in his earlier rage. With their echo of constitutionalist arguments
which sought to constrain the power of the monarch in agreement with
the 'ancient constitution', and their insistence that crimes are no less crimes
however successful they may be, the latter lines proffer a vital conception
of the poet's role within the state. Although it would be an overstatement
to claim that the poem is not royalist in its sympathies, it argues finally that
the poet's duty is to a nation defined less by the figure of the monarch than
by the abstract and enduring structures of the law.

   A notorious crux in interpretations of 'Tom May's Death' is that it
apparently contradicts the politics of 'An Horatian Ode upon Cromwell's
Return from Ireland', which Marvell wrote at around the same time. Recent
critics, however, have valuably situated it in a turbulent and uncertain political context. David Norbrook suggests the two poems should be read
as 'rival experiments'; Warren Chernaik sees them as 'in many ways companion pieces, reflecting a similar time of disorder and uncertainty'; while
Elsie Duncan-Jones argues that 'they constitute the most striking example

---

[51] *Ben Jonson*, VIII.395; *Marvell*, Smith's introduction to 'Tom May's Death'.

of "making the same thing serve" for opposite purposes'.[52] Certainly, each poem registers a political culture riven by intense controversy, within which conflicting discourses posited widely divergent versions of truth. And certainly, many contemporaries at this time held competing discourses within their minds, testing them against each other in the light of changing circumstances. Earlier in the century, this mentality prompted writers to pen alternate assessments of a statesman after his death, or to produce single poems which tease the reader with their ambiguities.[53] Marvell's poems might in some respects be situated in relation to this tradition; however, as I have argued, 'Tom May's Death' is also more than merely a polemical exercise. While so many of the texts considered in the course of this book were written for a clear political purpose, Marvell's libel rather argues against the subordination of poetry to politics. It looks back over a generation of political writing, allows Jonson his say, then condemns the servile May to hell.

Like the other texts considered in this Epilogue, 'Tom May's Death' prompts us to look backward as well as forward. In the Restoration, writers such as Cleveland and Marvell provided exemplars of a native tradition of political satire, and their works influenced much of the great outpouring of Augustan public poetry. Yet, as this book has been concerned to demonstrate, these poets were equally indebted to early Stuart traditions of unauthorized writing. Within these traditions, contemporaries not only responded to political events and arguments, but helped to ascribe meaning to their unstable times. A study of the unauthorized texts of this era, therefore, is a study of the construction – and contestation – of England's political truths.

---

[52] *Writing the English Republic*, p. 280; *The Poet's Time: Politics and Religion in the Work of Andrew Marvell* (Cambridge, 1983), p. 177; 'Marvell: A Great Master of Words', 284.
[53] See above, esp. p. 49.

Bibliography

A. PRIMARY SOURCES

I. MANUSCRIPTS[1]

Bodleian Library, Oxford
  Ashmole 36, 37
  Ashmole 38
  Ashmole 47
  Don.c.54
  Douce 173
  Eng. poet. c.50
  Eng. poet. e.14
  Eng. poet. e.97
  Eng. poet. f.10
  Malone 19
  Malone 23
  Rawlinson D 1048
  Rawlinson poet. 26
  Rawlinson poet. 212
  Tanner 299
  Tanner 465
British Library
  Add. 15226
  Add. 15476
  Add. 22118
  Add. 22601
  Add. 22603
  Add. 23229

---

[1] This is a list of manuscripts cited in the book, not of all manuscripts that have been found to be useful for a study of early Stuart political poetry. For more exhaustive information about sources, see 'Early Stuart Libels: An Edition of Political Poems from Manuscript Sources', ed. Alastair Bellany and Andrew McRae, *Early Modern Literary Studies* (forthcoming).

Add. 25303
Add. 25707
Add. 26705
Add. 29492
Add. 29996
Add. 33998
Add. 44963
Add. 61481
Egerton 923
Egerton 2230
Egerton 2725
Harley 1221
Harley 4955
Harley 6038
Harley 6383
Harley 6920
Harley 6947
Sloane 542
Sloane 826
Sloane 1446
Sloane 1792
Stowe 962
Cambridge University Library
  Dd.xi.73
Folger Shakespeare Library
  v.a.89
  v.a.103
  v.a.125
  v.a.170
  v.a.275
  v.a.345
  v.a.418
Huntington Library
  HM 116
  HM 198
National Library of Scotland
  2060
  Advocate's Library MS 19.3.8
Rosenbach Library, Philadelphia
  239/22
  239/27
  1083/16
Yale University, Beinecke Library
  Osborn b.197

2. PRINTED BOOKS

Adams, Thomas, *Workes* (1629)

Aristotle, *Aristotle on Rhetoric*, trans. George A. Kennedy (Oxford, 1991)

___, *Politica*, trans. out of French by I. D.? (1598)

The Arundel Harington Manuscript of Tudor Poetry, ed. Ruth Hussey (2 vols., Columbus, OH, 1960)

Aubrey, John, *Aubrey's Brief Lives*, ed. Oliver Lawson Dick (London, 1987)

Austin, Samuel, *Austins Urania* (1629)

B., A. D., *The Court of the Most Illustrious and most Magnificent James, the First* (1619)

Bacon, Sir Francis, *The Essays*, ed. John Pitcher (London, 1985)

___, *A Letter of Advice Written by Sir Francis Bacon to the Duke of Buckingham, When he became Favourite to King James* (1661)

___, *Works*, ed. J. Spedding, et al. (14 vols., London, 1857–74)

Barkstead, William, *That Which Seemes Best Is Worst* (1617)

Barnes, Barnabe, *The Devil's Charter*, ed. Jim C. Pogue (New York and London, 1980)

Bastard, Thomas, *Poems English and Latin*, ed. Alexander Grosart (Manchester, 1880)

Bastwick, John, *The Letany of John Bastwick* (Leiden, 1637)

___, *The Letany of John Bastwick [the second part]* (Leiden, 1637)

___, *A More Full Answer* (Leiden, 1637)

___, *The Vanity and Mischeife of the Old Letany [the third part of the Letany]* (Leiden, 1637)

[___], *A Briefe Relation of Certaine speciall and most materiall passages, and speeches in the Starre-Chamber* (1638)

Beaumont, Sir John, *Bosworth-field* (1629)

Blount, Thomas, *Glossographia* (1656)

Boccalini, Traiano, *The New-found Politicke*, trans. John Florio (1626)

Bolton, Edmund, *Nero Caesar or Monarchy Depraved* (1623)

Bond, John, *The Poets Knavery Discovered, in all their lying Pamphlets* (1642)

Brathwaite, Richard, *A Strappado for the Divell* (1615), ed. J. W. Ebsworth (Boston, Lincs., 1878)

Breda, Corneille de, *Is. Casauboni Corona Regia* (1615)

A Briefe Description of the Notorious Life of John Lambe (Amsterdam, 1628)

Britanniæ Natalis (1630)

Brooke, Christopher, *The Ghost of Richard III* (1614)

Browne, William, *The Shepheards Pipe* (1614)

Burton, Henry, *An Apology of an Appeale* (Amsterdam, 1636)

___, *Babel no Bethel* (1629)

___, *The Baiting of the Popes Bull* (1627)

___, *A Brief Answer to a Late Treatise of the Sabbath Day* (1635)

___, *A Divine Tragedie Lately Acted* (Amsterdam, 1636)

___, *For God, and the King* (1636)

__, *Israels Fast. Or, a Meditation Upon the Seventh Chapter of Joshuah; A faire Precedent for these Times* (1628)

__, *A Narration of the Life of Mr. Henry Burton* (1643)

__, *A Plea to an Appeale* (1626)

Carew, Thomas, *Poems*, ed. Rhodes Dunlap (Oxford, 1949)

Carpenter, Nathanael, *Achitophel, Or, The Picture of a Wicked Politician* (1629)

[Cavendish, William], *A Discourse Against Flatterie* (1611)

[__], *Horæ Subsecivæ: Observations and Discourses* (1620)

Chamberlain, John, *Letters*, ed. Norman Egbert McClure (2 vols., Philadelphia, 1939)

Cleveland, John, *Poems*, ed. Brian Morris and Eleanor Withington (Oxford, 1967)

The Constitutional Documents of the Puritan Revolution, ed. Samuel Rawson Gardiner, 3rd edn (Oxford, 1906)

Corbett, Richard, *Poems*, ed. J. A. W. Bennett and H. R. Trevor-Roper (Oxford, 1955)

__, *Poetica Stromata* (1648)

__, 'Richard Corbett's "Against the Opposing of the Duke in Parliament, 1628" and the Anonymous Rejoinder, "An Answere to the Same, Lyne for Lyne": The Earliest Dated Manuscript Copies', ed. V. L. Pearl and M. L. Pearl, *Review of English Studies*, 42 (1991), 32–9

Cornwallis, William, *Essayes of Certaine Paradoxes* (1617)

Cotton, Robert, *A Short View of the Long Life and Raigne of Henry the Third* (1627)

The Court and Times of Charles I, ed. Thomas Birch (2 vols., London, 1848)

Davenant, William, *The Shorter Poems*, ed. A. M. Gibbs (Oxford, 1972)

Davies, John, of Hereford, *The Scourge of Folly*, ed. Alexander Grosart (London, 1878)

A Declaration of the True Causes of the Great Troubles, Presupposed to be Intended against the Realme of England (Antwerp, 1592)

Dekker, Thomas, *Satiromastix*, in *'Poetaster' by Ben Jonson and 'Satiromastix' by Thomas Dekker*, ed. Josiah H. Penniman (Boston and London, 1913)

Devereux, Robert, 'The Poems of Edward DeVere, Seventeenth Earl of Oxford and of Robert Devereux, Second Earl of Essex', ed. Steven W. May, *Studies in Philology*, 77 (1980), 'Texts and Studies' supplement

D'Ewes, Sir Simonds, *Autobiography*, ed. James Orchard Halliwell (2 vols., London, 1845)

Digges, Dudley, *A Speech Delivered in Parliament* (1643)

Documents Relating to the Proceedings against William Prynne in 1634 and 1637, ed. Samuel Rawson Gardiner (Camden Society, London, 1877)

Donne, John, *The Complete English Poems*, ed. A. J. Smith (London, 1986)

__, *Letters to Severall Persons of Honour* (London, 1651)

Dow, Christopher, *Innovations Unjustly Charged upon the Present Church and State* (1637)

Drayton, Michael, *Works*, ed. J. William Hebel (5 vols., Oxford, 1931–41)

Drummond, William, *Poetical Works*, ed. L. E. Kastner (2 vols., Edinburgh, 1913)

Dryden, John, 'Discourse concerning the Original and Progress of Satire', in *The Works of John Dryden, Volume IV: Poems 1693–1696*, ed. A. B. Chambers and William Frost (Berkeley, 1974), pp. 3–90

Du Refuge, Eustache, *A Treatise of the Court or Instructions for Courtiers*, trans. John Reynolds (1622)

Dyke, Jeremiah, *Good Conscience: Or a Treatise Shewing the Nature, Meanes, Marks, Benefit, and Necessity thereof* (1624)

Earle, John, *Micro-cosmographie* (1628)

Eglisham, George, *The Forerunner of Revenge* (Frankfort?, 1626)

Elizabeth I, Queen, *Poems*, ed. Leicester Bradner (Providence, Rhode Island, 1964)

G., C., *The Minte of Deformitie* (1600)

G[ainsford], T[homas]?, *An Answer to Withers Motto* (Oxford, 1625)

Gainsford, Thomas, *The Rich Cabinet Furnished with Variety of Excellent Discriptions* (1616)

Gee, John, *The Foot out of the Snare* (1624)

Gibbon, Charles, *The Praise of a good Name. The reproch of an ill Name* (1594)

Goddard, William, *A Neaste of Waspes* (Dort, 1615)

—, *A Satyricall Dialogue* (Dort, 1616?)

Grymeston, Elizabeth, *Miscelanea. Meditations. Memoratives* (1604)

Guilpin, Everard, *Skialetheia or A Shadowe of Truth, in Certaine Epigrams and Satyres*, ed. D. Allen Carroll (Chapel Hill, 1974)

Hakewill, William, *The Libertie of the Subject* (1641)

Hall, Joseph, *Collected Poems*, ed. Arnold Davenport (Liverpool, 1949)

Harington, Sir John, *A Briefe View of the State of the Church of England* (1653)

—, *Epigrams* (1618); facsimile edn (Menston, 1970)

Harrison, William, *The Description of England*, ed. Georges Edelen (Ithaca, 1968)

Hayward, John, *Henry IIII* (1599)

Hell's Hurlie-Burlie (1644)

Hepwith, John, *The Calidonian Forest* (1641)

Heylyn, Peter, *A Briefe and Moderate Answer* (1636)

Holles, John, *The Holles Account of Proceedings in the House of Commons in 1624*, ed. Christopher Thompson (Orsett, Essex, 1985)

—, *Letters*, ed. P. R. Seddon (3 vols., Nottingham, 1975–86)

Hooker, Richard, *Of the Laws of Ecclesiastical Polity*, ed. Arthur Stephen McGrade (Cambridge, 1989)

Howell, James, *Epistolæ Ho-elianæ: The Familiar Letters of James Howell*, ed. Joseph Jacobs (2 vols., London, 1892)

Hubert, Sir Francis, *The Historie of Edward the Second* (1629)

Hudson, William, 'Treatise of the Court of Star Chamber', in *Collectanea Juridica. Consisting of Tracts Relative to the Law and Constitution of England* (2 vols., London, 1791), II.1–240

James VI and I, King, *The Kings Majesties Declaration to His Subjects, Concerning Lawfull Sports to be Used* (1618)

—, *Poems*, ed. James Craigie (2 vols., Scottish Text Society, Edinburgh and London, 1955–8)

__, *Political Writings*, ed. Johann P. Sommerville (Cambridge, 1994)

Jonson, Ben, *Ben Jonson*, ed. C. H. Herford, Percy and Evelyn Simpson (11 vols., Oxford, 1925–52)

__, *The Complete Masques*, ed. Stephen Orgel (New Haven, CT and London, 1969)

Josephus, *Jewish Antiquities, Books XV–XVII*, trans. Ralph Marcus, ed. Allen Wikgren (Loeb Classical Library, Cambridge, MA, 1963)

__, *The Jewish War, Books I–III*, trans. H. St J. Thackeray (Loeb Classical Library, Cambridge, MA, 1967)

Juvenal, *Juvenal and Persius*, trans. G. C. Ramsay (Loeb Classical Library, Cambridge, MA, 1918)

Lane, John, *Tom Tel-Troths Message, and His Pens Complaint* (1600); reprinted in *Shakespeare's England*, series 6, no. 2, ed. Frederick J. Furnivall (New Shakespeare Society, London, 1876)

Laud, William, *A Speech Delivered in the Starre-Chamber* (1637)

__, *Works*, ed. W. Scott and J. Bliss (7 vols., Oxford, 1847–60)

Leighton, Alexander, *An Appeal to the Parliament, Or Sions Plea Against the Prelacie* (Amsterdam, 1628)

__, *Speculum Belli sacri: Or The Lookingglasse of the Holy War* (Amsterdam, 1624)

[__]?, *The Interpreter. Wherein three principal Terms of State, much mistaken by the vulgar, are clearly understood* (1622); reprinted in *An English Garner: Stuart Tracts, 1603–1693*, ed. C. H. Firth (London, 1903)

Loe, William, *Vox Clamantis* (1621)

M., T., *The Life of a Satyrical Puppy, Called Nim* (1657)

Manningham, John, *The Diary of John Manningham of the Middle Temple 1602–1603*, ed. Robert Parker Sorlien (Hanover, NH, 1976)

The Marprelate Tracts, ed. William Pierce (London, 1911)

Marston, John, *Poems*, ed. Arnold Davenport (Liverpool, 1961)

Marvell, Andrew, *Marvell: The Poems of Andrew Marvell*, ed. Nigel Smith (Harlow, 2003)

Matthieu, Pierre, *The Powerfull Favorite, Or, The Life of Ælius Sejanus* (London?, 1628)

Maynwaring, Roger, *Religion and Alegiance: in two sermons* (1627)

Mead, Joseph, 'A Critical Edition of the Letters of the Reverend Joseph Mead, 1626–1627, Contained in British Library Harleian MS 390', ed. David Anthony John Cockburn (unpublished Ph.D dissertation, University of Cambridge, 1994)

Melton, John, *A Sixe-Folde Politician* (1609)

Middleton, Thomas, *A Game at Chess*, ed. T. H. Howard-Hill (The Revels Plays, Manchester, 1993)

__, *A Game at Chess*, ed. R. C. Bald (Cambridge, 1929)

__, *The Witch*, ed. Elizabeth Schafer (London and New York, 1994)

Milton, John, *The Complete Prose Works*, ed. Don M. Wolfe, *et al.* (8 vols., New Haven, CT and London, 1953–82)

Niccols, Richard, *The Beggers Ape* (1626)

__, *The Cuckow* (1607)

Original Papers Illustrative of the Life and Writings of John Milton, ed. W. Douglas Hamilton (Camden Society, London, 1859)

Osborne, Francis, *Traditionall Memoryes on the Raigne of King James* (1658)

Overton, Richard, *A New Play Called Canterburie his Change of Diot* (1641)

The Penguin Book of Renaissance Verse, selected by David Norbrook, ed. H. R. Woudhuysen (London, 1992)

A Pepysian Garland: Black-letter Broadside Ballads of the Years 1595 to 1639, ed. Hyder E. Rollins (Cambridge, 1922)

Perkins, William, *Works* (Cambridge, 1603)

A Plaine description of the Auncient Petigree of Dame Slaunder (1573)

Poems and Songs Relating to George Villiers, Duke of Buckingham; and his Assassination by John Felton, ed. Frederick W. Fairholt (Percy Society, London, 1850)

'Poems from a Seventeenth-Century manuscript with the Hand of Robert Herrick', ed. Norman Farmer, *Texas Quarterly*, 16.4 (1973), supplement

Poems on Affairs of State: Augustan Satirical Verse, 1660–1714, ed. George de F. Lord (7 vols., New Haven, CT and London, 1963–75)

Proceedings in Parliament 1610, ed. Elizabeth Read Foster (2 vols., New Haven, CT and London, 1966)

Proceedings in Parliament, 1626, ed. William B. Bidwell and Maija Jansson (4 vols., New Haven, CT and London, 1991–6)

Proceedings in Parliament: Commons Debates, 1628, ed. Mary Frear Keeler, *et al.* (6 vols., New Haven, and London, 1977–83)

Prynne, William, *Anti-Arminianisme* (1630)

___, *A Briefe Survay and Censure of Mr Cozens His Couzening Devotions* (1628)

___, *An Humble Remonstrance to his Majesty* (1641)

___, *Lame Giles His Haultings* (1630)

___, *A Looking-Glasse for all Lordly Prelates* (London?, 1636)

___, *The Perpetuitie of a Regenerate Mans Estate* (1627)

___, *A Quench-Coale. Or A Briefe Disquisition and Inquirie, in what place of the Church or Chancell the Lords-Table ought to be situated* (Amsterdam, 1637)

[Prynne, William], *A New Discovery of the Prelates Tyranny* (1641)

[Prynne, William], *Newes from Ipswich* (1636?)

Puttenham, George, *The Arte of English Poesie*, ed. Gladys Doidge Willcock and Alice Walker (Cambridge, 1936)

___, *The Prerogative of Parliaments in England* (1628)

Raleigh, Sir Walter, *The Poems of Sir Walter Ralegh: A Historical Edition*, ed. Michael Rudick (Tempe, Arizona, 1999)

Les Reportes del Cases in Camera Stellata 1593 to 1609, From the Original MS. of John Hawarde (London, 1894)

Reynolds, John, *Votivae Angliae* (1624)

___, *Vox Coeli* (1624)

Rous, John, *Diary*, ed. Mary Anne Everett Green (Camden Society, 1861; reprint edn, New York and London, 1968)

Rowlands, Samuel, *Complete Works* (3 vols., Hunterian Club, Glasgow, 1880)

[Russell, John]?, *The Spy* (Strasburg, 1628)

Scot, Thomas, *Philomythie or Philomythologie* (1622)

Scott, Thomas, *Aphorismes of State* (1624)

___, *The Belgicke Pismire* (Holland, 1622)

___, *The High-Waies of God and the King* (Holland, 1623)

___, *Newes from Parnassus. The Political Touchstone* (Holland, 1622)

___, *Robert Earle of Essex His Ghost* (1624)

___, *The Second Part of Vox Populi: or Gondomar appearing in the likenes of Matchiavell in a Spanish parliament* (1624)

___, *Sir Walter Rawleighs Ghost* (London?, 1626)

___, *Vox Dei* (Holland?, 1623?)

___, *Vox Populi: or newes from Spaine* (London?, 1620)

___, *Works* (Utrecht, 1624); facsimile edn (Amsterdam, 1973)

Shakespeare, William, *The Norton Shakespeare*, ed. Stephen Greenblatt *et al.* (New York and London, 1997)

Sidney, Sir Philip, *Sir Philip Sidney*, ed. Katherine Duncan-Jones (Oxford, 1989)

Spenser, Edmund, *Poetical Works*, ed. J. C. Smith and E. De Selincourt (Oxford, 1970)

Stafford, Anthony, *Staffords Heavenly Dogge* (1615)

Stanyhurst, Richard, *Thee First Foure Bookes of Virgil his Aeneis* (Leiden, 1582)

Stuart Royal Proclamations, ed. James F. Larkin and Paul L. Hughes (2 vols., Oxford, 1973–83)

T., I., *The Just Down[fall] of Ambition, Adultery and Murder* (1616)

Taylor, John, *Crop-Eare Curried, Or, Tom Nash His Ghost* (1644)

___, *A Reply as true as Steele, To a Rusty, Rayling, Ridiculous, Lying Libell* (1641)

___, *A Swarme of Sectaries, and Schismatiques* (1641)

___, *The Whole Life and Progresse of Henry Walker the Ironmonger* (1642)

Tisdale, Roger, *Pax Vobis* (1623)

Tom Nash his Ghost (1642)

Tom Tell Troath or A free discourse touching the manners of the tyme (Holland, 1630?)

Tom-Tell-Troath, or a Free Discourse Touching on the Murmurs of the Times (1642)

Townshend, Aurelian, *Poems and Masques*, ed. Cedric C. Brown (Reading, 1983)

'Two Unpublished Poems on the Duke of Buckingham', ed. J. A. Taylor, *Review of English Studies*, 40 (1989), 232–40

Vaughan, William, *The Spirit of Detraction Conjured and Convicted in Seven Circles* (1611)

Walker, Henry, *An Answer to a Foolish Pamphlet Entituled A swarme of Sectaries and Schismaticks* (1641)

___, *Taylors Physicke has purged the Divel* (1641)

Weever, John, *Faunus and Melliflora*, ed. Arnold Davenport (Liverpool, 1948)

Weldon, Sir Anthony, *The Court and Character of King James* (1651)

Wentworth, Thomas, Earl of Strafford, *The Earl of Strafforde's Letters and Dispatches*, ed. William Knowler (2 vols., Dublin, 1740)

The Whipper Pamphlets, ed. Arnold Davenport (Liverpool, 1951)

White, Francis, *An Examination and Confutation of a Lawless Pamphlet* (1637)

Whiteway, William, of Dorchester, *His Diary 1618 to 1635* (Dorset Record Society, 1991)

Wilson, Arthur, *The History of Great Britain, Being the Life and Reign of King James I* (1653)

Wit Restor'd In severall Select Poems (1658)

Wither, George, *Abuses Stript, and Whipt* (1613)

—, *Britain's Remembrancer* (1628); facsimile edn (Spenser Society, New York, 1967)

—, *Juvenilia* (1622)

—, *A Satyre: Dedicated to His Most Excellent Majestie* (1614)

—, *The Shepherds Hunting* (1615)

—, *Wither's Motto* (1622)

Wroth, Lady Mary, *The Countess of Montgomeries Urania* (1621)

Wybarne, Joseph, *The New Age of Old Names* (1609)

Yonge, Walter, *Diary*, ed. George Roberts (Camden Society, London, 1848)

B. SECONDARY SOURCES

Anselment, Raymond A., 'The Oxford University Poets and Caroline Panegyric', *John Donne Journal*, 3 (1984), 181–201

Atherton, Ian, 'The Itch Grown a Disease: Manuscript Transmission of News in the Seventeenth Century', in Raymond, ed., *News, Newspapers, and Society in Early Modern Britain*, pp. 39–65

Beal, Peter, ed., *Index of English Literary Manuscripts. Vol. 1. 1450–1625* (2 parts, London, 1980)

—, 'Massinger at Bay: Unpublished Verses in a War of the Theatres', *Yearbook of English Studies*, 10 (1980), 190–203

—, 'Notions in Garrison: The Seventeenth-Century Commonplace Book', in W. Speed Hill, ed., *New Ways of Looking at Old Texts: Papers of the Renaissance English Text Society, 1985–1991* (Binghamton, 1993), pp. 131–47

Beer, Anna R., *Sir Walter Ralegh and his Readers in the Seventeenth Century* (London, 1997)

Bellany, Alastair, 'Libels in Action: Ritual, Subversion and the English Literary Underground, 1603–42', in Tim Harris, ed., *The Politics of the Excluded, c.1500–1850* (Basingstoke, 2001), pp. 99–124

—, 'The Poisoning of Legitimacy? Court Scandal, News Culture, and Politics in England 1603–1660' (unpublished Ph.D dissertation, Princeton University, 1995)

—, *The Politics of Court Scandal in Early Modern England: News Culture and the Overbury Affair, 1603–1660* (Cambridge, 2002)

—, '"Rayling Rymes and Vaunting Verse": Libellous Politics in Early Stuart England, 1603–1628', in Kevin Sharpe and Peter Lake, eds., *Culture and Politics in Early Stuart England* (Basingstoke, 1994), pp. 285–310

—, 'A Poem on the Archbishop's Hearse: Puritanism, Libel, and Sedition after the Hampton Court Conference', *Journal of British Studies*, 34 (1995), 137–64

Benet, Diana, 'Carew's Monarchy of Wit', in Claude J. Summers and Ted-Larry Pebworth, eds., *'The Muses Common-Weale': Poetry and Politics in the Seventeenth Century* (Columbia, 1988), pp. 80–91

Bogel, Fredric, *The Difference Satire Makes: Rhetoric and Reading from Jonson to Byron* (Ithaca and London, 2001)

Bradford, Alan T., 'Stuart Absolutism and the "Utility" of Tacitus', *Huntington Library Quarterly*, 46 (1983), 127–55

Bredbeck, Gregory W., *Sodomy and Interpretation: Marlowe to Milton* (Ithaca and London, 1991)

Brettle, R. E., 'John Marston and the Duke of Buckingham', *Notes and Queries*, 212 (1967), 326–30

Brooks, Harold F., 'Verse Satire, 1640–1660', *The Seventeenth Century*, 3 (1989), 17–46

Bruster, Douglas, 'The Structural Transformation of Print in Late Elizabethan England', in Arthur F. Marotti and Michael D. Bristol, eds., *Print, Manuscript, and Performance: The Changing Relations of the Media in Early Modern England* (Columbus, OH, 2000), pp. 49–89

Burgess, Glenn, *The Politics of the Ancient Constitution: An Introduction to English Political Thought, 1603–1642* (Basingstoke and London, 1992)

Burke, P., 'Tacitism', in T. A. Dorey, ed., *Tacitus* (London, 1969), pp. 149–71

Butler, Martin, 'Late Jonson', in Gordon McMullan and Jonathan Hope, eds., *The Politics of Tragicomedy: Shakespeare and After* (London, 1992), pp. 166–88

___, '"Servant, but not Slave": Ben Jonson at the Jacobean Court', *Proceedings of the British Academy*, 90 (1995), 65–93

___, *Theatre and Crisis 1632–1642* (Cambridge, 1984)

Bynum, Caroline Walker, *The Resurrection of the Body in Western Christianity, 200–1336* (New York, 1995)

Calhoun, T. O., 'Cowley's Verse Satire, 1642–43, and the Beginnings of Party Politics', *Yearbook of English Studies*, 21 (1991), 197–206

Capp, Bernard, *The World of John Taylor the Water-Poet 1578–1653* (Oxford, 1994)

Chartier, Roger, *Cultural History: Between Practices and Representations*, trans. Lydia G. Cochrane (Cambridge, 1988)

Chernaik, Warren, *The Poet's Time: Politics and Religion in the Work of Andrew Marvell* (Cambridge, 1983)

Clark, J. C. D., *Revolution and Rebellion: State and Society in England in the Seventeenth and Eighteenth Centuries* (Cambridge, 1986)

Clark, Sandra, *The Elizabethan Pamphleteers* (London, 1982)

Clegg, Cyndia Susan, *Press Censorship in Elizabethan England* (Cambridge, 1997)

___, *Press Censorship in Jacobean England* (Cambridge, 2001)

Clucas, Stephen, and Davies, Rosalind, eds., *1614: Year of Crisis: Studies in Jacobean History and Literature* (Aldershot, 2002)

Cogswell, Thomas, *The Blessed Revolution: English Politics and the Coming of War, 1621–1624* (Cambridge, 1989)

—, 'England and the Spanish Match', in Richard Cust and Ann Hughes, eds., *Conflict in Early Stuart England: Studies in Religion and Politics* (London, 1989), pp. 107–33

—, 'The Path to Elizium "Lately Discovered": Drayton and the Early Stuart Court', *Huntington Library Quarterly*, 54 (1991), 207–33

—, 'Politics and Propaganda: Charles I and the People in the 1620s', *Journal of British Studies*, 29 (1990), 187–215

—, 'Thomas Middleton and the Court, 1624: *A Game at Chess* in Context', *Huntington Library Quarterly*, 47 (1984), 273–88

—, 'Underground Political Verse and the Transformation of English Political Culture', in Susan D. Amussen and Mark A. Kishlansky, eds., *Political Culture and Cultural Politics in Early Modern England: Essays Presented to David Underdown* (Manchester, 1995), pp. 277–300

Coiro, Ann Baynes, '"A ball of strife": Caroline Poetry and Royal Marriage', in Thomas N. Corns, ed., *The Royal Image: Representations of Charles I* (Cambridge, 1999), pp. 26–46

Colclough, David, '"Better Becoming a Senate of Venice"? The "Addled Parliament" and Jacobean Debates on Freedom of Speech', in Clucas and Davies, eds., *1614: Year of Crisis*, pp. 51–62

—, '"The Muses Recreation": John Hoskyns and the Manuscript Culture of the Seventeenth Century', *Huntington Library Quarterly*, 61 (2000), 369–400

—, '"Of the alleadging of authors": The Construction and Reception of Textual Authority in English Prose, c.1600–1630. With special reference to the writings of Francis Bacon, John Hoskyns, and John Donne' (unpublished DPhil. dissertation, University of Oxford, 1996)

—, '*Parrhesia*: The Rhetoric of Free Speech in Early Modern England', *Rhetorica*, 17 (1999), 177–212

Collinson, Patrick, 'A Comment: Concerning the Name Puritan', *Journal of Ecclesiastical History*, 31 (1980), 482–8

—, *Elizabethan Essays* (London and Rio Grande, 1994)

—, *The Puritan Character: Polemics and Polarities in Early Seventeenth-Century English Culture* (Los Angeles, 1989)

—, 'Ecclesiastical Vitriol: Religious Satire in the 1590s and the Invention of Puritanism', in John Guy, ed., *The Reign of Elizabeth I* (Cambridge, 1995), pp. 150–70

Combe, Kirk, 'The New Voice of Political Dissent: The Transition from Complaint to Satire', in Combe and Connery, eds., *Theorizing Satire: Essays in Literary Criticism*, pp. 73–94

—, and Connery, Brian A., eds., *Theorizing Satire: Essays in Literary Criticism* (Basingstoke and London, 1995)

Condren, Conal, *The Language of Politics in Seventeenth-Century England* (New York, 1994)

Connery, Brian A., and Combe, Kirk, 'Theorizing Satire: A Retrospective and Introduction', in Combe and Connery, eds., *Theorizing Satire: Essays in Literary Criticism*, pp. 1–15

Corns, Thomas N., 'Thomas Carew, Sir John Suckling, and Richard Lovelace', in *The Cambridge Companion to English Poetry: Donne to Marvell*, ed. Thomas N. Corns (Cambridge, 1993), pp. 200–220

Cressy, David, *Travesties and Transgressions in Tudor and Stuart England: Tales of Discord and Dissension* (Oxford, 2000)

Croft, Pauline, 'Libels, Popular Literacy and Public Opinion in Early Modern England', *Historical Research*, 68 (1995), 266–85

__, 'The Reputation of Robert Cecil: Libels, Political Opinion and Popular Awareness in the Early Seventeenth Century', *Transactions of the Royal Historical Society*, 6th series, 1 (1991), 43–69

Cromartie, Alan, 'The Constitutionalist Revolution: The Transformation of Political Culture in Early Stuart England', *Past and Present*, 163 (1999), 76–120

Crum, Margaret, ed., *First-Line Index of English Poetry 1500–1800 in Manuscripts of the Bodleian Library Oxford* (2 vols., Oxford, 1969)

Cust, Richard, *The Forced Loan and English Politics 1626–1628* (Oxford, 1987)

__, 'News and Politics in Early Seventeenth-Century England', *Past and Present*, 112 (1986), 60–90

__, 'Politics and the Electorate in the 1620s', in Richard Cust and Ann Hughes, eds., *Conflict in Early Stuart England: Studies in Religion and Politics* (London, 1989), pp. 134–67

Davies, Richard A., and Young, Alan R., '"Strange Cunning" in Thomas Middleton's *A Game at Chess*', *University of Toronto Quarterly*, 45 (1976), 236–45

Doody, Margaret Anne, *The Daring Muse: Augustan Poetry Reconsidered* (Cambridge, 1985)

Duncan-Jones, Elsie, 'Marvell: A Great Master of Words', *Proceedings of the British Academy*, 61 (1975), 267–90

Elliott, Robert C., *The Power of Satire: Magic, Ritual, Art* (Princeton, 1960)

Erickson, Robert A., *The Language of the Heart, 1600–1750* (Philadelphia, 1997)

Erskine-Hill, Howard, *The Augustan Idea in English Literature* (London, 1983)

Evans, Robert C., *Ben Jonson and the Poetics of Patronage* (Lewisburg, PA, 1989)

Faber, Benne Klaas, 'The Poetics of Subversion and Conservatism: Popular Satire, c.1640–c.1649' (unpublished DPhil. dissertation, University of Oxford, 1992)

Farley-Hills, David, ed., *Earl of Rochester: The Critical Heritage* (London, 1972)

Farr, Dorothy M., *Thomas Middleton and the Drama of Realism: A Study of Some Representative Plays* (Edinburgh, 1973)

Fielding, John, 'Opposition to the Personal Rule of Charles I: The Diary of Robert Woodford, 1637–1641', *Historical Journal*, 31 (1988), 769–88

Fish, Stanley, 'Author-Readers: Jonson's Community of the Same', *Representations*, 7 (1984), 26–58

Foster, Stephen, *Notes from the Caroline Underground: Alexander Leighton, the Puritan Triumvirate, and the Laudian Reaction to Nonconformity* (Hamden, CT, 1978)

Foucault, Michel, *Discipline and Punish: The Birth of the Prison*, trans. Alan Sheridan (London, 1991)

Fox, Adam, 'Ballads, Libels and Popular Ridicule in Jacobean England', *Past and Present*, 145 (1994), 47–83
___, *Oral and Literate Culture in England 1500–1700* (Oxford, 2000)
Frank, J., *The Beginnings of the English Newspaper, 1620–1660* (Cambridge, MA, 1961)
Frearson, Michael Colin, 'The English Corantoes of the 1620s' (unpublished Ph.D dissertation, University of Cambridge, 1993)
Freist, Dagmar, *Governed by Opinion: Politics, Religion, and the Dynamics of Communication in Stuart London, 1637–1645* (London, 1997)
Gardiner, Samuel R., *History of England from the Accession of James to the Outbreak of the Civil War, 1603–1642*, reprint edn (10 vols., New York, 1965)
Gibson, Leonie J., 'Formal Satire in the First Half of the Seventeenth Century. 1600–1650' (unpublished DPhil. dissertation, University of Oxford, 1952)
Gilbert, Allan H., 'Jonson and Drummond or Gil on the King's Senses', *Modern Language Notes*, 62 (1947), 35–7
Gittings, Claire, *Death, Burial and the Individual in Early Modern England* (London and Sydney, 1984)
Goldberg, Jonathan, *James I and the Politics of Literature: Jonson, Shakespeare, Donne, and Their Contemporaries* (Baltimore and London, 1983)
___, *Sodometries: Renaissance Texts, Modern Sexualities* (Stanford, 1992)
Gray, Douglas, 'Rough Music: Some Early Invectives and Flytings', in Claude Rawson, ed., *English Satire and the Satiric Tradition* (London, 1984), pp. 21–43
Greenfield, Matthew, 'The Cultural Functions of Renaissance Elegy', *English Literary Renaissance*, 28 (1998), 75–94
Griffin, Dustin, *Satire: A Critical Reintroduction* (Lexington, KY, 1994)
Guy, John, ed., *The Reign of Elizabeth I: Court and Culture in the Last Decade* (Cambridge, 1995)
Habermas, Jürgen, *The Structural Transformation of the Public Sphere: An Inquiry into a Category of Bourgeois Society*, trans. Thomas Burger (Cambridge, MA, 1991)
Halasz, Alexandra, *The Marketplace of Print: Pamphlets and the Public Sphere in Early Modern England* (Cambridge, 1997)
Hammer, Paul E. J., *The Polarisation of Elizabethan Politics: The Political Career of Robert Devereux, 2nd Earl of Essex, 1587–1597* (Cambridge, 1999)
Hammond, Gerald, *Fleeting Things: English Poets and Poems 1616–1660* (Cambridge, MA, 1990)
Hammond, Paul, *Figuring Sex Between Men from Shakespeare to Rochester* (Oxford, 2002)
Heinemann, Margot, *Puritanism and Theatre: Thomas Middleton and Opposition Drama under the Early Stuarts* (Cambridge, 1980)
Helgerson, Richard, *The Elizabethan Prodigals* (Berkeley, 1976)
___, *Self-Crowned Laureates: Spenser, Jonson, Milton, and the Literary System* (Berkeley and London, 1983)
Highet, Gilbert, *The Anatomy of Satire* (Princeton, 1962)

Hill, Christopher, 'Parliament and People in Seventeenth-Century England', *Past and Present*, 92 (1981), 100–24

Hirst, Derek, 'Revisionism Revised: The Place of Principle', *Past and Present*, 92 (1981), 79–99

Hobbs, Mary, *Early Seventeenth-Century Verse Miscellany Manuscripts* (Aldershot, 1992)

Hodges, Devon L., *Renaissance Fictions of Anatomy* (Amherst, 1985)

Holstun, James, *Ehud's Dagger: Class Struggle in the English Revolution* (London, 2000)

—, '"God Bless Thee, Little David!": John Felton and his Allies', *ELH*, 59 (1992), 513–52

Howard-Hill, T. H., *Middleton's 'Vulgar Pasquin': Essays on 'A Game at Chess'* (Newark, 1995)

Hutson, Lorna, *Thomas Nashe in Context* (Oxford, 1989)

Ingram, Martin, 'Ridings, Rough Music and Mocking Rhymes in Early Modern England', in Barry Reay, ed., *Popular Culture in Seventeenth-Century England* (London and Sydney, 1985), pp. 166–97

Kantorowicz, Ernst H., *The King's Two Bodies: A Study in Mediaeval Political Theology* (Princeton, 1957)

Kaplan, M. Lindsay, *The Culture of Slander in Early Modern England* (Cambridge, 1997)

Kernan, Alvin, *The Cankered Muse: Satire of the English Renaissance* (New Haven, CT, 1959)

Kishlansky, Mark, 'The Emergence of Adversary Politics in the Long Parliament', *Journal of Modern History*, 49 (1977), 617–40

Knowles, James, 'To "scourge the arse / Jove's marrow so had wasted": Scurrility and the Subversion of Sodomy', in Dermot Cavanagh and Tim Kirk, eds., *Subversion and Scurrility: Popular Discourse in Europe from 1500 to the Present* (Aldershot, 2000), pp. 74–92

Knowles, Ronald, '"The All-Attoning Name": The Word *Patriot* in Seventeenth-Century England', *Modern Languages Review*, 96 (2001), 624–43

Lake, Peter, 'Anti-Popery: The Structure of a Prejudice', in Richard Cust and Ann Hughes, eds., *Conflict in Early Stuart England: Studies in Religion and Politics* (London, 1989), pp. 72–106

—, 'Constitutional Consensus and Puritan Opposition in the 1620s: Thomas Scott and the Spanish Match', *Historical Journal*, 25 (1982), 805–25

Lamont, William M., *Marginal Prynne 1600–1669* (London, 1963)

Lanham, Richard A., *A Handlist of Rhetorical Terms*, 2nd edn (Berkeley, 1991)

Limon, Jerzy, *Dangerous Matter: English Drama and Politics in 1623/24* (Cambridge, 1986)

Lindley, David, *The Trials of Frances Howard: Fact and Fiction at the Court of King James* (London and New York, 1993)

Little, Ruth Marion, 'Perpetual Metaphors: The Configuration of the Courtier as Favourite in Jacobean and Caroline Literature' (unpublished Ph.D dissertation, University of Cambridge, 1993)

Lockyer, Roger, *Buckingham: The Life and Political Career of George Villiers, First Duke of Buckingham 1592–1628* (London and New York, 1981)

Loewenstein, Joseph, 'Wither and Professional Work', in Arthur F. Marotti and Michael D. Bristol, eds., *Print, Manuscript, and Performance: The Changing Relations of the Media in Early Modern England* (Columbus, 2000), pp. 103–23

Love, Harold, *The Culture and Commerce of Texts: Scribal Publication in Seventeenth-Century England* (Amherst, 1998)

Loxley, James, *Royalism and Poetry in the English Civil Wars: The Drawn Sword* (London, 1997)

McCabe, Richard A., 'Elizabethan Satire and the Bishops' Ban of 1599', *Yearbook of English Studies*, 11 (1981), 188–93

MacDonald, Robert H., 'Amendments to L. E. Kastner's Edition of Drummond's Poems', *Studies in Scottish Literature*, 7 (1970), 102–22

MacLean, Gerald M., *Time's Witness: Historical Representation in English Poetry, 1603–1660* (Madison, 1990)

McRae, Andrew, *God Speed the Plough: The Representation of Agrarian England, 1500–1660* (Cambridge, 1996)

___, 'The Poetics of Sycophancy: Ben Jonson and the Caroline Court', in David Brooks and Brian Kiernan, eds., *Running Wild: Essays, Fictions and Memoirs Presented to Michael Wilding* (Sydney, 2003), pp. 29–42

___, 'The Verse Libel: Popular Satire in Early Modern England', in Dermot Cavanagh and Tim Kirk, eds., *Subversion and Scurrility: Popular Discourse in Europe from 1500 to the Present* (Aldershot, 2000), pp. 58–73

Main, C. F., 'Ben Jonson and an Unknown Poet on the King's Senses', *Modern Language Notes*, 74 (1959), 389–93

Manley, Lawrence, *Literature and Culture in Early Modern London* (Cambridge, 1995)

Marcus, Leah S., *The Politics of Mirth: Jonson, Herrick, Milton, Marvell, and the Defense of Old Holiday Pastimes* (Chicago and London, 1986)

Marotti, Arthur F., *Manuscript, Print, and the English Renaissance Lyric* (Ithaca and London, 1995)

Maus, Katharine Eisaman, *Inwardness and Theater in the English Renaissance* (Chicago and London, 1995)

Mendle, Michael, 'De Facto Freedom, De Facto Authority: Press and Parliament, 1640–1643', *Historical Journal*, 38 (1995), 307–332

Metcalfe, Jean Le Drew, 'Subjecting the King: Ben Jonson's Praise of James I', *English Studies in Canada*, 17 (1991), 135–49

Milton, Anthony, *Catholic and Reformed: The Roman and Protestant Churches in English Protestant Thought 1600–1640* (Cambridge, 1995)

___, 'Licensing, Censorship, and Religious Orthodoxy in Early Stuart England', *Historical Journal*, 41 (1998), 625–51

Morrill, John, 'The Religious Context of the English Civil War', *Transactions of Royal Historical Society*, 5th series 34 (1984), 155–78

___, *Revolt in the Provinces: The People of England and the Tragedies of War*, 2nd edn (London and New York, 1999)

Mousley, Andrew, 'Self, State, and Seventeenth-Century News', *The Seventeenth-Century*, 6 (1991), 149–68

Neill, Michael, *Issues of Death: Mortality and Identity in English Renaissance Tragedy* (Oxford, 1997)

Nixon, Scott, 'The Manuscript Sources of Thomas Carew's Poetry', *English Manuscript Studies, 1100–1700*, 8 (2000), 186–224

Norbrook, David, '*Areopagitica*, Censorship, and the Early Modern Public Sphere', in Richard Burt, ed., *The Administration of Aesthetics: Censorship, Political Criticism, and the Public Sphere* (Minneapolis and London, 1994), pp. 3–33

___, *Poetry and Politics in the English Renaissance*, revised edn (Oxford, 2002)

___, *Writing the English Republic: Poetry, Rhetoric and Politics, 1627–1660* (Cambridge, 1999)

O'Callaghan, Michelle, '"Now thou may'st speak freely": Entering the Public Sphere in 1614', in Clucas and Davies, eds., *1614: Year of Crisis*, pp. 63–80

___, *The 'shepheards nation': Jacobean Spenserians and Early Stuart Political Culture* (Oxford, 2000)

Parry, Graham, 'Cotton's Counsels: The Contexts of *Cottoni Posthuma*', in C. J. Wright, ed., *Sir Robert Cotton as Collector: Essays on an Early Stuart Courtier and his Legacy* (London, 1997), pp. 81–95

Patterson, Annabel, *Censorship and Interpretation: The Conditions of Writing and Reading in Early Modern England* (Madison, 1984)

Patterson, W. B., *King James VI and I and the Reunion of Christendom* (Cambridge, 1997)

Pebworth, Ted-Larry, 'Sir Henry Wotton's "Dazel'd Thus, with Height of Place" and the Appropriation of Political Poetry in the Earlier Seventeenth Century', *Publications of the Bibliographical Society of America*, 71 (1977), 151–69

Peck, Linda Levy, *Court Patronage and Corruption in Early Stuart England* (London, 1993)

___, 'Kingship, Counsel and Law in Early Stuart Britain', in J. G. A. Pocock, ed., *The Varieties of British Political Thought, 1500–1800* (Cambridge, 1993), pp. 80–115

___, *Northampton: Patronage and Policy at the Court of James I* (London, 1982)

Pelling, Margaret, 'Appearance and Reality: Barber-Surgeons, the Body and Disease', in A. L. Beier and Roger Finlay, eds., *London 1500–1700: The Making of the Metropolis* (London and New York, 1986), pp. 82–112

Peltonen, Markku, *Classical Humanism and Republicanism in English Political Thought 1570–1640* (Cambridge, 1995)

Perry, Curtis, *The Making of Jacobean Culture: James I and the Renegotiation of Elizabethan Literary Practice* (Cambridge, 1997)

___, 'The Politics of Access and Representations of the Sodomite King in Early Modern England', *Renaissance Quarterly*, 53 (2000), 1054–83

Perry, Kathryn, 'Political Animals: Spenserian Beast Satire 1591–1628' (unpublished Ph.D dissertation, University of Reading, 2000)

Peter, John, *Complaint and Satire in Early English Literature* (Oxford, 1956)

Pocock, J. G. A., *The Machiavellian Moment: Florentine Political Thought and the Atlantic Republican Tradition* (Princeton, 1975)

___, *Politics, Language and Time* (London, 1972)

___, *Virtue, Commerce and History* (Cambridge, 1985)

Poole, Kristen, *Radical Religion from Shakespeare to Milton: Figures of Nonconformity in Early Modern England* (Cambridge, 2000)

Potter, Lois, *Secret Rites and Secret Writing: Royalist Literature, 1640–1660* (Cambridge, 1989)

Powers, Doris C., *English Formal Satire: Elizabethan to Augustan* (The Hague, 1971)

Pritchard, Allan, '*Abuses Stript and Whipt* and Wither's Imprisonment', *Review of English Studies*, n.s. 14 (1963), 337–45

Rabb, Theodore, 'Revisionism Revised: The Role of the Commons', *Past and Present*, 92 (1981), 54–78

Rambuss, Richard, *Closet Devotions* (Durham and London, 1998)

Randall, B. J., *Jonson's Gypsies Unmasked* (Durham, NC., 1975)

Randolph, Mary Claire, 'The Medical Concept in English Renaissance Satiric Theory', *Studies in Philology*, 38 (1941), 127–59

Raylor, Timothy, *Cavaliers, Clubs, and Literary Culture: Sir John Mennes, James Smith, and the Order of the Fancy* (Newark, 1994)

Raymond, Joad, *The Invention of the Newspaper: English Newsbooks, 1641–1649* (Oxford, 1996)

___, ed., *News, Newspapers, and Society in Early Modern Britain* (London and Portland, 1999)

___, 'The Newspaper, Public Opinion, and the Public Sphere in the Seventeenth Century', in Raymond, ed., *News, Newspapers, and Society in Early Modern Britain*, pp. 109–40

Rees, Christine, '"Tom May's Death" and Ben Jonson's Ghost: A Study of Marvell's Satiric Method', *Modern Language Review*, 71 (1976), 481–8

Rhodes, Neil, *Elizabethan Grotesque* (London, 1980)

Richards, Judith, '"His nowe Majestie" and the English Monarchy: The Kingship of Charles I before 1640', *Past and Present*, 113 (1986), 70–96

Roberts, Josephine A., 'Lady Mary Wroth's *Urania*: A Response to Jacobean Censorship', in W. Speed Hill, ed., *New Ways of Looking at Old Texts: Papers of the Renaissance English Text Society, 1985–1991* (Binghamton, 1993), pp. 125–9

Rosenheim, Edward, Jr., *Jonathan Swift and the Satirist's Art* (Chicago, 1963)

Russell, Conrad, *The Crisis of Parliaments: English History 1509–1660* (Oxford, 1971)

___, *Parliaments and English Politics 1621–1629* (Oxford, 1979)

___, *Unrevolutionary England, 1603–1642* (London, 1989)

Sacks, David Harris, 'Parliament, Liberty, and the Commonweal', in J. H. Hexter, ed., *Parliament and Liberty from the Reign of Elizabeth to the English Civil War*, (Stanford, 1992), pp. 85–121

Salmon, J. H. M., 'Stoicism and the Roman Example: Seneca and Tacitus in Jacobean England', *Journal of the History of Ideas*, 50 (1989), 199–225

Saslow, James M., *Ganymede in the Renaissance: Homosexuality in Art and Society* (New Haven, CT, 1986)

Sawday, Jonathan, *The Body Emblazoned: Dissection and the Human Body in Renaissance Culture* (London, 1995)

Schifflett, Andrew, *Stoicism, Politics, and Literature in the Age of Milton* (Cambridge, 1998)

Scodel, Joshua, *The English Poetic Epitaph: Commemoration and Conflict from Jonson to Wordsworth* (Ithaca and London, 1991)

Selden, Raman, *English Verse Satire, 1590–1765* (London, 1978)

Sharpe, Kevin, *Criticism and Compliment: The Politics of Literature in the England of Charles I* (Cambridge, 1987)

___, ed., *Faction and Parliament: Essays in Early Stuart History* (Oxford, 1978)

___, *The Personal Rule of Charles I* (New Haven, CT and London, 1992)

___, *Politics and Ideas in Early Stuart England: Essays and Studies* (London and New York, 1989)

___, *Reading Revolutions: The Politics of Reading in Early Modern England* (New Haven, CT and London, 2000)

___, *Remapping Early Modern England: The Culture of Seventeenth-Century Politics* (Cambridge, 2000)

___, *Sir Robert Cotton 1586–1631: History and Politics in Early Modern England* (Oxford, 1979)

Sherman, Jane, 'The Pawns' Allegory in Middleton's *A Game at Chess*', *Review of English Studies*, n.s., 29 (1978), 147–59

Shuger, Debora, 'Civility and Censorship in Early Modern England', in Robert C. Post, ed., *Censorship and Silencing: Practices of Cultural Regulation* (Los Angeles, 1998), pp. 89–110

Sisson, C. J., *Lost Plays of Shakespeare's Age* (Cambridge, 1936)

Skinner, Quentin, 'Meaning and Understanding in the History of Ideas', *History and Theory*, 8 (1969), 3–53

___, *Reason and Rhetoric in the Philosophy of Thomas Hobbes* (Cambridge, 1996)

Smith, Bruce R., *Homosexual Desire in Shakespeare's England: A Cultural Poetics* (Chicago and London, 1991)

Smith, Nigel, *Literature and Revolution in England, 1640–1660* (New Haven, CT and London, 1994)

___, 'The Uses of Hebrew in the English Revolution', in Peter Burke and Roy Porter, eds., *Language, Self, and Society: A Social History of Language* (Cambridge, 1991), pp. 50–71

Smuts, Malcolm, 'Court-Centred Politics and the Uses of Roman Historians, c.1590–1630', in Kevin Sharpe and Peter Lake, eds., *Culture and Politics in Early Stuart England* (Basingstoke, 1994), pp. 21–43

___, *Court Culture and the Origins of a Royalist Tradition in Early Stuart England* (Philadelphia, 1987)

Soens, A. L., Jr., 'Criticism of Formal Satire in the Renaissance' (unpublished Ph.D dissertation, Princeton University, 1957)

243

Sommerville, C. John, *The News Revolution in England: Cultural Dynamics of Daily Information* (New York and Oxford, 1996)

Sommerville, Johann P., 'Parliament, Privilege, and the Liberties of the Subject', in J. H. Hexter, ed., *Parliament and Liberty from the Reign of Elizabeth to the English Civil War* (Stanford, 1992), pp. 56–84

___, *Royalists and Patriots: Politics and Ideology in England 1603–1640*, 2nd edn (London and New York, 1999)

Stallybrass, Peter, 'Reading the Body: *The Revenger's Tragedy* and the Jacobean Theater of Consumption', *Renaissance Drama*, n.s. 18 (1987), 121–48

Taylor, Joseph A., 'The Literary Presentation of James I and Charles I, With Special Reference to the Period c.1614–1630' (unpublished DPhil. dissertation, University of Oxford, 1985)

Test, George A., *Satire: Spirit and Art* (Tampa, 1991)

Thomas, Keith, 'Cases of Conscience in Seventeenth-Century England', in John Morrill, Paul Slack and Daniel Woolf, eds., *Public Duty and Private Conscience in Seventeenth-Century England: Essays Presented to G. E. Aylmer* (Oxford, 1993), pp. 29–56

Thompson, Christopher, *The Debate on Freedom of Speech in the House of Commons in February 1621* (Orsett, Essex, 1985)

Tricomi, Albert H., *Anticourt Drama in England 1603–1642* (Charlottesville, 1987)

Tully, J. H., ed., *Meaning and Context: Quentin Skinner and his Critics* (Cambridge, 1988)

Tyacke, Nicholas, *Anti-Calvinists: The Rise of English Arminianism* (Oxford, 1987)

Underdown, David, *A Freeborn People: Politics and the Nation in Seventeenth-Century England* (Oxford, 1996)

van Dülmen, Richard, *Theatre of Horror: Crime and Punishment in Early Modern Germany*, trans. Elisabeth Neu (Cambridge, 1990)

Vickers, Brian, 'Epideictic and Epic in the Renaissance', *New Literary History*, 14 (1983), 497–537

Wear, Andrew, 'Puritan Perceptions of Illness in Seventeenth-Century England', in Roy Porter, ed., *Patients and Practitioners: Lay Perceptions of Medicine in Pre-Industrial Society* (Cambridge, 1985), pp. 55–99

Whigham, Frank, *Ambition and Privilege: The Social Tropes of Elizabethan Courtesy Theory* (Berkeley and Los Angeles, 1984)

White, Beatrice, *Cast of Ravens: The Strange Case of Sir Thomas Overbury* (London, 1965)

Whitlock, Baird W., *John Hoskyns, Serjeant-at-Law* (Washington, DC, 1982)

Wilcox, John, 'Informal Publication of Late Sixteenth-Century Verse Satire', *Huntington Library Quarterly*, 13 (1949–50), 191–200

Wilks, John S., *The Idea of Conscience in Renaissance Tragedy* (London and New York, 1990)

Williams, Franklin B., Jr., 'Thomas Rogers on Raleigh's Atheism', *Notes and Queries*, 213 (1968), 368–70

Williams, Gordon, *A Dictionary of Sexual Language and Imagery in Shakespearean and Stuart Literature* (3 vols., London and Atlantic Highlands, 1994)

Wiltenburg, Robert, '"What need hast thou of me? or of my *Muse?*": Jonson and Cecil, Politician and Poet', in Claude J. Summers and Ted-Larry Pebworth, eds., *'The Muses Common-Weale': Poetry and Politics in the Seventeenth Century* (Columbia, 1988), pp. 34–47

Woolf, D. R., *The Idea of History in Early Stuart England: Erudition, Ideology, and 'The Light of Truth' from the Accession of James I to the Civil War* (Toronto, 1990)

Worden, Blair, 'Ben Jonson Among the Historians', in Kevin Sharpe and Peter Lake, eds., *Culture and Politics in Early Stuart England* (Basingstoke, 1994), pp. 67–89

___, *The Sound of Virtue: Philip Sidney's* Arcadia *and Elizabethan Politics* (New Haven, CT and London, 1996)

Woudhuysen, H. R., *Sir Philip Sidney and the Circulation of Manuscripts* (Oxford, 1996)

Yachnin, Paul, '*A Game at Chess*: Thomas Middleton's "Praise of Folly"', *Modern Language Quarterly*, 48 (1987), 107–23

Young, Michael B., *King James and the History of Homosexuality* (New York, 2000)

Zaller, Robert, 'The Concept of Opposition in Early Stuart England', *Albion*, 12 (1980), 211–34

___, *The Parliament of 1621: A Study in Constitutional Conflict* (Berkeley, 1971)

Zaret, David, *Origins of Democratic Culture: Printing, Petitions, and the Public Sphere in Early Modern England* (Princeton, 2000)

Zwicker, Steven, *Lines of Authority: Politics and English Literary Culture, 1649–1689* (Ithaca and London, 1993)

Index